ZACH
GOOD THINGS COME TO THOSE
WHO WAIT. GREAT THINGS COME
TO THOSE THAT FIGHT FOR
WHAT THEY WANT!
CRUSH IT!!

MZKILLIAN
Mzk
20160201

From
I-YAH
TO
OO-RAH
MEMOIRS OF A
BLACK BELT
TO
UNITED STATES MARINE

Hey!

My name is Matthew Killian and it's a pleasure to meet you. Before I write another word, I would first like to say THANK YOU for diving into this book. I truly hope you enjoy reading it as much as I have enjoyed writing it. My hope is that you can relate to some of my trials and challenges and will in turn be able to share in the joy and adrenaline of success. I have never thought of myself as a writer so if something doesn't make sense or my insolent computerized spell check failed me, my bad.

This story is about the journey of making my dreams come true.

I don't know if joining the Marine Corps is anyone's dream, but it is mine. Knowing that my parents will still love and support me even though one (Love you mom!) may utterly despise what I'm doing is mine.
This is my journey in finding and keeping the things that are invaluable to my life. I've learned so many lessons along the way.

Throughout the writing process, one of my goals was to keep the content's integrity factually (Sweet, that's a word!) in check. Another goal was to make sure **YOU** didn't have to read through nonsense. I hate reading a book that makes you wade through pages of over-expressed pointless detail. Here, it's cut and dry.

Be warned, the opinions expressed in this book are of my own. If you don't like it or you don't agree, that's totally cool. I've changed the names of those that show up throughout the book. Outside of the names, I assure you the content is absolutely accurate to the occurrence.

If you have any questions or comments, please feel free to contact me.
Killian3014@gmail.com

One last thing before I turn you loose. Being the son of a preacher man, I never got into the habit of using bad language. However, just because I don't use bad language, doesn't mean everybody else doesn't either. I didn't sugarcoat or edit any quotes so stand by. You've now officially been warned.
Enjoy!

Sunday June 3rd 2007
The Beginning

Done!

It's just now 3:35PM, and I've finished my second birthday party for the month. Little did I know the fun and adventure that would come with being a Professional Martial Arts Instructor. Teaching Martial Arts is a blast, but there is nothing like teaching twenty 6 year olds a sport they have never done, with rules they have never followed, in a place they have never been, with a Black Belt Instructor they have never met. Not to mention that at the halfway point, I compound the general excitement by getting them all jacked up on sugar from cake and ice cream. But, I absolutely love it. It's great! Over the years, I have learned what it takes to keep them totally focused on me and actually get them to participate to the best of their abilities for the entire two hours. Some kids are easy from the start. Some kids have to be "convinced". No matter what, by the end of the party, EVERYONE has had a blast and the ones that were the worst hellions typically enroll for classes that same day or soon after. It takes a lot of energy and it's not easy, but it's a great way to teach kids the rewards of being respectful and it's a challenge that I thoroughly enjoy.

As I sat down, I realized that in 25 minutes I would be leaving from the school to tackle another challenge. I had set a goal that I would run 1 marathon every month for 6 months and this was lucky number 6. The Marathon started at 4 o'clock, so I had a little bit of time to relax before blast off. As I sat there in my chair, I realized that my life has always involved challenging myself and trying to improve myself physically, mentally, and spiritually.

My personal motto has always been-

If at first you do succeed, try something harder.

At that moment, a thought that has been in my head for years and years suddenly sparked an insignificant interest. No big deal really. My mind just said- *Hey, you've got some time. Let's check this out.*

So I conceded and started typing-

www.google.com   (enter)
Marine   (enter)

     Several choices popped up and I clicked on the one that looked the most "official." Suddenly the background of my screen went black and all that could be seen was a grey Eagle, Globe, and Anchor. Underneath that, a loading bar flashed and I knew something big was coming. And then BAM! The next thing I saw was 5 Marines standing tall and proud in front of that world famous statue of those warriors driving the American flag into the ground. That was easy. I started navigating the sight not really caring what order I went in. I just wanted to absorb as much as I could in the little time that I had. I scanned through a brief overview of what Basic Training was like, the significance of the Eagle, Globe, and Anchor, about this grueling 54 hour event known as "The Crucible", and about the history of how the Marine Corps started and what it stands for today. Needless to say I was thoroughly impressed. It was awesome. Under the category of "Recruit Training", it said-

This is the proving ground. If you are to become a Marine, you must first pass through the fire of recruit training. You must prove you belong.

     That's what I'm talking about! At that moment, I officially started the chain of events that would bring me to a very new and different today. I filled out a basic information request, clicked send, and closed out. I looked up at the clock. It said 3:57. I'm good to go. I filled up my camelback, grabbed my sunglasses, and headed out the door to the start line, which was right outside in the parking lot. Very Nice!
     For the whole run, all I could think about was if someone would call me back with information, if I would do anything about it if they did, if I would have to leave my job, if I was ready to leave my job, if it was the right move to make at this stage of my life, how my family would react to it, the thoughts went on and on. Wait... Actually, the only thing on my mind for the first 8 miles was: What the heck am I doing? I'm running another friggin Marathon. I forgot how much this sucks! But then, like always, I found my rhythm, my body adjusted to the work, and I was good to go. It also helped that I had my good buddy Cowboy riding along with me. Cowboy was responsible for confirming my

course, fluid and fuel intake, and just being someone to talk to. Cowboy is one of the Black Belts at my school, a seasoned Triathlete, and always wears a cowboy hat. He's owns a company that builds docks, loves anything extreme, and is easily qualified as a machine. Don't let the shorts and sandals hippy look fool you, the guy's nonstop. He's the one that helped me train and finish my first Olympic Distance Triathlon right here in Annapolis. So, when he found out that I had set a goal for running a lot of Marathons just for the heck of it, he was excited about the challenge. There was no way that he wanted to run them all with me but he sure didn't mind riding his bike along and just being a part of the fight. We talked a lot for the first part of the course but then we sort of drifted in our own thoughts. I started thinking about my life here in Maryland and teaching at the school. It's a wonderful job, but I found myself having issues with a few things.
My dad said it best-

Son, the only way you're going to make the money you feel you deserve is to make it happen for yourself. You have to be the Boss. That doesn't mean you have to pack up and leave the organization, it just means you at least have to put yourself in a position to run the show.

From that point on I knew that my life was going to have to reach a new level. It would have to take a turn in a new direction. Then, I started thinking about my life in the Marine Corps. Even though I didn't have concrete expectations, I knew that this was something that had "ME" written all over it. I had put it off for so long that I had finally come to a point where I said-

Matt, it's now or never brother. If you don't jump on this then you know you're going to regret not stepping up and doing it when you had the chance.

That is not the kind of feeling I want to carry with me for the rest of my life. I have always thought of myself as being a "go getter". I haven't been the best at everything and that's nothing but normal, but anything I have truly wanted or worked for, I have achieved to some level of satisfaction. So this was it. It suited my desires for a career. If I was going to do anything else besides teach and inspire kids via Martial Arts training, then it would have to be something where I was giving myself to something that would improve the world in which I lived. Fighting for my country was a great forward step in the life of Matt Killian.

That night, I fittingly watched the first 45 minutes of Full Metal Jacket. Everyone knows the rest of that movie is meh. But I was so jacked up and excited about the Marine Corps that I wanted to fuel that fire. I wanted to keep visualizing myself truly being a part of that life. The military life. I have always loved the Martial Arts because it is a world where I get to live and breathe respect and discipline. I like treating others at the highest possible standard. Where saying Yes Sir and No Sir is standard and as common as breathing. Everything has structure. Everything is solid. Granted, things change day to day and we're constantly welcoming challenge, but that challenge comes with terms that are regulated and requires correct and decisive action. You can't do anything half way. It's simply all or nothing. When you have to do a job, you have to do it RIGHT. This is what I was looking for. Well enough for today. I have 26.2 miles to recover from so it's time to crash.

Monday June 4th 2007
The Call

Well, just as I had guessed, Monday morning came with a vengeance. It felt like I had just closed my eyes when my alarm clock started singing its tune. Oh well. Might as well get this party started. Suddenly, as soon as my feet hit the floor, I started seeing things a little bit differently. I was trying to imagine what waking up in a barracks would be like. How the Gunnery Sergeant Hartmans would be waking us up and getting us moving. How little it would matter that I wanted to hit snooze. That it would be GET UP NOW! This is the point that a man usually looks at his life and says-

Man, I've got it made. My life is so warm and fuzzy. Why in the world would I want to put myself through something as miserable as Basic Training?

Well, that came and went. The fact is that nothing lasts forever. Sure, it's going to suck fruit loops when I'm going through it, but it won't last forever. I guess it's just like a Marathon. It's rough in the process but once you get used to it and you're close to the finish, it becomes easier to man up and gut it out. With all that in mind, I made my way to the office. Every Monday we have a business meeting to see how things are and see what we can do to maximize the upcoming week. I actually enjoy it. However, this morning I really wasn't focused on it. All I could think about was the Marine Corps. When the meeting wrapped up, I got my stuff together and made my way to my desk to make some calls and get some business moving. I had just turned on my IPod when I heard-

Mr. Matt, you have a call on line 1.

Sa-weet! I had made a lot of calls last weekend so this has got to be a future student calling me up to schedule an appointment to come in. Great way to start my Monday!
I answered the phone and said,

Good morning, this is Mr. Matt. How may I help you?

The Voice-   Is this Matt Killian?

Yes Sir it is. How may I help you?

The Voice-   This is Staff Sergeant Something-or-Other and I'm calling on behalf of the United States Marine Corps. I'd like to ask you a few questions. Do you have a few minutes?

Yes Sir. Just one moment please.

At that moment, I knew I needed to relocate to a private area. So I headed to the Main Training Floor of the school. At this point, my interest in the Marine Corps was not what I needed the staff at the school to catch wind of. Things can get turned upside down mighty fast and the last thing I need is for my job to shatter prematurely. As soon as

I was set I told the Staff Sergeant to go ahead. I started to receive nothing short of a battery of questions from the Staff Sergeant. He asked question after question starting with my name, age, date of birth, occupation, years in college, criminal record, middle school, high school, criminal record, tattoos, body piercings, oh yeah, and he asked me some questions about my criminal record. I guess he had never spoken with a guy that had a clean record. I was no troublemaker. Then he asked me a very interesting question. He said-

Mr. Killian, have you ever done illegal drugs?

I thought-
Crack? No.
Acid? No.
Marijuana? Uh-oh

At this point, I didn't see any of my previous answers as deal breakers until this question hit. The problem wasn't that I had smoked pot on two separate occasions in college. The problem was if I should fess up to it right now. How would they ever know? I could go in with a totally clean record. It wasn't even that big of a deal. I went to a party; some friends asked if I wanted to try it, I said, ok. I tried it, didn't like it, the next morning they tried again saying it was better in the morning. I tried it, didn't like it, and then I decided right then and there that it just wasn't for me. Since I didn't think it was that big of a deal, I figured I could have probably gotten away with just saying no. But then it occurred to me. The military has polygraph tests and drugs to make you tell the truth. How would that look if I was found to be a liar on my first day? Nope. I might as well explain myself now and man up to the consequences. Luckily, there were no consequences. Even the Staff Sergeant said-

Yeah, me too. That was then, this is now. We all make mistakes along the way. Don't worry about it.

Whew. BIG sigh of relief. After making some notes and a slight pause, the Staff Sergeant said-

Mr. Killian, I have some unfortunate news. You are no longer qualified to enter this Program.

I said- *Program? What program?*

He said- *The Officers Program. In order to enter this particular program you....*

I cut him off and said-

Oh, I'm sorry. I wasn't looking for the Officer's program. I was just looking for information on how to join the Marine Corps. (By the way, that would be the last time I would EVER cut off a Marine!!!)

Relieved, he said- *So you are just looking to join the Marine Corps?*

I said, Yes Sir!

He said- *Outstanding. Just wait 5 minutes and a recruiter from your area will call and give you that information.*

Apparently, "Outstanding" is a word that Marines like to use...a lot. Note to self. So I hung up and headed back to my desk to make some calls. Keeping an ever-anxious eye on the clock, I waited.

1 minute went by.
2 minutes.
3 minutes had passed.
4 minutes.
5 minutes.
6 minutes.

No one's calling. Man, I've been here waiting and... (Ring-Ring). Finally, now we're in business. His name was Sergeant Peterson. He confirmed who he was and then fired into the same exact line of questioning as the other Staff Sergeant. After the revisited interrogation, he asked me when it would be possible for me to swing by the office so we could sit down and discuss my future in the Marine Corps. Since I had to work the rest of that afternoon and evening, I would need to go in on the following day. So BAM! There you go. At 9:00AM, I've got a meeting with the Marine Corps. For the first time, I felt like I didn't need to consume my mind with the military. Now that I had an appointment, I could let things settle since all would be revealed tomorrow.

Tuesday June 5th 2007
The Meeting

At 8AM I shot out of bed and got myself ready for the day. I arrived at the Recruiters' Office Depot (**ROD1**) at 8:45 AM. It was upstairs in a local strip mall that was right down from Best Buy. Very Nice! I flew up the stairs and bounced my way down the hallway. Turning the corner I saw the sign for the United States Army. Very cool. The very next sign was it. It simply said, MARINES. I walked up to the door, took in a deep breath, smiled, and pulled...a locked door. What the--? Just on the other side of the door was a sign that read "Back at 9:00".

Looks like I have some time to kill. So in the meantime, I popped over to Best Buy to check out the New Releases and play a round or two on Guitar Hero II. Just so you know, that's the best game in the world! However, it's wicked hard. There's this song called Jordan that seems to be my nemesis. I have beaten it at home but never in a group setting.

You ain't done nothing unless eyes besides yours have witnessed it.

Some day. After that, I checked the time, grabbed a Mountain Dew, and headed back to the **ROD1**. This time I turned the corner and the door was open. Halle-friggen-lujah!

As I walked in, I immediately got bearings on my surroundings. The room was no more than 900 square feet. To my immediate right was a rack full of pamphlets detailing information about the opportunities offered by the Marine Corps. To the back of the office was a door leading to a hallway that joined the offices of the four military branches. To the back left was a private office that at this time was closed. To the left of that and coming forward was a pull up bar mounted to the wall. You just don't see that every day. And finally, to my immediate left, was a gentleman sitting at a desk. I walked up and introduced myself-

Hi. My name is Matt Killian. I'm here to see Sergeant Peterson.

The man stood up and introduced himself-

Yes sir, he will be coming here shortly so I'm going to be helping you out until then. My name is Staff Sergeant Garfield, but you can call me Staff Sergeant G.

Staff Sergeant G explained that people often times mispronounced his name so he simply Men-in-Black'd it to make it easier. Staff Sergeant G was a nice guy based on first impressions. Based on his looks, he wasn't at all like the Marines I had seen in the movies. However, the way he carried himself and the way he spoke verified that he was in fact the real deal. Personally, I was planning on meeting a recruiter dressed in a starched and pressed uniform. Staff Sergeant G was wearing a grey Marine Corps T-shirt with track pants. He had just gotten to the office straight from working out at the gym and was going to change over after he checked his messages. In all truth, that actually made things more comfortable. Instead of a job interview, it was more like a conversation with your buddy.

After the small talk, Staff Sergeant G jumped into the same line of questioning as the other two. For a moment, I thought that maybe this was just standard protocol for every Staff Sergeant to fire through upon meeting a future recruit. But luckily, this was just to make sure that all the information gathered about me was true, accurate, and consistent. After he made his final notes he said-

Well Mr. Killian, I'd love to tell you all about the Marine Corps, but before I do, I need you to step inside that office and take a computerized test to make sure you are qualified to join the Marine Corps.

Sound good?

I said- *Sure. Sounds good.*

We walked in and he told me that this was actually a practice test. The test consisted of four parts, I had a time limit on each section, and he showed me how to hit the correct keys in order to reduce the possibility of errors. No problem! I'm a pretty smart guy. I did great in college and I have plenty of scratch paper. No worries. Well, the test was actually more challenging than I had anticipated. Out of 40 or so problems, I actually had to guess on 2 of them but I still got them right. I just wish I would have known that right then. At this point, I had no idea how I did. All I knew is that I felt good about it. Most of the stuff came back to me as soon as I had given it some thought. There were a lot of math and problem solving questions.

Apparently, the Marine Corps wants to know that you have the capacity to figure out problems based on logic. Not so much formulas, but if this happens and this happens, what will you do to get this? Sure, there were factoring problems, fraction problems, conversion problems, but overall, I felt the majority of questions were geared towards solving every day life problems, under stress, as quickly as possible, without error. As soon as I completed it, Staff Sergeant G came in and took a look at the numbers that represented my results. I couldn't make them out from my point of view or understanding but judging by his body language, they seemed to be...(you guessed it) outstanding. After a moment he looked up and said-

Mr. Killian, I have good news and I have bad news.
(My heart dropped a mile.)

What do you want first? He asked.

I said- *I want the good news.*

He said- *OK, the good news is that there isn't any bad news. You did great! Based on this test, you won't have any problem whatsoever with the ASVAB.*

It was a homerun! Matt 1- Test 0. Believe it or not, this was actually a huge relief. I knew two things-

1- This type of test kicked my butt in high school and I wasn't going to let that happen again.
2- I was not going to pull a Billy Madison and go back to school to relearn any of it if I jacked it up too bad.

But since I had done well, I was good to go. After a quick bathroom break, I walked back into the office and saw another gentleman there. He walked right up and introduced himself as Sergeant Peterson. Apparently, Sergeant Peterson was actually new to this office and so Staff Sergeant G was going to handle the rest of my proceedings and Sergeant Peterson was going to help out with the paperwork. Sergeant Peterson walked into the mini office and got to work on my personal information while Staff Sergeant G leaned back in his chair and asked me a bomb of a question.
He asked- ***Mr. Killian, what do you want from the Marine Corps?***

I was stunned. I thought: What do I want? I don't know what I want exactly. All I know is that I want to go through Basic Training, become a Marine, and—wow, what do I want? It occurred to me that I do have a great job and I love working with kids, but if I'm going to become a Marine, then I'm going to have to figure out where to go with it once I achieve that goal. I believe Staff Sergeant G could feel my state of perplexity and handed me a book that had all the jobs that I was qualified for in the Marine Corps.

He said- *Look that over and see if you can find anything that interests you.*

I took the book and found a job that would actually be right up my alley. I knew that I wanted to do something that directly helped other people. No offense, but there was no way I wanted a job that put me behind a desk. I'm a mover and prefer something that keeps me going. It took a matter of seconds and then BAM! There it was-

Aircraft Fire and Personnel Rescue

I could definitely get into that. That's cool. I also found out that I could be involved in training future recruits the Martial Arts that they receive in Basic Training. The program is called MCMAP (Marine Corps Martial Arts Program). That would be even better. Teaching Martial Arts to kids is one thing, but teaching full on gung-ho recruits is quite another. This is a good start. I have found two jobs that would make all of this make sense.

After pointing them out to Staff Sergeant G, he said-

Outstanding. Now that you know you can have a job that you'll really be into, **IS THIS WHAT YOU WANT TO DO?**

Just so you know, he wasn't yelling this. This just seems to be the way I heard it. It was a huge question that seemed to carry an enormous amount of weight behind it. Here I am, merely interested in the Marine Corps, filled out some info, showed up for an appointment, took a test, passed it, and now this guy is asking me if I want to leave my job and my cushy life right NOW and enlist in the United States Marine Corps. This might have bothered me under any other circumstance and I might have walked away to think it all through and then come back and discuss it further, but the bottom line is this IS what I want to do.

I said- *Yes Sir it is.*

He asked- *Well, when did you want to leave for Boot Camp?*

I asked- *When can I leave?* (Thinking it would somehow be like school where you enter in the fall!)

He said- *This Thursday.*

Whoa. Back the truck up!!!

I said- *Ok, I'm not that ready. I actually have a good job and I'll need at least 2 to 3 months in order to get a replacement so I can leave on the best of terms. My job has been great to me and I would like to return the favor.*

He said- *No problem. Then when do you think you can go?*

How does November sound? I asked.

That'll be great! He said with a relieved smile.

I think he might have thought I'd be one of those wishy-washy indecisive guys that say they are not sure and nothing ends up happening and it becomes a huge waste of time. Well not me. I wasn't going to waste my time and jerk him around with something if I truly just didn't want to commit. At that point, Staff Sergeant G picked up the phone, dialed a few numbers, and said-

Hello Sir, It's Staff Sergeant Garfield. I have Mr. Killian here and he wants to be a Marine. Can I get him in? (Pause) *Outstanding. Thank you sir.*

After that, he put down the phone, looked me in the eye, and said- *You'll need to miss work tomorrow.*

I asked- *What for?*

He said- *I have to get you up to MEPS.*

Obviously, my next question was
_____?
You are correct if you answered-
What is MEPS?

He said-

MEPS (Military Enlistment Processing Station) *is the place where you will need to take the ASVAB exam and undergo a full physical.*

I told him that there was no way I could miss work and asked if there was any possible way we could do it on the weekend. Incidentally, this was the last test for new recruits for this year so, if I didn't make it up this weekend, it wasn't going to be looking good. So after looking at our schedules, we agreed that I would meet here this Friday night at 8:00PM, be driven to Fort Meade, stay in a hotel, get up "early", take a bus into Fort Meade, take all the exams, and be good to go by the end of the day. Sounds fun! And it actually did.

After that, I shook hands with Staff Sergeant G, thanked him for all of his help, and went into the office to start the paperwork with Sergeant Peterson. You may think you have a lot of paperwork to fill out when you buy a house, but you have nothing on the Marine Corps! There is no such thing as scratching or crossing something out and then fixing it. The documents that are submitted must be absolutely pristine. I felt so bad for Sergeant Peterson because we had to redo one form at least four times. I would write something that was not the military way and he'd have to print a new form out so we could fix it. He kept apologizing because when you do things for so long a certain way, you have a tendency to expect that everyone else does it the same way. He was totally cool about it.

He would say- *Uh Oh. I forgot to tell you. You have to write it like this.*

He would show me, and then I'd fix it. Man, am I glad that's over. As soon as I finished the initial paperwork, I double-checked the plans for this weekend, shook hands with Sergeant Peterson, thanked him for all his help, and bounced my way to my car like a kid before Christmas. Friday is the day!

Thursday June 7th 2007
Calling The Big Man

At this point, I was set to head up to MEPS on Friday. I was excited about it. It's funny how sometimes you get nervous when you don't know what's going to happen while other times it's actually exciting. Since there wasn't any pressure on me to enlist or sign my life away, I was looking forward to the silver lining in this trip. For the past couple of weeks, I had wanted to go in and get a check up just to make sure that everything in me was functioning correctly. Typically, a general physical like that is about 300 bucks. Not now! I was going to be able to get a complete physical for free. Awwyeah!

However, with every good comes a challenge. There was going to come a time where I let the family in on what I was working on. By far, my father is the safest confidant when it comes to issues that are very personal to me. He has this uncanny ability to just listen to what I have to say and then offers me the feedback that makes the most sense to me. Whether I'm right in my pursuits or I'm way off, he simply lets me know how it is. Unlike most people, he doesn't base his advice on biased opinions or from having an emotional bond with the solution, he just says this is right and this is wrong. And if it's a decision where there isn't exactly a defined right and wrong like adjusting your career path, he simply says to look at both sides, sit on it for awhile, pray about it, ask God for some direction, and then do what you know is right. My dad's a brilliant man. You might not always sense it from a first impression, but he is truly the wisest man I know when it comes to questions about life. I'm positive that he has forgotten more words of wisdom then I have learned entirely. So, now it's time to talk to pops.

A wise man once told me-

If you fail to plan, you plan to fail.

There was no way I was going to speed dial El Padre unless I have my stuff in order. And there was no way he would support my decision of pursuing the military unless I had given this path a lot of thought. After a bit of strategizing I pounded some keys-

Contacts-
(Enter)
(Down)
(Down)
(Down)
(Down)

(Down)
(Down)
(Down)
(Down) ...deep breathe
(Send)

As always, my dad answered the phone just the same as he has for the last 18 years. He said-
This is Brother Mike.

He's always got a way of putting you at ease the moment you hear his voice. Well, the moment I said, *Hey dad* he knew something was up. Whenever I have something important to discuss with him that always seems to be the way it starts. So I proceeded to tell him how I've always had this deep desire to be in the military, how he knew that I had tried once before but mom had just put up too much of a fuss and now that I'm older, it's something that I really want to consider. He listened just like he always does. I told him how I had never gotten into the service before simply out of respect for mom, but now I'm just at the point where if I don't do it now, I'll have to shoulder that regret. He understood. He just gave me that same-

Uh huh. Well son, seems like you need to weigh this thing out and sit on it for a while.

I asked him if I was just chasing a fools dream or if I may have been kicked too many times in the head at work. He said-

No son, I understand what you're saying. You know I was in the military and I know what you're going through. Just remember that the military really doesn't have a whole lot to offer you like it does most kids going in. It's not going to make you any more of a man than you already are today. Sure, you'll pick up some new skills here and there but that's about it. I'm so proud of you. Don't forget that your life has purpose. I have never seen anyone motivate and inspire kids the way you do. You have a gift son.

Then, I proceeded to tell him that I wasn't really interested in full time enlistment but more interested in joining the Reserves. That way, I

21

could still run a school and teach kids but also have a hand in the Marine Corps. I think that relieved him. I believe deep down that he was afraid I might run off and join some Special Forces group. He saw me die in a play and from a father's perspective; I believe he could live out the rest of his days without that mental image. So could I for that matter. I told him about going to MEPS and he said-

That's all well and good; just don't go enlisting without sitting on it for a while.

I said- *Yes Sir.*

Before I got off the phone, I said- *By the way, how do you think mom will take it?*

After quite a bit of silence he said- *Well, it'll be hell.*

With that I said- *Well how about we keep it between us until I know for sure what's up. There's no reason to worry her if we don't have to you know?*

He said- *Sounds good.*

With that, I told my dad I loved him and I would keep him up on everything that was going on. And that was that. I have to tell you that I am so proud that he is my father. He is the closest thing to Jesus I have ever met. Don't get me wrong. He can't walk on water, perform miracles, or call himself the son of God. Or claim to do such. BUT, he does have unconditional love. And that means more to me then anything else in this world.
Thanks dad.

Friday June 8th 2007
The Nightmare Before MEPS

Friday morning I woke up and blasted out the door. I had to work

22

out and then my buddy Erin and I were heading out to see Ocean's 13. I had tried to jam pack my day so I wouldn't have to feel the pain of it dragging by like it normally does when I'm excited about something. Luckily, the day flew by and before I knew it, I was wrapping up the Competition Team workout and heading out the door. I flew home and grabbed my overnight bag and headed out to meet Sergeant Peterson at the office. As soon as I arrived, Sergeant Peterson and I jumped in the van and took off to the Glen Bernie Recruiters' Office Depot (**ROD2**) where we were to pick up a young lady that was joining the Marines as well. On the way, we talked a lot about what he enjoys the most about the Corps and what I had to look forward to. One thing that I had really liked about Sergeant Peterson and Staff Sergeant G was the fact that they didn't sugarcoat anything. Most recruiters will offer you the world and try to guarantee this and that. I've actually witnessed that. Not these guys. In fact, some of the things they told me might have made anyone else say, "Screw this. I'm out of here." It said on the website that Marines were about Honor and Integrity and I could see that. They said that if they had lied or made something out that wasn't true, then it was there name as well as the Marine Corps' name that was in the mud. That was something that I did appreciate. Plus, Sergeant Peterson said that based on his luck, the moment he fed a new recruit a load of crap and they found out the truth, they would be just the type of person to come back from Boot Camp and be sitting on the top of a building looking for him through a scope.

As soon as we got to Glen Bernie, we picked up the young lady from that office and proceeded to the Hotel. Upon arrival to the Comfort Inn, Sergeant Peterson walked us in and checked us at the front desk. Apparently, the Comfort Inn houses men and women coming and going to MEPS on a daily basis. We walked down to the basement, headed through a corridor, and took a left into a room where 20 -30 special forces guys were firing fully automatic weapons and testing explosives. OK, you're still with me. Just checking. Actually, it was a rather small room with posters on the wall of the Marine Corps, Army, Navy, Air Force, Coast Guard, and even the National Guard. There was an older lady sitting at a desk at the end of the room. Sergeant Peterson gave me the rules and regulations sheet detailing acceptable behavior during our stay at the Comfort Inn. She then gave me my room key, explained about the dinner and breakfast tickets in the envelope, and then warned me that if I was caught on the girls' floor or girls were found on my floor that we would be asked to leave. Bummer, but check. Then she said that we needed to be back down in that very room at 0400 in the morning to drop off the key and jump on the bus. I said-

4:00, no pro--- 4:00 as in AM?

She looked up at me with that "Hello, this IS the military!" look.

Ok. 4:00 it is. I'll be here I said.

In all actuality, it didn't matter at all. I have no problem getting up in the morning so I was good to go. From there I exited the room, walked back through the corridor and up the elevator to MY floor. My room was the first one to the left off the elevator. Sa-weet. As soon as I entered the room, I dropped my bag down on the bed, emptied my pockets, laid out my clothes, and headed right back out so I could go grab a bite with my free dinner ticket. Wow did I get a hook up. The kitchen was closing up and so I got the last of everything out. Typically you are only aloud to take one of everything, but since I was the last guy, I got 2 brownies. What now! I could have gotten more but I really wasn't that hungry and I had no frig. Plus, it was 9:58PM. The next thing that happened could be classified as completely normal, but it was something that I would never want to relive. As I got back to my room, I sat down to eat my dinner and at that moment I felt completely...

A l o n e

Here I am. I'm 28 years old. I'm not entirely happy with my job. My family is nowhere near close enough to visit any time soon. I just broke up with my girlfriend. And now I'm going to join the Marine Corps. You would think a guy my age would be settled into his career and starting to make serious money for his family. Not me. I'm the guy in my family that has struck out on some unbeaten path. Don't get me wrong. I'm thankful for everything that has happened in my life, I just hated the feeling of starting this adventure and having no one to share it with. Then from bad, came worse. In the Marine Corps, I can die. That could destroy the strength of my family. Sure, they would rise again through the grace of Almighty God. I would just hate to put them through that. I remembered the awful screams of my friend's mom when she heard the news that her son had died in the Marines. And he wasn't even in combat. He died in an unfortunate training exercise. That night, the world was dark in the world of Matt Killian. I distinctly remember thinking

I should just get up right now, get out of here, run away, and get back to my cooshy little existence!

For 2 hours, my emotions were on some misguided rollercoaster ride. At moments I would feel entirely scared. After that, I would have this feeling of peace wash over me and knew that I was doing the right thing and everything was going to be OK. Then the darkness would return. I would think of all the "What if's" that could happen. I would think about all the bad things that could happen to me. I felt like I reached the bottom of **FEAR**'s barrel and then found a way to drill deeper and deeper. Then I would realize that my life is not in my control and all those things could happen at any moment. The uncertainty of existence was staggering. Who was I to think that I controlled when I tap out of this life. I have no control over that what so ever. Crap! I felt like I had Pre Military Syndrome! Then I had had enough. I made up my mind that I wasn't going to live in the shadow of fear. I needed to trust in Almighty God. I needed to just leave the answers to Him and live my life while I'm blessed with each new day that comes. I closed my eyes and prayed-

Almighty God, please come and give me the strength to get through this. Help me to put my mind at ease. I can't do it without you. I know you have a plan for my life. I ask you now to give me the courage and confidence to do what's right. Thank you for sending your son to die for me. Thank you for coming in and being in control of my life. It's in Your name I pray.
Amen.

Just as soon as I said the word Amen, my mind flooded with scripture versus. First came **2nd Timothy 2:22** which says-

For the Lord did NOT give me a spirit of fear, but a spirit of POWER in mind, soul, and strength.

Then came **Philippians 4:13** which says-

I can do ALL things through Christ who gives me strength.

And that was that. God gave me the strength to shut my mind up. Enough was enough. He did just as He promised He would. The Bible says-

Come to me you who are weary, and I will give you strength.

The Lord answers prayers and He did. I fell asleep at peace and woke up in peace...

Saturday June 9th 2007
Welcome to MEPS- Day 1

...At 3:50AM that is. And just like I called it: the alarm went off and I was out of that bed. I cleaned up, threw on the clothes I had set out, brushed my teeth, and got down to turn my key in with 2 minutes to spare. No problem. I went over to grab breakfast and found myself surrounded by future recruits heading into one of the 4 branches of the military. Not a whole lot of talking was going on, but when it did it was just cool. You could sense an underlying pulse of excitement growing as the dining hall started to fill. After I finished my eggs, toast, bacon, and a glass of Orange Juice, I headed out to the parking lot. There were already sub groups here and there of men and women just talking about the service they were going to enter, when they would be shipping off, and so on.

At 4:40, a big red bus pulled up to where we were and opened its doors. An older black gentleman about 2/3 my size bounced down the stairs and off the bus. As soon he hit the ground, he looked straight up at me and said-

Going to Fort Meade?

I replied- *Yes Sir!*

He said- *Good. Now get your cracker-ass on the bus and bring your friends! I've got to take a piss.*

With that, I looked behind me at the stunned assembly and led the way. To this day, I don't know the name of that bus driver. Even after all the trips I've made since. Maybe I'll get a chance some other time. He was great. He wore civilian clothes. It was always the same black shirt with flames on it and a pair of black jeans. He was definitely in the routine. Every time I saw him, he would look me in the eye, ask me if I was going to Fort Meade, get us on the bus, go in and use the restroom, come back out with a plastic cup that was never filled but he always placed it on the console by the windshield, closed the door, drove us to Fort Meade, told us to get out our ID's at the checkpoint entrance, and brought us to a halt at the MEPS building. Sometimes we would get a story along the way of when he was this great Drill Instructor, sometimes he would sing this incoherent love song, and sometimes he wouldn't say a word. He was definitely a box of chocolate. Same box every time, just different stuff inside.

Well the first time I arrived at the MEPS drop-off, an Army officer in fatigues bounded up the stairs and, with a very direct and authoritative voice, briefed us on what we would need to do upon entering the MEPS building. Basically, you have 10 seconds to get your paperwork out, get off the bus, get in line, shove your bag through the x-ray, drop the bag off in the holding room, have a gentleman with a metal detector survey you, and then have a seat at a desk in the conference room. Oh yeah, and NO CELL PHONES. Wow, these guys were serious about that. 2 things the military is particular about- your criminal record and cell phones. You can't have either at MEPS.

As soon as everyone was seated in the conference room, a liaison from each branch would come in one at a time and call the role for future recruits on their list. The order was always Air Force, Army, Coast Guard, Marines, and then Navy. I must say that I was impressed with my liaison. He was this stocky little black guy that looked like he could rip a man's head off if provoked. That's what I'm talking about! His name was Staff Sergeant Wilson. When he talked, he spoke soft, quick, and said, "friggin'" a lot. He was like a Black PG-13 Speedy Gonzales.

It was interesting to me how everyone responded during the role call. It could have just been me, but when Staff Sergeant Wilson called our names and we had to walk up and set our paperwork on the podium, it was like everyone looked at us and privately thought, "Yep, there goes the friggin' crazy ones!" It wasn't like that with the Navy, Army, Coast Guard, or Air Force recruits. But with us, it was like everything got a little extra quiet like they were watching to see what we would do. Personally, it made me feel pretty good. I walked up to the front of the class with pride. The way I see it, if I'm ever called to go to war, I would rather be taught by the most feared military branch known to man. Well after the role call, the officer that met us on the bus asked for all those that needed to take the ASVAB to follow him. That's me; I'm out of here. We followed him out of the room, down a long hallway to a room that had a sign that read-

Silence, testing in progress. Violators will be shot...survivors will be shot again!

We walked in and were assigned computers. Excellent! The officer in charge was from the Navy. Just like my liaison, her exterior was cool and calm but she had a distinct hint of, "I'll rip your heart out if you mess with me" mixed with this, "Can I get you more scratch paper honey?" thing.

The **ASVAB**! (Armed Services Vocational Aptitude Battery) This test totally kicked my butt and asked for seconds in high school. If you don't know what it is, it is a proficiency exam that will let the military know that you are/ or are not intelligent enough to solve problems, find solutions, and make decisions based on military standards. It also qualifies you for the MOS (Military Occupational Specialty) you can get after Basic Training. In short, this test was a deal breaker for me in two ways-

1- If I didn't pass this test, I had no intentions of going back to school and learning what was needed to pass the test. It would be a closed case.

2- If I didn't receive a score that would qualify me for the MOS I wanted, then I would have to bounce. There is no way that I was going to take a job that I had no interest in.

So, as you can see, this test would dictate my future in the Marine Corps. I wanted to kill it. I didn't want this to be a repeat butt kicking and I didn't want to just do OK. I wanted to own this test and prove to myself that I could do it. I got my scratch paper and as soon as I got the go ahead, I tore into that test. I would like to say that I blew every question out of the water to get the score I did, but in all truth, there were a few questions that I know I guessed on and I guess I just got lucky. It was much harder than I anticipated. The hardest thing for me wasn't the questions being asked, rather, the time given to solve those problems. You were bound by a relentless clock and the questions only got harder as you went on to the next. There were absolutely no breaks and no going back. It was an awesome challenge, but I **KILLED** it!

As soon as I finished, I picked up my folder with my results and headed back to the front desk. From there, I was directed to Medical. Medical is this wing right across from the ASVAB testing room. Everything you needed to have checked out would happen in that wing. Start to finish. My group started in this classroom. As it turned out, we would work through all the tests together through to the end. That was actually pretty cool. The way I saw it, the team mentality started right there. Between tests, we would sit down for a while and be able to compare what the guys and girls had to do. Good times. For some reason, the guys (including myself) were totally in to asking the girls to describe in detail the breast cancer check, what it was the gynecologist was looking for, and the infamous "duck walk". The females were happy to toy with our minds. I guess it was just a way for all of us to deal with the uncomfortable feeling of what we had to do in this now strange environment. In short, we simply resolved to what we knew best. The guys were busy being guys and the girls were busy playing with the guys.

The first thing I learned in the classroom was how the military writes the date. When I had first walked in the room, I had noticed some numbers right below the TV and thought nothing of it. But when the doc went into describing what it should look like when we wrote it on our forms, he pointed to those 8 numbers that I thought were nothing and it all made sense. It goes YEAR, followed by MONTH, followed by DATE. It's actually pretty easy. On my first try, I thought it might be a bit confusing or that I might accidentally put the month and date backwards, but after I wrote it about 50 times, it was a cakewalk.

Civilian   June 9th 2007   -or-
            06/09/07   -or-
            06-09-2007 (or some similar variation)

Military   20070609   -or-
            20070609   -or-
            20070609

It was made very clear that this is how ALL of our documents had to be noted. While we were filling out general medical information, there was a doctor coming around taking our blood pressure. While he was doing that, he made a point to tell us semi privately not to keep anything back about our medical history. The military has to know about every single thing that has ever happened to you. From the time the doctor smacked you on the butt to this very day, it all had to be there. I later found out that the Chief Doctor's job is to look for reasons to keep you out of the military. The military wants people that are 100% healthy. They don't want to put up with recruits that have a bad this or that. They are looking for a smooth running machine. Even the littlest things had to be documented- broken bones, stitches, concussions, aches, pains, soreness, sprains, hospital visits, pins and plates, surgeries, everything. And if anything came up that may serve as a stumbling block to proper motor function, Hasta la Vista. Oh yeah, another little thing was that everything had to be painstakingly consistent. All the dates had to match up as well as the number of occurrences in which they happened. So on one sheet you would say that this happened twice and this was the result. A few days later, you would be required to write down the same exact information otherwise you would be called on it. And you DID NOT want to be called on anything. Some recruits found that it felt as though the Med staff was trying to trick you or twist something around to make you a liar. This was of course to make sure you were telling the truth, but it was a nightmare if they got a hold of you. Luckily, I remembered exactly when everything had happened so I was good to go. I wish it was because I had such a terrific memory, but it wasn't. The fact is that not much has ever happened to me and the stuff that did was easy to remember. When it came to dates that I wasn't sure about, I pinpointed a date that would be super easy to remember. Done deal!

After we got our crash course in military notation and our blood pressure checked out, we were taken through a door and asked to have a seat in front of these two doors that looked like dressing rooms. We could see something going on under the doors but no one knew what it was. Soon enough, a woman came out from the door on the left and I walked in. As soon as I sat down I found that both of the dressing rooms were actually connected to a larger room. They were simply divided by a small partition to service two people at once. I took a glance around and recognized what was about to happen. It was time for some blood work baby. The lady that played vampire was a pleasant woman but not too talkative. She seemed like her job was some endless mindless task and she was just in a daydream until she could go home and watch Lifetime. However, she was good at it. She swabbed my arm, shoved a straw in my vein for a quick fill, slapped a Band-Aid on my arm, and sent me on my way. It was interesting to me in the since that everyone looked mean. I've gone to give blood before and the ladies are very sweet and offer a sense that they will cater to the fact that you don't like needles going into your arm. These ladies here were a tad different. Two words- strictly business. They "secured" your arm with an almighty death grip. They grabbed their needle and popped the cap one handed, smiled, and shoved it into your arm before you could say a word. I got the impression that they were not interested in what anyone had to say and the sooner you sat down and shut up the faster they would be done with you. It was over so quickly that we didn't even have a chance to cuddle afterwards. She just kicked me out the door and on my way to the next station. I felt used. What ev's.

After that little field trip, the girls and boys were split up for a urinalysis test. We were given these little plastic cups with a line about halfway up. We were instructed to fill it up and if we couldn't, we were required to stand by this table filled with bottles of water and drink them down until we had to go. Yeehaw! Luckily, I had to go so I didn't have to do the table dance. As soon as we filled the cup to the line, we had to stand in line and wait for our turn to have it checked, bottled, and verified that we had completed the process. I started with a folder holding my test results and basic medical history, but after every station I cleared, more papers were added and my folder was growing. After the fluid check, I headed out that door and into a small hallway with 2 doors at the end. Not anything strange here except for the fact that all the guys had their shoes off. What the--? It was odd how we would receive instructions but have no idea what was going to happen. The only time we knew was when the first person came out and gave everyone the heads up. Apparently, this was where the doc was going to make us cough. However, the guys that came out had this peculiar look on their face so there had to be something else. Were they going to say? Nope. They all just replied- "You'll see." Finally, it was my turn. I walked in the office barefooted. I smiled an uneasy smile at the doc and he just grinned at me. He was an older gentleman and he was actually cool to talk to. It wasn't just strictly business with this guy. He could sense the nervous tension of all the guys coming through and tried to make things as easy as possible. As he carried a casual conversation with you, he would motion what he needed you to do. He would jabber on as he did his work and that was that. I've done the cough test before and that was normal. However, I was not prepared for the turn around, bend over, and spread your cheeks apart thing. I don't know what he was looking for, but whatever man. As long as I'm not getting the finger I'm good to go. Interestingly enough, he read on my profile that I was a Professional Martial Arts Instructor and talked about a book he had read about the Martial Arts called "Iron and Silk" and how much he enjoyed it. So, to take the edge off of what was going on, he just asked me about what I did on a day-to-day basis and it was over before I knew it. At the end, he shook my hand and thanked me for talking to him and I was out the door. When I came outside to see the guys that had just arrived, they asked me what had just happened. I got this peculiar look on my face and replied- "You'll see."‖

Just when I thought things couldn't be pushed into weird world any further, I walked into the next room. It cracks me up just writing about it now! I walked around the corner into this room and saw all the guys at the back end of this 30X30 foot room. The room is empty except for the bench that runs the length of the back of the room. All I see is a bunch of guys sitting on a bench stripped down to their boxers or briefs. At first, I couldn't see their shorts from the way they were sitting and I honestly thought everyone was stripped bare. All I could say was- *"All right, now I've seen everything!"*

The guys cracked up because there really isn't anything you can say after being stunned like that but you feel like you have to say something in order to show that it doesn't bother you. Again, whatever man. However, it was fun to see the rest of the guys come in and get that stunned "what the--?" look on their face. Turns out, we all had to get weighed in and have our height recorded. We couldn't do that with clothes on so we just had to strip down and wait for the doc. Waiting was murder.

I believe only guys can truly appreciate what I'm about to say. But if you asked anyone there what would have been the absolute worst, the results would have been unanimous. Everyone was praying-

Please Lord, don't let me get a stiffy.

Oh the horror of standing up to get weighed in just to find out that you were not the only one "standing at attention." Why would this be so bad? Because even though all the guys would have known it was from the temperature change in the room, you would automatically be labeled gay and even though everyone knew you probably weren't and even if you were no one would have cared, you would have instantly become the focus of everyone's conversation. There are probably a few people out there that would say "There's nothing wrong with that. Why would you make a gay person be the brunt of a joke? You're just homophobic." Well guess what? It has absolutely nothing to do with being gay or straight. Nothing. One of the best parts of the Marine Corps is its ability to take everything back to square one. Guys are guys and if we can make fun of something to help us feel more at ease, we will. That's what guys do. It's not really designed to make anyone feel bad, it just amuses everyone and keeps you occupied. Luckily, it didn't happen to anyone. After our info was collected, we had to line up 5X5 and the doc had us run through a series of exercises to prove our joints and ligaments were in check. We did stuff like arm rotations, toe touches, squats, and finally squat and rotate 360 degrees only on our tiptoes without using our hands. For a moment I felt like a ballerina. But it was all just part of the deal. We all took this big awkward uncomfortable horse pill and choked it down as a team.

One thing I noticed was that everyone I came into contact with, as far as the staff was concerned, was that they were very direct with everything they did. I'm sure that they could come across as cold and insensitive but I see it a bit differently. The military has the responsibility of stripping everything away from you that characterizes you as a total individual. It wants you to think and respond as a unit. The military is all business. Check your emotions at the door. It's just business. If you need something, you get it. No excuses. If you have a problem, you fix it. Now. If you need help with something, you take the responsibility and ask the right person and find the help you need. There is no room for weakness or apprehension. The world is full of idiots that want people to do every little thing for them. No sir. Not in military world. I would pay so much money to go through Boot Camp with a celebrity. It would be awesome to see a Drill Instructor put them in check and make them do everything for themselves. Go ahead and finish this equation:

Marine Corps Boot Camp + Self Entitled Celebrity =_____

That's what I love about the Marine Corps. It brings you back to the most basic elements of life and teaches you to be grateful for it. To respect yourself and the people that have tried to help make a difference in your life. Some people call the Marine Corps mentality being brainwashed. I disagree. I think it's the Marines doing the job that their parents never did. The Marines teaches you that only 3 words matter the most- Honor, Courage, and Commitment. It was cool to watch some kids come to MEPS all hardcore and found that the longer they stayed, the more they tried to do the right thing so they wouldn't get yelled at. Everyone did exactly what they were supposed to do. The staff understood this transformation. That's why they would always smile at you and get you going in the right direction. There was a lot to get done and no time to waste time.

The next test reminded me of being in the 3rd grade. I walked into a room and we had to have our hearing checked. Everyone has done it. You put these headphones on and signal to the examiner when you hear a pitch. However, this time around was different. It was the same in that you pushed a button to signal when you heard the sound. The primary difference was that the tones were not the same. The tones went through a complete range of pitches at random. Each time you would hear a tone, it would come in the form of repeating beeps. Your job was to push the button as soon as you heard the first one. I swear this test messed with you because you would be so paranoid if it was a tone you were hearing or if you were just imagining you heard something. And you couldn't cheat. The computer would automatically reject any button push when there wasn't a tone. To make things more challenging, the tones came at different volumes as well. Some would be loud while some were super hard to hear. You had to really pay attention. However, I did pretty well with this test. I only missed two tones and that was exceptional. Score for the home team! So after I took the go-go gadget ear test, I headed off to take the vision test... CRAP!

I know for a fact that my eyesight isn't the best. For that reason, I thought this might just be the test that would boot me out. I wore glasses when I was a kid, but when I went to high school, I actually learned how to focus so I didn't need them. That's all well and good and I think there's actually a medical word to describe automatically correcting your vision through focus, but that goes right out the door when they cover an eye or make you keep your head straight. So I did the best I could and I actually passed. My depth perception was down the tube but it was correctable. My MOS didn't require me to get glasses and that's cool but even if I did, I wouldn't have to pay for it. Uncle Sam would have shouldered that bill and I'd still be in the Corps. Awesome!

Well I had all this stuff done and I passed everything with flying colors. Now, I have just one more thing to pass. MEPS does everything it can to make sure that the right candidates go through the process. The next "test" would solidify my future in the Marine Corps. Drum roll please... it was time for my final chat with the Chief Doctor. It was time for MEPS to know that what you had said, who you were, and what you were capable of was put into the spotlight for the last time. When I sat in the row of chairs and saw everyone in front of me go in and come out a short time after, I really didn't think too much about it. But then I noticed that some would come out smiling big and others would come out looking rather upset. I turned to the guy that was next in front of me and asked him what this was all about. He told me it was the "Burner". You go in and the Doc grills you on everything and if even the slightest thing is inaccurate or out of place, you're going home early. Wow, that sucks! I didn't even know it was going to happen but that was the final step. I didn't know what to expect so I figured not worrying about it and just going in and putting everything on the table would do the trick. Luckily, it wasn't bad at all when I went in. When I was called in, I made eye contact with the Doc, smiled, introduced myself while shaking his hand, and answered his questions. He went through all my papers that I had collected throughout the day and asked very direct questions about everything that happened.

My battle plan- 2 words- Honesty and consistency. The military wants to know that what you say is what it be. They have no room to cater to people that lack the intelligence nor the integrity to man up and state "This is who I am." And that's what I did. I answered everything he asked of me, he smiled, shook my hand, told me I was good to go and good luck, and I was out the door.

After that final meeting, I was really glad I made it through. This entire process taught me so much about myself that even if I had failed something, I would have known more than if I wouldn't have come out and tried at all. It was a great process. What's even better is that now this part is over... or at least that's what I thought when I left the Doc. Staff Sergeant G came and picked me up from MEPS at 1PM. It was wild how a new recruit wasn't aloud to leave the building for any reason without his/her recruiter. The only way you could go outside was if the building was on fire! Besides that, you might as well just park it in front of the big screen and wait for your ride. Staff Sergeant G picked me up and asked me how everything went. He could totally relate to everything I was telling him and we shared similar stories about the MEPS experience. It was a good ride back to Annapolis.

Right before Staff Sergeant G dropped me off, he informed me that my work at MEPS was not complete. I had to go back on Monday morning and finish everything up. I still had to have my paperwork finalized, get fingerprinted, and officially be sworn in. I told him that was impossible because I had to work Monday morning; however, I could come back up Monday night and stay Tuesday morning no problem.

BAM! Just like that, date with MEPS... again. Yeehaw!

The rest of the weekend flew by. Sunday came and went, and by the time I had settled into Monday starting the week, it was already over and I was heading to **ROD1** to meet up with Staff Sergeant G. He was reading some emails from a friend he has over seas. His friend is stationed at a place known as "Camp Cupcake"‖ because they actually have a Subway Restaurant and Cable TV. Very Nice! So I threw my stuff in his car and we headed to MEPS... again. I checked into the Comfort Inn... again, but this time it was different. My first night was brutal because of the emotions I was trying to sort out. Now that I had been in the mix and gotten used to everything, I had no worries at all. It was a pleasant change.

20070612 (Tuesday)
Welcome Back to MEPS- Day 2

3:50AM came early as always but just as before I shot out of bed and was anxious to start the day. Now that I knew the system, I was able to relax a bit more and take my time with breakfast and making my way out to see my friend and the big red bus. Sure enough, everything happened like clockwork. The bus was right on time, the driver bounced off the bus and he and I exchanged pleasantries, he went inside, we got on the bus, he came back, put his empty plastic cup on the console, and off we went. Today he wasn't telling stories so it was just me and Limp Bizkit. I was feeling the need for some old school and Significant Other was going to do the trick. I remembered to bring my IPod to get me through the down time and that was a nice alternative. We arrived at MEPS and headed for the conference room. Just as before, the liaison's called role and we were split into our groups. Even though most stuff was the same, today was a big ship day so there were a lot of new recruits heading off to Basic Training. How does that affect me? My group was put at the bottom of the list of priorities because we were not the ones shipping out. So after we got split from the group, we were dropped in the cafeteria. Great! Now I get to hang out for hours on end with the Breakfast Club Posse. This wasn't bad at all though. At first, no one was really saying anything. But then, we all started talking and getting to know everyone. No one talked using names. We referred to everyone based on the branch they were going into. So we had 2 Marines, 4 Armies, 2 Coast Guards, and 3 Navies. So it went like this-

Marines-   *Hey Navy, is this your first time at MEPS?*

Navy-   *Hell no! I've been here for 3 days and I'm ready to GO! What about you?*

Marines-   *Second day for me. I've just got to get final paperwork done and sworn in and I'm out.*

Army-   *Yeah me too. I was supposed to be sworn in yesterday but it didn't happen because of the shippers heading out today.*

Navy-   *So where are you from Marines?*

Marines-   *Right here in Annapolis.*

Navy-   *That's not fair! You can go home every night. I've been stuck at that hotel for 4 days!*

For the next two hours, we just sat there in the cafeteria just talking about this and that. Then, one of the Program Directors came in and sent us on our way to where we needed to go to finish up. 2 Army's, 2 Coast Guards, 2 Navy's, and 1 Marines were sent to medical while the rest of us headed back to Liaison Central. Liaison Central was just a big room with a big screen at one end, chairs set up to watch whatever was on, and offices around the parameter of the room for each branch.

Staff Sergeant G told me that he would come and pick me up by 3PM and get me back to the Karate school whether I was done or not. In the meantime, all I could do was just hang out and wait for Staff Sergeant Wilson to get me in gear. Then, just like that, Staff Sergeant Wilson came out and we were able to get things moving. How fast? That was yet to be determined, but since I was getting serviced, it didn't matter.

Life always has a way of keeping your mind occupied when you have nothing to do. In this case, the 2 Navy's and I had our hands full with B2K (not the group). This kid was put with us from the start of the day. He was totally cool at first because he was sleeping in the cafeteria. Then… he woke up.

That's when everything changed. It was like a flip was switched and he went from completely brain dead to B2K. I swear he would not go away. He took a liking to the 3 of us and decided for the remainder of the day that he would serve as the world's most annoying recruit. At first, we called him Billy the Kid because he was 18 and joining the Marine Corps. Billy the Kid was totally gung-ho about killing some insurgents or blowing something up. I'm kind of glad he was serving our country because without that outlet, he would definitely be the future mascot of Mass Murder University. Then, the name Billy the Kid became entirely too long to say so we shortened it to B to the K. Shortly after that, he just became B2K. B2K was like a kid with ADHD on speed suffering from turrets. Here's just a taste of the fun we had-

Navy-   *SHIT! Here he comes!*
B2K-   *What's up guys? Check it out. I got this Gideon's Bible from the guy handing them out. Do you want one?*
Marines-   *No thanks man, he ju…*
B2K-   *It's even camouflage! A camouflage Bible! That'll be sweet because if I was in the field about to invade some town, I could totally read it while I was hiding and no one would be able to see me. Plus, I could use the pages as toilet paper just in case. I could also use the pages to roll cigarettes and stuff because they only have European cigarettes in places like Japan. You gotta be resourceful over there you know?*
Navy-   *So when are you shipping Marines?*
Marines-   *November at this point, but I'm going to try and kick it up to Octo…*
B2K-   *Wow, check this shit out! If I turn the Bible sideways it looks like a tent!*

I would pay so much money to go to Boot Camp with B2K. 1 of 2 things would happen. Either he would become the official Marine recruit piñata, and we could take out our daily aggression on an idiot, or the Marine Corps would totally straighten him up and he would work out in the end. It's a Win/ Win either way. I swear he was just always there. I would get up to use the bathroom and he would follow me to the bathroom and wait for me to come back out just to follow me back to where I was sitting. He would be talking the entire time never offering a reason for you to respond, just talking. In a way, I felt sorry for him because no one wanted to be around him. So whether I liked him or not, I let him feel welcome in our little group. After all, there could come a day where it was his responsibility to watch my back. I would hate for him to think of me as the guy who snubbed him. You never know in this life. You got to be good to everyone no matter how much you want to strangle them. Oh well.

Nothing happened for 2 more hours. Then I got a big surprise. Some shippers had come back into Liaison Central and they were getting their first look at what they were about to get themselves into. The nice Marine Liaison that had been helping them all morning came out of his office and this time without a smile. He looked totally different. Before, he was somewhat nice and eager to help you along the way. This time, he came out yelling at the top of his lungs which totally startled everyone in Liaison Central. Even B2K stopped talking to see what was going on. He was telling them to stand in a straight line by the wall and to do one thing and one thing only-
He yelled- **Shut up!** (That got everyone's attention!)

He walked over, shut off the TV, and then whipped back around to face the shippers. His eyes were razors and his demeanor was screaming with intensity. You could see the white bones shining through his clenched fists. Everyone in the room froze as if they were paralyzed. There was no way anyone was going to do anything to bring negative attention to themselves with a rabid bulldog in the room. He started telling them that they were about to jump on a bus, check in at the airport, get on a plane, get on another bus, arrive at Parris Island at 0200 (2AM), and the only thing that was required of them was to keep their mouths shut and stay in their groups. He turned to one shipper and in a really hushed and direct voice said-

If one of you fucking idiots gets lost, the other four in the group better be fucking lost as well. Starting now, you idiots are to work, think, and respond as a hardcore fucking team. No one fucking stands alone in the Marines. NOW MOVE!

After that, the room was buzzing with excitement and anticipation. It definitely gave us another solid hour of conversation material to say the least. All the guys that were enlisted for Marines were floored by the Staff Sergeant. It was exciting. That's exactly what we wanted. Everything was getting a little too warm and fuzzy and his display snapped us back into reality. It was great. As far as all the other Army, Navy, and Coast Guard recruits, you could sense the divide. Some saw the display with envious eyes. Deep down, you know they wanted a piece of that. On the other side of the spectrum, you could see that some were glad that wasn't them. They didn't sign up for that. They simply wanted to serve their country without the intensity the Marine Corps carries. That's the great thing about our US Military. There is no such thing as a bad service. No matter what your background is and what you desire, there is a service that will fit you to the T. All you have to do is pick the one that will maximize your potential and step up to bat.

Finally, it was time for me to finish up my processing papers. I headed back to the processing center and sat down in front of a brand new 23-year-old secretary. Great! She was a sweet girl but you could tell that the ink on her Certificate of Completion was still warm. However, she went straight to business and proceeded with guiding me through a battery of question. I guess this was just to finalize and solidify my history. On several occasions, she had to have another secretary come over and get her screen to move forward. I tried as best as I could to let her know that even though I was in a rush to finish, it didn't bother me that she was struggling. As soon as that was done, it was off to get fingerprinted. This was actually really cool. Back when I was in school, you simply touched an inkpad and then pressed your finger on a piece of paper. This time it was completely digital. The newbie secretary grabbed the appropriate finger, rolled it on a plexi-glass surface, and my fingerprint appeared on the monitor in real time. That was actually pretty cool. The process sounds easy too. But it wasn't. First she had a problem getting the program to respond. Then, she couldn't get the pressure right and it came out too dark or too light. It just wasn't going to happen today. We ran out of time, which means I would have to come back tomorrow, same time, same place, and hopefully finish everything up.

Staff Sergeant G took me straight to work from there. It was interesting in the since that I hadn't told anyone at work about my plans to join the Marine Corps, my trips to MEPS, or anything else that was going on. At this point, I didn't want my job to be in jeopardy until I knew that I could make it in and everything would be set to go. If for some reason something came up and I was rejected and a replacement had already been set up to take my place, I would be dead. For that reason, I set my ship date 3 months ahead. That way, once I knew I could make it in, I could still give 90 days notice and bring someone in, have them fully trained, and leave on the best of terms. So as far as my work was concerned, they knew that I took a physical and Wednesday I'll be going to pick up the results. No harm no foul. When I left work that night, I ran by the house, picked up MORE clothes and headed to the recruiting office one last time to meet Staff Sergeant G and head to MEPS. At least I was praying this would be the last time. Luckily, all I had to do the next day was finish being finger printed and get sworn in. Staff Sergeant G informed me that he had someone coming in for the sole purpose of swearing me in and then BAM! It was going to be a done deal. I was excited about that.

Well that night I got to the Comfort Inn, got signed in, headed to my room, and found a change in plans. This time I had a roommate. For the past few visits I had been in a room by myself. This time I walked in and found company. That's just great. I introduced myself and that was really that. He said his name was Mirko. You could tell by first glance that Mirko was just out of high school and heading off to the Navy. His mom kept calling and even though I couldn't hear what she was saying, he kept saying that he was fine; the room was nice, the food was good, he had all his stuff, and he felt great. You know, stuff you say when your mom is asking you if everything is ok and seeing if you are emotionally stable. To me, he looked worried. But since his mom was asking all the questions and acting more nervous, it must have helped put him at ease. Suddenly, I started remembering what my first night was like. At least he had a mom to talk to.

And then it hit me. I reached in my bag, grabbed some paper, asked Mirko for a pen, sat down at the desk, hit my IPod, and started on this little masterpiece that you are presently reading. So many cool things had happened that no matter what the outcome was, I had to write it down while everything was still fresh on my mind. Even if no one ever reads it, it just might be something cool to look at and read later on down the road.

20070613 (Wednesday)
Last Day at MEPS- Day 3

3:50AM came early. But just as always, I jumped out of bed and waltzed right in to my morning at MEPS ritual. Everything was the exact same. At this point, I actually started to feel sorry for the people that worked there. I had only been there a few times and the monotony was unnerving. Same thing (x3) every day. You could tell that the staff really enjoyed when something out of the ordinary happened. Having new blood in there certainly catered to that. You would always see a newbie that was just as lost as can be (just like me when I first showed up) and they would jump in to show the new recruit what needed to be done and keep them pointed in the right direction. And the new recruit was always thankful. The way I saw it, there was only one way to truly describe the mentality of a new recruit. If you put a new recruit in a round room and stripped him/ her of her clothes and gave them 2 BB's, within five minutes they would lose one and break the other. I can't say much because this world was just as foreign to me. You had no idea what to do and since everything was done with such an unwavering sense of urgency, it was easy to be careless over the most simplistic of tasks.

Today was different for some reason. It was as if everything had really settled down after the shippers had left the day before. Not as many people were talking and there seemed to be a lack of energy in the air. It was almost as if there was more a feeling of utter relief. I must say that I was put to the test on finding ways to keep myself busy and my mind moving. At first, I started to drift in and out of sleep but then decided that that was not the best use of my time. So, first I broke out the IPod and listened to some stand up comedy. When I got in trouble for having an IPod (which was not on any poster but strictly enforced) I started jamming on the Rubik's Cube. I was seeing if I could solve it in less than 3 minutes. My best time that day was 2 minutes 14 seconds. Not too bad. But then I realized that that was actually making my brain tired so I put a halt to that. Finally, I got called for fingerprinting. I made my way to the back just as before and this time, I had a new person helping me and that was great. He made it happen the first time every time and I must say that I was impressed with how it turned out.

After that process was out of the way, it was back to liaison central for me. Upon arrival, I saw that Staff Sergeant G was there and he was working hard to get all of my papers in order. It was time to sign off on my MOS, complete my forms, and sign the final papers. Then I received the **black** question. The question that everyone seemed to side-skirt, tip toe around, or avoid all together. That question was-

Who would you like your belongings to go to if you die?

I'm fairly certain that the question was posed in a much less threatening manner, but when it all comes down to it, that's what it's all about. If I die, who do I want my stuff to go to? WOW! Let me just say that that questions sucks! I for one do not want to be reminded of the fact that I am enlisting in one of the most dangerous jobs in the world. Yes, I understand that its terms are based on a volunteer basis and it's what I want to do. But it's just like having surgery. You know you have to go in and get taken care of and you'll be better on the other side. But you don't want to have a conversation where a doctor says-

...and then we're going to take a sharp instrument out and slice you wide open, play tic tac toe with your internal organs, finger paint with your blood while we discuss our golf handicap, and then sew you back together so you'll be good as new.

I'll pass. However, I had to answer the question so I simply said- *"My dad."* I gave his full name, address, and phone number and that was that. In retrospect, it was a simple question that required no real

44

thought what so ever, but it still made you think for a moment. Oh the dark side of life. Yahoo! After that, I signed a few more papers and was... again... sent back to liaison central.

I sat down in a chair replaying everything in my mind and decided it was in my best interest to get my mind off of it. Just then, two Navy's that I had met earlier in the day saw me sitting there and came over to join me. Excellent! That's what I'm talking about. I don't know what it is, but Navy girls are always cuter than most other military girls... actually they... well... yup, they got it going on! So they sat down and I start in like a geek playing Tetris. They start telling me about the last few tests they took. For example, one of the girls wanted to be in the linguist department and said she had to listen to these recordings of someone speaking a foreign language and she had to decipher if the voice's tone was hostile, intimidated, happy, sad, stuff like that. As it turns out, the language wasn't even foreign by country standards. It was just a made up gibberish language used for that particular exercise. Just about that time, Staff Sergeant G showed up after having to step out to pick up some things and starts in on me.
He says-

What's up with that Killian? I brought you here to be a Marine not a pimp. Look at you working your game.

I told him it was cool. We were just talking about nothing. No big deal. He laughs at me a bit and said-

Oh ok. I was just checking.

He smiled again and then went on with his business. As he was walking away, Staff Sergeant Wilson was coming toward me. He was looking at some papers and had an odd look on his face. He said-

Killian, I need you to do something for me. You told me that you had been to court and I need you to write out every friggin thing that happened. Don't leave anything out ok.

I knew exactly what he was talking about. It's funny how just when you think you can put something behind you, all of the sudden it comes back and says "Remember me?" This is when you were retarded. I had worked so hard to right the things I have done wrong in this life and I wasn't really happy about bringing it up yet again. It's simply embarrassing. However, it all has to get done so... whatever. I was given a pen, paper, and specific directions to be completely thorough. I took a deep breath, sat down in a chair, and hammered it out-

To whom it may concern,
        Last November, I went to pick up my mom from the airport. I pulled up to the curb, got out to give her a hug, and as I was loading her bags in my car, I noticed an Officer walking towards me. Oh CRAP! Just my luck. I closed the trunk, opened my door, put on my seatbelt, started the car, and right when I was about to pull away from the curb felt the Officer tap on the back of my car and ask me to stop right there. I'm DEAD and I knew it. He walked up to my side and said-
Sir, may I see your license and registration?
I started to get out of the car explaining that my license was in my back pocket. He took a look at my license and told me that I had an expired tag. I said I know. Worse yet, he asked-
What's up with the sticker?
I could have lied. I could have made up a half-truth story. But I didn't. I just told him the deal. I said-
Sir, that's just a poor excuse to buy me some time. I had done it myself. I took a black pen and turned the '06 into an '08.
With that, he called for back up. Not because I was some huge threat, but just to show the new Officers on staff just how retarded a white boy can be. I sat in the car humiliated. My mom was scared for me. She works in the Tag office in Florida and is fully aware of the ramifications of what I had done. It was my fault. As soon as everything was set, the Officer called me out. I walked up knowing full well I was in for it. He said-
Mr. Killian, are you aware that what you did is a federal offense?
I said- *Yes Sir.*
He said- *Mr. Killian, are you aware that I could take you to jail right now for this offense?*
I said- *Yes Sir.*

He said- *Mr. Killian, you don't even have insurance on this vehicle. I ought to throw some cuffs on you and take you in. But I'm not. I'm going to give you 2 tickets. The first is because you tried to fraudulently fix your tag. The second is for not having a current registration on this vehicle. I'm not going to cite you for not having insurance if you will just get it done. Now listen to me. The only reason I'm not placing you under arrest is because you told me from the very beginning what you had done and you were honest about everything else. But just so you know, if you would have made up anything but the truth, you'd be sitting in jail tonight. Do you understand?*

I said- *Yes Sir.*

He then told me that my car was going to be towed to the Maryland State Inspection Facility to make sure that it is in appropriate working order. I was going to have to arrange a ride for my mom and I to get back to Annapolis. Wow what a mess. My mom was glad I wasn't going to jail but she was disappointed that I had tried to shirk responsibility. We didn't talk about the ordeal but it weighed heavily on the both of us. After that, I immediately took care of my car. I got the registration updated, got it inspected, and got insurance for it. I didn't want to play around with that at all. I then paid the fines that could be paid before the court date. I also acquired an attorney to stand for me during court. My lawyer was a genius. As soon as he saw the Officer on the day of court, he started talking to him about the incident. They agreed that since I had been honest about it and that I had taken care of everything that we simply stet the case. I didn't really know what that meant but I didn't care. The penalty for my actions was a minimum of $10,000 and up to 1 year in jail. I didn't want either. Instead, the judge ruled that I keep my nose clean for 1 year and they will drop all charges against me. I simply agreed. So I didn't have to pay any fines, do any time, and all I had to do was be good for a year. I can do that! All it cost me was $750 to get my car up to Maryland code and $1000 for my lawyer.

I wrote all this down and submitted it to Staff Sergeant Wilson. After reading it, he looked relieved. And he was. He didn't know the details of my run in with the State and thought it would have been much worse. But it was going to be ok. For a moment, I thought this might kick me out of being in the military but it wasn't. I was good to go.

Staff Sergeant Wilson then faxed what I had written to "who knows." He then got on the phone with "who knows" and discussed everything I had written. Then it was a done deal. Staff Sergeant Wilson hung up the phone, looked me in the eyes, and said that was done. I guess he didn't know if someone needed to sign off on the fact that everything was ok, so he wanted to check just to make sure. Finally, I was going to be able to put that to rest. That was the last ring of fire to pass through before completing this process of being accepted. Everything was done. I had made it!

Then he told me the time had come. It was time for me to be officially sworn in. A big dog from Marine Headquarters had driven down just to finish me up and get me on my way. I introduced myself and made short conversation about my experience so far.

One thing about the Marines is that they talk more at you than with you. They ask a question, you answer the question, they ask another question, you answer that question, and they say "Outstanding." Then the conversation is over. I mean, you smile and everything, but it's strictly business in this world. So it's off to the Ceremony Room. I had walked by it a hundred times while here at MEPS. It's a 30 x 15 foot room. The Marine Corps, Army, Navy, Air Force, and Coast Guard flags are represented at the front of the room. Red carpet lines the floor and there is an elevated podium at the flag end.

He first showed me how to stand at attention. It was a bit different then how we stand in the Martial Arts school because our toes and heals are together, whereas here, you put your feet at 45 degree angles. That was cool. And in the Karate class we have our hands open, fingers straight, and pressed to our legs with our fingertips pointing down. Now, I had to make fists and hold them to my sides. The thumb of your closed fists is straight and runs down along your trouser seam. OK, I think I have it.

Then it started. Unlike all the other times I'd seen this room in action, I was standing by myself. Every other time, there was always a nice group of people, moms and dads shedding tears for their beloved sons and daughters, and friends were right there to take a picture to commemorate the moment. I was solo, And that's ok! He took his position at the podium, had me raise my right hand, and then asked me to repeat him swearing upon this oath-

I, Matthew Killian,
do solemnly swear...
that I will support and defend the Constitution of the United States...
against all enemies, foreign and domestic;...
that I will bear true faith and allegiance to the same;...
and that I will obey the orders of the President of the United States...
and the orders of the officers appointed over me,...
according to regulations...
and the Uniform Code of Military Justice...
So help me God.

I don't know about you, but this was very powerful to me. It was almost sobering. I had been thrown here and there at MEPS and at times, reality seemed to be lost. When it came to swearing on this oath, everything became very real. This is the big leagues. It's very serious and something you don't play with. It meant a lot. I was practically overwhelmed with a sense of pride to honor my country. All the thoughts of fear and uncertainty escaped me. This is what it was all about. I shook hands with the Officer and that was it. I was FINALLY DONE. That in itself was just great. I didn't want to be spending any more nights in the Comfort Inn any time soon. I didn't want to spend any more time with the Breakfast Club Posse in the cafeteria, or sitting around for hours on end in Liaison Central, or spinning my wheels in nowhere conversations with guys like B2K. I'm just ready to go. I walked out of the Ceremony Room and Staff Sergeant G came up and shook my hand with a word of congratulations. It was official. In just a few short months, I was going to be heading off to Boot Camp! Staff Sergeant G said that we had to do just one more thing. We had to head over to Marine Headquarters and pick up my New Recruit Package. That's cool.

I gathered my belongings and said goodbye to MEPS. As we got to the door, we were joined by two other Marines. Both had JUST gotten out of Boot Camp and were enjoying their first break. They were in need of a ride back to town and when Staff Sergeant G told them that I was enlisting, they asked if they could tag along. Apparently, they wanted to see how I was responding to getting ready to go. They asked me a ton of questions like-

What did I think about the MEPS experience?

Am I looking forward to Boot Camp?

Why did I want to become a Marine?

Do I train now?

It was cool. In turn, I got to ask them all kinds of questions about their experience and they were excited to tell me everything. It was inspiring. They told me about "the Crucible" (A 54 hour endurance challenge filled with obstacles, challenges, and scenarios where you had to rely solely on your team to reach the finish), "Attitude Adjustments" handed out by the DI's (Drill Instructors), that 4 people had quit in the middle of Boot Camp, and then they proceeded to offer me a few Do's and Don'ts. For example-

- Always say- "Aye Sir!" Even if you have no clue as to what they are screaming at you.

- Never ever say "I'm sorry." The Marine Corps doesn't want you to be sorry. They want you to fix it, learn from it, and move on.

- Never volunteer for anything. This actually got a rise out of Staff Sergeant G. The reason this was said is because every time volunteers were asked for, it was always for some torture exercise. Staff Sergeant G said that this was most likely a subtle difference between DI's because volunteering helped him finish at the top of his class. So I guess we'll see.

- Always try to outrun the DI's. They like to see that you still have some hustle in you since they are kicking your butt 24 hours a day.

It was great talking to them. One of the Marines was totally horse even as we spoke. He said that the last couple days had been just awesome. Everybody was amped at the graduation screaming their heads off and congratulating the new family of brothers and sisters that they were now a part of. They were finally able to say- "We did it! We survived!!"

When we got to Marine Headquarters, we got out of the car and instead of going straight in, Staff Sergeant G and I headed to the pull-up bars. He had to see me throw down on the bars to finish up my physical. I asked him how many I had to do. He just smiled and said- Don't worry about that. Just do as many as I can. Well, I'm no pro so I shot for 10. I got to 10 and realized I had 1 more in me so I finished at 11. Not bad. From there we went inside and found our way to the back offices where

I met a lot of Marines who all seemed excited to have me on board. It was great. If I can say anything, the Marine Corps sticks together! I took a seat and I swear I waited there for about 2 hours. No one came in and I wasn't supposed to get up and go anywhere. I was just sitting in this conference room, twiddling my thumbs, and praying any second a Marine would walk in and let me know it was time to go. After two hours I started getting antsy and walked up to the front desk. The moment I turned the corner, the Marine behind the desk said-"Hey, are you with Staff Sergeant G?
I replied- Yes Sir.

He then informed me that everything had gone through and we could bounce. AWESOME! After that, I was given a Marine Corps Tin, a Certificate, and a T-shirt. Sweet. The tin held all the important information I would need prior to arriving at Parris Island. It contained a work out training log, a Manual filled with guidelines and protocol, and a couple "Proud to be a Marine's Parent" stickers. After I got my stuff, we headed back to the car and took off to Annapolis. On the way, the Marine I was sitting next to started telling me all about the stuff that was in my tin. He told me about having to memorize the 11 General Orders, how to remember the rank structure, about the workout log and making sure to work on some of the calisthenics before Boot Camp so I would be used to them. It was great! Like I said, if you fail to plan, you plan to fail. I wanted to know as much as possible so that when it was my turn to run, I'd be good to go. When I got back to ROD1 to pick up my car, I was left with a feeling of pure excitement. I had set a goal to get myself involved, I did everything that was necessary to make it happen, and now I'm set to jet. Now, the only thing I have to do between now and then is train my body specifically for the rigors of Boot Camp training, memorize everything that was highlighted in the Manual, and figure out what to tell momma dukes. Should be fun!

20070624 (Sunday)
Salvation

I had started going to a church because I was tired of running from it. Being a Killian, I had always gone to church. My parents always

51

made sure that Sunday was the day that the family got up, got dressed, and went to church. My dad wasn't always a preacher. In fact, he was actually a UPS driver for the first 8 years of my life. When I turned 8, he was called to the Ministry, we packed up, and we moved to Fort Worth Texas so he could become a bona fide Baptist Preacher from the Southwestern Baptist Theological Seminary. My parents made sure that I stayed actively involved in the church until I was 18. It was cool.

Growing up as a preacher's kid can be interesting. Call me biased, but my father is by far the best preacher in the world! I could never get tired of hearing him preach. Like I said, he always had a way of saying things that gave me food for thought or a better understanding. But I couldn't find a church home that gave me that feeling of being spiritually satisfied.

There just came a point in my life where church had just become boring. I didn't want to stray from my beliefs or deter how I wanted to carry myself as a Christian. Far from it. I just couldn't stand going to church. Hearing the same stories every Sunday for 20 sum odd years became a drag. I love it when you go to church and you get to get up and sing and fellowship with other Christians and celebrate God's love. That's my kind of church. Unfortunately, I hadn't found that here in Maryland. There seemed to be a bipolar sort of selection here in Annapolis. I went to one church and even though it said contemporary, it was flat out traditional. I don't know what they thought was contemporary about it, bit it wasn't my cup of tea. I went to another church and they were out of their minds. They were hollering out in the middle of the service claiming to be speaking in tongues (Bull crap, I heard that guy say hakuna matata!) and doing all sorts of stuff that I just don't want any part of. For a moment, I thought hope maybe lost. Oh contraire. I'm a firm believer that if you want to get your life in check, God will hook you up.

On Friday, I went and saw a movie and before it started, one of the advertisements said that there was a church group that held a service right here in the theaters. Awesome! So I checked it out. Result, it was fantastic! After the service, I was invited to go to lunch with a group that obviously hung out all the time and we all sat around and talked and got to know everyone. They told me that they were in need of another musician to complete the band and I jumped on that like a fat kid on a cupcake! Not only did I find a church that fueled the fire in me, but now I was given the opportunity to plug in.

This was a huge answered prayer. That feeling of alone that I had mentioned before was gone. It seems to me that the moment you stop trying to control everything and trust in God by following what you know is right, he blesses you! My buddy Jason, a great friend and awesome Pastor, always told me-

Thank God that He's faithful even when we are not.

In this case, I was faithful in getting my sorry self back in church and He was faithful in blessing me with feeling absolutely whole. Physically, Mentally, and now Spiritually.

20070808 (Wednesday)
A Small Reunion

I got a call from Staff Sergeant G and headed up to ROD1. It had been awhile since I had seen him because of everything that was going on at the Karate School. As soon as I walked in I smiled, shook his hand, and introduced myself. I said-

Hi, my name is Matt Killian. What can you tell me about joining the Marine Corps?

He said- *Nothing man. You're out of luck!* and smiled real big.

Since he was eating lunch, he asked me to tell him about everything that had been going on. I told him about my Nationals trip. I had taken 36 kids down to Fort Lauderdale Florida to the AAU Nationals Tournament. The best kids in the nation were down there and we wanted a piece of that action. My team competed in Forms, Point Sparring, and Olympic Sparring. We brought back 14 Bronze medals, 12 Silver medals, and 11 Gold medal National Champions. In short, we rocked the sauce! In one division, 3 of my Black Belts swept the entire division. Meaning, our school took 1st, 2nd, and 3rd in that ring. The other 21 competitors in that ring didn't have a prayer. Next year may be an entirely different story because everyone always gets there day in the sun but this was clearly our day! Plus, this is my story so I feel as though I can brag on my guys all I want and it won't be bad for them...so what now? I'm proud of my kids.

Staff Sergeant G was excited to hear about our success because he knew how hard we had been training for it. After that, he gave me the run down on what was going on between now and my ship day. Staff Sergeant G and some other future Marines were meeting on Saturdays and, since I was clear on this Saturday, he wanted to invite me to come out and do some training. You bet I do! That would be awesome. Anything I could do to better prepare myself for Basic Training was up my alley. At that point, he took the Manual that I had been reading like the Bible and highlighted some areas that I needed to have memorized by this weekend. Sounds good. Luckily, I had most of it but it would be no problem to knock out the other stuff. With that, I put it on the schedule and made arrangements to meet up at 9:30AM on Saturday. When I got back to the school, I got my Manual out and made up some flash cards to help me memorize the stuff I needed. Rank structure and the General Orders were at the top of the list of things to get down. The rank structure was completely new to me while the General Orders were something I had been working on for a while. Believe it or not, the flash cards really helped out a lot. Whenever I had a free moment, I took out the stack and flipped through them trying to commit to memory all the details on the cards. So kindergarten teachers DO know what they are talking about! Son of a--!

20070810 (Saturday)
Training Day with the DEP #1

What a beautiful morning! I woke up and jumped out of bed with a smile on my face. Today, I got to participate in my first group meeting/training session with all the new recruits in the DEP (Delayed Entry Program). As soon as I stepped out the door I received the greatest surprise of all- a cool breeze! It had been so HOT the last couple days. It's going to be a good day!

Since I really didn't know what to expect, I bounced over to the gas station across the street and got me one of those Rockstar energy drinks. WOW! That stuff is awesome. Even though it does taste kind of like liquefied Nerds. Anyway, I then made my way across town to hook up with Staff Sergeant G. I was to meet him at the office at 9:30AM. He was there right on the dot and we were off. On the way, we got to talk about this and that and he was telling me about this new program he was going to start on Monday. It's called P90X. It's a conditioning program that is supposed to get you in go-baby-go shape in 90 days. He was excited about it. Being a recruiter, his hours make it incredibly difficult to set a scheduled workout session. I totally empathized. But the cool thing was that even though he had a tough schedule, he still fought to find a way to make it happen. And it's not like he's in bad shape at all. I guess he just wants to hit that next level. Good for him!

On the way to the meeting, we picked up another new recruit named Patterson. This kid was young. He looked like he was right out of High School. I guess that's because he was. He was talking about how his parents are getting him his first car and his graduation party. All I could think was that I was going to have to watch out for this kid. You could tell he meant well and the Marine Corps was right for him because it would square him away, but he also had this look that made you just want to break him in half. He couldn't have weighed more than 120LBS.

When we arrived at ROD2, we found ourselves in a great turnout. There were at least 16 of us. Both guys and girls were jumping in the mix. Awesome. When I walked in, something strange had happened. For some reason, all the Recruiters were coming up to me and carried somewhat of the same conversation with me. It went like this-

Recruiter-   *Hi, what's your name?*
Me-   *Matt Killian*
Recruiter-   *Ah, So you're Killian. I've heard a lot about you.*

They were all doing it. They said they had heard about me and gave me this really weird smile. Just then, Sergeant Peterson came up to say hi and I asked him what the deal was. He said that Staff Sergeant G had been throwing my name around to everyone saying that I'm really fast and I teach Martial Arts. That's just GREAT!

Rule Numero Uno- Attention can be a blessing or a curse. Be decisive in knowing when to acquire it and when to avoid it.

It's not a problem to perform without any prior impression. In that case it's not bad. It's quite another story when you have a reputation and it's based on what someone said and not by current visual testament. Now it all makes sense. I was getting sized up to see if Staff Sergeant G was telling the truth or full of it. Or worse yet, if I was telling the truth or full of it. That would be totally screwed up if I told Staff Sergeant G one thing just to find out I was making it up when it came down to the moment of truth. Well, there's nothing I can do now except sit and wait for this show to start. Right about then, Staff Sergeant Benette introduced me to Travis. Travis is this big black guy that looks like he's a football player. Staff Sergeant Benette then proceeds to tell me that Travis has set the mile and a half record at 9 minutes. Perfect. He then tells me that we are competing today in the run. Then he looks at Travis with an ice cold stare and says-

You better not let him win!

Well this is just fantastic. It's my first day with the team and I already have this behemoth black guy wanting to smoke me on the course. Awesome. Luckily, after Staff Sergeant Benette had walked away, Travis looked at me and gave me this "Sorry little man" look, shook my hand, welcomed me to the family, and then yelled at everyone to get to the front of the office. Up at the front, there are two pull up bars and a pull up machine for people that can't do standard pull-ups. We were ordered to make two straight lines in front of the bars and do 3 sets of a minimum of 10 pull-ups. You could tell a couple guys were thinking-
"What? 10 pull-ups? When do we just get to start at 1?

I found my way to the middle of the lines so I could see what everyone else was able to do and then base my work off that. If they blew 10 away then I was going to have to grit my teeth and make some magic happen. However, it wasn't going to be bad at all. The first few guys knocked out about 4-8. I know for a fact I can do 10 so that's cool. Oh yeah, if you can't do all 10 then Travis or one of the other Recruiters pushes you up and helps you grind out the remaining pull-ups making you do as much of the work as possible. That way, you always walk away with 10 under your belt. The result, you force yourself to always hit your goal and the Recruiters will invariably have to help you less and less until you are strong enough to do it all on your own.

When it was my turn, I stepped up, grabbed the bar, and looked back at the team, I found myself looking face to face with "the man." He was a stocky bald headed black guy that was cut like a tree and looking to squash someone for looking at him the wrong way.

Who are you!
Matt Killian Sir (Shook hands)
I'm Sergeant V. I've heard a lot about you. Now get some!

With that, I fired into my pull ups. I knocked out a clean 15, struggled on 16, and bailed after 17. The moment your form goes to crap, you're done. He looked at me with an "Good, he's in shape. We'll see what he's got" looks and I returned to the back of the line. Man I'm glad I started working on pull-ups before I showed up today. I would have hated to let Staff Sergeant G down. Not to mention the fact that some guys couldn't do 4 and that was bad for them. The Recruiters fired into them like you see in the movies. They were utterly relentless. But, they got it done. I personally believe that guys do really well with that type of hard-core motivation. The meaner the Recruiters got, the more the recruits would dig to prove they belonged with the team. And we were a team. Even Sergeant V jumped up there and knocked out a set. He cleared everyone out of the way and said-
Watch out now, even the big man is gonna get some!

We finished our 3 sets and headed out to the sidewalk. We formed 3 lines on the sidewalk and were told to stand tall and straight. The **ROD2** was located among other shops and offices in a strip mall. We were right next to a grocery story and so there was plenty of traffic walking by. People would stop to see what was going on, smile, and then go on their way. Staff Sergeant Hendrickson, the only female

Recruiter present, let the females know that when we got back after the run, they all had to do the flexed arm hang. I think the girls thought they were going to get out of it and, when Staff Sergeant Hendrickson reminded them, you could tell they were excited! Interestingly enough, females don't do pull-ups in the Marine Corps because they say that the flexed arm hang is a better test of overall strength. Cool.

After we got lined up, Sergeant V told everyone to grab some sidewalk because we were about to do some push ups. The almighty trademark military exercise. However, this experience was AWESOME. We got on our faces and when Sergeant V yelled- PUSH UP!, everyone pushed up to the ready position while shouting **"MARINE CORPS!"** It gives me chills right now just thinking about it. It definitely made people stop in their tracks when walking by. It's amazing how loud a unified team of 16 can be. However, not everyone knew we were supposed to shout that. Including me. So it wasn't as loud as it could have been and everyone knew it. So Sergeant V goes into his pep talk. He says-

All right, I'm going to tell you guys the troof .You guys know how Sergeant V likes it. I want you to be loud! I want all the people walking by to hear you. To see you training. I want you to make them wish they weren't the fat ass lazy degenerate motherfuckers that they are. I want you to inspire them. To make them want what you are working for right now. So this time, when I say Push up, you fuckers better let me hear you shout MARINE CORPS!

You got it?!
yes sir
No, maybe you didn't hear me. I said Do YOU got it?!
Yes SIR!
No, no, no. I said DO YOU GOT IT?!
YES SIR!!!!!!!

This time, when he yelled- Push up! EVERYONE sounded off full tilt. It was awesome! Then we started the 4 count push-ups. On 10, we held it out for a while. Then we V'd our bodies up and held that for a while. Then we held it at Half Arms for what seemed like forever. Then we got to rest on our faces. It was hard work. Sergeant V started coming

around and asking us how we were doing. He asked-
Killian, how you doing?
I said- Good to go Sir!

He smiled with that "Thank God he can do push-ups" look. Step 2 for me is complete. All I have now is the run. I had been hanging hard core with Travis the whole way. Both of us were keeping an eye on each other seeing if there was the slightest hint of quit to be seen. Not today.

We jumped into some cars to head out to the running trail. Sergeant V assigned me to his car. Sweet. I get to ride with the man. On the way, he asked me about what I taught at the Karate School and seemed pretty interested. Then he asked me about Marathons. I answered his questions and everything was just Kool and the Gang. When we got to the trail we unloaded, circled up, and Travis led us through a warm up. After that, Sergeant V called me, Travis, and a few others over to him. He said that since we were most likely the best runners so we needed to do a couple things-

1- Mix in with the other not-so-good runners and help encourage them. Got it? (Aye Sir!)
2- Work as a team. We stay together for the whole run. Got it? (Aye Sir!)
3- If I come down on anyone and make them do extra pushups, you are to jump right in with them. Don't even think twice. Just do it. Got it? (Aye Sir!)

After that, we formed up into two single file lines and took to the trail. The pace was easy and everyone was doing really well. Then, we got to the bridge. The bridge is a sidewalk overpass that goes over the highway. It's about 100 yards long and looks like a big hump. So you are running uphill halfway and then downhill halfway. Sergeant V put us two by two and our orders were to sprint across the bridge and whoever came in second had to do 10 pushups. Staff Sergeant Benette partnered us up and as soon as Staff Sergeant Carter saw my partner he said- "Hell NO!" He calls Foster, this other guy that came with a camelback, and told me we were running together. He glares at Foster and said- "You better not let him beat you!" All I was thinking was IT'S ON NOW. If I let this guy beat me then I'm letting Staff Sergeant G down. Not today. As soon as he said GO! I tore off with everything I had. Not only did I beat Foster, but I also blew past the team that had started before us. It was awesome. I wish I could take all the credit but I think it was just the hand of God giving me some love because I had never run so fast in my life. Now it was show time. If I outright beat Travis, then he would look bad in front of everyone and I might come off as some pompous hot shot. The Recruiters knew that, but they still wanted to see who was the fastest. So they sent us off one at a time. They let Travis go in front of me. When Travis got about 10 yards out they sent me. I caught him and then ran in side by side with him. I didn't want to bring the spotlight anymore on me so I figured that if we tied, then the Recruiters would know what was up but no one would look bad. I saw the movie Drumline. I know how this works. And I was right. When we got to the finish, Sergeant V tore into Travis and said that he was lucky we tied because if I would have beaten him, he would be sorry. From that point on, Travis and I were a great team. There was nothing else to prove.

When everyone was done with the bridge sprints, we kept on path for another mile. Next was the Indian sprint. That's when you run single file and the one in back has to sprint to the front of the line as quickly as possible while everyone else runs at a set pace. That was hard-core. We were already tired from the running and the sprints and now we had to do this. Well, bring it! When we got to our destination and had a chance to rest, Staff Sergeant Carter made a point to make sure that everyone KNEW not to EVER put theirs hands on their head. He said that putting your hands on your head was a sign of surrender and MARINES never surrender. We then partnered up and did 3 sets of 25 sit-ups. Good times. Williams was my partner and we worked really well together. When that was done, it was time to head back to the start. I was right behind Travis and was required to keep the pace steady when he had to go back and yell at anyone who was walking or slowing down. At the last quarter mile, I got a cramp in my side and had to slow down. This pissed me right off. I'm a Marathon runner. I don't get cramps. Oh well. So I slowed down and let 3 guys pass me. Come to find out, we were the only four left. Everyone else had stopped or slowed down. That made me feel better. However, when I got to the finish line I headed back to support the ones who were struggling. I would go back, run one in, and then head back for another. It was a total Forrest Gump moment. But it made me feel better for dying out when I was finishing. When I went back the last time, I found Travis and this girl making their way in. Travis was yelling at her relentlessly saying- *Keep moving! Stop walking! Boot camp isn't going to be any easier! Move it!*

You know- typical stuff. I just shadowed back and let him do his thing and before long, we had joined back with the team at the finish. From there, Sergeant V gave us very simple instructions- Get a full bottle of water in your right hand. Unscrew the cap with your left. Drink it! All of it! When you're done, hold it over your head and turn the bottle over. He said we're not leaving until he sees an upside down bottle over everyone's head. One kid said he wasn't thirsty. Sergeant V said-

I didn't ask if you were thirsty. I told you to drink a bottle of water and hold it over your head when it's empty. Now do it!

After that, Travis took us through a cool down stretch. Then, Sergeant V stood up and said that the Marine Corps is about Honor. Living by rock solid Integrity. He said-

In the Marine Corps, you must always tell the troof. ALWAYS! No matter what. Now, I have just one question. And you better tell me the troof. Raise your hand if at any point during the run you put your hands on your hips.

We all raised our hands. We were really good about remembering about the rule when we found ourselves for a split second with our hands on our hips and didn't get caught, but since we had done it, we were all guilty. What does that mean? PUSH UPS!
Sergeant V told us to get on our faces. He said- PUSH UP! We shouted **"MARINE CORPS!"** While we were doing the push up exercises he was telling us that if we were ever squad leader, 2 things would face us.

1- We were guaranteed to get smashed if our squad messed up in any way. The Drill Instructors wouldn't punish the squad; they would punish the squad leader. So, if we were ever squad leader, we had to remember to keep an extra eye on the team otherwise we would pay for it.

2- He said- *If the squad fucks you, to fuck 'em back.*

For example, the most cherished moment in boot camp is chow time. That was the only time to sit down, rest a bit, and eat undisturbed for 20 minutes. Once the squad leader is done eating, everyone is done eating. So if you need to teach them a lesson, eat an apple or two, drink some fluid, and head back out. No matter what, the squad will have to stop eating and fall in. Checkmate.

When we got done with the push up routine, he told everyone that we were a family and we had to work together no matter what. Then he said-

For 10 seconds I want you guys to show me you're a family and for 10 seconds, I want you to scream as loud as you can!

So we huddled up and when he said go, we let her rip! We screamed as loud as we could. It was awesome. After I got a ride home, I thought about everything that had happened and I realized one thing. I was made for this! The whole experience was like heaven to me. YES- it sucked having to work hard but that's what it's all about. I loved the energy of everyone, the camaraderie, everything. I am so glad I took this step.

20070814 (Tuesday)
Lunch with the Boss

Today was the day. It was do or die. I was not about to let another day go by without taking care of business. And believe it or not, this was single handedly the hardest conversation I had to execute to date. I'm not exactly sure why, but it was. I got to the school at 6:50AM and proceeded to warm up for my Instructor's Training class. Today was Forms day and that was all well and good. Even though my mind was focusing on making sure I didn't forget any moves, I still felt preoccupied.

Mission-
I had to find a way to tell my boss that I needed to leave the school for up to 6 months and then come back and resume my position.

That was the big deal. Even though I was totally amped about being a part of the Marine Corps, I still had to find a way to keep my relationship stellar with my professional occupation. If I wanted to enlist full time with the military then I wouldn't even worry about it, but I have been extremely blessed with working with kids and as long as I'm able to make a difference then that's what I want to do. So this was going to take a little finesse. After all, this whole thing could blow up in my face. There were a million "what ifs"‖ that could potentially pop up. For example-

What if he cuts my hours because he knows I won't be staying?
What if he tries to outright fire me? Even though he couldn't because the law prohibits that when it comes to military duty. He HAS to hold my job. But what if?
What if it shatters any hope of opening a school when I get back?

These are the things that I wanted to handle delicately so I could maintain a strong relationship with the Martial Arts School. We had scheduled a time to meet at 10:45AM but that didn't work out because he had an ad to crank out. So we rescheduled to 12:15PM. I used this extra time to think through my battle plan and organize the order of what needed to be said. When it came down to game time, I was ready to go. We went to Potbelly's to grab lunch and as soon as we were done eating, I went to work-

I need to talk to you about something that has really been eating at me for the longest time. I've never told anyone about it because it was something that was just personal to me. But now I'm at the point that if I don't do anything about it, I'll have to let it go. If I jump on this opportunity, I would be gone for 6 months tops, and then I would want to come back and resume the work that I have invested the last two years of my life in.

But here's the thing. You know that I'm loyal to the school. You know I wouldn't intentionally do anything to hurt it.
If you think that my leaving for 6 months would hurt it or cause too many problems, then I won't do it. However, if you think that I will be able to do this and then come back and everything will be fine, then that's great. What do you think?

(At this point, you notice I haven't even said what it was I wanted to do. That's not important yet. I wanted him to be thinking yes or no first without being able to be swayed either way by an emotional bond to what it was. The only thing that matters is the time I'm gone and whether or not I'm planning on coming back. I also wanted him to know that I cared about the school and want only the best for it. I think I covered everything.)

When would you have to leave?

November 4th.

(Thinking) *Well, that gives us three months to plan for it, get everything in line, and then make it happen. I think that'll be OK. What is it you want to do?*

I want to join a Reserve Unit of the military.
Oh OK. Which one?

Marines.

(Eyes Widen) *Really. What will that entail?*

Well, I'll have to work one weekend every month and two weeks out of the year in the summer time.

(We have a woman right now that is in the Navy Reserves at the school so he knows about what I'll have to do based on his experience with her. And since he doesn't have a problem with her, I figure he shouldn't have a problem with me.)

I think that'll work just fine. I appreciate you telling me now because that makes it so much easier to plan. We could make this a big deal in the school. Towards the end of October, we'll make an announcement that you'll be participating in the most elite training known to man and that you'll be back in 6 months. That way, all the students can get behind you and we can throw a party when you go. We shouldn't lose any students or business if they know you're coming back. That should be cool.

And imagine what our Warrior Boot Camp will be like when I get back. How cool will that be?

That'll be INSANE!

After the dust had settled and the tension was gone, we were able to continue on and just talk about this and that. It was cool because, before I left, I told him about the training I had the previous Saturday. He was totally excited about it. He told me that he would have done the same thing but his mom was just like mine and gave him too much static about getting involved. In the end, he was happy for me and we were going to be able to work on this together. Score!

20070815 (Thursday)
Got it...Finally!!

Today, I finally memorized everything I needed before Boot Camp. This was a huge goal for me ever since the drive back with those two Marines after MEPS. They had told me that if I took the time to memorize everything, that it would take some of the pressure off of fighting for it under pressure. I'm all about it baby! I mean I know it'll be a great accomplishment just to get through, but my goal is to do the best that I'm capable of. To me, I don't want to go through Basic Training and merely survive; I want to be the BEST! So ever since I got the Manual, I had been working on getting everything down. Like I had mentioned before, I had even made flash cards to help me out. They totally paid off because now I'm finally done with the hard part of memorizing everything. The following is what I had in front of me. I started off with the easiest thing and perhaps the most important of all-

The Marine Corps Birthday-
November 10th 1775. AKA 17751110

After that, I started knocking out the 11 General Orders. These looked to be the hardest thing to memorize, so I started on them the day I got the Manual. I had only started on the Rank and Grades after Staff Sergeant G had pointed it out a few days ago.

Marine Corps General Orders
1- To take charge of this post and all Government property in view.
2- To walk my post in a military manner. Keeping always on the alert. And observing everything that takes place within sight and hearing.
3- To report all violations of orders I am instructed to enforce.
4- To repeat all calls from posts more distant from the guardhouse than my own.
5- To quit my post only when properly relieved.
6- To receive, obey, and pass on to the sentry that relieves me all orders from the Commanding Officer, Officer of the Day, and Officers and Noncommissioned Officers of the guard only.
7- To talk to no one except in the line of duty.
8- To give the alarm in case of fire or emergency.
9- To call the Corporal of the Guard in any case not covered by instructions.
10- To salute all Officers and all colors and standards not cased.
11- To be especially watchful at night. And during the time for challenging, to challenge all persons on or near my post. And to allow no one to pass without proper authority.

These were actually more difficult to memorize than I would have thought. Some of these tend to be rather sketchy because they are actually several statements put together instead of just being long one-liners. 5, 7, and 8 were rather easy to memorize. The others took a bit more thought because you had to say the words just right. They didn't roll out with ease. 4 and 11 are still a pain in the butt. Both 5 and 6 can be found in the movie Full Metal Jacket. Private Pyle nailed #5 while Joker butchered #6 and had to pound out 25 push-ups.

Marines' Hymn (Verse 1)

From the halls of Montezuma
to the shores of Tripoli
We fight our country's battles
In the air, on land, and sea
First to fight for right and freedom
and to keep our honor clean
We are proud to claim the title of
United States Marines

I used to play this tune all the time when I played trumpet in High School. That made it easy to memorize because the melody was already cemented in my mind. It then just became a matter of putting the right words in the correct place. Interestingly enough, this is the only Military anthem that is classified as a Hymn. All the other branches refer to theirs as a song while the Marine Corps embraces it with great pride and solemn reverence. Thus the title Marines' Hymn.

Marine Corps Ranks and Grades

N/A	Pvt	Private	E-1
	PFC	Private First Class	E-2
	LCpl	Lance Corporal	E-3
	Cpl	Corporal	E-4
	Sgt	Sergeant	E-5

SSgt	Staff Sergeant		E-6
GySgt	Gunnery Sergeant		E-7
MSgt	Master Sergeant		E-8
1st Sgt	First Sergeant		E-8
MGySgt	Master Gunnery Sergeant		E-9
SgtMaj	Sergeant Major		E-9
SMMC	Sergeant Major of the Marine Corps	E-9

(Gold)

(Silver)

(Silver)

(Gold)

2ndLt	Second Lieutenant	0-1
1stLt	First Lieutenant	0-2
Capt	Captain	0-3
Maj	Major	0-4

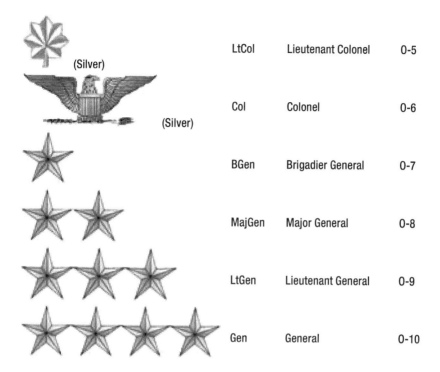

	LtCol	Lieutenant Colonel	0-5
(Silver)			
(Silver)	Col	Colonel	0-6
	BGen	Brigadier General	0-7
	MajGen	Major General	0-8
	LtGen	Lieutenant General	0-9
	Gen	General	0-10

One thing that helped me with the top brass General structure was to remember-
Be My Little General
- Brigadier General
- Major General
- Lieutenant General
- General

For the rest of the ranks, I drew the picture on a flash card and all the information on the back.
Since I had never had a clue as to the rank structure of the Marines, or any other for that matter, it was cool to finally be able to recognize the "Brass" and Bars. I would catch myself identifying the Ranks of Officers in military movies without even thinking about it. I remember when I thought that a Brigadier General was the highest because it sounded the coolest. Yup- wrong about that. Now it all makes sense.

20070817 (Friday)
Challenge #2...Game On!

Memorization? Check. The next battle will be more of a necessary nightmare to survive. It isn't exactly required, but it's a goal that would be top shelf awesome to achieve. In the Marine Corps, you have to take an IST (Individual Strength Test) just to be qualified to enter into Recruit Training. So if you can't make the minimums, you can kiss Boot Camp goodbye. The PFT (Physical Fitness Test) which is the test you have to pass in order to be a Marine is comprised of 3 events.

Running   **Sit Ups**   **Pull Ups**

Recruits receive a score based on the number they are successfully able to perform in each area. There are different target goals between ages of men and women. A perfect score is a 300. In order to score a 300, I must be able to perform a minimum of 20 Pull Ups, 100 Sit Ups in 2 minutes, and run 3 Miles under 18 minutes. Holy Dog Crap! At this point, I can knock out 15 Pull Ups, I can complete the 100 Sit Up requirement, but I'm at 21 minutes for the 3 Mile run. So I'm close but I'm not THERE. It's one thing to run a 6 minute mile (which I can do), it's quite another to do it 3 times in a row. Knowing that my IST would be coming up in about a month and a half, I decided to schedule a personal trainer to help me set a workout routine and training schedule that would get me there. In order to be able to do that, my trainer had to see first hand where I was and what I would be capable of. In short, he had to put me through "The Works." And he was good at it! I consider myself to be in pretty good shape but my trainer knew how to push me so that I would work my guts out.
It was great- what I would call "Happy Misery."
I started out on the rowing machine. I did 5 minutes of that just to get my heart going and pump some blood to all the big muscles. After that, Ben threw me into a Pyramid Burpee routine. Sounds simple- very hard to complete. It goes like this-
1- you jump straight up in the air as high as you can.

2- you shoot down to a push up position and do a push up.

3- you get back to your feet and jump as high as you can.

4- you shoot back down to a push up position and perform 2 push ups.

5- you continue this process by increasing the number of push ups each time you go down until you get to 10 push ups.

I finished the first set, took a swig of water, and then jumped into the second set. The second set is what kills you. I believe that just about anyone can get through the first, but finishing a second, that's when things get raw. Not to mention the fact that it's actually easier to do in reverse. It's actually not as challenging if you start with 10 push ups and work back to one. So if you want to really get at it, then 1-10 is the way to go!

After that, we made our way over to a machine where you sit down with your chest against an upright and you pull the handles toward you. My goal was to complete sets of 20. The first set went pretty well even though I was stuck in a rhythm of 2 seconds in and 2 seconds out. That was actually harder then just pumping away. I took a 30 second break and then fired into the second set. However, this time, Ben reduced the weight. Cool. 20...19...18...17...16...15...stop. What? Ben then cut my distance of stroke in half isolating the work to a whole new level of Hades I had never experienced. Ben told me to do 15 as fast as I could at this range. As soon as I hit 15, he put me back at full range stroke and I continued from 15 on my way to 1 without skipping a beat. That was INSANE! It's amazing how just making a simple adjustment can make such an incredible difference.

As soon as that bit of fun and adventure was over, we headed to the free weights. I jumped on the declined bench and did a cycle between declined dumb bell presses (20) and straight into a short set of push ups (10). I did this twice. On my second set of push-ups, my arms were spent. They were far beyond tired and well into complete exhaustion. So what do you think super Ben had me do next? That's right. He said the next event on the agenda was to head on over to do some pull-ups. Great. We headed to the pull up bar and I was already thinking to myself how I was going to squeeze out just 1. He showed me what he wanted and I jumped in the mix. My goal was 20. I have no idea how I'm going to get there, but whatever. It's got to get done. I did 5 clean pull ups and then my form took a hike. When Ben saw this, he grabbed my ankles and held them at his waist level height. From there, I was actually able to pound out the next 15. It wasn't pretty...at all, but it got done. I took a 30 second break and then proceeded with the jumping pull-ups. I had to jump up and get my chin above the bar. Then I had to hold myself up for 2 seconds, and then I would slowly let myself back down. The first 8 were ok. The next 4 were a fight. The final 8 took everything I had left just to finish the exercise. To finish out, we did some leg lifts to work out the abs. I hit the floor, grabbed the supports, and started working floor to rack keeping the heels off the floor. 40 straight and it was a done deal. Hallelujah!

I thanked Ben for all his help. He was great at keeping me going and giving me the advice I needed to stay as proficient as possible. It's one thing to go into a gym and do your own thing. It's a completely different story when you have someone to keep you moving and pushing you into that next level. Well I did my sit ups and pull-ups. The only thing left is to see where I'm at on the run. I've run long distances and never really worried about speed as much as I did endurance when it comes to Marathon training. Now I was facing a new challenge. Instead of running a sub 9-minute marathon pace for 26.2 miles, I needed to start running a sub 6 minute pace for 3 miles.

I jumped on a treadmill and punched in 18 minutes. I set the speed for a 7 minute and 30 second mile. I kept that pace for 13 minutes and from there bumped it up to 7-minute miles for the final 5 minutes. Since I hadn't been running regularly, I decided to start at a pace that I could comfortably maintain and then bump it up for the final 5 minutes. Then, on my next visit I'll be able to start a bit faster and bump it up from there. For some reason, I have a hard time starting fast off the bat so I warm myself up and get used to the pace first. Then I kick it up. It seems to be working pretty well. The first couple minutes are always tough. Your body seems to ask you repeatedly what the heck you're doing. It tells you that it would feel so much better to stop just for a little bit and then you can keep going. It tempts you severely. You keep telling it not to worry. It'll all be OK. We'll keep pushing. We're not going to over do it, but we're also not going to quit. Finally, there comes a point where your body just screams "Please STOP!" By training like this, it becomes that much easier to simply say no.

After the run, I was able to walk out of the gym proud of the day's accomplishment and looking forward to the training that was to come. I just kept reminding myself how good it will feel if I can knock out these physical goals. Accomplishing these goals would put me in the top percentile and that's where I want to be. The top!

20070819 (Saturday)
Track Practice

Given the fact that I am currently unable to run 3 miles in 18 minutes, I knew that I was going to have to make a few visits to the track. Using the track, however disturbingly boring it may be, is a great agent for fine tuning your time, pace, and overall endurance. If you can do anything for more than a mile on a track repeatedly without wanting to put a gun barrel in your mouth then you're the man... or woman.

Black Belt Testing went well into the afternoon, and then we had the after party for all the students that had passed the test. When all was said and done, it was about 6:30PM. Afterwards, I headed to the track. The weather was on the verge of raining which was really good because it cooled everything off. Plus, if it did rain, I got Pina Coladas.

I took an easy warm up lap around the track. Then, another one on the stopwatch. I wanted to find out my "worst case scenario" pace which put me at 2 minutes and 9 seconds. So my recovery pace in case I gassed out or ran into some other minor problem would put me at a 2:09 lap. Since 3 miles is only 12 laps, there was no reason to make my recovery pace at walking speed. So now the foundation is set. 2:09 is the bottom.

My next goal was to find out how well I could pace myself. I was watching the clock and all I had to do was take a lap and see how close I could come to 1:30. 1:30 was my target speed that would put me at a 6-minute mile. Eventually, my goal would be to beat that every lap so that I would have a window on my last lap if I slowed down. On my first trial lap, I clocked in at 1:34. Not too bad at all. When I finished that lap I felt like I could have pushed a lot harder. That's good because if I'm not going full out, then that means I can sustain that and push it if needs be. My next lap put me at 1:39. Uh oh. That's not really good because now I have a 5 second loss. To monitor that, I decided to run 2 laps straight. I would stop and restart the clock each time I came through making a note of what my lap time was for each lap. My first was 1:34 and my second was 1:36. Ok we're doing better. Based on my numbers, I'm averaging between 1:34 and 1:39. That's a good start because it's close to my target and I'm feeling pretty good after each lap. So now the middle ground is set. My sustainable pace is between 1:34 and 1:39.

Now I have to set the max limit. My next lap brought a time of 1:20. This would be difficult to sustain. Luckily, my target is 1:30 so I won't be looking to sustain 1:20 at this point. As my father would say-

Praise the Lord and pass the ammunition!

This was a great training session because it set the framework for what I had right now and what I needed to hit my goal. The next stage of this process will be focused on completing more than 3 miles at my target pace. I figure that if I can do 4 miles at a 6-minute per mile pace, then I will have no problem with the PFT test. I don't want it to be where I can just barely make the requirement. No sir. I want it to be where I could do it at least twice. Why? Because the run is not guaranteed to be the first test. It could be the pull-ups then the run. Or it could be the sit-ups, then the pull-ups, and then the run. The point is that I don't know what shape I'll be in when I start the run so I want to be as well off as I possibly can be.

Just for the heck of it, I took out my track chute and took a lap with that. Wow was that hard! This mini parachute adds a level of resistance to your training that makes you work full tilt. Not only does it pull you back, but it also pulls you to the sides based on the direction of the wind. And if the wind is at your back, then you have to run faster just to get it off the ground. Good times I must say!

20070825 (Saturday)
Training Day with the DEP #2

I thought I might be going out of town this weekend but it didn't happen. That was a bummer. Looking on the bright side; however, it gave me another opportunity to train with the guys in the Delayed Entry

Program. That's awesome! So I woke up early because I had to meet Sergeant Peterson at the ROD1. He said he would meet me there at 9AM. I got there at 8:45AM just to be on the safe side. I HATE being late. I hate it with a passion. The problem with that is that I also hate it when other people are late. This morning I was getting tested. 9AM rolled by... then 9:05... then 9:10... then 9:15. At this point, I decided that if I waited any longer, I would need to just drive myself. But first I wanted to call the ROD2 and see if he forgot or if he was just running late. I called the ROD2 and Staff Sergeant Benette picked up. I told him the story and he put me on the phone with Staff Sergeant G. He didn't know either so while he had me on the phone, he gave Sergeant Peterson a call to see what the deal was. When he got back on the phone, he told me that he had to pick up a couple other people first and then he would be there for me. Awesome. I'm so glad he didn't forget. I had a high expectation that the Marine Corps was not known for being forgetful and I was right. When Sergeant Peterson pulled up, we had just enough time to get from the ROD1 to the ROD2 in the knick of time so we were good to go.

Upon arrival, I saw some new faces as well as some I hadn't seen before. That was cool. I walked into the Marine Corps Office and right away saw Sergeant V. Awwyeah. The first thing he said when he saw me was-
Uh Oh. Watch out! Kung Fu Joe is up in here!
Kung Fu Joe huh?

I walked up and shook hands with him first and then headed around to see everyone else. Today was going to be an easy day. Everyone was doing really well in the training so the Recruiters were going to take us to the Coast Guard yard to have some fun. It's not really a yard. It's more of an industrial complex with a recreation center in the middle of it. With that, he hollered at everyone to get out to the sidewalk so we could split up in cars and take off. We got out and lined up in rows. Sergeant V said-
Oh yeah, before you go, I gotta make sure you still got your game in check.

He told us all to get on our faces and he let us know that this better be really short or he was going to ruin our day. I guess he just wanted to make sure that we were still watching our P's and Q's. He told us to show him how motivated we were by how we sounded when we did our push ups. As soon as he yelled- "Push Up!" We yelled, **"Marine Corps!"**

However, it clearly wasn't as loud as it could have been. Crap! At that, Sergeant V said-

Aww hell no. We gonna be out here all day. And if you make me miss my football game, I'm gonna fuck you up!

He gave us the same exact speech as last time and gave us a second shot. The second time was much much better. After that, we had to do some Down/ Ups. That's where he says "Down" and you get on your face as fast as you can, and when he says "Up", you get to your feet as fast as you can. And he doesn't play around. You have to be quick. And then the moment I dreaded occurred. The kid next to me got into a small dispute with Staff Sergeant G.

Staff Sergeant G called him a pretty boy for fixing his pants when he should have been standing at attention. The kid was claiming the reason why he was fixing his pants was because he was going to trip if he didn't. The next time we did a Down/ Up, he pointed it out to Staff Sergeant G and showed him it was the truth and that he wasn't trying to make excuses. That was all well and good. But then he got retarded. When Staff Sergeant G said-

So you were right and I was wrong?

The kid should have said, "No sir, you were right. I shouldn't have worried about it." But he didn't. He told Staff Sergeant G he was in fact wrong. Ahhhhhhh! Are you STUPID? I could have punched this kid in the eye. Staff Sergeant G stopped in his tracks, glared at him, and again questioned him. The kid was oblivious to the fate he was heading toward. Behind him, I was frantically whispering- *Shut up! Shut Up! Tell him NO!*

But he didn't. That's when Staff Sergeant G looked at Sergeant V and told him that this kid said he was wrong. You should have seen the look on Sergeant V's face! I was thinking- *Here we go!*

Sergeant V didn't get pissed off and chop heads; instead, he got in his face real cool and calm.

Without breaking his stare with the kid, he told Foster, another future recruit, to come over and get on his face in a push-up position and hold it halfway. Foster was to hold this position until Sergeant V took his sweet time in saying why you never ever correct a Senior. He told everyone that when someone gets stupid, he's not going to discipline the stupid one, he's going to discipline the person that is in charge of the stupid one. I jumped on my face too because if I didn't, I knew what was coming if we didn't support Foster like a family. The other guys followed in as well. I believe because of that, Sergeant V didn't kill the rest of us in the example proceedings. Hopefully, it sank in and that kid will never make the same mistake again. Hopefully.

Unfortunately, this was only the beginning. It seemed like today was the day for people to lose their minds. When we got separated into our ride groups, we were told that we were going to a military instillation and that we needed our ID's. This will come back shortly. In the meantime, I got into the car with a couple other Deppers. As soon as the driver started the car, he started smoking a pipe! Luckily it was tobacco. But I was thinking to myself-

What are you thinking? You are enlisting to become a Marine and you know full well Boot Camp is coming. Correct me if I'm wrong, but I'm pretty sure that the Drill Instructors at Boot Camp don't allow you to smoke. Awesome!

Smoking doesn't bother me at all. The problem is that the Marine Corps is going to strip away every sense of civilian individuality that you have spent the last 5 years ingraining and instead of making it easier on yourself and preparing for it, this guy is still trying to be an individual just like everyone else. The result, he's the kind of guy that will make everyone else who's working hard do lots and lots of push-ups. What an idiot. I could have nunchucked him. He has no idea. He's the type of person that I could get to believe that seatbelts are a stupid waste of time and you don't need to wear them.

Just then, we stopped at a red light and I asked the kid next to me if he had his ID. He had to have been right out of high school. He got this "Uh Oh" look on his face, checked his pockets, and said he left it at the office. GREAT! I knew that if we got to the Coast Guard Yard and he didn't have an ID after Sergeant V told everyone they needed it, we were going to pay. So I jumped out of the car, ran up to Staff Sergeant Carter's car, and told him the story. Luckily, someone else forgot theirs as well so it was going to be Ok. So we turned around, picked up the ID's from the ROD2, and got back on the road. I couldn't really say anything because I've done the same exact thing. What a sinking feeling. On the road again! However, this time I road with Staff Sergeant Carter. There was no way I was going to ride with tweedle dumb and tweedle dumber if I didn't have to.

When we got to the yard, we parked the cars, and headed in. It looks like we're playing Wallyball. That's AWESOME! I love Wallyball. If you haven't played, it's just like Volleyball except you play it in a racquetball court so you can play off all the walls. Only major rules say that-

You can only hit the ball 3 times before it goes back over the net.

The same person can't hit it twice in a row.

You can't hit the sidewalls or ceiling on a serve.

Besides that, everything else is fair game. We split up the teams and we were off. During the first game, everyone revealed their hands. Some were pretty good. They could keep the ball moving towards the net. They could judge how the ball was going to bounce off the wall. They were good to go. The others, well, they tried man. No one quit and everyone was supportive of everyone no matter what so it was cool. Plus, it was funny to watch some of them eat the ball off their own hands. Turns out it was on between Sergeant Peterson and myself. He was coming with it and I was on. I wish that I could say it was just mad skills and I'm really good. But I can't. I was just really lucky today. A few shots that I thought I would screw up turned out good so I'm not complaining. The secret: in Wallyball you can hit the ball as hard as you like so it takes the need for finesse and throws it right out the window.

We played 6 games switching teams and sides just about every time. Everybody improved during the games and we all made really good plays and we all screwed up at one point or another. Everybody got to play and nobody got hurt. That's a good day in my book. When we finished, we piled back in the cars and headed back to the ROD2. I was taking my sweet time walking to the back main Office and as soon as I turned in to the room I saw that everyone was talking about the game. Staff Sergeant G looked up and said-

What's up Ryu?

Ryu? Why is he calling me Ryu? It turns out that everyone was telling the Recruiters that didn't go about my serve. I was lucky with my serves. I would throw the ball up, blast it in a straight line about 1 inch over the net, and it would rebound off the back wall all the way back to the net. It was really hard to return. The first time I served, everyone including Sergeant Peterson ducked out of the way. The ball sounded like a bomb off the back wall. Very nice! It spooked the girls and some of the guys so I knew they wouldn't try to play it. The only ones that figured out the return were Sergeant Peterson and Foster. My team loved it! They didn't have to do a thing except to point and laugh at people ducking for cover. The smoker that I had to ride with first got big surprise. I blasted it off the back wall and when he turned around, the ball rebounded off the wall and he took a direct shot to the nuts. It wasn't hard enough to really hurt him but definitely hard enough for him to react to it and give everyone a good laugh. Yeehaw! Welcome to Wallyball.

Everyone carried on with who they were talking with and so I took this chance to ask Sergeant V about all the DEP's coming to my School on a Saturday to train. I thought it would be cool for everyone to hit some targets and stuff. He thought it was a great idea. Sweet. We started talking about MMA training and they started asking me how the Martial Arts has evolved in the last couple years. I told them how everything is transitioning from Traditional training to more Sport and Street oriented training. Traditional skills are becoming the vast minority and Sport Martial Arts like the UFC and Street Self Defense classes are on the rise. It's great for our school because that's what we major in when it comes to adults. Then, Staff Sergeant G wanted to see some examples so he told Swett to grab a hold of me. I thought he was just joking around, but then the other Staff Sergeants started paying attention and everyone was watching me. Swett came up and grabbed me by the arm. I asked Staff Sergeant G what he wanted to see. He didn't care. He just wanted to see what I would do if someone grabbed me. He just told me not to really hit him. That's cool. I looked up at Swett and within a second I took the arm he was grabbing and grabbed his bicep for control while my other hand went straight into his face. It was just enough contact for him to know he had been hit. Swett freaked out. It shocked everyone watching. It was a lot faster than they had expected but also a lot easier. I think they all wanted to see me do some kind of defense where I would grab his arm, sweep the leg, and then punch him with an old school yell. Not happening.

Everyone liked it a lot. It even got Sergeant V's attention. Sergeant V told Swett to charge in and grab me around the waist like he was going to pick me up and slam me. When he did, I shot in under his arms and scooped him up in the air. As soon as he was up in the air I looked for a clear spot on the floor and dumped him on the ground. When we hit, he went to grab me around the neck. As soon as he did that, I realized he wasn't going to stop so I shoved my forearm in his throat to make him release his grip on my neck. As soon as he let go, I threw my right leg over his head and put him in an arm bar. He still didn't want to quit since I wasn't cranking on his elbow so I sank his arm under my shoulder for more pressure, tightened my right leg around his neck forcing it the opposite direction of the arm that I was cranking, and since he couldn't reach to tap anything with his hands, he let out this weird "Arrg" noise and started snapping his fingers. That was it. It all took less than 8 seconds and he was baptized. By this time, everyone was watching and really digging everything. Even Swett was excited about being the defense dummy. I don't think he had ever trained any street defense and so it was really cool to actually do.

Then, Sergeant V asked me about my choke out time. I told him I could have someone out in 2 to 3 seconds. So he wanted to see that. Swett actually volunteered. There was no way I was really going to choke him until he was unconscious so I told him to tap his leg as soon as he felt he was in trouble. I stood behind him with my arms to my sides. Swett stood in front of me. I told him to just relax. Staff Sergeant G started giving me a count down. He said 3...2...1...go! As soon as he said "go", I had him in a full out rear naked choke. Swett naturally grabbed my arm with his hands out of reflex and started kicking the ground with his feet. I let him go right away. There was no way he was getting out of that and everyone knew it. Swett was floored. He couldn't believe that something of that magnitude could happen so fast. He was tapping before Staff Sergeant G got to the "O" in GO. To be honest, I wasn't happy inside because I was thinking that I was the man, or that I was Superbad, or anything like that. I was happy because the Martial Arts can allow a guy my size to have a fighting chance. Practical Self Defense gives you a window of confidence in adversity. I say a window because if you don't take advantage of it, it can close and you can get into serious trouble. Sergeant V and Staff Sergeant G were both impressed. I think this really greased the wheels with getting them behind me in bringing everyone to Annapolis for training. I know I'm not going to be teaching anyone anything because that is the job of the Marine Corps, but at least they will all be able to come in and hit some targets and do some fun stuff. It'll be a BLAST!

20070917 (Monday)
Moment of Truth #1 (Day 1)

The time was going to come sooner or later so when I got to the office, I decided it had to be sooner. Everything was set with me getting ready to go and there was just one more thing to do- get momma dukes on board. My mom believes in our country. She supports the President whether she voted for him/her or not. And she takes pride in being an American. She just has a hard time with certain aspects of the military life. I don't know all the details, but I do know that it runs deep. I could come up with my own assumptions such as-
My father was in the Air Force. He served in Vietnam.
My close friend Eric. He died in a training exercise while serving in the Marine Corps.
Who needs more reasons than that? A woman's heart is an ocean of emotions that can be swayed in a moment. So how do I bring it up to mom that I want to get involved with something that she detests? Good question. It took some time and preparation. Sure, I could just dump it on her and decide not to care what she thinks, but as you know, that doesn't work. I wanted to get her on board and at least have a hint of support that may lead into an open door. She doesn't have to like it or love it, but my ultimate goal is to have BOTH parents behind me. So here's the plan. My mom works best when she can read big news through email. That way, she can sit on it, think through everything, and then come back with the best possible response after she has had time to see a clearer picture. Here we go-
(The following is a cut and pasted original)-

Hey mom,

I have some stuff in front of me and I need you to be a part of it. Regardless of whether your initial feeling is for or against it, I need you to get through this with me and then we can go from there. Ever since I was 18, I have always wanted to be involved in the military. It's a lifestyle that I always wanted a part of. However, I didn't do it out of respect for you. You always threw such a fit and had such a terrible distaste for it that I let it go.

Now I'm a little bit older and I'm getting to the point that it's kind of like now or never. I feel that if I don't do it then I'll live with a level of regret that I want no part of. I don't want to live out my days knowing that I could have done my part. I started checking things out in June of this year. I found out that I could go into the reserves and keep my career as a professional martial arts instructor. As my military job in the reserves, I would have two opportunities-

1 I would be a certified trainer for new recruits/ Marines in military martial arts.

2 The second thing I could do is be a fire and rescue specialist. They essentially help the guys that are out in the field and keep them safe.

I think these are honorable jobs in which I can give some time to my country and help people. I have talked to dad briefly about this just because he would understand what's in my head. Besides that, you are the first to know. I didn't want to say anything to anyone until I knew that this was really what I wanted to do and I had some months invested in thinking about it. I also wanted to make sure that I was qualified for the job I applied for.

Now that I have done both, it's time to discuss it with you because I would have a terrible time with anything without your support. I need you with me. I will be happy to give you all the details you want AFTER you absorb this and give it some time in prayer the way I have. Give it a couple days. I'm positive God will give you the same security in your heart that he has given me. I'm totally excited about it!

I look forward to hearing from you.

Your crazy-never-stop-always-doing-something-else son,

MZK

Ok. This is a good start. I said everything I needed to say and I gave it a positive feel. Not too bad. And hey, it only took me an hour and a half to write. I must say that there was lots of backspacing and rewriting. Oh well. It got done. Now, do you honestly think she would wait a couple days to get back to me? You are correct. NO WAY!

20070918 (Tuesday)
Moment of Truth #1 (Day 2)
(not a couple days later)

I went for a quick 3 miler before I came in to work. I had set up my battle plan for what I wanted to do to get my running time down and today was the day to see where I was. The track for the IST will be a standard quarter mile track, which means two things- nice and flat. Actually, it's not nice at all but it is flat. So it only makes sense to me that I should train on a course that is nothing but hills. If I can maintain my target time on my target distance on a completely undesirable course then I'll be whistling Dixie. Hills are so much more fun. On a flat course you just keep going. You tend to get lost in your thoughts and before you know it, you're done. This doesn't happen to me on a hills course. All I'm thinking is what kind of shape I'll be in at the top of the hill so that when I get to the bottom I can decide how I want to tackle the next. It makes things very interesting. My goal for today was to pace the course. I didn't want to go all out. Instead, I just wanted to find a pace that I could hold throughout the course whether I was going up or down. And one more thing- NO STOPPING! This was a run till you get to the end training session. No stops, breaks, chats, or changes to the plan. It was go time. My goal was to run it with an 8:45 pace which would give me a 25:35 finish. On a hills course, I didn't know if that was going to be easy or hard so I just went with the recommendation. I took on the course no problem and when I got back, I saw that I had finished with a 7:36 pace which gave me a finish time of 22:07. Rock On! That was good news to me. It showed me that my training had been paying off and my legs were in fact getting stronger because I felt great when I completed the course. Very cool. So now the next course of action will be to keep this new time and try to beat it on the next time out. Should be fun!

As soon as I got to the office and sat down, there it was. Mom had already gotten back to me. I have no idea why I told her to think about it for a couple days. I knew she was going to whip it back. Well let's see what she has to say-

Good morning son,

I didn't get your e-mail until late afternoon and we were swamped so I could only read it and then wait until I could get back today. I did read it carefully, and I understand what you're saying. I've always appreciated the fact that you have respected my feelings. This is an issue where dad and I will NEVER agree and you probably won't understand. I don't care how much time you give me to pray about it, my (hostile) feelings about the military will never change. If this is a decision that you want to fulfill then I won't even try to stop you...you're a grown man and must do what your mind and heart tells you. But you do it with the understanding that as much as I love you and believe in you, I will not support you.

I told Dad that I'll give in as long as I don't EVER (and EVER means EVER) want to see you in a uniform. He says that's asinine and gets quite hostile himself. I don't care. I cannot even begin to tell you how much I loved Gary and Eric...and how their senseless deaths affected me. To see them in uniform in their casket was a lasting impression and to this day I grieve for Eric. Now I know that when it's your time to go, God will take you, no matter where you are or what you're doing. It just so happened that Gary was overseas in a tank that got blown up and Eric was on a maneuver...they could have just as easily gotten killed on the highway or even in their own home. But the last time I saw them was in a funeral service, which was controlled by the government, forcing them to be buried in uniform, and having the last say-so.

The "control" is something that I have the hardest time with. And that's from experience. I suffered through four years of hell with your dad and I endured a year of rehabilitation because of what he experienced in Nam. Your life won't be your own and for you to think that even in the reserves you'll do what you want just confirms you have no idea what you would be getting into. To help the guys out in the field puts you out there with them....how else could you help them? When you sign your name on the dotted line you have just booked your ticket to the war. Yes, what you want to do sounds honorable. But like I told

84

you before, you don't have to enlist to achieve the same thing.

It breaks my heart that you have pursued this...but since you have, then I will stand in the background. Nothing will ever change my extreme love and pride for you...not because you're a man serving your country (that doesn't impress me in the slightest) but because you are my son who has an enormous amount to offer others. In Dad's heart, he had to serve his country, too. That's something that most women don't have a passion for. We're always the one left behind so we can pick up the pieces down the road. Don't be so positive that God will give me the same security in my heart...He will give me peace so I don't worry about you, but my distrust and aversion towards the military dwarf the walls of Jericho. Granted those walls were broken down, and maybe God will break down these walls, too... I'm not saying it can't happen; I'm just letting you know that right now not even a giant could stand on tiptoe and look over them.

I'm sure there's more to say because I always want to keep communication open...but for now I think this is enough. Stay in touch with me.....and be careful!
Love you,
Mom

Believe it or not, that went better than I thought it would. So I thought about it for a few moments and then boomeranged this back-

Hey mom,

Well that wasn't so bad at all. I feared the absolute worst and just as you always seem to do, you surprised me. To be honest, I thought I was going to get something else. I know that we are born to have different likes and dislikes and that's totally normal. It's what makes us so tremendously unique. Why am I telling you this? Because, no matter what, I really care about what you and dad have to say. It means a lot to me. I don't know what it would do to me if I didn't have you and dad together behind me. That doesn't mean that you'll jump for joy with every single thing I do but it's enough for me to know that you're still proud of me and you're not going to turn your back on me. That means more to me than anything.

So even though you say you won't support me, it's a relief that I know you'll still be a mom for life. I don't expect you to turn a new leaf and just be hunky dory with everything and I certainly won't try to get you to see things the way I see them. That's fine and dandy. Ever since I started this process I have been through an absolute whirlwind of emotions. It has been something I have never been through. I have reached a level of fear that I never knew I could experience as well as felt a wave of comfort that was able to bring everything back to square one just like that. It had such an impact on me that I have documented everything to this very moment. I have to say it's a GREAT read. Turns out your boy may have inherited some of those Sandra K writing skills. The point of this is that I have exhausted every thought of BAD that could happen to me. I'm tired of that. It's so easy to think of only the bad. That's why I see this as something positive and see it as something to be excited about. I understand what "signing the line" means. Dad spoke to me in great depth about that and saw to it that I understood the "truth" that is often covered up when the military is involved.

However, there has to be a purpose greater than my understanding why I am drawn to it and I'm sure that answer will reveal itself in due time. We'll see. In the meantime, thank you thank you thank you for at least hearing me out.
I'll keep you up on everything.
Love you bunches-
MZK

I'm happy to say that all went well. I called her up and she was just fine and dandy. I'm really glad my mom listens to me. It would be hard to go into this knowing that she has shunned me or something like that. That's what we call unconditional love right there. Even though she doesn't like it at all, she has found a grain of support. That's a WIN in my book!

20070924 (Monday)
So many Fires, So little Time

It's funny how life makes sure it keeps you on your toes whenever everything is going so well. Up until now, things had just gone great.

Almost too great. So it almost seemed natural that right before I left, I would face some adverse challenges to keep me grounded and focused. I was originally going to leave this section out, but I figured it would keep a certain balance by addressing a few speed bumps that came along the way.

Now that we are nearly a month away, it was time to get the school on board. This, similar to informing my family, was a situation that had to be handled quite carefully. It's a simple fact that if the students believe the teacher is going to bounce, then they will generally follow suit. Not all of them of course, but you always get a handful. Well, I didn't want any of them to stop their training for the months I was out. I wanted my students to be focused on the goal of why they were there, not just who was there to lead them at that time. For example, I just finished my first Triathlon. I had two trainers that helped me maximize my ability. How sad would that have been if, right before the race, one of my trainers pulled out? Would I abandon the race just because I didn't have a trainer? That's a negative ghost rider. So I have a greater challenge. The way I see it, I'm going to reach my goal no matter what. Some parents don't see it that way and I understand that, but the kids have to believe in their goal more than anything else, not just who's along for the ride. Besides, it's an awesome Martial Arts School and I'm fully confident that the Instructor that takes my place will be able to make it happen.

To make things even more interesting, two whirlwinds had attacked the atmosphere of the school at the same time! Each challenge had to be handled just the right way because if they weren't, it would positively shatter the plan that we had made. So here's what happened. During a Wednesday night class, I was teaching the Black Belts just like always. Towards the middle of the class, I introduced this new challenge where all the Black Belts get into a push up position on their elbows instead of their hands. Then, the shortest person in each line walks down the line of Black Belts by stepping over the middle of their waists. I didn't know this until the next day, but one of the Black Belts woke up feeling a bit sore. The mom, obviously concerned, contacted the school to let us know she was sore. That was totally understandable; I would have done the same without question. The problem was the dad. He totally freaked out and ordered an emergency hospital visit on the spot.

So even though the daughter actually felt fine besides being a little sore, now it turned into this huge thing.

I totally understand being concerned about the daughter, but I think I would have saved my panic attack until after I got the results. Personally, I would have felt absolutely horrible if the results came back where she had in fact been injured in the training. I truly care about all my students and I don't want to see any of them injured, ESPECIALLY because of me. I prepared myself for the worst just in case the results came back positive for injury. I would have faced the consequences and done whatever was necessary to make things right.

However, the results came back with NO injuries what so ever. That's just great! I took the necessary precautions to make the drill as safe as possible, everyone thought it was the coolest thing after the class, a girl felt sore the next morning, and now I got a parent coming at me as if she's paralyzed. So now because of the heat, the owner of the school thinks I'm endangering the kids in the class because he was only present to catch the aftermath. He pulls me off the floor until stuff died down a bit. I didn't complain at all. Then he starts getting blasted by the dad who was saying that I was going to shut his school down. This is coming from a guy that hardly attends his daughter's classes. His wife comes to ALL the classes and I believe that's why she was so cool about the whole thing. She knows what goes on in the class and knows that even though we do advanced stuff, we always take the right precautions. No one has **ever** been injured or broken a bone in my class. I've been a guest at other schools and have witnessed absolute negligence by the Instructors.

- At a Black Belt test, a guy was sparring, fell down, and broke his arm.
- At a competition class, the son of one of the Senior Instructor's got knocked out.
- In a regular class, a Blue Belt was sparring a White belt. Neither had protective gear, and the Blue Belt kicked the White Belt in the face and chipped his tooth.
- In a kickboxing class, a man was taking his first class and fell and broke his wrist while trying to kick a target while moving backwards.

The point is that unfortunate accidents can happen. We do everything we possibly can to prevent them. So it makes no sense to start fires when there is no need. It's just not right. Within my first month of starting at a new school, we started this new Sword Fighting Class. You get to sword fight full contact with padded swords. It Rocks! We did a demonstration at a movie theater to show off the new sport. I was set up to fight with an Instructor from the school. WE went hard. It was fun! The cool thing about it was having the ability to wear full body protective equipment so you can wail on each other and you don't feel a thing. It's like being invincible. The following Monday, he came in to work with an air-cast on his arm saying his wrist was broken in several places. I've broken my arm twice and always had a solid cast but maybe times had changed. However, I felt awful.

I apologized relentlessly and did everything I could to make things right. The mom told everyone in the school that I was a dangerous Instructor and to watch out. I felt terrible. What a first impression! For another year and a half I was in their debt. At the two-year mark, the mom tried to sue for damages to her son. It went to court and we found out that his arm was **NEVER** even broken. We got the x-rays back and there wasn't even a hairline fracture. The wrist was bruised but there was no damage what so ever. When we showed up for court, the kid was scared to death. He knew he was lying when he said he swore to tell the truth on the Holy Bible. And you can best believe that his Instructor, the one that taught him everything, was sitting front row staring at him.

Needless to say, the Judge found that if he was cleared to join the Army, then he was cleared to get out of the courtroom without a dime. To this day, I have never expressed my feelings about this situation or asked for retribution. But they got served! What a family. A lying mom that happily leads her kids into everything that Black Belts stand firmly against. And to make matters worse, she home-schools her kids! I believe there are a lot of great parents that have done a fabulous job teaching their kids; however, this is not one of those cases. There is no such thing as honesty and integrity in that family. I feel sorry for the kids. His sister is a sweet girl and has never done anything wrong. His younger brother may be the devil. The dad is actually really cool, but you never ever see him at all. The mom- she's rotten to the core. Good thing the son joined the Army. That'll straighten him up and teach him what his mom was incapable of.

I firmly believe that the strength of a Nation is built on the integrity found in the home.

That kind of mom is the reason why the kids of today will be the ruin of the future. That is, unless we do something about it. I hope and pray that if you are a parent, you set an example that will return honor to your family name. If you don't have kids, I hope that when you do, you'll be a Super-Parent.

Next on the skillet, another individual went around telling everyone that I wasn't teaching the Black Belt class ever again. PROBLEM! It was true that I wasn't going to be teaching that class as often simply because another Master Instructor needed to take over and get used to the class until I left for Boot Camp- Not because of a problem with my teaching. I was confronted about whether or not I said that I wasn't teaching, and after I assured the boss I hadn't said a word, he went on to inquire within the staff to find out who did. The truth came out that I had never said such a thing and we all found out who had started it. Stupid people ruin everything!

Then, it got really exciting. Another person, or perhaps the same person, circulated the fact that I had been FIRED! What the fudge dude? That was totally ridiculous! But oh well. We all had a good laugh about it when we found out that everyone could just fire me when they felt like it, but it was totally unnecessary. It causes so much tension when you're trying to teach classes knowing that everyone is watching you to make sure nothing bad happens. Oh well. Both of those situations got worked out by simply finding out who said what and that was that.

When we gathered up for the staff meeting, the first order of business was to make sure that the staff all knew the story and how everything was going to work for when I left for Boot Camp. That way, when someone had a question, we could all say the same thing. Since all the staff was not aware of my plans, the Boss reaffirmed to the team that I was leaving on November 4th. Everyone was totally positive about it. The second order of business was to make a flyer that we could hang around the school that would inform all the students.

Now that the flyer is up, all we have to do now is pull the pin, chunk the grenade, hold our ears, and see what happens. As it turns out, everyone in the school was totally excited for me. There were so many people that would come up and tell me a story about themselves, a family member, a friend, or they would give me a word of advice about getting through Boot Camp. It was great. There was so much support in the school... after they knew I was going to come back after training. I had one mom make me pinky swear that I was indeed coming back. It was cool.

Overall, I was proud of the fact that everyone in the school was so patriotic. It would have been a total bummer if anyone would have copped an attitude or had something negative to say about the Marine Corps. I sent a few emails to some close friends and I'll never lose this simple reply that a dear pistol sent back-

Wow!
And as you know Walt and I and how we think and feel..... THANK YOU FOR SERVING YOUR COUNTRY IN HER TIME OF NEED!!!!! WE LOVE YOU FOR IT!!!! But please be safe. You are too precious to us! -Tricia

Thanks Trish!

20070927 (Thursday)
Homework 101

You know the part in the movie Forrest Gump where Bubba is talking to him while he's whipping his rifle together fast as lightening? That is the guy I want to be. Not in the sense of being Forrest Gump, but being able to know everything there is to know about my service rifle. I want to be able to tear it down and put it back together at warp speed. The problem is- I know nothing about M-16's. I'm sure I could find all the information in the world about the subject, but that's not the same as getting one in my hands. Hmm... Let's see what we can do about that!

Welcome to M-16 land! As you may well know, the Marine Corps requires that all enlisted men and women must first be bona fide riflemen. You CANNOT be in the Marine Corps and not know how to use this weapon under the strict standard that is required. Sure, anyone can point the dangerous end down range, squeeze the trigger, and come close to a target or possibly hit it, but the Marine Corps demands that you kill the target in a single shot. It's called accuracy baby! That's what separates a man with a gun and a Marine. Marines shoot with profound accuracy.

However, that is all to be taught in Boot Camp. For now, I decided it was in my best interest to learn everything I could about this weapon before I got to Parris Island. Fortunately, one of the school's Black Belts has a father that is the top dog all pro master Jedi Naval marksmanship coach. If anyone could help me the most, it would have to be him.

Wednesday night he was at the school. The man's name is Bill. The guy is a human machine as well as a walking talking Wikipedia when it comes to weapons. We call him Coach Bill because he is a shooting coach as well as a volunteer coach at the school. Coach Bill is 6 foot-ish and solid rock. He trains every day and always has a smile on his face. To this day, I have never seen him not wear something Navy. He's always got his Navy Rifle hat or his Navy shirts. So I knew what to look for. As soon as I saw the hat, I B- lined it right toward him.

I walked up and asked him if he had a moment. He sure enough did and so I started in on him. I told him that I needed to learn everything there is to know about an M-16A2 (The field service rifle of the Marine Corps) After the shock had set in, he asked me what for? He hadn't yet heard that I was leaving and so I simply pointed to the sign that gave the rundown. He read it and got the biggest smile on his face. After that, he looked at me and said- "You got it!" With that, we made arrangements and the very next day I was to meet him at the Armory on the Naval Base. Rock on!

The next day, I found myself just as excited as when I was going to MEPS. I couldn't wait to dive in and learn everything there was to know about this particular weapon. Sure, I had BB guns when I was young, shot shotguns when I was older, and paintball guns in college, but this is a serious gun! Yeehaw!

I got to the Armory early and decided to use the time to study the 11 General Orders and keep them fresh on my mind. As soon as he showed up, we were in business. We briefly discussed exactly what I wanted to know. I told him that I wanted to know what everything was called, how everything worked, and how to handle it properly. Coach Bill said-

No problem! It'll take about an hour and a half. Do you have that much time?
I said- *Yes Sir!*

And off we went. He took me to this back room, asked me to wait just a second; he walked away and then came back in a blink with an M-16A1. He told me it wasn't an A2 but the differences were not that great in terms of what I wanted to learn today. Sounds good to me, here we go!

The first thing we discussed was the nomenclature of the weapon. He wanted to make sure we used the same exact terms when we were talking about the parts of the weapon. As he went from the bottom to the top, he would point to the part and then call its name. Then every so often he would back up a few parts and continue on. That way, we hit everything several times and it was much easier to memorize. And let me just tell you, he continually quizzed me on all this material. It was great because I knew that when I left, I would be able to remember everything better than if we just went over stuff and nothing more. I was thoroughly impressed with this weapon.

Once I got the basic nomenclature, we continued on with how to handle it properly. That included how to hold it, load the magazine, ground a used magazine, strip it down, put it back together, make it ready for inspection, and we finished by dry firing it. It didn't matter how much I knew going in, Coach Bill simply told me everything as if I didn't know anything so that nothing would be left out. Now, I have to continually review this information so that when I arrive at Boot Camp, I'll be prepared to do the best I possibly can. As I was leaving Coach Bill's office at the Armory, he told me that I should try out the "O" Course the next time I came out.

What the heck is the "O" Course? I asked.

Coach Bill just smiled. Check. He asked me if I would like to come out the following Tuesday and run the course. I was all over it. We set up the time and squared everything away. That night, I dug out a book that I had picked up way back in June.

I picked it up because I wanted to get used to the rigors of Marine style warm-ups and workouts. I have to say that it was a solid investment, and after I found out the "O" Course was detailed in it, it turned into solid gold.

Now some may say that doing all this research and practice will give me an unfair advantage over the recruits that have never done any of it. And being able to be pretty good at the challenges will make me look better than I truly am. The way I see it, if you want to be the best, you have to prepare. You don't go to war without knowing your enemy. You train. You practice. You monitor yourself. You get advice. You study. Then, when it's time to go for it, you can kill it. I want to kill it!

The book gave me some great tips so that I would have a good idea of what I was getting myself into when I got there.

20071002 (Tuesday)
Marine Corps Obstacle Course ("O" Course)

I showed up a couple minutes early to the Armory and Coach Bill was ready to go. He grabbed a stopwatch and we were out the door. The Course was actually just a couple hundred yards away. We turned a corner and BAM, there it was. Wow!

It looks a lot bigger in real life. The book gave it no justice what so ever. It's funny because even though the obstacles look pretty harmless, doing them one after the other as fast as you can is hardcore. However, at this point, I had no idea.

Coach Bill started out by walking me through the 8 obstacles (*14 total if you count the low jumps that separate most of the Main Obstacles*). We went one by one, and he told me how I needed to

94

negotiate each obstacle. It didn't look too bad at all. In fact, I was excited to get it on. We got to the final obstacle, which was the rope climb. He explained that I could either use the snake method or, since I was young, "arm it!" I had never climbed a rope without my legs so I gave it a shot. About 4/5ths of the way up I got my legs in the mix. That's tuff. 25 feet is no joke man! Just as we were walking back to the start of the course, a Marine Corps Major and a young lady walked up to the course. Apparently, she was in the Navy and was looking to cross over and this was the only thing that was keeping her back. She was failing on the time requirement. The Major then went on to tell me that the qualification time for the entire course was in his words- *"One minute to pass and two minutes to fail."*

So the bottom line says that I have to finish this course in less than 2 minutes. I looked at Coach Bill and there was nothing more to be said. It was time to see what's up.
The order of events is as follows-

1 LOW HURDLE
2 SINGLE HIGH BAR
3 COMBINATION SLANTED BAR/ BALANCE LOG
4 WALL
5 SINGLE HURDLE
6 MULTIPLE HURDLE
7 DOUBLE HIGH BAR
8 ROPE CLIMB

The course is set up in a straight line with about 10 yards between each obstacle. The entire course is set in loose sand so you find yourself in a catch 22. On one hand, all the high falls are supported by a soft landing. On the other hand, it makes moving feel like you're in slow motion and jumping just sucks. All the obstacles, for the most part, are constructed out of 12-inch logs and 3 inch steel bars. For the first run, Coach Bill just wanted to see how long it would take me worse case scenario. He told me to take my time so we could have a good point to start from clockwise. I can do that. We let the young lady get far enough into the course and then Coach Bill gave me the go ahead with the stopwatch running. I made it through everything and we took a look at the clock. 2:20. Not too bad really. But I need 1:30. We took a look at how I went through, discussed some ways to cut some time and then I got ready to tackle it again. This time, it kicked my butt. The first time I went through smooth and easy. This time I tried to hammer it. True, I made up huge time but by the time I got to the rope I was out of gas. I made it half way up the rope and my forearms gave out. I said c'mon, let's go. They said, nope.

Then the Major gave me excellent advice. He gave me a tip on the body mechanics on my rope climb and how I could improve my technique. As soon as I felt like I understood what he meant, I went back to the start with Coach Bill and it was time to try again. This time, however, I was to just maintain proper technique and not worry about the time. Here we go-

O1 Low Hurdle
This is the calm before the storm. The object is to negotiate a log that is about 3 feet high. It's really not that big of a deal. However, it's just tall enough that it's tough to simply jump all the way over when you are gassed. You can either jump up with one foot and then step over (what I did), or you can put one hand on top of it and hop over the top with both legs. No big deal. I was over it and on my way to O2.

O2 Single High Bar
There are two ways to get up and over this 8-foot bar. You can swing up underneath it and catch it at your hips similar to doing a back flip motion over it, or you can use the chicken wing approach. The Chicken Wing approach is easier but it takes more time where as the back flip motion is faster but takes more energy. Catch 22... again. So I chicken winged it. I jumped up, hooked my elbow, swung a foot up and over, and then rotated my body over. That's done. On to O3.

O3 Combination Single Slanted Bar/ Balance log
This is pretty tough. Not so much because of how hard it is, but because it just takes time to complete it. First, you jump up on top of a log similar to the first low hurdle. Then, you jump out and grab a horizontal bar. You then swing both legs up and hook your heels on two slanted parallel bars (not just one). You then pull yourself up in between them

and shimmy down the two bars. At the bottom of the two slanted bars is a platform that is about 7 feet off the ground. You climb up onto the platform and walk down a 10 foot slanted log. This is the part that you really have to watch your balance. One slip and it's a long way down. At the bottom of the log (about 4 feet off the ground), you then jump out to a log and catch it with your stomach. You throw your leg over and it's an 8-foot drop. This one takes some technique because you really don't want to slow down at all, but you also have to keep your balance or you'll fall off and have to start all over. Ok, this one is in the bag so it's on to O4.

O4 Wall
No obstacle course would be complete without having to jump and climb over a 6-foot wall. This was pretty tough because this wall wasn't completely solid. Instead of a flat wall to get over, this one was constructed with round logs as the base and 2 2x8's on top. The logs were used so that you couldn't rely on running up the wall and grabbing the top. On this obstacle, you had to run, jump up and get your forearms on top of the wall, and then you swing your right leg over the top and drop off the other side. It would have been much easier to run up the wall but that opportunity was not present here. Once I hit the ground it was off to O5.

O5 Single Hurdle
This was just like the first one except it is 5 feet high. So I jumped up, planted my hands on top, swung my right leg up, threw my left leg through and I was done... only to face O6.

O6 Multiple Hurdles
This was a killer. By this time I was already being worked. Now it was time to send it into overdrive. There are 4 logs you have to clear that fall one after the other. There is just enough room in between each one to land and then jump over the next. The logs are about 4 feet off the ground. There are a couple different techniques you can employ. The first is the step through which I had used on the single hurdle. Again, that is where you jump up with two hands and swing your right leg up to the top of the log and simply pass your left leg through. The second

way is to swing your leg over from the ground so you become horizontal with the log and just roll over it to the other side. The first way is slower and you have more control. The second way is faster but you get awfully dizzy. Choose your poison. Well those are done so it's on to O7.

O7 Double High Bar

This isn't too bad. It's just hard to do fast. All you do is run up to the obstacle, jump up with one hand and grab the first bar. You then power up and reach the second higher bar with your right hand. Once you get that, you are home free. You then swing your right leg up to catch the lower bar, stand up to the higher bar keeping as tight to it as possible, passing the right leg over that bar, and then jumping out and away from the obstacle. No need to climb down- just jump. Once I hit the ground it was on to sudden death. O8

O8 Rope Climb

By here, you're already feeling the work. The last 7 obstacles have taken their toll and you only have one more to go. 25 feet to freedom. I stepped up, grabbed the rope, took a deep breath, and jumped into the mix. The first time I attempted the rope, I made it. The second time, I got about half way up and bailed. This time, I knew just what to do and I was going to make it. Sure enough, I got about half way up and realized the technique adjustments were on the spot and I was going to make it. I gave the top log a love tap and started making my way down. Done.

Coach Bill smiled and told me my time was 2:10. Even though that wasn't good enough to pass, it was still good. Why? Because now I knew I could finish it even if I was gassed out. I didn't know what I was doing in my first attempt. I rushed myself in the second attempt. My third attempt was smooth and precise. Smooth and precise is a lot easier to speed up. With a little practice, I'll get the techniques down so I can conserve as much energy as possible and then shoot for the time. I found that when I rushed myself, my movements were much more chaotic and it cost me time. When I concentrated on staying low profile and doing it right, I was much faster. No matter what, this obstacle course is no joke. You can't take it for granted because the moment you do, it'll kick you in the junk and laugh at you.

When we were done, Coach Bill and I parted company with the Major and headed back to the Armory. Coach Bill informed me that I was welcome to come up whenever I had the opportunity to practice on the course. And if he had the time, he would be more than happy to come out and time me. Awesome. I can already see that I'm going to be out here as much as possible.

Step 1- get it under 2 minutes.

Step 2- chase the Major. He did it in 1:30. Game on!

20071004 (Thursday)
Marine Corps Obstacle Course #2

So I took Wednesday off so that I could recover from Tuesday. Tuesday was a big day. When I got done, it felt like I had been at the gym for a monster workout session. It's funny the difference between doing a training session with weights and doing a training session based on sheer body weight. BIG difference. I totally prefer staying out of the gym. Body weight training is so much more fun and you don't really notice the length of time you have been working out until you're ready to bounce. Not to mention the fact that you feel like you're able to do something with your muscles when you can vault yourself over a 6-foot wall instead of doing 50 curls with a bar. I found that a lot of people work out at the gym and get weight strong, but then they get tested in an atmosphere where they use that muscle and it's not as effective as they would have guessed. I discovered the value of learning how to use my body strength together instead of simply being awesome at individual exercises. I was fortunate that I had the opportunity to come out and hit this Course because it taught me the almighty lesson of practical application. Until this point, I thought I was in great shape. The course gave me a great left hook and told me otherwise.

This morning, I made sure I ate breakfast. That was a huge problem on Tuesday. I knew better. This time I made sure I stacked some fuel. I got out to the course and set everything out. I had a stopwatch, a bottle of water, and 8 obstacles to tackle. The first time through the course, I just wanted to go slow and smooth. I just wanted to remember how everything was supposed to work. I got through and, to my surprise, I actually did really well. I wasn't timing myself just yet, but it felt really good. I could feel a huge difference.

The next time I went through, I put a little jack on the speed and just as before, I finished feeling good. Awesome! On my way back to the start, the young lady I had met the previous day had just pulled up and was walking on to the course. Cool. I said hi and she said she had remembered me from Tuesday and that I was looking a lot faster. Really? I asked. That's pretty sweet. I wasn't even going at it and it appeared I was getting it done. Even better. I told her my name and she told me that her name was Nicole. She was having a terrible time with the rope. She could get everything else done but every time she got to the rope, she would get about half way up and then simply gas out. It was hard to watch because you know she wanted it bad and she really was trying but she was just mentally giving up. That is definitely one thing that I do love about Marine Corps Training- Just when you think you have given all you possibly can, The Marine Corps demands you give more... and you do. Somehow, you learn to dig just a little bit deeper and venture into the world that is beyond your best.

I was feeling really good about everything and figured I needed to get some validation on my ability to knock out this course. No effort counts unless you have a witness. I figured Coach Bill had to be working at the Armory so I ran on over to see. When I got there, I hit the buzzer, waited a few seconds, the door swung open, and tada! He greeted me with a big smile and asked me what I was doing. I told him that I had been pounding the course and wanted to see what he was up to. I took a seat in his office while he was finishing up some stuff and as soon as he was done, he asked how the course was coming. I told him that I had really made some great improvements since the last time. I swear, the first thing he said was- *"Let's go time it!"* He had the biggest smile on his face. I didn't even have to ask if he would. He hustled me out of that office so fast and onto the Gator (military golf cart with 6 wheels) and we were off to the course.

As soon as we got there, I sat my stuff down and he was all set to go with the stopwatch. He told me to start whenever I was ready. Since the time starts the moment you touch the first log, I was able to begin wherever I liked. So I started about 5 yards back from the log, took a deep breath, slapped my hands together and off I went. Everything went according to plan. I leaped over O1 no problem. Got to the high bar and swung myself up and around it just like Coach Bill taught me. I hit the ground and was so happy that I cleared the high bar so fast that I actually tripped a bit and had to drop a knee. I regained my balance and tore off to O3. I jumped up to the bar, swung my heels up and hooked them, shimmied down the bars, jumped to the platform, ran down the log, and hurdled the leap of faith for an 8-foot drop. I was on fire. I cleared the wall at O4. I made my way over the O5 single hurdle, bounced right through the O6 multiple hurdles, and got to the O6 double high bar. When I got to O6, I used a better technique than the chicken wing approach. I reached the first bar with my left hand, powered my right hand to the second bar, and then swung my right leg straight to the bar without hesitation. I was up and over and off to O8. At this point, Coach Bill hollered out that I had just hit 1 minute. YEEHAW! That was music to my ears. It was just what I needed to jump up and make my way up the O8 rope. As soon as I started climbing, I heard Coach Bill yell- *"You got it!"* My technique was much better today. Even though the last 2 feet of climbing seemed like an eternity, I hit the finish log and started sliding my way back down. Coach Bill looked at the clock and just shook his head. He then looked up at me still sliding down and told me my time. 1:09!!!

Yeah! That's what I'm talking about. We were both floored by the result. From there, I just jumped down the rest of the way off the rope. I was so happy I didn't care. When I got to Coach Bill he gave me some knuckles and we both just smiled. Tuesday, I was sucking holes with a time of 2:10. Today, even after a few times through, I killed that time by a full minute. From this event, I can tell you that NOTHING beats practice and experience. You have to practice to get good at what you want. And I believe you have to have the wisdom of someone that has actually done it to help you along the way. It's all about the tricks of the trade baby!

This was an enormous accomplishment in the world of Matt Killian.

On Tuesday, I was killing myself trying to figure out what it would take to break 2 minutes just because I was having a terrible time with the rope. In truth, the guidance I got from Coach Bill and the Major made all the difference in the world. With practice on top of that, I was good to go. I said in the last input that I wanted to break 2 minutes and then chase 1:30. Having hit a 1:09, I was amped!

It looked to me that Coach Bill wanted to have a go so I said the one thing that I knew he would jump on. I asked him- *"Hey, you wanna race?"* He got this big smile and without saying a word, he started stripping off his sweatshirt and stretching out. As soon as he was done stretching, he gave me that look like **"It's on now!"** we got to the line and he said- *"Whenever you're ready."*

I gave the 1,2,3 go and we were off. We side by sided the first obstacle. No big deal there. On the high bar, he got a jump on the swing and gave himself a small lead. I chased him to O3 and caught him on the shimmy down and got back to side by side from the drop on the end. We stayed that way all the way to the single hurdle past the O4 wall. As soon as we got over the O5 single obstacle, we headed to the hurdles and that's where the fun began. He saw me pulling away and I don't know what happened but all I heard was **Ughh!!**

I didn't stop or look I just kept right on going into the O6 hurdles. I heard him coming so he had to be ok. I made my way to the O7 double high bar and he was hot on my trail. I jumped up and as I was jumping off the other side, I could see now that he was just clearing the top and I had a couple seconds on him. I got to the O8 rope and I was looking good. I started my way up and then I heard it. When a rope tightens up you can clearly hear the fibers squeeze together. I couldn't believe it. He caught me! I didn't have time to look. I just kept going. I had about 4 more feet to go and all the sudden the rope noises behind me passed my rope noises. **NOO!!!** Just when I was making my last heave on the rope, I heard Coach Bill's hand tag home. Son of a--! Oh well. I tagged home without missing a beat and looked down to see him a mere second in front of me. Good man!

When we got to the bottom we were both gassed. Neither of us could talk because we were too busy catching our breaths. We both had a seat on the home stretch log and started recounting the battle. I asked him what the commotion was and he said that he had simply misjudged the take off on the single hurdle before the multiple and took it in the chest instead of going over it. I told him how I could hear him catching me just by the noise of the rope and how I was screaming to myself in my head to go faster. We both had a good laugh!

You can say what you want about age, but Coach Bill is a friggin machine. I was so impressed with him. Not only did he take a hit near the end, but he still managed to catch me and pass me on the rope. Judging from our speed, we had to have finished about 1:04. We totally rocked the sauce going head to head. We congratulated each other on a job well done and just enjoyed the fact of knowing that we were living the dream. I had just overcome the fear of not being able to finish the course with a sub 2 minute time and he was happy knowing a ~45 year old could get the job done in phenomenal time. It was a great day. After that, I had to head back to work and we parted ways.

I really can't thank Coach Bill enough for helping me the way he has. He has really gone above and beyond and I'll never forget that. Thanks Coach Bill!

20071016 (Tuesday)
2 Weeks to Go Time!

That's right. Two weeks and I'm out of here. Rock On! It cannot come fast enough. I'm tired of planning and getting stuff ready. In the past couple of weeks, I have been able to knock out a lot of stuff. I jumped out to the "O" Course and busted out a 60 second finish. That was my ultimate target and today I made it happen. I remember the first time I did it and thought my 2 minute 10 second finish was pushing tin. Now I'm knocking on sub 60 second's door. I believe a perfect run for me will bring a sub 60-second time so we'll see if I can get lucky at least once or twice. I also stepped up my rope-climbing workout. Instead of just climbing the rope, I threw on a 25-pound pack and climbed the rope with that. Wow! That was hardcore. 25 pounds doesn't seem like a whole lot, but you have 25 feet of rope to get up, it does some magic.

I read a book that totally blew my mind. The book is spectacular. It's a 200 something page book but it flies by. It's about this guy named Martinez who grows up a full blown gangster, turns to the Marines in his junior year of high school, heads out to Boot Camp after his senior year, turns hard core grunt, heads out to the sandbox, and becomes a hero receiving the Navy Cross. It's an incredible story. I would recommend that book to ANYONE who is even remotely interested in the Marine Corps.

I was finally able to invite all the DEP's out to the Karate School for some training. Good times I must say. They were totally amped about the chance to hit some stuff. They all showed up for the 8:10 class right on time. The look on the faces of the parents and the students who were getting out of the last class was priceless. They ALL wanted to see the next training session that was about to get underway. When it was time to get started, I rallied everyone together so I could say a quick word. I introduced myself to the ones I didn't recognize and welcomed them to the school. I also made a point to tell them that even though I was going to be leading the class, I was just one of them. I told them I couldn't wait to ship and that I didn't think I could watch Full Metal Jacket one more time. That loosened them up and we got started. It was cool because even Sergeant V jumped in the mix.

We ran some laps around the class, stretched out from head to toe, and then ripped into the targets. I told them that the Drill Instructors at Parris Island would teach them everything, but I was going to go ahead and show them a few things that would give them a head start. We touched on making a good fighting stance, keeping the hands up when you punched, and basic body mechanics for engaging your whole body. Everyone understood and we were ready to throw down. We did a few punching drills, some cardio up and downs, some football style aggression drills, some body conditioning, and finished with punching and kicking combos. By the end of class, everyone was smoked. They were glad it was over. When we circled up for the close, I thanked everyone for coming out and told them they were all welcome to come back and train any time between now and the day we shipped. They were thrilled. The class was nothing like they expected. I guess they thought it was going to be a bit more traditional or conservative and that didn't happen. It was Go Go Go! They had no idea it would be so hard. But since it was fun, they coped really fast. We all had a blast.

There is nothing like clenching your fists up tight, gritting your teeth, and laying in to a target with everything you've got... and then doing that repeatedly for an hour. Good times. Just when we thought we were done, in comes Sergeant V. He had that smile on his face. That smile that said- "Oh we ain't done boys and girls." He thanked me for the opportunity to have everyone together. And then the line that everyone was hoping they wouldn't hear came on out. He smiled and said- *"Everybody on your faces. You didn't really think you were going to get out of this did you?"*

We all yelled- **"No Sir!"** He went into his usual deal by telling us this would be over real quick or we were going to be here for a long while. We got on our faces and when he yelled- "Push-Up", without missing a beat we yelled, **"Marine Corps!"** We knocked out a clean set without having to play any extra games and we were done for the night. We made the big man happy! Even though we had a rock solid class and everyone was spent, we still had enough to show some love for the Corps. Personally, I had a lot of fun working out with everyone. It's one thing to train with guys that are here for a good sweat. It's quite another to train with guys that want to kill stuff. There is nothing like it. But even beyond that, there are already the beginnings of family in the team. Everyone watches out for everyone and we all support each other no matter what. When someone is getting in trouble, we jump in and take it as a team. It's an attitude that is hard to find in every day life. It's sad when the only place you can be taught that type of friendship and teamwork can only be found in an environment that most people are too afraid to pursue.

After the training, we all sat around and talked about this and that. The Recruiters were bombarding me with questions about my training background such as what I've done, what I'm certified in, how long I've been training, what I like the best, what advice I would suggest about this and that. It was great. The last thing the Recruiters told me before I left was to make sure that I didn't tell any of the Drill Instructors at Parris Island about my background in Martial Arts. They said for me to keep it totally to myself. They said this for two reasons-

1. So I wouldn't be put into an unnecessary spotlight or bring negative attention to myself.

2. So that if I ever get a chance to roll with the Drill Instructors, I might be able to surprise a few of them. That sounds good. Based on what I've read from Marines that have gone through the process, they said they would have paid a lot of money just to get a few shots in on the devil.

20071020 (Saturday)
I.S.T- Final Day with the DEP

Today was going to be a huge day. It's time for the BIG IST (Individual Strength Test). This is the test you have to pass in order to ship for Boot Camp. If you failed this, you would have to keep moving your ship date until you could meet all the requirements. All the information as far as minimums and maximums came in a flipbook out of the Marine Corps tin I received from Headquarters. Ever since I got that I have been training for this test. I didn't want to just pass it, I wanted to kill it!

I had a huge event at the school the night before so I wasn't worried at all about being too excited to get some good rest. The moment my alarm went off, I jumped out of bed ready to go. I remembered the last time I met Coach Bill at the "O" Course and how bad my performance suffered because I hadn't fueled up before hand. I wasn't going to make that mistake this time. I don't know why but Apple and Cinnamon Oatmeal does the trick. I ate a couple packs of that and I was set. I was scheduled to meet everyone at the ROD2 for the IST at 0800 on the dot. So I jumped in my car and hit the road.

Upon arrival, I found that I was early because I didn't see anyone except 2 people in the parking lot. Oh well. If you're early you're on time so that's cool. About 10 minutes later, Sergeant V pulls in. He looked a bit rough getting out of the car and walking up, but as soon as he saw that Josh brought him Krispy Kreams doughnuts, he was the happiest man alive. He smiled, opened up the building, and we headed back to the Marine Corps office. Apparently, there was miscommunication with some of the guys and everyone else wasn't going to get here until 1000 to start the IST. Great. But no worries, Sergeant V had some MMA Fight Videos, he had some doughnuts, and so we watched them and chit chatted about the fights while the time flew by. Soon enough, more people started showing up and it was getting close.

Then, we were graced by the presence of two brand new Marines that had just graduated Boot Camp. Everyone called the girl "Mouse". I guess because she was really tiny and actually kind of looked like one.

The other Marine named Powell was just a young kid but you could tell that there was something different about him. Even though he looked 19, he carried a seasoned demeanor about him. Powell didn't talk too much, he laughed along with the guys, but when it was time to come correct, he was razor sharp. There was a profound difference between these two. Mouse was going on and on about her experience in Boot Camp. It was actually hard to listen to. She talked about how her DI's truly didn't like her because she gave them static, how the Crucible was too easy because she was a girl, and at about that point I started looking for new company to hang around with. That girl was simply annoying. She's the perfect example of someone who barely passed everything but comes off as being the top of the class. And since she has finished Boot Camp, she wants to come here and try to make us work as hard as she claimed she did. Whatever. Powell was cool. He was much more relaxed, only talked about Boot Camp because you asked him a direct question about it, and you could actually see that he was there to motivate everyone through the IST.

And then it was Go time. Sergeant V gave Travis the order to get us formed up in the front and get started. So we hustled to the front and lined up out on the sidewalk just like we always do. Once everyone was formed up, Travis led us through a warm up routine. Upon completion, Sergeant V came out and gave us a pep talk. He said-

All right, here's the deal. You all sounding like you ain't got it today. Like you ain't got heart. I want all them Navy fuckers to here you in their little meeting. They think their gonna meet? Naw, we gonna give them a little interruption. They ain't like us. We work! Our heart is what makes us the few, the proud. So from now on, if you wanna be Marines, you better start actin like Marines and sound the fuck off!

Sergeant V always did have a way with words. After that, we let it rip! And sure enough, the Navy poolee's jumped ship and gave us all these mean little looks when they left. After that, Sergeant V led us back in to the pull up bars. Game time!

Sergeant V told us how it was going to go. First we were going to hit the pull ups, then we do the sit-ups, and then we run. The minimum requirements are as follows-

Pull ups- 3
Sit ups- 44 in 2 minutes
1.5 mile run in less than 13 minutes

     It all sounds easy doesn't it? But that's the Marine Corps. Those figures are simply the minimums. There's a little thing called Maximum Output Potential. Your Recruiters know full well what you're capable of and that's what they want to see. So if you do 3 pull ups and jump off the bar knowing you can do 10, you're going to get kicked in the nuts. Maximum Output means the maximum number of reps you can do, even if it gets a little ugly. You'll have guys yelling and sweating and doing whatever they can to squeeze out just one more good one. When it came my turn to do my max set of pull-ups, the top number so far was 12 (with only Travis following me), Sergeant V looked at me, and asked if I was going to give him more than 12. I said- *Yes Sir!* I didn't know how hard it was going to be but I was going to have to make it happen. So I jumped up and started pounding them out.
     1...2...3...4...10...11...12...16...17...18...and 19. That was it. 19 was all I had without my form going out the window. I jumped down and Sergeant V just shook his head like always. I cannot believe how my pull-ups have improved. Before, I was lucky to get past 14. Now, I'm knocking on 20's door. Yeah! Travis finished at 22. That guy is just a guerilla. The DI's in Parris Island are going to have their hands full with him. But he did what he should have done. You don't want to leave for Boot Camp with a sub 20 pull up max. You need to have that under your belt. And that's what Travis did. Good man.
     Even the Recruiters got in the mix. However, it should have been only Sergeant V because he was the only Senior to clear 13. The other Seniors sucked! It was actually disheartening. Here they are screaming at us and they suck at PT! Sergeant V is twice our age and still able to hit his number. What's up with the other Seniors? It was just what I needed to understand that you always have to be ready to throw down because everyone's watching. And even if they say it's ok that you can't keep up, deep down they are full of it. The guys wanted to see their Recruiters perform what we couldn't, but that didn't happen. It was like watching Michael Jordan miss 9 out of 10 free throws. We killed them! Deep

down, I think they knew it. Hopefully that'll make them step up. To drive this lesson of preparation and humble pie home, Sergeant V told Mouse to get up and do her flexed arm hang. She was bragging about how she pulled a 74 second for her PFT. Everyone was impressed with that so we wanted to see it. Since she had been harassing the girls with sub 74 performances, the girls wanted to see Mouse show them how it was done. The first thing she said when she got up to the bar was that she wanted to respectfully decline because she was on leave. Sergeant V said-

Now that's some Bullshit. Get up there and show them how it's done!

Mouse gets up to the bar slowly and turns to look at all of us. In a way I kind of felt sorry for her because we were heartless. When everyone else went, there was nothing but encouragement coming from the team. When she grabbed that bar, it was dead silence. When she called the ready, Travis stepped away so she could start the exercise. She actually started off great looking quite confident. She had started with Herrick (another girl) at the same time. Both were looking good until Mouse made a big mistake. I guess since she was feeling good, she started heckling Herrick. This was a mistake because this only fueled Herrick's drive to beat her... whatever it took.

Mouse realized this when Herrick said nothing back. Herrick's teeth clenched and her eyes screamed determination. Then it happened. Mouse's arms started to shake. It's funny how you feel great one moment, and then the very next, your body starts to shut down and all your confidence goes right out the door. Right then, everyone knew she wasn't going to make it. For that, everyone started giving her static. WE were all yelling-
To Mouse- Where you at Mouse? You look worried!
To Herrick- Keep it up! You're going to make it!
To Mouse- You're shaking too much Mouse! You better control it!
To Herrick- Let's go girl! You can beat her!

After that, Mouse couldn't hold on. Time- 48 seconds. Someone yelled from the back- **YOU SUCK BITCH!** It got ugly. Herrick kept right on going. There was NO quit in sight. Finally, she dropped at 86 seconds.

Not only did she set a new personal record, but she also beat the piss out of Mouse's 74. What now? Everyone lost their minds for Herrick.

Mouse didn't say anything but words of sincere encouragement for the rest of the day. Don't get me wrong, no one said anything bad to Mouse or did anything disrespectful afterward. She's still family. Even more so because she is a no joke Marine now and we are still waiting to go. After she was put in check, she was cool.

Travis informed everyone that we were to head out to the back to do the sit ups. We started moving back and I guess that speed wasn't good enough because he then proclaimed that if we didn't get back there in 30 seconds, it was time for some push-ups. I started to move but the idiots in front of me were thinking Travis wasn't really going to back it up. They jammed the hallway and we were stuck moving at push-up speed. Sure enough, we got outside and as soon as everyone formed up, Travis told us to get on our faces. He said 35. I heard a couple groans in the guys and Travis just smiled. We started in and when we got to 34 he just waited. I knew what he was up to and so did the slow pokes. They were learning their lesson. Finally he said 35 and we were done. No one said a word. Everyone knew that this wasn't civilian life where the hammer doesn't reinforce consequences. It's simple. You do what you are asked and you move with a purpose. Otherwise, you get the hammer.

When Sergeant V got outside, he told everyone to partner up and get into the start position. I was first two go. To be honest, I'm not really good at sit-ups. I had been working hard because I knew it was my weakness. My goal was to hit 80. I kept telling myself: No matter what, just hit 80. As soon as I got the GO, I got to work. The first 30 were a breeze. 50 came tuff, and the burn started at 75. Fortunately, I hit 80 and had time to spare. Rock On! I had 15 seconds left and knocked out another 9 before time was up. My ultimate goal is to surpass 100, but for this day, 80 was the goal and it was met. Hallelujah! Petterson came around and got our numbers and then it was time to switch it up. When we got the GO I got hit with a dose of serious inspiration. A Sergeant came in to encourage everyone and he jumped in the mix for the sit-ups. Holy Crap! That Sergeant was a machine. Since everyone had to count out loud you could hear the difference in his blistering rhythm. It's hard to explain on paper except for this-

If everyone was at a pace of	1....2....3....4....5....6
The Sergeant was going at a pace of	1..2..3..4..5..6..7..8..9..10

Wow, that was easier than I thought. When we were ordered to give our numbers, I heard things like 45, 93, 104, 35, and then when he got to the Sergeant, his number was 138. I don't care who you are, that was inspiring. That gave me such a kick to start working on my sit-ups so I could turn out a number like that. That's awesome!

After everyone closed their mouths, Sergeant V told us to head to the start line of the run. It was time to knock out the 1.5 Mile run left on the schedule. As soon as we got to the start, we noticed some subtle differences to what we expected.

Dream- Flat quarter mile track with easy gradual turns. Smooth pace throughout.
Reality- Two trip out and back that would require a stop and go. Steady uphill out, same steady downhill back.

Sergeant V gave us the run down of how it was going to work. We would run out to the Marine, go around the island where he is posted, head on back, do it all again, then finish it up. Check. Everyone got into the start position and we were ready to go. Just as I expected, Sergeant V put us into two groups- slow and fast. There were five guys in my group and we were all issued a 10-minute limit for the 1.5 miles. Anything over that and we would have to come back and try again. Sergeant V gave the GO and we were off.

The 4 other guys tore off ahead leaving me at the caboose of the fast group. At first, I was shocked. These guys just tore out like there was no tomorrow. I'm screwed. I started widening my stride a bit and that seemed to knock off a couple feet at a time from the group. Then I started to get closer and closer. Then it occurred to me, the guys were running anxious. This was not their true pace. Sweet. Sure enough, they started slowing down and I passed all but two of them. Travis and Foster. As soon as we circled the Marine, I caught Travis. I continued with the length of my stride but pushed the cadence up just a bit. Sure enough, I crept passed Foster and then Travis. I was gaining. I wasn't forcing it, but I did get out front. As soon as I got in sight, Sergeant V yelled- *"That's what I'm talking about! Get it Killian!"*

I got to the home turn around and headed back out. I was in a comfortable lead all the way to the Marine. Then it happened. Travis and Foster started creeping back up and slipped passed me in the final hundred yards. It was my fault. I had let them draft me thinking that they had reached their speed when I made my move. As it turns out, they simply let me hold the pace, drafted off of it holding as much energy as they could until the end, and then used the last reserve to overtake my position. It was the right strategy all the way. As soon as we crossed the line, Travis turned and smiled at me. I smiled back and asked him what was up with sandbagging me? He told me that since we had never raced, he gave up the lead to see if I would tear away or cruise. Since I cruised, he sandbagged it. We gave each other a high five and laughed about it. No matter what, we finished with a time of 9:30 so we were good to go.

As the others were just coming in, we headed back out to encourage everyone else. Everyone had heart that day. No one was walking. As soon as they saw the finish line, the looked down, grit their teeth, and when their head came back up, they sprinted it out to the finish. After they finished, they were given permission to blow chow. That was some nasty junk. It was like Sergeant V turned on the mains to a couple faucets. Whatever. As soon as everyone rallied up, Sergeant V told us to head in, use the head, and then line up at the pull-up bars.

Sergeant V welcomed us to Death Valley. Everyone looked confused. Then he told us it was the name for the ladder style drill we were about to perform. We were then divided into groups according to ability. My group was Travis, this new guy, myself, Foster, Peters, and finally Sergeant V. The directions were simple. For my group it was –
7 pull-ups hands toward you.
6 pull-ups hands away
5 pull-ups hands toward you.
4 pull-ups hands away
3 pull-ups hands toward you.

Then you go back up starting at 3. It was hardcore. Going down was easy. Going up was tuff. They have to be correct pull-ups. We finished that exercise well spent. It was a GREAT day! We finished our time there with Sergeant V giving us our results from the day. He had us all sit down the way they make you sit in Boot Camp and told us not to move from there. He went through his sheets telling everyone what they did and what they needed to do for the next IST. Like I said, it's not overcoming the minimums. It's all about reaching the maximum. He encouraged everyone by pointing out a few people that sucked holes when they first started coming and now they were hitting it. It was simply to motivate us. For example, he made one guy stand up and talked about how he couldn't do 1 pull-up. Now he can do 10. It was great.

He then told us what to concentrate on as far as our next goals and told everyone that no matter what, they have to be able to hit 100 sit-ups. He said it's too easy to max out your score by hitting 100 sit-ups so just make it the goal no matter what. After that, he told Travis to stand up and come to the front. He announced that he was shipping tomorrow and let him know that we all wished him the best. Sergeant V then did the unexpected. He thanked us for our hard work and told us how proud he was of our scores. Everyone killed it in their own way. Not only did they meet the minimums but they surpassed them. Sergeant V said-

That is the difference between the Marines and everyone else. We don't just do what's required, we go above and beyond. We don't stop at OK. We stand up for each other. When one struggles, we jump in the fight any way we can. No one stands alone. That is the number one reason why I train with you and push you the way I do. We're a family. We live off each other. We live for each other. Our bond as a family is what makes us Marines.

Like I said, Sergeant V has a way with words. It motivated everyone. Everyone left with a great feeling of accomplishment. It was a great way to finish my training with the Delayed Entry Program Recruits. Two more weeks and I'm off to Boot Camp. I can't wait.

20071028 (Sunday)
Party People!!!

Today was perhaps, one of the BEST days of my life. I went to my last Sunday morning church service and it was phenomenal. Interestingly enough, the preacher spoke on trusting God and pursuing your passions with confidence. The Lord did not give us a spirit of fear but one of power! He was saying that the Lord has a mighty plan for you: not one that will harm you, but one that will strengthen you. What that means to me is that you may be put in harms way, but with his guidance you'll make it through better than when you started. At the end of the service, we started to leave but I couldn't. Something was holding me back. I couldn't explain it, but if I had to try it was as if I felt there was unfinished business. My dad always told me that when you get that feeling, shut up and pray and God will tell you what you need to do. So I walked up to my buddy, Pastor Jason, who was talking to a couple other fellas I'd played with in the band. I asked him if he wouldn't mind to just pray with me that God would guide me in this journey, keep me safe, and get me back. They were all over it. It was awesome! We spent a few moments in prayer and they prayed for me with utter sincerity and it was like a flip of the switch. As soon as we said amen, I felt a rush of relief and a charge of confidence. I needed to start this journey with God in control and the nail was hit on the head. As I was walking out, I was just thinking to myself- *"if God is for me, than who can be against me?"* This is a rhetorical question but the answer is no one. When God is behind you, you are unstoppable because His **will** is unstoppable.

The school threw a party for my eminent departure. To be honest, I had no idea who would even show up. I simply told everybody that we were going to have it no matter what and to make sure they brought food. In my past experience, the organization I was with in Florida never made a big deal out of someone leaving whether the reason was good or bad. One day you were here, the next day you were gone. It was hard sometimes. But this time, we were going to have a party. It turned out to be a Grand Slam! Everybody and their brother came. And it wasn't like everyone came because they had to. There was just a great atmosphere here and you could tell they wanted to come. Wow! I had no idea it was going to be so big. It took up both training floors of the school and everywhere in between.

The party kicked off at 3PM. A few people came before that

because I announced that I was picking up Guitar Hero 3 at 12 Midnight and would then be playing that until everyone showed up the following morning.

As soon as the school started filling, I jumped off the game for some meet 'n' greet time. Everyone was smiling. The food tables were totally packed with all kinds of stuff. There was music playing, everyone was in great spirits, it was going to be great. As soon as the majority had shown up, I packed all the kids on one floor and then got the parents started on the food lines. That way, they could get their food in peace. I walked back in the room and proceeded with telling everyone the scoop. First off, it's time to play the greatest schoolyard game in the world- The game that is used to forge the Leaders of tomorrow- The game that separates the weak and the strong- The one and only- Dodge Ball.

It was a blast. I separated the swarm into two teams. The two teams were the winning team (My team), and the team that wanted the chance to take the "Master" down. For some reason, the opposing team was seriously stacked. As soon as we started, I knew I was in trouble. Everyone started sending balls my way trying to take me out. They didn't even care about anyone else on my team. Sure enough, BAM! I got tagged by one of my own Leadership team members. Instantly, he became a star! Everyone was cheering and screaming for him. Good man!

After that, I let everyone continue playing while I started making my rounds again with the people that had just shown up. I figured that would keep them busy for at least 4 or 5 hours. It was so cool talking with the parents. They expressed their gratitude for me helping their kids and I told them that I really appreciated their support for their kids. It was great being able to say where they came from and where they are now. Some kids were the type that would be good no matter what. Other kids started out as Satan's red headed hyperactive stepchild and eventually squared themselves away.

About an hour in, one of my Black Belts wanted to play me in Guitar Hero. Bring It! This kid is amazing. He's only 11'sh years old and he's a prodigy. I've never seen any other kid his age that equals his ability. So we have a great time because we can both rock out on Expert. It was awesome. We got a huge crowd packed in a little room.

Everybody was placing bets to see if he would beat me this time. This past summer, he was helping in summer camps and he tore my score up for Sweet Child of Mine by GNR. Good man! But today, I was looking to take the crown back! It was just fun!

To cap off the Guitar Hero time, we attempted Jordan. Jordan is the hardest song in the entire game. If you get a chance, just go to www.youtube.com and type in "Guitar Hero Jordan expert". You'll see just what kind of nightmare it is! Until this day, I had never beaten the song in a crowd setting so I told them that there was a huge probability that I might fail it. Everyone wanted to see us have a go at it and so we jumped in. We started the song and it really wasn't looking too good. Both of us missed the first power-up but then recovered well and got the second and third. That's better. We got to the first solo and decided to save it until the monster solo that was yet to come. This means that we were going to have to really nail the "A" solo section, kick in my boost at the end of "B", and then really nail "C". After that, we knew we could hammer the final solo sections D, E, and F because we had learned to beat them with no star power. You know? A lot of people have no idea the strategy and focus required to beat elite games. But it's worth it. Who needs a social life when it comes to becoming the master of a plastic guitar!!!

When we got to the break before the solo section, I just took a deep breath and relaxed. The tighter I was, the slower I would be. That wasn't going to be helpful in finishing this song. Well, I stuck to the game plan and ripped through the "A" solo. Holy Crap! I couldn't believe it. Everyone was losing their minds. It was crazy. When we got to the end of "B", we kicked in the juice and drove through. We finished the "B" and "C" solo and the crowd was a roar. No one had ever seen anyone get through "B" and "C". After "C" comes the calm before the storm. It's a good place to recover if you barely got through "C". The final sections came and we made it through to the last section. The last section is wicked hard. You really have to concentrate on making your pinky fly. Before I had even realized it, it was over. You end the song playing the chorus riff and the crowd knew it. I couldn't believe it. Jordan was beat!

I hit the last note of the song and the crowd went into a whole new world of chaos. I felt like I was in the end zone after the winning touchdown at the Super Bowl. It was truly awesome!

After that, it was time to play some Warrior Sport. Break out the swords campers, it's time to beat some heads in. I soon found that even though the room was huge, there were just too many people and someone was going to get hurt. So I spun the rules. We played a game called "Pig Slaughter". I'm the Butcher and they are the Piggies. I'm the only one with a sword and all they have top do is be the last one to survive. I explained the detailed rules and we were off. The good thing about that game is I can actually decide who is going to win because all I have to do is not go after them. That way, I can usually pick the kid with the most heart (not always athletic ability) and make them a superstar. They loved it. After the game was done, I gathered everyone up for a final heart to heart. I told them-

Guys, you can never control everything in life. Life happens and all you get to do is decide on how you respond to what happens. Good things happen to good people. Bad things happen to good people. Everyone has their days in the sun and unfortunately in the gutter. But the difference between average people and Black Belts is how we respond to what happens to us. We have to fight for what's right. If we fall short of our goal, then we adjust our attack and jump back in. We never give up. You will decide what person you will become. The world will not decide that. You will decide that. It's your choice. I believe there are only two types of people in this world. The people that make it happen, and the people that don't. You are the only one that can make the choice.
Will you be weak, or will you be strong?
Will you be one that makes excuses, or a person that someone can depend on?
Will you be lazy, or someone that does whatever it takes to get things done?
You'll have to make that choice. My hope is that I've shown you that you have everything it takes to be a WINNER. You guys got it?

Everyone shouted, **"Yes Sir!"**

After that, Mr. Palmer, the other Senior Instructor of the school, came in and said they had something special for me. Everyone cleared the floor. The doors opened up and out marched a team of our Black

Belts all in uniform. Mr. Palmer put them into the ready position for a Form. They were going to perform Koryo. It was flawless. Everyone moved together as a unit. I was thoroughly impressed. Even Ben, my Guitar Hero buddy, had learned it the previous day without me knowing so that he could perform it with the team. I was floored. The last move has a yell. When everyone yelled, instead of yelling- **"I-yah!"** they yelled- **"Semper Fi!"**
Everyone clapped and cheered for them. No one expected that and they said it clear as day. It was a flawless performance.

After that, one of the moms presented me with a scrapbook filled with tributes of all the students in my honor. I had never gotten anything like that. Each student told me about how I had helped them in some way. It was staggering. Luckily, I didn't have to read any of it out loud because it would have broken me. I'm so proud of all the kids in the school. They are truly remarkable. That scrapbook was the single greatest gift I have ever received. It was so much better than any thing someone could give me. I kept my composure and humbly thanked them for coming to the party and allowing me the opportunity to help them in the journey of becoming the best they can be. I was truly grateful for each of them. I have a picture at my house of a young child looking into a river. It reads-

A hundred years from now, it will not matter what job I had, how much money I made, what car I drove, or what kind of house I lived in. But the world may be different because I made a difference in the life of a child.

My ultimate goal had come true. I had helped to make a difference. That means more to me than anything else in the world. To me, there is nothing more important, or more fulfilling, then to make a difference in someone's life. I thanked God for this opportunity. It was truly amazing. After that, everyone had a chance to come up and say whatever they wanted to say and I gave each one a few encouraging words. It was phenomenal! I have to really enjoy things now because starting next Sunday, my life is going to suck! At least for 13 weeks that is. What a way to end my time at the Martial Arts School. I know I'll be able to come back and teach when I get done, but the sheer fact that the students really want me back and that I'll be welcome will make it better than ever. I finished with having a lot of fun, spending time with people that I care the most about, and for once in my life had nothing else to worry about. Now, it's all about looking forward to Boot Camp.

20071104 (Sunday)
Thanks... Matt Killian, Out!

If you are reading this, it means that I have left for Boot Camp. There are only two ways out of Boot Camp- Graduation or a Grave. Since my family hasn't given me permission to tap out of this life, that kind of narrows my options. This experience has taught me so much. I learned how to communicate with my family
and found that, despite their natural fears, their unconditional love for me and Faith in Almighty God will overcome. I learned that when you take care of business and honor God through your actions, He will bless you beyond measure. I learned that whenever you do what's right, everything else will fall into place. I learned that age is only a state of mind. You can do so much more than you think you're capable of if you will simply get out of your own way and just try. I learned so much in these past few months.

To end this part of the story, I would like to thank the people that have helped me beyond the call of duty.

I would like to thank my Father for understanding my goals and offering sound unbiased advice when I have needed it the most.

To my Mother- Thank you for not throwing a tantrum when you found out that I wanted to be a Marine. Even though you don't support the decision itself, I know you support me and that's good enough for me.

To my extended family- Mark, Janelle, Cati, and Christian. Thank you for believing in me and supporting this entire venture despite the loss of PFC. Eric Davis, US Marine.

To Mr. Palmer, my golf trainer/ movie quote rival/ ingenious idea sharer/ diplomatic advisor/ video game assessor/ Boot Camp partner in crime- thanks for everything. You've Jedi mind tricked/ guided me when things have been challenging and helped me to come out on top. We've had some good time my brother from another mother. I can't wait to tell you all about it on the golf course when I get back.

A huge thanks goes to Coach Bill- Thank you for taking the time to teach me about the M-16A2 and helping me to kill the Marine Corps "O" Course. You helped me to achieve what I thought was beyond my reach.

To RJ- Thank you for guiding me in finding an MOS that I feel would maximize my desire to help other Marines. Thank you for supplying me with the study materials that will help me to become the Marine I see in my mind.

To my Martial Arts Family, thank you for the love! You guys are the best! To the parents who have given me invaluable tips to keep me out of trouble, thank you so much.
To all my students- Enjoy the ride now because when I get back, you'll be in for a whole new world of fun and adventure- Grrr!

I would like to thank everyone, past and present, in the Army, Navy, Coast Guard, Air Force, and the Marines, for serving the United States of America. You are my heroes! To all the mothers sending their "kids" off to fight for what's right, thank you for your unwavering strength and support.
(To all those opposed, don't bother wearing a seat belt.)

A special thanks goes to all of the Recruiters here in Maryland that have helped me along the way.
Sergeant Peterson- Thank you for calling me and setting up my first appointment.
Also, a big thanks goes to Staff Sergeant Benette, Staff Sergeant Carter, Sergeant McIntyre, Staff Sergeant Hendricks, and a HUGE thanks goes to Sergeant V (You're the MAN!)

Last but not least, Thank You Staff Sergeant G. Thank you for explaining everything to me so I could make my dreams come true. Thank you for your honesty. You are a Marine's Marine.

I could not have made it to where I am without the help of everyone around me. I am truly blessed. Thank you. With all of my heart, thank you.

At this time, you have walked with me from the moment I went on the internet looking for information about the Marine Corps up to the point I left for Boot Camp. I didn't know if I would be able to record what happened in Boot Camp but, as you can see by the number of unread pages still in your right hand, I found a way. It was extremely difficult, but the job got done.
So I invite you to walk with me a bit more.

20071104 (Continued)
Sunday Matt Killian Out!

My bags are packed and I'm ready to go. I jumped in the car and headed for the ROD2. I walked in the front door and, as the door shut behind me, I entered into a whole new game. A game where I would find the consequences utterly severe and the lessons learned by the fire of pain. I had no idea what I was getting myself into. I walked into the office and it was packed. All the guys I had been training with and their families were all waiting around watching the Patriots and Colts game. Apparently, we had some time to kill before we took off so we did whatever we could to amuse ourselves. We found a foot counter leaning against the wall. It's nothing more than a handle attached to a wheel that you push along the ground and it counts how many feet you've gone by how many revolutions the wheel makes. It's basic trig at its best. The game was to hold the handle off the ground and spin the wheel with your other hand as fast as you possibly could. Several different grips were tested for maximum results but we soon found the two-fingers-on-the-spoke spin worked the best. Boggs and I were battling for the record. Little did I know that this friendly competition would help us help each other all through Boot Camp. While we were playing our games, the parents were playing "ask the recruiters a million questions" game. Staff Sergeant Benette had his hands full. They wanted to know everything just like you would expect normal parents would. The moms asked all the questions and the dads just hung back and listened and tried to calm the moms between questions. Then the moment we had all been waiting for came. Sergeant V came in and told us it was time to bounce. Hallelujah! We all loaded up, said goodbye to the parents, and we were out. We were finally on our way.

On the way to the Comfort Inn, Boggs dropped a bomb. He came clean and told Sergeant V that he had hooked up with a girl that was shipping in a few weeks. Up until then, it had been speculation. But now the truth was out. Sergeant V was pissed in a fun way. He said-

How you gonna keep that shit from me? How can I watch your back and keep you out of shit if you be fuckin bitches that are gonna be shippin? She's gonna pay now!

Boggs lost his mind. *"No, don't tell her. She'll kill me. Don't tell her."*

Nope, tomorrow I'm gonna get her in PT. She's gonna be sayin "BOGGS! That no good punk fuck! I'm gonna beat his ass!"

We all laughed about that. We all knew it didn't really matter but it was fun. We had more things in front of us to worry about. We pulled up to the Comfort Inn and this time it was different.
I was not ... a l o n e.

Thank God I'm not alone. The last time I was here, all I could think about was how I was going into this thing with no one beside me. This time, I had the love of my life saying her prayers for me. I was good to go! It gave me strength and confidence I had never felt before. I could go forward full steam ahead knowing that there was someone special waiting for me on the other side. It was great! As soon as we were checked in, we walked back to the foyer and Sergeant V gave us a speech we didn't expect. With an iron face, he said-

I'm gonna tell you the troof. Tomorrow, you guys are going to leave. As far as I'm concerned, the only way I want to ever see you again is when you come back with the title "United States Marine." If you give up or quit or say you're going to kill yourself, don't ever show up to my office. I don't want to see you ever again. Like I said, you come back a fuckin Marine. When you do, I'll stand up, shake your hand, give you a hug, and call you by your title whatever it is. You worked too hard to do anything but succeed. It's gonna be the hardest thing you ever done. That's why we prepared you the way we did. You are ready.

With that, he turned and walked out the door. Myself, Boggs, and Gram were speechless. After a moment we parted ways to our rooms and got ready for tomorrow.

The last few times I was at the hotel, I had an overnight bag, a change of clothes, and the essentials I needed such as spending money, my cell phone, and my wallet. This time it was much different. All I had was-
- The close on my back
- My Social Security Card
- My Driver's License
- 20 dollars in cash
- A pocket Bible with everyone's address written on the back cover

This is all we were allowed to bring. No extra clothes. No cell phone. No extra money. No toothbrush or toothpaste. No change of underwear. We weren't even supposed to bring deodorant! We had no idea what to expect. It seemed really strange to know you're going on a 3-month trip and having nothing more than the clothes on your back. Really strange.

But those were the directions and we stuck to it. We were told everything else would be issued to us upon arrival to the Island. So for now, all we needed to do was go to sleep, wake back up, and get ready for the world to change.

20071105 Monday
Ship Day is Here!

3:50AM came with a quickness. I was ready for it. Today was the day. I met everyone downstairs for breakfast and the room was buzzing with excitement. We ate with some urgency and headed out to wait for the bus to come and get us to MEPS. The bus showed up on schedule. However, this time it was a different bus driver. Oh well, it had been a couple months since the last time I was at MEPS so it was to be expected. We jumped on the bus and headed down the road. As soon as we arrived at Fort Meade, we unloaded and headed in. By now, I bet you could tell me the order of events going into MEPS. We found our way into the cafeteria awaiting our directions for shipping. After about 45 minutes, Staff Sergeant G came in and called the roll. After the roll was called he took a couple steps toward the door and turned around to my directions. He scanned the room, saw me, and informed me that he needed to speak with me. OK.

I followed him back to Liaison Central and, upon arrival, he said there could be a problem. The recruiting office had dropped the ball with my paperwork and apparently I had to get an age waiver signed off before I could ship. It's 6AM. I have until 10AM for the paperwork to be faxed to Headquarters, signed, faxed to Parris Island, signed, sent back here, authenticated, and put in my packet for me to ship. The office in those two places doesn't get up and running until 8AM. That means that there will only be 2 hours to get it done and my name isn't even on the top of the list for priorities. What does that mean for me? I'll have to sit around and wait to see if it can get done.

In the meantime, Major Thomas briefed us all. He told us the rules while we were at MEPS such as no leaving the building under any circumstances, no bad language, keeping the noise down, and staying awake. Then he went into some tips once we got to the Island. For example, begin everything you say with Sir! No matter what. Sound off at all times. And be honest when they grill us. Apparently, they will put us in a room and ask us--- demand us to verify everything we said to make sure it's true. Major Thomas said that 1 out of 3 will be back by Friday because they lied. Good to know.

As we sat there watching the time pass by, it became apparent that I was not shipping today. I sank. My new friends Boggs and Gram, the guys I was planning on showing up to the Island with, would now be going today and I would leave tomorrow on my own. There must be another word for disappointed. It was a terrible feeling. 10AM came, their families came up and sent them off, and then everyone was gone.

Whatever! I came to be a Marine with or without anyone else. It was my first lesson in mental fortitude. I could sit around and wallow in being disappointed but that's not me. I'll get there soon enough. I got my friends and family praying for me and I'm not letting them down. Screw it! I waited around MEPS until 1PM and then was taken to Headquarters. I was to wait there until the paperwork got back from Parris Island. At 6PM it arrived. I friggin waited around twiddling my thumbs for 5 hours straight.

This day was gone. I now had to return to the Comfort Inn for yet another night. I was good to go. I had learned my lesson in staying strong and that was an accomplishment. I got back to the Comfort Inn and it was time to grab some chow. The chow hall was run by the chow nazi. No one knew why she was so feisty but whatever it was, it did the job. She was as mean as mean could be. She would tell you to come in, shut up, get your food, don't even think about looking at the TV, just eat, and get out. In turn, everyone was as nice to her as they could possibly be. It took the wind out of her sails and amused us at the same time.

After I finished chow, I headed for the gym. Even though I was coping with the frustration of waiting around all day, it still left me with some pent up energy that could be put to good use. I pounded the weights and 45 minutes later I was good to go. I headed back up to the room and prayed that tonight would be the last night. Tomorrow had to be the day.

20071106 Tuesday
Ship Day is Here... Take 2!

Once I got to MEPS, I noticed I felt relaxed. I didn't have that same anxiety of not knowing if today would be the day I would actually ship. I would get there sooner or later and it made no sense in killing myself over something I had no control over. The hardest part was not being able to call my family.

Now all I could do was sit around and watch the same crap that was on yesterday. It was an endless cycle. Each show was on for 1 hour and after the rotation would end it would start all over again. It went Charmed, Angel, ER, Law and Order, and then back to Charmed. Put a gun barrel in my mouth and put me out of my misery. You can only take so much of that crap. Then, just like magic, our names were called to ship.

I'M OUTTA HERE!

But first, all the shippers had to clean up. We filed into the bathroom and had a cold shave. None of us cared because we were shipping. We then went into a conference room and were given our flight information. We were put into our groups and then given a few other briefs before we left. There were two other guys in my group. Greys and Jones. Both were laid back recruits that were in no hurry to be in any kind of spotlight. They just worked under the radar and that was good. We were loaded on the bus with guys going to other branches and they were loud and obnoxious. One guy was popping off as this- "I'm going into the Army and I know everything there is to know about it. In fact, I know so much that I'll tell you what you'll do when you get to Parris Island. I know everything."

Everyone wanted to kick him in the nuts. Luckily, the bus driver told everyone to shut up so we didn't have to hear it. Off to the airport we go. There was no time for playing around once we got there. We got through security, rotated turns through McDonalds for some chow, and then sat back and waited to go. We chit chatted about why we were going in and told our stories of where we came from. It was cool. It occurred to us that this was the last time we would be walking in our own individual way. We agreed that the Marine Corps would bring us together and everything we had been through and what made us what we were was about to become in a way insignificant. It didn't matter what we had done or what we had. Even though we were entirely different, we would all be working to become the exact same thing- a United States Marine. Just about that time, we were called to board. AWESOME! We're finally getting out of here.

We jumped on the plane on our way to Atlanta International. It was to be the halfway point on our way to Savannah. All 3 of us knew that we were in for a long haul so we all slept on the plane. Reserving as much energy was priority numero uno. We touched down in Atlanta and proceeded through the terminal. Little did we know that we were about to receive one of the greatest gifts/ luxuries unbeknownst to any of us. We were walking around looking for a place to grab a bite to eat and a lady came up and asked if we were looking for the USO. She said she noticed we were all holding folders that said "Marines" across the top and figured we were looking for it. Dumbfounded, we asked what the heck the USO was. She smiled, and simply pointed up some red-carpeted steps to the 2nd floor. We thanked her and headed that way. None of us knew what it was so we figured what the heck, let's check it out. We walked up the stairs, turned the corner, and saw a man sitting behind a desk. He smiled and said- "Welcome to the USO gentlemen." We said thank you, signed in, and preceded down the narrow hallway past the desk. As soon as we turned the last corner we stopped dead in our tracks. We had arrived.

The USO is a military lounge. But it's not some uppity high brow joint. It's awesome! Big screen TV's locked on NFL games, Lay-Z-Boy recliners set up in a theater setting around a huge flat screen, Playstation 3's, X-Box 360's, internet stations to look up whatever you wanted, a solid wall of books and reading material, and last but not least, free food. There was food everywhere. Whatever you wanted. Soda, chips, cake, coffee, tea, subs, fruit, candy, pizza, burrito's, and it was free. Just when I thought it couldn't get any better, I walked up to the man at the desk and asked where the nearest pay phone was. He looked at me, smiled, opened a drawer, and said, "Right here son." The drawer had about 9 cell phones in it. He handed me one, asked to hold my ID, and said bring it back whenever you're done. I was floored. I LOVE the USO!

The 3 of us made our rounds on the internet, used the cell phones, and we watched football. We knew the next few days were going to suck so we might as well live it up now. After a bit we decided to grab some real food. There was a Mexican restaurant in the food court and we had a voucher to use so we jumped on that. It was pretty good for our last meal before boot camp. As an added bonus, there was a bar there and so we were able to get some Red Bull. Our master plan was to get off the plane and pound the Red Bull so we would be supercharged for the night ahead. While we were waiting for the plane, I noticed a man on a cell phone that was wearing a Marine Corps polo. He kept looking over at the 3 of us so I held up my Marine folder. He flashed a smug smile and went back to his conversation and didn't look back again. At the time, I thought he was smiling because we were excited about our journey into the Marine Corps. Today, I'm positive he smiled because 3 garbage civilians were about to enter hell and that's always amusing. We jumped on the plane, fell asleep again, and woke up landing in Savannah. We were here!

It was just past 11 and we were ready to go. We got off the plane and headed down the terminal. We saw the baggage claim sign and right underneath the sign stood a Marine. That must be our check in guy. We walked up and I said- Good eveni...||SHUT THE FUCK UP! He yelled.

Everyone else in the terminal froze in their tracks. He told us to follow him and keep our mouths shut. We turned a corner and we were ordered to make a single file line in front of him. We faced him in line and he whipped out a trashcan. He told us to empty all of our pockets and throw away everything except our ID, Folder, and Social Security Card. Everything else had to go. So long Red Bull. After we were cleaned out, we went into a room and checked in. The Marine behind the computer asked for our SS# and to verify our last name. After we checked in, he got on the phone and told the person on the other end something I will never forget.

He said- *"Good evening Sergeant. 3014 has arrived."*

He told us to get out of the office and return to the waiting room. But it wasn't your typical waiting room atmosphere. No one said a single word. Everyone was sitting in tightly lined rows of chairs and everyone was seated with their backs perfectly straight. You weren't allowed to fall asleep or talk. There were these racks of chow you were welcome to eat if you were hungry but no one was eating anything. The guys that had been there were watching Marine Corps Boot Camp DVD's. It got us all jacked up and ready to go even though we couldn't say a word. After about 35 minutes, we were ordered to stand up and get ready to go. The time had come. We were heading to the Island. The 2 Marines that checked us in didn't come on the bus with us so we were on our own. Next stop, Parris Island.

It was pitch black outside because we were outside of any city lights or civilization for that matter. So we had no idea where we were going. But it didn't matter, we were amped. The anticipation was staggering. We had been driving around for what seemed like forever, and then, we saw it. We pulled up to the front gate of Parris Island.

A guard stepped up onto the bus, took a look at us for a moment, smiled, and said-

Welcome to Parris Island. Ya'll ready to become Marines?
The bus boomed **YES SIR!!!**
He smiled and simply said- *"Very well, enjoy your stay."*

He stepped off the bus and we pulled away. We were in a frenzy until we hit the bridge. Once we started over the bridge it was like someone hit a mute button. No one said a word. We could see the lights of the Island and now we knew we were past the point of no return. Up until the airport, any one of us could have walked away and said never mind. Once we passed the bridge and were officially on the base, we knew there was no turning back. Up ahead, we saw lights in front of a building. I recognized that building from all the YouTube videos I saw about Boot Camp. But now, it's real. The bus pulled up and came to a halt. I was on the right side of the bus and directly out my window on the ground were a whole bunch of yellow footprints.

The infamous yellow footprints.

I looked up and saw two Marines stand up, came out of the building, and were B-lining straight for the bus. You could say they were walking with "urgency."

Here it comes! The Sergeant tore up the stairs of the bus and, with a cold steel and totally direct voice, he stated-

Welcome to Marine Corps Recruit Depot Parris Island. The only words you will say is, "Yes Sir, No Sir, and Aye Sir." In 10 seconds your bodies will be locked on my yellow footprints. NOW GET THE FUCK OFF MY BUS!!
We flew off the bus. Everyone was ready to go. We jumped on the footprints and locked our bodies. From there, we got our official

introduction speech. The Marine said-
Welcome to Marine Corps Recruit Depot Parris Island. Congratulations on your endeavor to join the world's finest fighting force. It will be challenging, but by maintaining the Marine Corps values of Honor, Courage, and Commitment, you too can earn the title United States Marine.

With that, we were then ordered to run over to the silver hatches in front of the processing building and made two single file lines while maintaining a heel to toe distance.

Doors are now called Hatches. Every order came loud, fast, and one time. The Sergeant never repeated himself. If you didn't get it, you better be watching everyone else and follow suit. We were told that we would walk through these hatches one time. After that, everyone uses the hatches on the sides. This was to be the official transformation from civilian to recruit.

Over the silver hatches it reads-
Through these portals pass prospects for America's finest fighting force.
United States Marines

The silver hatches flew open and we ran into the building. We were ordered to sit down in metal desks with recruits that had already been there for a while and we were to wait until called.

They called us up one by one to verify our last name and SS#. Then we went back to the desks. Once everyone was done, we were split into two groups. The two groups made up the origins of Platoon 3013 and my Platoon, which was 3014. At this time, there were only 27 recruits in my Platoon. During the next few days, that number would climb to 81 in our Platoon. Tonight, Platoon 3014 was born kicking and screaming.

From there, we were given to the Sergeant that got us off the bus. His job was to get us through the processing phase. We left the main room and went to make our arrival phone call. There are about 15 phones mounted to the wall and a script on the inside of the lid.

The Call Script reads-
Hello (person's name)
This is (your name)
I have arrived safely at Parris Island.
Do not send mail.
I will contact you later.
Thank you for your support.
Goodbye.

We were ordered to scream this at the top of our lungs, word for word, and then hang up. If you said anything not on the script then the Sergeant would hang up the phone and you would be done. Most of us couldn't even think straight. We had just spent the last hour getting yelled at by the pit bulls. Every time we turned around we were getting yelled at. They would throw our stuff, then scream at us to pick it up, and then throw it again. Their job was to put as much stress on us as they could. They did a great job. No one wanted to look like an idiot so we all just did things as fast as we could and tried to stay out of trouble. It was nuts. When it came time for me to make the call, I couldn't remember any numbers off the top of my head. I had dialed those numbers a million times, but right at this moment, it wasn't coming together. So I just pretended to dial a few numbers, I screamed my lines out, and then hung up the phone. No harm no foul. I'll be in touch with my family soon enough. And to be honest, that's not really the way I would like to leave a message. My family would have just worried that much more about me. We then finished final paperwork with a Corporal. He was cool because he knew what we were feeling. He was the comic relief. While everyone was trying to treat us like the Sergeants, he talked to us like our Recruiters. Easy and to the point. He got us through the paperwork because it had to be completed without errors due to stress and then we were handed back over to the Sergeants. The Sergeants greeted us by making us throw away any and all contraband still in our possession. That means goodbye address book. We could keep our SS# card, ID, cash and coins, and paperwork. Everything else was thrown in the trash. How am I going to write anyone?! This SUCKS!... but I'll figure something out.

FORMING

20071107 Wednesday
(Straight continuation from Tuesday midnight)
Welcome to Parris Island

At 12:30, we got out first haircut. We walked into this room and there were about 6 chairs and that line was cooking. I swear each cut took on average about 35 seconds. Before I knew it I was up next and getting yelled at for not moving to the next open chair. Right before I sat down, I caught the reflection of myself in the window. 35 seconds later, I stood back up and I was officially bald. My hair had never been that short. Luckily, everyone looks just as dopey with a bald head so it's all good. The barbers aren't paid to be gentle either. Everyone gets the same exact haircut and the clock is ticking. They don't say you're done. They just pat you on your back and you're out of the chair.

At 1AM we went to clothing. It was here that we would get everything we would need until we were picked up by our Drill Instructors. And by that I mean, from now until we picked up our Drill Instructors, we would carry every single thing we were issued at all times. There was no place to call home where we could keep it locked up. We carried everything everywhere we went. We were issued 2 sea bags that would be used to hold everything we were about to get. First we got our utility green and desert uniforms. I noticed right away that they didn't say US Marines or our names and quickly learned that we didn't rate name tapes or the title so they were just bare. Without the luxury of changing rooms, we stripped completely out of our civilian clothes, put them in a brown paper bag, and said seh-la-vee. I could tell some recruits were self-conscious and the lesson here was the Marine Corps just doesn't have time for that. You can just throw your modesty right out the window with my address book.

From now on, it was military issue. Everything we wore from head to toe was Marine Corps issue. After our cammies, we got our running shoes, which our now called "Go Fasters." We were to check off the Go Fasters on the inventory sheet with our Ink Sticks (aka Pens). After we had something on our feet, we then got our personal items. That included-
More Ink sticks- writing paper- laundry bag- laundry pin- marking kit-

Neosporin- moleskin- hygiene bag- diddy bag- medical tape- soap-
deodorant- nail brush- hygiene towel- scuz towel- scuz brush- tooth
brush- sewing kit- razor- blades- shower shoes- shaving crème- soap
box- laundry detergent- toothpaste- marker- cuticle scissors- Marine
Corps Handbook- Green Monster- 2 canteens- hand sanitizer- jock
straps- skivee shirts- skivee shorts- belts- drill boots- jungle boots-
folder- 3 locks and a cable- 6 inch ruler- boot socks- black socks- pt
socks- 8 point covers- boonie covers- knowledge guide- money/
valuable bag- and a glow strap

     We were all lined up in front of these cubby partitions. We would
get a piece of gear and then bring it back to our cubby. Then we'd get
something else and bring it back until finally, we had all our stuff. It was
interesting to me because as we would walk back and forth getting gear,
we would pass by this huge open hatch. Every time we would pass by,
you could hear way off in the distance ----left...left...left right left...left---
- It was then that I learned that Parris Island never sleeps. There is
always a Platoon moving here or there... always.

     Then the Sergeant flew in the door and gave us 120 seconds to
put all that stuff in our sea bag. Being counted down applies to
everything. And counting down does not mean by standard clock time.
It means that the Sergeant counts down as fast as he can from a given
number to 0, and you better be done when he gets there. 120 seconds
really means 30 seconds. 30 seconds really means 10 seconds. We
learned fast. Anyone who wasn't done would have his stuff thrown back
out of the bag and given another chance to get it done in the given time
while being screamed at.

     Good times. All this took until 4AM. After we got our personal
gear, we were taken over to get our field gear. We walked into this
fenced in area that had two warehouses joined in the middle by a roof
and a concrete floor. We staged on the concrete floor and took turns
going into the warehouses with the other 3 forming Platoons. 3012,
3013, and 3014 had come together. 3rd Battalion Follow Series was
born. We got all of our stuff and inventoried it. It included-

LV Pack which is the huge hiking pack- day pack- drill belt- canteen
pouches- magazine pouches- H harness- dry bag- canteen cups- butt

pack- rifle gloves- polypro top and bottoms- green gloves- gortex top and bottom- iso mat- and a beanie

All this gear had to be packed in the LV pack. The LV pack went on your back. You carried the sea bag. All this gear would go everywhere we went. Throughout the next couple days, we would constantly have to unpack and repack our gear so we could get used to everything we had and learn how to pack it efficiently for time and space. Once I got all my gear I was introduced to the worst pain/ feeling you can experience in Boot Camp. I had to go to the bathroom. Since I had my stuff and everyone else was still getting theirs, I figured it was a good time. I had been holding it since 2AM. At that time, I got screamed at for not knowing it's a "head call", not "needing to use the bathroom." So this time I felt better when it was time to ask. At first I was told NO but when I asked again, he let me go. He was just messing with me. I truly wish I would have known the rules of making a head call going in, so I'll tell you.

Here's the deal. They have to give you a head call if you ask for it. If they don't, they get in huge trouble. The Mothers of America have them by the balls these days when it comes to head calls. Back in the day, they would tell you to go ahead and take a dump in your shorts. Not now. The only problem is that I did not know this at this time. Oh well. So I asked, I got yelled at for having to make a head call, and then I could go. You just have to know you're going to get yelled at for everything. Who cares what they say. You get to go. Since they know they have to let you go, they're going to yell at you. Just keep asking and they'll let you go. IF for some reason they don't after the 3rd time you ask, simply sprint to a nearby head. YES, they'll chase after you, (make sure you lock the door if it's a port-a-jon otherwise you'll get ripped out.) They'll pound and beat on the walls, they'll yell at you to hurry up, take care of business, and then sprint back to the Platoon. I've done this myself. You'll be fine.) Just don't move slow because if the Drill Instructors believe you are taking your time, they'll make the rest of the Platoon pay for it and then you're life will suck.

Once we got all of our main equipment, it was time to say goodbye to the receiving Sergeants. It was now time to get introduced to our "Drop Hats."

Drop Hats are the Drill Instructors that get you prepared to meet your official Drill Instructors. Drop Hats teach you the basics such as how to get into Platoon formation, how to start marching together, what all your gear in your sea bag is and what it's used for, getting all your final paperwork done, and how to talk and what not to say. So by the time you meet your official Drill Instructors, you have a pretty good grasp on how you are supposed to carry yourself. We had two Drop Hats. Sergeant C and Sergeant V. Sergeant C was the one we met first. He was this short little Mexican that fed us a lot of knowledge. He was great. He really made sure we were good to go for Saturday when we would meet our official Drill Instructors. He didn't have to yell at us too much because everyone did what they were told.

Then there was Sergeant V. That Marine was just crazy. He found ways to make you scream without raising his voice. He would just keep saying-

"Oh you'll scream... now scream... I said scream... c'mon girl scream... now scream!

He would just say that over and over and you'd scream just like he told you. And even though he was short, that Marine would climb up into anyone's face and put them in their place. He did his job well. When we first got picked up, Sergeant C fed us our first Parris Island meal... box chow. Every day until Saturday afternoon, we would eat box chow for breakfast, lunch, and dinner. The first day and a half was OK but after that, we were sick of box chow. Literally. We would open it up and just get nauseous.

After we met our Drop Hats, Sergeant C took us to the "Burner". I looked at the clock and it was about 9AM. We got through the night. The burner is your final screening. You sit in a class room and they call you up one by one and make you tell them whatever it is that you lied about coming in or what the Recruiter told you not to tell anyone once you did get in. This includes but is not limited to broken bones, stitches, surgeries, drug use, criminal incidents, etc. Apparently, a lot of recruits had left information off of their paperwork. So it all had to get fixed. There were two recruits in my Platoon that had showed up high and they knew they would pop positive. So, they came clean about it, the Marine Corps generated a waiver, and they could stay in training. The ones that lied about it would receive negative paperwork under article 134 of the UCMJ and be sent home. That's BAD!

It was time to come clean if you weren't. It was time to practice having a little honor and courage and taking it like a man and declare what you did so you could get it behind you. Even if you put everything in there like I did, they would still grill you about the times, dates, and occurrences until they were satisfied that they had exhausted the truth. I could remember when I got that very first phone call and had to make the choice to just come clean from the start. I'm so glad I did because it made this process easy. Everyone else suffered because the Marines had a way of making them crack after they had been trying to hide the truth in lies. Once that was done, we were informed that we would be taking a piss test and if anyone had not been honest in the burner and the results popped positive, you were going home.

After that ordeal, we grabbed all of our gear and headed out. Finally, we got to leave the building. We had been there long enough. We started moving in Platoon formation to who knows where. We started in the front of the receiving building, hit the streets, walked down a dirt path through some trees, came to a street, and right across the street saw a few 3 story buildings. We crossed the street, headed to the 3rd floor of the building and it was there that we were informed that we were "home."

This was to be our home for the next 3 months. Up three flights of stairs and we're home.

Sergeant C welcomed us to 3rd Deck. When we arrived, 3rd Deck was completely empty. We carried in the Rack to sleep on, the Footlockers were issued, and we literally brought in everything we would need to live, clean, and maintain throughout our stay.

It was exciting to set up our racks and square our gear away. For the first time since showing up, we finally belonged some place.

The above picture is the view from inside the Drill Instructors' Office. From there, we spent the rest of the day getting the final inventory on our gear, finishing more paperwork, eating more box chow, and moving as fast as we could so Sergeant C and Sergeant V yelled at anyone but us. For the first time, we were allowed to sleep in a rack. We had been sitting in desks ever since we showed up to the Island. We hit the rack about 10:30 that night. It had been a long couple of days. I didn't know if it would be hard sleeping the first night there but as it turns out, sleeping is never a problem at Parris Island when you pass out.

20071108 Thursday
Goooood morning Parris Island

At 4AM I would be introduced to something that would happen **EVERY** single morning until the day I graduated Boot Camp. I don't know who, but it is someone's job every single morning to stand in between the buildings and scream **LIGHTS** 3 times at the top of his lungs when that clock hits 0400. From there, Sergeant C would echo **LIGHTS, LIGHTS, LIGHTS** at the top of his lungs. Let me tell you right now, that will get you out of the rack in a heartbeat. It rattles you. You'll be sleeping. You'll be totally dead to the world. Then, all of the sudden, the silence is shattered by someone screaming **LIGHTS, LIGHTS, LIGHTS!**. From that point, you have 10 seconds to be out of the rack and on line with your body locked. Then comes the BDR. BDR stands for Basic Daily Routine. There is one in the morning and one at night. BDR in the morning starts by counting off, making the rack (which we don't know how to do yet), getting dressed, shaving, brushing teeth, squaring away gear, and then you finish by standing on line. And don't you know that you are getting counted down for each one of these tasks. 200 seconds to make the rack, 120 seconds to get dressed, 90 seconds to shave, 40 seconds to brush teeth, 30 seconds to clear the head. Every time we were too slow, we simply started over and tried it again all the while being screamed at by the drop hats. Good times. Once that was done, it's time for box chow.

Today was awesome because we went to the armory. That's right ladies and gentleman. Today we got our M-16A2 Service Rifle. We marched into the armory, stepped in front of a barred window, out came our issued rifle, we took it over to the metal cleaning tables, put on the sling, and we were out. The rack number for my rifle was 3377. It was marked on the butt stock with a florescent green marker. That was the number I looked for when the rifles were stacked or I needed to find it quickly. Once we had our rifles, we had to memorize the Serial # on it. I will forever remember 10242754. If you didn't know your number well enough to rattle it off at a moments notice, you got served.

That rifle went with us everywhere. It never touched the ground. It was always leaning on something if it wasn't in your hand. If it did touch the ground, you got served. We spent the afternoon learning how to make our racks. It's not really hard at all. As long as you go step by step, you'll be good to go. It's actually hard to mess up. That whole "bounce the quarter" off the bed stuff, cakewalk. The hardest part was having to do it over and over and over. We would make the rack, strip it clean, make it again, and strip it again. We just did it over and over until everyone could do it RIGHT.

We made a visit to medical in typical hurry up and wait fashion. We flew to medical in a mad rush and then were ordered to sit down in Platoon formation until it was time to go in. That sucked!! We waited for a good 35 minutes and then filed in. We were told we were getting the peanut butter shot. It's actually the GG shot. (gammaglobulin) It feels like you're getting an ounce of straight peanut butter injected into your butt. Right after the shot, you pull your trousers back up and sit down in a single file line and rock back and forth to smooth out the lump. It's absolutely nuts smoothing out a big glob of peanut butter chilling out under your skin but that's what we did. Once we stood up, it felt a million times better. The rest of the day was marching, kicking knowledge, and of course ripping our rifle apart and putting it right back together. I swear we did it well over 50 times before evening chow, went for chow, came back, and then we learned how to clean it.

We cleaned every single piece of the rifle. We learned what to put CLP on, how to apply it, and how to get it right back off. We had a toothbrush that we used to clean parts of the rifle. When a recruit answered a question wrong, we'd hold the barrel over our head and scrubbed it until everyone sounded off with their rifle serial number by memory. Our Sergeant C would walk by and pick up our lower receiver and check the number while we were scrubbing the upper receiver, which was over our head. You'd think that a rifle weighing 7.5 pounds wouldn't be that much to hold over your head and scrub, but after 15 minutes that junk got heavy! He'd say **SCRUB!!!** And we'd sound off **HARDER FASTER SIR!!!**

From that point on, we would tear our rifle apart and clean it every single night. We scrubbed that rifle better than we scrubbed ourselves haha. Showers were 120 seconds depending on the Drill Instructor, but that rifle was pristine.

20071109 Friday
Say hello to my little friend... the "Grinder"

Today, after we went through our morning routine and started the day, we got in Platoon formation and headed out to the "Grinder." The grinder is the parade deck outside our squad bay.

It sits right in the middle of the 3rd Battalion houses. We had never really marched and today was the day. However, before we started, Sergeant C laid out some ground rules for us.
#1- Pay attention at all times so you don't look stupid.
#2- Never ever spit on the deck. This will get you served faster than anything else on the Island while in Phase 1.

You'll see the Drill Instructors do it all the time but they'll tell you it's because they have earned that privilege. Since we haven't, and in their eyes never will, don't even think about it. It was show time. Marching 101. Sergeant C gave us the instructions.

He would shout- "FORWARD!"

We would echo, **"STAND TALL LEAN BACK!"**

He would shout, "MARCH!"

And then we would echo, **"Annnd STEP!"**

It was just a simple diddy that would get us all going together. When it was time to stop marching, he would break out of the left... right... left and shout- "PLA-TOON... HAULT!" And we would echo, **"STEP FREEZE!"** and do our best to slam our heels together on freeze. We stopped and started and stopped and started and stopped and started over and over until everyone had it down without thinking. We didn't do any column rights or lefts with Sergeant C. His job was just to teach us the basics of how to start, stop, body position, arm swing, and just marching straight. We learned all about maintaining 40 inches back to chest and when we got the basics down, Sergeant C decided to go ahead and show us how to change directions and march to the rear. It was cool. All the other Platoons were out on the grinder and we were all garbage. Everyone was out of step, arm swings were all different, and no one could march straight ahead or keep the steps consistent. We were all garbage! Oh well.

One thing I noticed right away was the way the Drop Hats called cadence. In a way, I was expecting some old school Full Metal Jacket cadence, but that wasn't the case. I don't know how to describe it, but the Drop Hats had a way of singing cadence that was just awesome. No one called it the same way. They all had their own groove. It was cool. To this day, I still find myself humming or quietly singing their cadence to myself.

We spent the rest of the afternoon marching and then we got a welcomed surprise. We were introduced to the 3rd Battalion Chow Hall. Finally, no box chow! However, it came with a price. Before we could eat chow hall food, we had to learn how to go into the chow hall. Here's the directions-

FORM FOR CHOW!

FORM FOR CHOW AYE SIR! (*We would sprint to the steps of the chow hall and have 10 seconds to be locked in Platoon formation*)
TWO HATCH RECRUITS FROM THE REAR!
TWO HATCH RECRUITS FROM THE REAR AYE SIR!
(Two recruits from the back of the line would step out and scream-)
AYE SIR, AYE RECRUITS, CARRY ON RECRUITS!
(As soon as they screamed that, we would echo-)
AYE RECRUITS KILL!

All this was learned on the spot. It wasn't thoroughly explained, we were just told what to say and expected to have it down right then and there. That's one of the hardest things about Boot Camp. There is no such thing as "Let me try it a couple times and get it down." Your job is to get it down right away.

If you don't get it right and it's not your assigned job, then the Drop hats blast you for being a complete moron. If you don't get it right and it is your job, then you get fired on the spot and someone else takes your job on the spot.

It's no joke.

20071110 Saturday
(Marine Corps Birthday!)
IST/ MEETING OUR DRILL INSTRUCTORS

Today was a huge day. Not only is it the Marine Corps' Birthday, but it is also the day that we would take our IST (Individual Strength Test), and upon passing, earn the privilege to wear our combat boots, and finally meet our official Drill Instructors.

The IST was a cakewalk. We headed over to "Leatherneck Square." That's where you'll find the MCMAP Pit, the Confidence Course, and the Pugle Stick Pits. We formed up and broke into 3 groups. The order was simple: sit-ups, pull-ups, and then the run. We partnered up for sit-ups. All you had to do was get more than 44 in two minutes. No problem. My partner was Recruit Larson. With my partner came a lesson I will never forget. Always tell the truth... no matter what.

It seems obvious to think to always tell the truth. But I'm not talking about big stuff. I'm talking about being totally honest even when no one cares and you don't have to. It's the little things that make the difference. I came to the Marine Corps to become the best I can be. Here was the dilemma. I went first and Larson started skipping numbers to give me a higher score. To start with, I didn't need any help. Hitting 44 was a cakewalk. Plus, I wanted my score to be my score. I wanted to be able to stand by everything I did whether it be good or bad. The problem came when it was Larson s turn. He did need a little help and so I felt I had to skip numbers for him. If I didn't, I feared he would throw me under the bus for the score I got. It put me in a place I never wanted to be.

From that moment on, I vowed to myself not to get caught in something stupid like that ever again. Then came the pull-ups. All you needed was 2. Unlike the sit-ups, the Drop Hats counted those for you. Believe it or not, some heartless Recruiters sent their recruits up to Boot Camp without the ability of being able to perform 1 pull up. It was awful. The Drop Hats destroyed those recruits. Not only would they fail the IST, they wouldn't pick up with their official Platoon. Instead, they would drop into the PCP (Physical Conditioning Platoon). The almighty "Pork Chop" Platoon. That's where all the recruits go to work on their physical conditioning. Once they are able to do the bare minimums, they can join into the next available platoon. You do NOT want to go to PCP. Recruiters will say it's OK. That's wrong.

Finally came the run. It was a mile and a half. Good to go. Me and my buddy Boggs found each other and we ran it together. We stayed in the front all the way through and finished with a 10:05. Not bad at all. The coolest thing was that the Drop Hats gave us a bit of a nod for hustling. Let me tell you right here and now:

IT PAYS TO BE A WINNER IN BOOT CAMP.

If you perform when you're told, you'll just get hammered by the Drill Instructors when you screw up. If you're lazy and out of shape, the Drill Instructors won't stop until they send you to medical. Once everyone was done, they separated the recruits that failed the IST. They were given 1 more chance if they failed the pull-ups. We could not see it, but you could here the Drop Hats screaming at them to just get 2. 3 came back to our Platoon after passing on the 2nd try and they were welcomed back. They fought for it so no one gave them static. They made it fair and square. As for the others, they were gone. We would never see them in our Platoon again.

After all was said and done, we went back "home." To our surprise, more recruits came into our Platoon. They were consolidating after losing recruits to the IST. It was awesome. Boggs was one of the recruits that got moved over into my Platoon. We all cleaned up in recruit fashion and had our last box chow with the Drop Hats. After that, it was time to meet our official Drill Instructors. Sergeant V and Sergeant C split us up on the quarterdecks, sat us down, and told us not to move during the introductions. The anticipation was riveting. We were just sitting there waiting. Our Drop Hats had changed into their Service Charlies and were completely squared away. You could see on their face that this was a big deal. Both of them walked around with a bit more edge in their step.

Finally, it started. Sergeant V locked himself in front of the hatch leading into our squad bay. I'll never forget how his knuckles were stone white from clenching his fists standing at attention. The Captain came in and briefly introduced himself. He was speaking with a very pleasant tone and put everyone at ease. He welcomed us to Parris Island, congratulated us for completing the IST, and gave us the premise of Recruit Training. He told us that this would be the most challenging experience we have faced, but through teamwork and steadfast diligence toward excellence, we would succeed.

He then introduced our Drill Instructors.

Before I go on, I need to make this clear. Out of shear respect for my Drill Instructors, their full names will not appear in this text. I will refer to them based on the role they served. Some of the lessons they taught us may seem harsh, mean, or cruel. But to me, they were absolutely necessary to our success in becoming Marines. These men have served their country and their call to the absolute best of their ability and I don't want that to be taken away just because someone thinks that anything they may have said or done was wrong.

First, he introduced our Kill Hat. Our Kill Hat was a Sergeant. Even though he wasn't the tallest of the Drill Instructors, what he lacked in height, he made up in shear intensity. Looking back, he is by far the meanest, most intense Marine I have ever met to this very day. He was a machine on the PT field. Passing our Kill Hat on a run was a tremendous accomplishment held by few. In all facets of being a Marine, he was the epitome of "Squared away." That known fact is why all the recruits respected him so much. He was what we wanted to become. However, at this time, all we knew was that he was our Kill Hat. We called him our Kill Hat because as we were told, his only job is to put pain in our bodies. That's it. His job is to Kill us physically. He doesn't have to teach us a thing. He was the King in the Kingdom of Pain and his house was the Quarterdeck. He hated and utterly despised us. His only satisfaction came from making recruits scream for their lives until they passed out and were sent to medical: never to set foot in his Kingdom again. He loved to see recruits quit and go home due to some "medical condition." If he was the King, the Senior Drill Instructor was the Emperor. And our Kill Hat was an extremely loyal Marine. He was bound by a chain of shear discipline and respect held by the Senior. He was a ghost when the Senior Drill Instructor spoke. We felt "safe" when the Senior Drill Instructor was around. If the Senior Drill Instructor turned him loose, STAND BY!

Second, our Knowledge Hat came out. He was a Staff Sergeant. Our Knowledge Hat is tasked with the responsibility of making sure we learn all the knowledge and practical applications required to graduate Boot Camp. He stood a bit taller than our Kill Hat but his demeanor seemed identical. He was completely squared away. By the way, in the Marine Corps, there is no such thing as Black Marines. They are referred to as Dark Green. Both our Kill Hat and Knowledge Hat were Dark Green Marines. Getting back to the roll of our Knowledge Hat, he also taught us all the diddy's. Diddy's, as you may remember, are phrases to help us remember our knowledge. Our Knowledge Hat taught us the coolest diddy's. One of his other rolls was to help our Heavy Hat on the Drill deck. Our Knowledge Hat would march us all over the place when our Heavy hat was gone. Oh yeah, he also shared the roll of support Kill Hat. If you really screwed up and both our Kill Hat and Knowledge had ganged up on you, it's over. They'll just tag team you until you quit. Looking back, that's where our Knowledge Hat got his nickname. We called him Staff Sergeant Assassin. He was notorious for "killing" recruits. We expected it from our Kill Hat so we didn't give him such a nickname. But Staff Sergeant Assassin was smart. That's why he's the Knowledge Hat. And he would know exactly what to do to make you want to quit. However, at this time, all we knew was that he was in charge of filling our heads with what we needed to Graduate.

Third, our Heavy Hat came out. He was also a Staff Sergeant. He was definitely the most serious of the 4. He had a completely different walk than the other two. Our Kill Hat and Knowledge Hat marched out as if it was a performance. As for our Heavy Hat, he marched out a bit slower. He radiated discipline and perfection. You could tell he was seasoned. He was smooth and precise with everything he did. As our Heavy hat, his job is to get us from point A to Point B on time during the day, to make sure we have all the gear necessary for the day, and most importantly, he is tasked with teaching us to March and pop sticks (Rifle Manual). His position sits directly underneath the Senior Drill Instructor. He takes command of the other Drill Instructors when the Senior is gone. He is also responsible for relaying to the Senior our progress as a Platoon. Looking back, our Heavy Hat ran the Platoon. He was there more than the Senior and took care of making sure we had what we needed and got what we needed at all times. That included smoking the piss out of recruits that needed it. Of the 4 Drill Instructors, I hated getting smoked by our Heavy hat. The other Drill Instructors would smoke you physically until you couldn't function. Our Heavy Hat would do the same except he would climb up into your head and mess with you mentally. He knew how to play with your mind. We didn't know that at this point, but we would find out soon enough.

And last but not least, out came the Senior Drill Instructor. He was about the same height as our Kill Hat but a lot stockier. While all the other Drill Instructors wore a Green Drill Belt, the Senior Drill Instructor of a Platoon wears a Black Drill Belt. That way you can always spot who the Senior is. His job is the sole responsibility of the Platoon. If you have personal issues, family issues, or anything that the other Drill Instructors can't deal with, you go straight to the Senior. He makes sure that everything that is supposed to get done, does.

They stepped forward and went through their formalities of saluting. The Captain then went through a charge to the Drill Instructors that they would vow to teach us to the very best of their ability.

These Recruits are entrusted to my care.
I will train them to the best of my ability.
I will develop them into smartly disciplined,
physically fit,
basically trained Marines.
Thoroughly indoctrinated in love of the Corps
and Country.
I will demand of them
and demonstrate by my own personal example
The highest standards
of personal conduct,
morality,
and professional skill.

The four Drill Instructors raised their right hands and vowed compliance to this charge. With that, he said the words that I will never forget-

Drill Instructors, take charge of your recruits and make them into Marines.
AYE SIR!!!

It had become official. This marked the exact moment of our training toward Graduation. We were to be under the charge of our Senior Drill Instructor until he Dismissed the Platoon on Graduation day. Everything was dead quiet as the Captain left the Deck. Nobody moved. The hatch slammed shut and our Senior Drill Instructor yelled- **EYES!!**
We echoed- **OPEN SIR!!**
He then went into his motivated welcome speech-

My name is Staff Sergeant B and I am your Senior Drill Instructor
Along with me are-
Drill Instructor Staff Sergeant N
Drill Instructor Staff Sergeant R
And Drill Instructor Sergeant D

*Our Mission is to train each of you to **become** a United States Marine.*

A Marine is characterized as one who possesses the highest of military virtues.

He obeys orders, respects his Seniors, and strives constantly to be the best at everything he does.

Discipline and Spirit are the hallmark of a Marine.

And these qualities are your goals of your training here.

Every recruit here, whether you are tall or short, fast or slow, fat or skinny, can become a Marine if you can develop Spirit and Self Discipline.

We will give every effort to train you, even after some of you have given up on yourselves.

Starting now, you will treat me and all Marines with the highest respect and obey all orders without question.

We have earned our place as Marines and will accept nothing less than that from you.

I will treat you as I do my fellow Marines with firmness, fairness, dignity, and compassion.

As such, I will not threaten you with physical harm, abuse you, or harass you.

Nor will I tolerate such behavior from anyone else Marine or recruit.

If anyone should abuse you, or harass you, you will report those incidents to me.

Further, if you feel I have mistreated you,

you will report such incidents to the Series Commander.

My Drill Instructors now will be with you every day, everywhere you go.

I've told you what my Drill Instructors and I will do.

For your part, you will give 110% of yourself at all times.

You must do what you are told to do quickly and willingly.

You will treat all Marines and recruits with courtesy and respect.

You must be completely honest in everything you do. A Marine never lies, cheats, or compromises.

You must respect the rights and property of all other recruits. Marines never steal.

You must be proud of yourself and that uniform you are wearing.

You must strive hard to remember everything you are taught. For everything we will teach you is important. And must be remembered.

You must strive hard to strengthen your body.

But above all else, you must never quit or give up.

We offer you the challenge to become a United States Marine and the opportunity to wear the Eagle, Globe, and Anchor.
Do you understand that?

YES SIR!!! *(We BOOMED!)*

A few minutes ago, you witnessed my Drill Instructors and I reaffirm our pledge.
Now you're going to reaffirm your oath to the Marine Corps and to your Country.
When the Senior Drill Instructor gives you the command "READY MOVE" you will stand up in place.
Raise your right arm as such.
And repeat after me.
Do you understand that? **YES SIR!!!**
READY…..MOVE!!!

(At this time, we recited the Oath of Enlistment and then were instructed to sit back down)

From there, our Senior Drill Instructor turned around and called for our Heavy Hat. Our Heavy Hat marched up to him and locked into attention. Then our Senior said-

Drill Instructor Staff Sergeant N, take charge of MY Platoon and carry out the plan of the day!
AYE SENIOR DRILL INSTRUCTOR!!!

They saluted and then our Senior headed straight for the hatch. No one moved a muscle. The hatch slammed shut and that's when the Drill Instructors came UNLEASHED! They screamed at us to stand up, get on line, and lock our bodies out. Even now, I struggle with finding the right words to describe to you how intense our situation became. It was NUTS!

Our Knowledge Hat and Kill Hat were swarming around the recruits and making them scream for their lives. The Drill Instructors would ask them a question and the recruits had to sound off over and over. Our Senior came back out after a while and joined our Heavy Hat. They were starting at the front of the line looking for someone to be able to correctly introduce our Senior Drill Instructor for when he came on deck. They started with Boyd. Our Heavy Hat did all the shouting. He told Boyd what to say and made him repeat it. The problem was, under that level of stress, it was nearly impossible. Boyd would get about halfway through and then have to start over all the while screaming louder and louder. Then it happened. Boyd 's emotions started getting the best of him and the tears started to come. The utter frustration made it impossible to think through. Then, that was it. Our Heavy Hat won. He shouted at him and demanded he repeat it correctly otherwise he would kill him. Boyd tried but he was done. He simply collapsed and was out of the game. He was hyperventilating so much from screaming that he couldn't breath right and he was out. Bring on the medics.

Then, they asked if anyone else could do it. I thought I could so I raised my hand. They bolted over to me and sank their teeth in. The introduction goes like this-

HATCH!!! (Everyone echoes **HATCH**)
OUR SENIOR DRILL INSTRUCTOR, SENIOR DRILL INSTRUCTOR STAFF SERGEANT B ON DECK!!! (Everyone echoes)
GOOD AFTERNOON SIR!!! (Everyone repeats)

It sounds easy doesn't it? But, it's not. I screwed it up just like everyone else. The only difference is that they left me alone because I kept my bearing. You couldn't hear a thing from all the shouting going on. It was madhouse. Then the games came.

The Heavy hat would get us to get all of our gear on line, dump it all out, pack it all back up, and repeat. At the same time, our Kill Hat would be booting a recruits stuff all over the place and our Knowledge Hat would be making recruits scream just to make them scream. For the next 2 hours we were played with. By the end of it, 7 recruits' faces were covered in shaving cream, 2 more were sent to medical for hyperventilation, 5 recruits were completely soaked with canteen water, and the rest of us were just happy to have made it through. It was crazy.

One of the games they liked to play with us was the Indy 500. That's when you crush the house in so you have a track around the squad bay, you dump water all over the floor, then take your scuz towel, jump in a push up position, and use your legs to push yourself around the track while maintaining the push up position. We went around and around and around. Our Kill Hat would give us 20 seconds to make it all the way around. I remember going around and slipped through a corner. As I regained my balance, I looked up and saw my Kill Hat working on 2 recruits. He put them in the electric chair. That's where you stand on your toes and do squats in thirds. You start standing up, go a third of the way down, hold it for what seems like forever, go another third, hold it, go to the bottom, hold it, come back up a third, hold it, and so on. Tears were streaming down their faces as they were constantly screaming **"AYE SIR!"** over and over.

I doubt they even knew what they were saying "Aye Sir" to. They just knew that if they didn't sound off, it would never end. What actually surprised me was that it was my buddy Boggs. He's a beast physically. The Drill Instructors just know how to find your weakness. But Boggs never quit.

We would also dump all of our new gear in the middle of the racks, which is known as the Highway, and the Drill Instructors would go around kicking all of our stuff into a huge mess. Then we had to find all our stuff and get it back into our footlocker in the time given or we would start over. We did that for... awhile.

After we were done playing games, Our Senior cleaned us up, got us hydrated, and then sat us down on the quarterdecks. He then had a 1 on 1 chat with us. The other 3 went into the Drill Instructors room, which we called the "House." He looked at us and said-

Look at it this way gentlemen, it's you and me against those 3. If you stick with me and do exactly what you're told, you'll make it through Recruit Training. If you want to do things your way, I'll leave you alone to play with my Drill Instructors. You will not make it. I'll make sure of it. If you have a problem, a legitimate problem, let me know and I'll solve it. Don't be a little bitch. Be honest with me at all times. If you go above my head without giving me a chance to help, I promise you that I'll fuck you up. I'm the only one that will help you on this Island. Welcome to

Recruit Training.

That day we actually got to eat again in the chow hall. Awesome. No box chow tonight! However, when we got back, the Drill Instructors played with us again. We must have taken our cammies off and put them back on at least 40 times. On and off, on and off, over and over. Then it was the "on your face/ on your feet" game over and over. They would count us down time and time again. Finally that stopped and it was hygiene time. Our Heavy Hat led the rotations. One group was in the head "shaving" with our Knowledge Hat. One group was in the showers with our Kill Hat. The last group was making racks. EVERYTHING was by the numbers. If you were in the showers, our Kill Hat would stand in the middle so he didn't get soaked and say RIGHT ARMPIT, then LEFT ARMPIT, and so on until you got all the major spots. Then he would kick you out and bring in the next group whether you had all the soap off or not. It didn't matter. You had to learn. We were always counted down. Finally, the day was over. We were all exhausted. We were glad to hit the rack.

All I could think of that night was 1 day down... 12 weeks to go.

What have I gotten myself into?
Who cares.
I'm here.
I'll make it.
Oh yeah, today is the Marine Corps' Birthday.
Happy friggin birthday.

20071111 Sunday
SALVATION (On Parris Island)

Today is the first Sunday on the Island. We woke up to the lights, lights, lights deal, took care of the BDR, ate chow, and then formed up on the quarterdeck. Our Heavy Hat came out and passed the word-

Now pay attention. Today is fuckin Sunday. There are about 13 different kinds of church services that you fuckers can go to. We're only doin' 3. If you have a problem with that, fuck you! There is Protestant, Catholic, and Jewish service. Raise your hand for Protestant. Raise your hand for Catholic. Raise your hand for Jewish.

(After he saw that some hands didn't go up, he said this.)

I'm not sayin' you have to go to fuckin church. But if you stay here, you WILL play with the Kill Hat for 4 hours. If you bitches make him stay here, you're gonna play some fuckin games.

(All the other hands went up.)

That's what I fuckin thought.

My advice. Go to church. Whether you think you need it or not, go to church. After we got the church count, we were given the time to leave and instructed to clean the house until then. When it was time, we headed out and waited in our church formations. A Sergeant got the count, and marched us to church. I was in the Protestant group. We got to the RTF (Recruit Training Facility) and went inside. To my surprise, the Drill Instructors were not allowed inside. Hallelujah. When we got inside, we were separated into first timers and everyone else. Then we were taken into another auditorium for an intro service. In short, it was a motivated Gospel presentation. It was great. There was music playing when we came in, a Bible study leader that was NOT a Drill Instructor, jokes, football scores *BONUS*, and no stress. The only bummer was when the service time was over and the Drill Instructors kept popping their heads in to see if we were done. Finally, we had to meet them outside. When we were grouped back up in formation, we were marched over to the actual recruit Chapel.

On the way over, I noticed some recruits dressed like me but they were walking all by themselves. We had a Drill instructor marching us. These recruits were in their own formation and they were able to go where they needed to go all by themselves. I had no idea what their deal was but hopefully that would be us one day. Maybe when you get farther into training you're able to go to church without being marched by a Drill Instructor. Who knows?

When we got to the actual Chapel, a Drill Instructor started yelling at us just before we went in. He was saying that if we so much as said a word to any other recruits in church, he was going to bite our finger off at the first knuckle. His was blown off in Iraq and so he had an ET pointer finger. The reason he said he would be able to get away with biting our finger off is because Parris Island has great medical on base. Awesome.

When we walked into the chapel, it was like walking into another world. There was more music playing and all these civilian "moms" were walking around giving us hugs and telling us that everything was going to be OK. There were also a few biker veterans walking around thanking us individually for our service. The church auditorium seating was divided into 3 sections. In the very back looking at the stage it was all Phase 1 recruits on the right, all Phase 2 recruits on the far left, and all Phase 3 Graduating recruits and Marines were in the center. I say Marines because they were the recruits that had just finished the Crucible, received their EGA's, and were considered forever more United States Marines. All they had to do now was get to Friday and Graduate.

You could tell the 3 groups apart without a doubt. All of us Phase 1 recruits had this horrified look on our face. We were skittish and paranoid. We were still in culture shock. All the Phase 2 recruits looked relaxed, quiet, and calm. All the Phase 3 recruits and Graduating Marines were ALL smiles, laughs, and jokes. They were having a great time.

We opened with some familiar songs like "Lord I lift your name on high", "He's got the whole world in his hands" with all Marine Corps lyrics, and "I can only imagine". None of us Phase 1 recruits could sing. Our emotions prohibited it. We would try and just be overrun by tears and cracking voices. It was useless to try. When the minister came out, he plopped his Bible on the pulpit, walked over to us, and said something I will never forget. He said-

Gentlemen, your country needs you. Every one of you. You have answered the call to the United---States---Of---America. What makes you all special is the circumstances of your presence. You didn't come in

159

a time of peace. You didn't come because you were forced to. You chose to come here by your own desire to serve no matter what the circumstances. I applaud you. I thank you. I know a million things are going through your heads. I would guess the main thought being: what have I done? You're wondering why you are here. When you could be home relaxed with your family and friends. So why are you here? You came to be Marines. You came to be the best of the best. You wanted more and you got it. You wanted a new start... and you got it. This is your chance to take hold of your dream. Most importantly, and gentlemen listen to me, most importantly, it's because God has a plan for you and whether you know it or not, you're here to see that plan out. Yes, this will be the hardest challenge you have ever come up against. You will want to quit. But that's simply what makes Marines. Your presence here is not, I repeat, it is not a mistake. You are supposed to be here. 12 weeks from now, you'll see exactly what I mean. God bless you boys.

After that, he went on with his sermon, and we sighed in relief. It all makes sense. At the end of the service, there was an alter call. I'll have you know that 28 recruits accepted Jesus Christ into their hearts. Not a dry eye in the house. It was surely a moment of incredible change. As long as there is a Parris Island, there will be prayer and lives changed every single Sunday morning. On the lighter side, this was the first service I have ever been to in my entire life that did not have a time for offering. It was strictly the word of God and songs of worship. The BEST part of all was the end. At the end, we sang "I'll fly away" with a little Marine Corps flair. The center section was a riot. They were having so much fun. How could that be? I guess we'll see. At the end of the song, our peace was shattered by Sergeant ET finger. He stormed in with all the other Drill Instructors and started moving us out. He looked at all of us newbie recruits and with a sneer said-

Pray all you want you little bitches. God don't exist on this fuckin Island!

At this point, we could have cared less what he said, we were flying. And someday, we would fly away from this place. Someday. When we got back to the house, we found that it was time for day chow. Nice. Not only is church a breath of fresh air, but it also kills the entire morning. However, after we got back from chow, there is nothing else on the training schedule as far as events so it's off to the grinder. Our Heavy Hat would rally us up, get us out, and get us marching. Depending on how we did would ultimately determine how much our Kill Hat messed with us. That night, our Senior gave us "Stand by your devotions" time. That's when we get into our church groups and say 1 last prayer to end the day. We would have that every night till we Graduated. Sometimes it would last 3 minutes. Sometimes it was only a minute and a half. No matter what, we prayed every night for our loved ones back home, gave thanks for making it safely through another day, and prayed for continued safety through the next day until we came together again.

PHASE I

*If you **CAN'T** do it, you're either not **STRONG** enough or not **TOUGH** enough. Which is it?*
                                        -Dan Gable

20071112 Monday
TRAINING DAY 1

Today is the first day of no joke Marine Corps Boot Camp. As of now, everything counts. Brand new Drill Instructors, brand new day. We woke up early to the whole Lights lights lights deal. It's the world's craziest alarm clock. All you can do is wake up in a state of shock. The lights come on all at once, the Drill Instructors storm the deck, and yelling and swearing at slow recruits ensues. You're only job is to jump out of the rack, hit the deck without landing on the recruit below you if you're on the top rack, and get on line and lock your body in the position of attention as fast as possible.

The Drill Instructor gives the command **COUNT!**

We SCREAM **SNAP** and whip our heads to the Left and extend our left arm out toward the middle of the highway.

The Drill Instructor gives the command **OFF!**

Starting with the Guide, he whips his left arm down, whips his head to the front, and screams **"1"**.

Immediately, the count continues down the STARBOARD side of the highway, gets to the end, and comes back up the PORT side and ends with the 1st Squad Leader who screams his number as well as **LAST RECRUIT!**

If someone jacks up the count along the way, it start all over with the Guide. It's done over and over until we make it all the way around. The count usually gave us a good indicator of the mood the Drill Instructors. The more you jacked up, the more it irritated the Drill Instructors. We quickly learned to get the count done in one shot.

After the count, we learned about the BDR (Basic Daily Routine). Cleaning assignments are given. Starboard side would go hygiene which included shaving, brushing teeth, and filling up your canteens for the day. Then it would change over. Starboard would continue the cleaning while Port side would turn to Hygiene. Racks were made perfect, the highway was scrubbed, the ladder wells were swept with out boot brushes, everything was organized, and then it would be off to chow. There is no such thing as mops in Boot Camp so we filled up a bucket, poured in some Pine Green, a little bit of Aqua Velva, soaked up a couple towels, and then by making a push up position with the towel, we used our legs to go all the way up and down the highway until it was shining.

As soon as we got back from chow, our Heavy Hat started with getting us used to every single piece of gear that we were issued. He'd tell us to get a piece of gear out and then start counting us down. While he was counting, our Kill Hat and Knowledge Hat were swarming looking for anyone moving too slow. If they did, the Drill Instructors would start screaming at them until they did get it out.

Then our Heavy Hat would say what it was used for, when we would be using it, and then we would move on to the next piece of gear. It took forever. We have a lot of stuff! Not to mention the fact that our footlockers and sea bags must remained locked up, so every time we needed a piece of gear, that scramble always included unlocking your combination lock first, getting the piece of gear, and then locking everything back up.

After the gear orientation was done, we all went to the quarterdeck and had a period of instruction on the major do's and don'ts. For example-

1- Never ever scratch your face or wipe your nose with your hands. The only reason your hand should touch your head is when you salute. If you have to wipe your nose, pretend to sneeze into the pit of your forearm like Dracula.

2- Always repeat commands from the Drill Instructors. So when it's time to make a head call, your Drill Instructor will say-

Piss, fill, wash!

And you'll scream- **Piss, fill, wash AYE SIR!**

3- Never ever nod your head as you're being told something from a Drill Instructor. I got blasted for nodding while my Heavy Hat was talking. In civilian life, it shows understanding and that you're following along. In Boot Camp, it's a no go. He stopped in his tracks, looked me dead in the eye, and said-

Don't you nod your head at me you stupid fuck. At all times, you'll be hands on the knees, legs crossed, back straight, eyes forward say Aye Sir! **AYE SIR!!!!**

Do that shit again and see what happens say Aye Sir! **AYE SIR!!!!**

As soon as that class was done, we all went out to the Grinder

and our Heavy Hat marched us to see what he was dealing with. Wow do we suck. Oh my gosh. We were the furthest exact opposite of everything we would eventually need to be. Our Drop hats just showed us the basics of marching and they didn't teach us as if they were our Heavy Hat. It was way more relaxed with the drop hats. With our Heavy Hat, he was a precision monster! You could tell by the tone of his voice and the directions he gave that he was the end all be all of marching. It was incredible. It felt like we had gone from t-Ball to the Major Leagues. Because of his expectations and clear instructions, we got on his page fast! The harder he drove us, the more we wanted to show him that we got it.

Chow is crazy. It's the farthest thing from what I'm used to but it's been consistent so we should adjust soon enough.

Morning chow is around 0530.
Lunch chow is around 1130.
Evening chow is around 1830.

We hit the rack at 2100 sharp. Once the lights are off, it's game over. Most of us passed out from the day, and the restless tried to get to sleep as quickly as possible.

After marching, we rolled over to the PT fields and we were taught all the basic exercises we would be doing. It included push-ups, squats, burpees, side straddle hops, steam engines, and a lot more. It wasn't designed to be a work out for us today: it was just a simple here's how to do this so remember it.

We were also introduced to the "Silver Bullet." If you are working out in a PT session and you fall down from over exhaustion, pass out, or simply die, the Safety Officer will run over to wear you are, roll you on your stomach, whip down your pants and shove a silver thermometer up your tailpipe in order to see if you are truly dead or just mostly dead. It's jacked up. And don't think it'll come with lube. Luckily, I never had an encounter with the silver bullet. I can't say the same for some other recruits. Knowing the silver bullet was awaiting a fallout recruit was awesome motivation to stay hydrated, focused, and to keep moving.

When we got back from chow that night, the house was turned upside down and shaken. Everything was everywhere. Then we had a given amount of time to find all our stuff, get it back in our footlocker and back into our bags, and locked back up otherwise we would do it all again.

After that, our Heavy Hat came out and sat us down on the quarterdeck. He explained how the firewatch system works. As it turns out, we would have firewatch every other night from now until we Graduate. There are 4 positions. The scribe would be responsible for generating the list each night so you knew exactly when it was your shift. Each shift was an hour long. You were required to be up and ready to go 10 minutes before your shift started. That was not a problem because the firewatch would simply wake you up and tell you it was time to get ready.

20071113 Tuesday
TRAINING DAY 2

The day started off with the Captain giving a speech on Honor, Courage, and Commitment. These are the Marine Corps Values. He told us this before morning chow so that we would make every decision from that moment on based on those 3 values. Speaking of morning chow, it's getting a lot better. I'm getting better at shoveling more in at each meal. Chewing takes too long. It's easier to pick foods that you can simply swallow. Chow is not about eating food. It is your opportunity to see how much you can shovel before time is up. I remember when I was told that you have 3 meals a day and you get 20 minutes to eat. This is somewhat true. However, you are not told that the 20 minutes you get INCLUDES the time it takes to get your food, sit down and eat it, and evacuate the chow hall. When it all comes down to it, you have 6-8 minutes to inhale as much as you can before you are ran out of the chow hall. It's getting better. Our marching is getting a lot better as well. We march everywhere we go. We're starting to pick up on the details. To help, our Drill Instructor would say the key word and we would echo the rest-

COVER **DOWN!**- means you're standing directly behind the recruit in front of you.

ALIGN **RIGHT!**- means just that. You align to the right all the way to 4th squad.
TIGHTEN **UP!**- Pay attention. Look sharp. Move like you know what you're doing.

This would be the beginning of what's known as "Kicking knowledge" as well as working on volume. We had to scream everything at the top of our lungs. Anything less and we would play "games". Anytime we needed something pounded into our memory, we would kick knowledge over and over until everyone got it perfect. Our Drill Instructor would kick the key words and we would blast the definition. Here are some examples-

Step it out!
STEP IT OUT AYE SIR!

5 Navy Crosses!
SIR, 5 NAVY CROSSES IS, COLONEL CHESTY PULLER SIR!

Honor!
SIR, HONOR IS, THE QUALITY THAT DRIVES A MARINE, TO EXIMPLIFY THE ULTIMATE IN MORAL AND ETHICAL BEHAVIOR. TO NEVER LIE CHEAT OR STEAL SIR!

Sergeant!
SIR, SERGEANT IS, 3 STRIPES UP, CROSSED RIFLES IN THE CENTER, HE IS THE BACK BONE OF THE MARINE CORPS SIR!

There is A TON of knowledge to kick in Boot Camp! There is never a time when you are not learning knowledge. Even when you are going through the practice steps at Graduation, you are blasting out little diddy's to make sure you don't jack it up. I wrote down all the diddy's I learned from beginning to end and it's a staggering amount of knowledge. To be honest, I have no idea how we were all able to get it down so well. Unbelievable.

We started putting together a lot of pieces to identify who we are. Our Platoon is 3014. The 3 that starts that number indicates the Battalion you are in. So we are 3rd Battalion. The saying is-
1st Battalion makes men.
2nd Battalion makes Marines.
3rd Battalion makes machines.
4th Battalion makes babies. (This is said to help you remember that it's the only female Battalion in the entire Marine Corps.)

Today was the first day of MCMAP training. We did the shear basics like making the "Warrior Stance" and compass movement. Nothing really big just yet. After that, we marched back to the grinder and met with the Battalion Commander. He said-

In every war, there have been drafts. Not this war. We volunteered. We are to be commended. Thank you for your service.

And that was it. He must have been having a bad day and needed to get us out of the way. Oh well. Then, we marched all the way back to the RTF (A.K.A the House of Knowledge), we got a class on what it takes to be a Marine. We learned about some of the heroes that have given their lives up for the brothers to their right and left. It made everything a bit more serious. This certainly isn't a game. This is life and death. It made us think. When we got back to the house after dinner chow, we got smoke checked by our Kill Hat. But this time I noticed something. Last week, I wanted everyone to make it in Platoon 3014. I felt sorry for the weak ones. In my business at home, it's our responsibility to invite any willing beating heart to enter the world of martial arts training. We have nothing but time so we are able to turn the weaker ones into stronger ones over that time. We identify the weaker ones, give them a battle plan, and encourage them even if it means holding their hand a bit until they can walk on their own. It usually takes 3.5 to 4 years to go from White Belt to Black Belt and it takes a bit longer for some. But our goal is to guide them ALL to the same ultimate goal of becoming a Black Belt. And we accomplish that goal. We have rigid standards that must be met in order to wear an ECMA Black Belt. Even if it takes 5-6 years to meet those standards.

Well we don't have that luxury here. There is no room for terminal weakness. If you can't stand up to the challenge, the Marine Corps will break you in half and spit you back out into civilian life. The Corps only wants the hungry. The ones that are willing to do whatever it takes right now. Not next week or a year down the road. But right now. A Karate school has 3.5 years, the Marine Corps has 13 weeks. Now I understand.
I clearly remember thinking to myself-

Man I can't wait till all the pansies are out! If you can't take it, that's totally cool. But know where you belong. If you don't want to go through this to the best of your ability, then get OUT!

I don't know if that's right, but I do know that I don't want to die because of some accident. Because some idiot just didn't have it in them to give it all they've got. The Marine Corps finds a way to weed out the weak. I now see that the Marines can only be made of the strong.

20071114 Wednesday
LIGHTS, PT, SUICIDE!

Wake up as usual. **LIGHTS, LIGHTS, LIGHTS!** Grr. However, tonight I finally got my first full night's sleep. For the last week and a half I had been tossing and turning and waking up 3 or 4 times to use the head. It was just garbage sleep. Last night, it was phenomenal. I closed my eyes and I woke up to the LIGHTS deal. After morning chow, we headed to the PT field. PT officially begins. The series Gunnery Sergeant came out and lead us in the warm up we had learned on Monday. The Drill Instructors were swarming looking for some recruit to show the littlest sign of weakness. There was always someone getting grilled by 3 or 4 Drill Instructors.

For this morning's PT, we did a max set of pull-ups, 20 push-ups, and repeated that 3 times. After that, we did a max set of sit-ups in 2 minutes. Then another max set in 1:30. Then a final set in 1 minute. We finished with a 1.5-mile run. It was some good training. The entire PT session was based on your own output. I can dig it. However, our Heavy Hat kicked some cadence for us while we ran the 1.5-mile run. But it wasn't the cool cadence I had heard in the movies. And we had to sing whatever he said. By the way, the "Guide" is the recruit that is the leader of the Platoon. Oh well. It went like this-

Wake up in the morning to the Parris Island sun...
Our Guide looks strong but he's really fuckin dumb...
3014 ain't never comin back...
We're all gonna die when we go to Iraq...
Cause we are nasty...
We are stupid...
We're fat an ugly...
And we know how to prove it...

Oh well. It was messed up but who cares. It was funny and pretty clever since it came off the top of his head. After that motivating run, we kicked some MCMAP. Good times. After that, the strangest thing happened. The reveille kicked on the Island speakers and everybody froze, faced toward the sound, and stood at attention. Even the cars stopped in the middle of the road. It was no joke. Reveille and the National Anthem brought the entire Island to a complete halt. If you had never been there and you drove by the field, you would see nothing but Drill Instructors and recruits frozen solid staring off at the same thing. And then all of the sudden, everything instantly just carried on like nothing ever happened. It was like hitting PAUSE while you're watching an action movie, waiting about 60 seconds, and then hitting PLAY again.

When we got done with PT, we headed to the house and took a PT shower. That's when you strip down, walk single file into the head, circle through the showers, walk right back out, and get dressed. After that, we stepped to the RTF and learned the customs and courtesies of the Marine Corps. We learned when to salute, the different types of flags, and went over the rank structure for Officers. It just turned out to be more knowledge to kick. Yeehaw.

The last 3 days had been jam packed, and finally, we were rewarded in a way for our hard work. In Boot Camp, one of the most enjoyable events is to "Battle" another Platoon. You can do that in 3 ways-

1- **A Knowledge battle**- that's when you see which Platoon has memorized the most.
2- **A volume battle**- that's when you kick knowledge but the goal is to blast the other Platoon.
3- **A rifle battle**- this is the most important. You ain't jack if you can't pop sticks.

Well tonight, we battled our first platoon in poppin sticks and we destroyed them. They stepped on our deck and took the walk of shame back home. Even though it wasn't said, our Heavy Hat was happy with us. We made him proud. That night we had to learn the fire watch script on the spot. It goes like this-

Good evening sir.
Recruit Killian reports for Platoon 3014 all secure sir.
There are X# recruits,
X# rifles,
X# footlockers,
and X# sea bags all secure sir.
Nothing unusual has occurred during this recruits tour of duty.
The Platoon is currently engaged in Taps sir.
Good evening sir!

Sounds easy right? The recruit on duty was getting blasted for not memorizing it fast enough so after lights out, I stayed up to memorize the script by heart. I knew I had duty the following night so I made sure that wouldn't happen to me. By the way, firewatch can suck if you don't take advantage of it. There are 4 positions. Head, front hatch, rover, and back hatch. Each position has to be able to report the same exact thing. Fire watch is by the hour so every hour the 4 recruits on fire watch switch out with the next 4 recruits on the list. This means that you have fire watch every other night all the way through Boot Camp. Get used to it. How do you take advantage of it? Easy-

1 Become good friends with the scribe so that he puts you in 1 of the first 3 hours. You sleep better that way. If you have to wake up at 3 to hit the rack at 4 to wake up at lights at 5, well, that just sucks.

2 Try to be the rover. All you do is march up and down the highway. And believe it or not, I actually practiced marching. I would work on little details to sharpen up my steps. I would also use the entire hour to memorize knowledge. I memorized everything during firewatch. I would keep my knowledge in my blouse pocket, sneak a peak at a line and just remember it till I had it. And then I would move on to the next.

That night, Bartone tried to kill himself. He took a fork to his wrists. He almost got away with it but he made too much of a mess. Stupid kid. Not only because he tried to kill himself, but also because he had no idea where it would get him. We were told that if you try to kill yourself, you don't just get deemed crazy and go home. Nope. You get sent to the psycho platoon, sit around for an eternity, and then get evaluated. If you're crazy, you go to a loony bin for 6 months. If you are still crazy, then you stay longer. If you're not, you go right back into training, pick up a page 11 for being stupid, and continue on in training exactly where you left off. The bottom line is this; you won't get out for trying to kill yourself. Welcome to Hotel Parris Island.

20071115 Thursday
Movin on Up!

After chow, we headed out to Leatherneck Square. Turns out we're going to do some bayonet training. Our Heavy Hat had us. Great. Recruits wanted to move slow. Even more great! What does that mean? We get to learn a new game. Our Heavy Hat made us line up heal to toe. He would then give us 10 seconds to all get to 30 inches from heal to toe. Then back to heal to toe. Then back to 30 inches. We went back and fourth over and over and over and over. The longer we went, the more everyone got pissed off because our Heavy Hat would keep saying someone was moving too slow. We were turning into a frenzy. Finally, it was time to start our training so that game stopped. Good thing because it was about to come to swings between a couple recruits. This morning's event was all about the bayonet skills. We learned all the different strikes and that was actually cool. The only down side was having to wear this stupid mouthpiece. I don't know why, but for all MCMAP training as well as this event, we had to wear a mouthpiece. We didn't get to mold it to our teeth so it turned out to be this oversized rubber spit collector that you screamed diddy's through. Garbage. Oh well. Beyond that challenge, we got a surprise. Today was the first day we saw rain. The diddy for that-

RAIN!
SIR, IF IT AIN'T RAININ, WE AIN'T TRAININ SIR!!!

It was actually fun training in the rain. It gave us something we recognized from every day life. Training doesn't stop just because it rains. We were ordered to get on our gear and get out our issued ponchos. The ponchos weren't designed to wear; they were designed to keep your gear dry. If it rained really hard, we just put on our Gortex top and bottom. If it was just sprinkling, we didn't bother with anything. Our Heavy Hat always knew what the day was going to be like so, in the morning, he told us what to put in our daypack so we were never surprised by weather.

Next, we formed back up and stepped for haircuts. Yeehaw! We formed a barbershop line outside the barbershop and came face to face with another Platoon. What does that mean? It simply means it's time to turn up the volume. It's a battle baby. We kicked knowledge back and forth and it was a smoke session. We became known pretty quickly that we were the Platoon to try to beat. As I made the turn into the building, I'm not sure what happened but the 4th squad leader did something stupid and was fired on the spot. Next thing I know is that our Heavy Hat was looking for someone that could maintain order and keep the line moving. He started looking down the line and when we made eye contact, I didn't look away. I stared at him. I wanted it. And just like that, Bam! Recruit Killian is 4th squad leader. Good to go. I learned the flow and it was on. Squad leaders have a lot of responsibilities in the Platoon. For example, my position in formation is right behind the Guide. It's my job to keep him marching straight since he can't look back. I can do that. Bell was the Guide and he was a guy I got along well with so it was cool.

Just before we hit the rack, I learned a valuable lesson. The words you choose to use are far more important in Boot Camp than anywhere else I know of. Sometimes when a recruit gets lippy, the best thing, besides yelling at him, is to quietly walk up, get right in his face, and simply say, "Just let it go." You say it really quiet but with a bit of ferocity in your voice. It works really well. For some reason, THE most common phrase you will hear ALL throughout Boot Camp is **"Shut the fuck up!"** You hear it ALL the time. But I promise you; it's the worst thing to say. Not because it's got a bad word in it, but because telling someone to shut up is just weak. Like I said, it is said so often that it just becomes common. Getting in someone's face and just telling them direct and dead serious seems to do the trick. A couple other things I learned to keep in my back pocket were the following 2 principles-

1- Every Marine has the moral obligation to do what is ethically and morally right at all times. It's the law. As a Recruit, the faster you adopt this and just do what's right no matter what, the happier you will be. If that means throwing someone under the bus because they broke a rule, then so be it. You'll find out really fast that a Platoon will play games when no one tells the truth. You'll start to get a reputation for being hardline on always being honest and the result will be recruits not jacking up because they know for a fact you're not going to lie or hide anything.

2- Doing the right thing all the time gives you a clean conscience and you will always feel better because of it. Especially when you see recruits getting smoked for doing something stupid and trying to lie.

That night, me and Bell had fire watch. I was going down and he was coming up and since our racks were close, we would usually chit chat about whatever. He's big, fearless, and appears invincible. So it surprised me when he sat down next to me not saying a word. His head in his hands. Then he looked over at me, took a deep breath, and said-

Yo Killian, do you think we'll make it through this thing man?

174

I said-
Absolutely bro. It'll be rough but we just gotta stick together man. We'll make it.

I don't know if I was speaking the truth and it didn't matter. We both wanted to believe it. Sometimes it just helps to hear someone say it.

20071116 FRIDAY
Come and Get It!

We started out with some good ol' Friday morning PT. Today's PT was a circuit. The menu-

Sprint 800 meters. (1/2 mile)
20 Push Ups
20 Burpees
20 Lunges
20 Air Squats
Sprint 800 meters back.

Just so you know, the track that we ran on was not your typical high school track. The track we ran on was a 1-mile loop and it was sand and dirt.

There was no such thing as a rubber or concrete surface. It was just dirt. It made it much more difficult to run on especially when it rained. But I believe it helped get our legs stronger and it definitely made it more interesting.

For the 800-meter sprint, we started off in sticks of 10 recruits wide. When the Drill Instructor said go, we would fly down the track. The sticks took off every 10 seconds. I was the 4th stick to go. Every once in a while, the sun just seems to shine on you. Today was my day. As soon as we got the go, I took off. By the time I got to the 800-meter mark, I had caught the 2nd stick. The calisthenics were a cakewalk and I finished my lunges before the recruits that were in first place. That motivated me even more so I spread the lead during the squats. By the time I took off for the 800 meter run back, it was over. All I had to do was maintain my lead and I would come in first for the event.

As soon as I got to the line, the Drill Instructors were screaming at me to keep going so I turned and took off for a second time through. By the time I got to the Push Ups, I was about 30 seconds behind the last guy in the formation. I finished the Push Ups and was stopped by a Drill Instructor-

Hey recruit! Who are you?
(At this moment I noticed my Heavy Hat was standing right behind him. I didn't want to let him down.)

Recruit Killian, Platoon 3014 Sir!
Platoon what?
Platoon 3014 Sir! (This is when I should have just shut up!) **The WINNING Platoon Sir!** (Me and my big mouth.)
Oh, so you're saying my Platoon fucking sucks huh? Then why the fuck are you dead last?
Sir, this recruit is on his second time through!
Bitch! You're only supposed to go 1 time! Looks like you got too much energy left. Get on your face!

Even though he made me do some Push Ups, I heard him talking to my Heavy Hat and he said that they probably didn't stop me at the finish to play with me. Oh well. Drill Instructors do that all the time. They make you do push-ups or sit-ups so they can talk something out really quick. You're screaming numbers so loud that you never hear what they say so it's all good. He then told me to get up and I could see my Heavy Hat smiling a little bit. Good to go. Even though I was chased by the Drill Instructor all the way back, it was totally worth it. Mid day, we headed out to the grinder for some motivated marching. Our Senior had us.

We did pretty good. We're really starting to come together and get things tight. However, the Guide was having some trouble with the column rights and lefts. When we broke to go to the chow hall, we could all tell that our Senior was pissed off. He stopped us in front of the chow hall and said the Guide was now fired. He asked who among us could lead Platoon 3014 and be the Guide. My hand shot up like a rocket. He took a look at me and studied me just for a second. Then he said- *"Very well. Killian, you are now the guide."*
As I stepped up, he tied the 3014 brassard on my arm and gave me the Guidon (Pronounced guide-on)
(I don't think my computer knows Marine Corps terminology). Then he said-

No one can take this from you except me. If someone tells you that you're fired and it's not me, tell them to fuck off! You are the Guide now and only I can take that from you. You got it?

I sounded off and screamed- "YES SIR!" and then headed back to take my new position. As soon as we got inside and formed for chow, it was show time. I had to blast all the commands without error. One thing I learned in Boot Camp is that everything is easy come easy go. If I make the littlest mistake right now, it would be just as easy to pick some other recruit to be the Guide. There is no such thing as On the Job Training. Either you can do it because you've been paying attention, or you can't.

My Drill Instructors knew this all too well and stood by. My Knowledge Hat and Kill Hat studied me to see if I knew the commands for getting the recruits through the chow line. On one word I ran out of air from screaming and it sounded weak. This was just what they were looking for. They became unleashed. They were blasting me with questions like-

What's a matter Guide? Can't handle the Platoon? I guess we gotta get someone else. Where you at Guide? Why don't you take control guide?

I ignored everything they were saying. I recomposed myself and kept firing the commands as I should.

Who here can do a better job? -Said our Knowledge Hat.

A recruit's hand shot up and so our Knowledge Hat told him to get up to the front and take my place. The recruit scrambled up to the front and when he got to me I grabbed him by his throat and pushed him backwards into the Platoon. Our Knowledge Hat then said-

Good. Piss off the fuckin Guide! Better get your ass back in line.

He went back in line and the Drill Instructors left me alone. It was going to be a constant fight to stay as the Guide. Game on. To be honest, Platoon 3014 helped me more than anything else. They followed the commands perfectly and backed me up by sounding off. If not for them, I might have been screwed.

As soon as I sat down, my Kill Hat told me to hurry up. I had 4 minutes to eat and then we were out. I shoveled chow as fast as I could. True to his word, we were out as soon as the big hand hit 4 minutes. We marched back to the house and got the word to fly up the stairs and get in the house. We had 45 seconds to accomplish that. Sure enough, the last 2 recruits didn't make it. What does that mean? We got on line and our Knowledge Hat said something that I heard many times throughout the rest of training. He said-

Where you at Guide? Get yo' ass on the Quarterdeck!

I ran up to the Quarterdeck and met my Kill Hat. He told me that from now on because I'm the Guide, any time a recruit screws up, I'm gonna pay. Great! From there, it was a kill session. My Kill Hat and Knowledge Hat kept taking turns with me on the Quarterdeck. It went on for what seemed like forever. They kept telling me that I was free to quit any time and that would be OK. They would simply pick a new Guide because I didn't have to do it. But I didn't quit. Then they told me to quit. But I just ignored them and kept doing what they told me to do and sounding off. Finally, it was over. I'm not going to lie. I staggered back to my place. I was dead exhausted.

Since I was the Guide now and there was a position open for a new squad leader, the Drill Instructors appointed Jons to be 4th squad leader. HOLY CRAP! Let me tell you about Jons. That kid has more heart than words I can put into this book.

He does not quit. But as far as common sense is concerned, it's over for him. He is a guy that constantly makes mistakes. No matter what you do or what you say, he will always just be a hair too slow. We were always helping to dress and undress that kid so we wouldn't have to pay. I think Jons was born with an automatic 8-second delay. You would tell him to do something or say something, and it would take about 8 seconds for the information to compute and then he would do it. It was crazy. So as long as he was squad leader, I was going to be paying for everything he did. Whatever. I liked the kid's heart so I helped him as much as I could. Who cares? Someone had to be on his side and it was going to be me. He may have my back one day and I'll need him to keep me alive. That's what makes 3014 strong. It's US against the Drill Instructors. All of US.

20071117 SATURDAY
Take it up a Notch!

Today, we started with the strength circuit course for PT. It's no joke. It consists of stations all around the PT field. You don't go by reps. Instead; you go by time in each area. You have a motivated Drill Instructor in each area pushing you. Some of the exercises included the Military Press with a make shift Boot Camp Barbell. Barbell Squats and lunges. Barbell Curls. Step Ups with ammo cans. And we even hit some body weight work by doing Pull Ups and Dips. Good times. We went through the course twice and it broke us off.

Guide work is getting a bit easier. I'm learning how to get what I need from the Platoon and the Drill Instructors are finally leaving me alone. I'm still paying for recruits on the quarterdeck but that's fine. It's part of learning everything. I'm finding that even though I'm on the quarterdeck, it's based on something specific like recruits not moving fast enough, jobs done poorly, and other things that I can actually help to improve. Sure, sometimes they are just amused playing with me but that's becoming less of the case.

This one recruit named Icabola tried to jump out the 3rd deck window but we stopped him. Stupid kid. And one more recruit left for the hospital from hyperventilating. So the Platoon is thinning a bit. Good to go. If a recruit is having trouble, we will help them out. Once a recruit tries to kill himself, it's over. We can't help that.

The surprises kept coming. At the chow hall, we got pizza. No joke. I thought it might be a trick. Who cares? We tore it up. I'm learning more and more how I can eat more. Never eat with a fork. If you're using a fork, it takes too long. All you need is a spoon and food that is shovel-able. Chewing wastes time. Shovel and swallow. That is the Boot Camp way.

While marching, our Senior showed me Guidon technique. He showed me things like how to keep the pike straight, proper height of carry, grip position, how to punch the ground with some authority, and a few other tricks of the trade. It was cool. Recruit Moss took over as Squad Leader relieving Jons. Good to go!

We finished the day in a Rifle Battle with 3010. We kicked some new moves and it was awesome. When we did "Inspection Arms", we would be given the command to put our M-16's on kill. That means to take it off safe. When we did, we would lean forward, click the switch to fire, and say in a low voice-

"I got something for yo ass bitch."

It freaked out 3010. Nobody said anything during a battle. Now, we were taking it to the next level. It was a lot of fun. Our Heavy Hat was really happy with us even though he would NEVER say so. But when we kicked a move, he would grin at the sound of the cracks and he knew we would smash who ever we faced. The other Drill Instructors would hurry their Platoons off our deck in defeat. As a reward, he would kill us and say we needed to do better next time. We would all take turns on the quarterdeck. That's fine. We won!

We had just hit the rack and I looked over to the rack next to me and saw McKeney with his back to me. He was doing something but I could have cared less. Just then, a recruit walked up and asked what he was doing really quiet like. McKeney said he snagged some Peanut Butter packets from the chow hall and offered him some. The recruit said, "Peanut Butter huh?" McKeney said yeah. Then the recruit turned his moonbeam on to show his face. IT WAS OUR HEAVY HAT DRESSED UP AS A RECRUIT!!! McKeney just asked our Heavy Hat if he wanted Peanut Butter that he had stolen from the chow hall. Awesome! Our Heavy Hat then smiled and simply said- *See you in the morning.*

20071118 SUNDAY
Lessons to Learn.

Our Kill Hat woke us up and got us going. You never really knew who had you the next day. You would hit the rack with 1 Drill Instructor and be woken up by another. Every morning, Firewatch would have instructions to bang on the Drill Instructors hatch and notify them is was 10 minutes before Lights Lights Lights. You'd bang on the hatch 3 times really friggin hard and automatically say-
Good Morning Sir, time on deck is 0430!
GO AWAY!!
Aye Sir Good Morning SIR!
Based on the "Go Away", you knew who you'd have that morning and then let everyone else know during that 10 minutes before calling Lights. Word spread like fire because everyone was starting to learn what the Drill Instructors looked for and expected.
If it was our Heavy Hat, the only thing that matters is getting on line as fast as possible, locking our bodies out, and standing with some sense of good order and discipline. If we did that the way he expected, we were good to go.
-If it was our Knowledge Hat, the only thing that matters is volume. If we screamed our guts out, we were good to go.

-If it was our Kill Hat, we were screwed.

To no ones surprise, especially McKeney, it was our Heavy Hat. Our Kill Hat was also there so we had both of them there. Great. When we were cleaning the house, I noticed that my buddy McKeney was sitting on the quarterdeck with our Kill Hat.

Our Heavy Hat came on deck with a rather large box. He sat it down in front of McKeney and made him open it. It was a huge box of Peanut Butter packets from the chow hall. He made him start chowing down. We cleaned for about 30 minutes. The next time I walked by and snuck a peak, he must have eaten 30-40 packs of Peanut Butter. Man was he sick. I don't think he'll be doing that ever again. Lesson learned. Never, under any circumstances, steal food from the chow hall. Ever.

We got dressed and formed for chow. I think McKeney was good. He would be skipping chow this morning. Like always, another recruit screwed up by not moving fast and so our Kill Hat made us run all over the place. He would holler a location and then we would just run to it as fast as we could. Back and forth, back and forth, here and there then back again, over and over. The other Platoons just watched us. They didn't dare move a muscle otherwise they would be joining us. Oh well. There's nothing like a little PT before chow. To make matters worse, when we did get to the chow hall, we only had 5 minutes to eat. Great!

When we got back to the house, we hit the quarterdeck to pop sticks. We worked Inspection Arms A LOT. That seems to be the most difficult series of moves to execute so we hit it regularly. The timing is what will kill a Platoon. If you're not together even in the slightest, it will be amplified. Here's the diddy we learned to make us tight-

Inspection... Arms!
CRACK, snapshot, **PORT**, snapshot, **DROP**, snapshot, **CLAW**, snapshot, **PULL**, snapshot, **PUSH/ GRAB**, snapshot, **LOOK**, snapshot, **PORT** (freeze)

We would say snapshot between every movement so that the same amount of time was found between each move. We also said it because when you say snapshot you remembered to freeze like someone was taking your picture. Everything had to be sharp and precise.

Port...
DROP to the bolt **BANG, MOVE** to the cover **CLOSE, DROP** to the trigger **FREEZE**

Arms!
CLICK POP!

It was awesome when it was airtight. Our Heavy Hat used this huge stick he called the Drill Stick. He would bang on a footlocker to emphasize the "move" words listed above. The first sequence is the hardest because it requires you to lock the bolt to the rear and some recruit(s) always missed it. He would find out who it was, make a mental note to kill the recruit later, and then say the infamous "Get it back!" As in, send the bolt home and get back to the start position to try it again. Get it back... Get it back... Get it back... we heard it a million times throughout Boot Camp. But we got it... eventually.

One thing I learned very quickly about Boot Camp is that there is no such thing as down time. There is no point where you are not doing something. You are constantly on the move... except church. That is the one time out of the week that you can actually chill out for a short amount of time. No Drill Instructors. You are still doing something but it's a stress free environment.

So, it's back to church for this recruit. This time it was different. We didn't go to the "First timers" class like we did last week. We stayed with everyone else. Before church got started, we would share stories to recruits from other Platoons. It was cool. We found out quickly that even though we did pretty much the same stuff, our Drill Instructors were unique in the way they worked. A few things we talked about were-

1- Being recycled is the number 1 fear among all recruits. The thought of being sent back in training to another set of Drill Instructors and redoing all the tasks and games you've pushed yourself through would just SUCK!

2- Do not swing on a Drill Instructor. Period. They have to play by the rules right up until you cross the line. They have so much hate built up towards recruits that you just won't win. They are a pack of wolves. There is never just 1. Let's say you beat 1. Good on you. Now comes 9 more just from the floor below yours. If that doesn't do the trick, there are 4 more on the bottom floor. It's futile.

3- There are recruits that have been there for more than a year and a half. The easiest way off the island is to Graduate. Mommy and daddy will not come to save you. There is no way off the Island. Even if you ran away, they would find you and bring you right back. You belong to Parris Island now.

I never thought I would be happy to sing "Count your blessings." I have heard it all through the years growing up and was quite sick of it. This time, it was truly music to my ears. We also broke out our moonbeams and sang "This little light of mine."

Verse 2 was- "When I'm in the sand box I'm gonna let it shine."
Verse 3 was- "When I'm in the Crucible I'm gonna let it shine."
Verse 4 was- "On my Graduation Day I'm gonna let it shine."

It was great. Another thing I realized was that you do not pick to become a Marine. You volunteer yourself and the Marine Corps keeps the strongest ones. Recruit Bartone, the one that tried to cut his wrists, was dropped and we were told he will now be serving 4 years in a mental institution and he's not even sick. He just wanted a way out. It's simple. Learn the rules, give 100% effort all the time, sound off, move fast, and go to church. Simple. Who knows if that's the total truth about Bartone but you don't know what to believe in Boot Camp. So it's easy to believe anything.

After church, we tried to march and failed. The result was that we had to roll up the Guidon. That shows everyone else on the Island that you're a garbage Platoon and you pissed off the Senior. We beat 3013 in a Rifle Battle, got a little too cocky, and our Senior made us pay. But instead of physical pain, it was humiliation. We had to talk soft, drag our feet, and wear our covers crooked. That was actually worse than playing in the sand box. I was proud of 3014 and now we were forced to look like garbage. I was SO pissed off! When we were told to form up downstairs for evening chow, I asked if I could address the Platoon. Our Senior said- "Very well" and walked off. I turned around and once he was out of the house, I unloaded on them. I screamed-

YOU GUYS ARE A BUNCH OF PUSSIES! SOME OF YOU DON'T DESERVE TO BE HERE. ARE YOU HAPPY NOW? IF YOU DON'T WANT TO BE A MARINE THAT'S GREAT! GO HOME! DON'T MAKE THE ONES THAT ARE PUTTING OUT HAVE TO PAY FOR YOU BECAUSE YOU ARE A PUSSY! YOU NEED TO STAND UP AND SOUND OFF! I'M SICK OF PAYING FOR GARBAGE RECRUITS! IT STOPS NOW! GO AHEAD AND SCREW UP AND SEE WHAT HAPPENS! NOW GET DOWN THERE AND MAKE IT HAPPEN! MOVE!!!

Everyone knew I was addressing the ones that got us in trouble so it was well received. It was just the right kick in the butt we needed. From that point on, when our Senior told us to look like garbage, even though we said, **"Aye Sir!"** We didn't. We kept looking strong. He saw what I told the Platoon to do and he was cool with it. Lesson learned. Never look bad because you're told to. Even in the face of following orders, do the right thing.
When we got back, I addressed the Platoon again. This time, I wanted to motivate them in a positive fashion. I said-

If you fail to plan, you plan to fail. We all know what our Drill Instructors want from us. Our Kill Hat wants us to put out and move fast on the quarterdeck. Our Knowledge Hat wants us to memorize our diddy's and sound off. If I hear "No volume!" one more time I'm gonna snap. Our Heavy Hat wants us to pop sticks and march like there's no tomorrow. Our Senior wants us to give him naked pics of our girlfriends. (That got everyone smiling.) We know what we have to do. You have to be loud. You have to move fast. You have to have your game face on. I've worked with a lot of people. I know what it takes to win. 3014 has it. WE have it. So let's make it happen!

It worked. The Platoon started really working together. They knew I was fighting for them, and they had my back. It was good to go. My buddy Ferguson's legs were killing him. He had a wicked case of the shin splints. So before we hit the rack, we prayed together over his shins and that God would take the pain away so he could get through training. There is nothing worse than being in pain in a place that is hard enough on its own. That night, I remembered thinking to myself-

I gotta take it one day at a time. Sunday to Sunday. Just get to Sunday. It's so easy to lose track of time because you never wear a watch and no one tells you what time it is. Sunday is the only time I know what day it is. Just get to Sunday and you'll be fine.

Before lights out, our Heavy Hat came through and wrote our weight on our hand. I wonder what that's for.

20071119 MONDAY
HIT 'EM TILL THEY STOP YOU!

Today, we started with some motivating Rifle manual in the squad bay. Unfortunately, some recruits were failing to get the bolt back and this was pissing off our Senior. It wasn't too long before we heard-

If you recruits don't care then I don't care. Get outside!

That only means one thing- to the sand box we go. This got us good and pissed off because no one wanted to start the day in the sand box. However, I now see the genius behind it. It was just a game. Our first event today is Pugil Stick fighting. You've seen it in movies. You get all this gear and you have a stick with two Fred Flintstone sized pads on the ends. What better way to show up at the pits then all pissed off? We wanted to kill someone for having to play stupid games and now we got our chance. Brilliant!

As soon as we got our safety brief, we were split into our weight divisions and told to sit down and shut up. That's what the number was for on our hands. Good to go. Our Heavy Hat and our Senior were in charge of my ring. They explained that they wanted to see a good fight. Today we would fight our own Platoon. Next time, we would square off against other Platoons. You had 3 rounds to fight.

Round 1- Red was attacking- Black was defending.

Round 2- Black was attacking- Red was defending.
Round 3- Both were attacking.
  - You had 30 seconds for each round.

I was fighting in the 160 division and felt pretty confident going in. We had done this a lot at the Karate school so it was nothing new. The first couple fights were horrible. No one knew what they were doing and it was pissing our Senior off. He would holler stuff in the ring but no one was able to follow. Our Drill Instructors wanted blood. This event was another opportunity for a recruit to get hurt and dropped out of training. They wanted to thin the Platoon out.

My turn came up and I was ready to go. I figured I might be able to put on a pretty good match. My first round I was on offense. We ran in at each other and I got pretty lucky with a clean back of the head shot. This dazed my opponent, so when I hit him in the face he dropped to his back. I stuck my boot on his chest and started smashing him in the face. I doubt it hurt him at all because of all the gear we had on so I tried to break his junk. This got the attention of the Drill Instructors who at that time were planning our deaths. At the end of the first match, I came to the realization that you really couldn't get injured with all the gear we were wearing. We were issued football helmets that were reinforced so you can blast the opponent full on in the head but wouldn't feel the impact that would cause any head trauma. Word got passed along to the other recruits and that was the ignition source that gave more exciting matches.

In the second round, my job was to play defense. He came at me pretty well but kept leaving himself wide open. I rolled the dice and turned the tide on him. 4 quick headshots and he was down. The Drill Instructors were loving it.

For the last round, my opponent was wobbly so it was over in 3 headshots. It was fun. As it turned out, I was faced up against my buddy Branning. I couldn't even tell because of the gear. I asked if he was cool, and he said he was just exhausted. Good to go. Continuous attacks win this game. Shoving back and forth gets you nowhere.

The rest of the fights went really well and as a reward, we got an introduction to the Confidence Course. This is the one I was excited about. The "O" Course is cool but the "C" Course is just awesome. You actually get to see a lot of it in Full Metal Jacket. The events are as follows-

1- The Dirty Name- (This is the one that Pyle has a hard time getting on. You jump up, climb up, jump up again, climb up, and over you go.) Interestingly enough, it's one of the most challenging obstacle for most recruits because of the amount of consequence that surrounds it. it's so easy to fall off. There's no easy way outs on this one. You have to jump up and catch the first log with your hips. Then, it's a leap of faith to catch the next log with your hips. Otherwise, you'll come short and slip off having nothing to hold on to and do it all over again.

2- Stairway to Heaven- Climb up a 35 foot oversized ladder and come down the other side.

3- Un-upright short wall- It's a 6-foot wall slanted toward you. No big deal.

4- Un-upright vertical ladder- This was cool. Imagine over sized monkey bars going straight up about 12 feet. It's tilted a bit toward you so you can't use your feet. You just gotta climb up with your arms.

5- Cargo Net- This I had done before on the "E" Course back home.

Remember to grabe the vertical ropes and climb the horizontal ropes.

6- Rope Swing. You run, jump out, catch the rope, and swing the rest of the way.

7- "A" Frame- This is a combination obstacle. You climb a 25-foot rope, walk over logs, climb a wood ladder, reach out and grab a rope, and slide down to the bottom. (Also in Full Metal Jacket)

8- Arm walker- It's like the parallel bars in gymnastics.

The only difference is that you walk with your hands down to the end of the bars, you actually drop down to a next set of bars without touching your feet, walk down to the end of that set, drop down to a third set, walk down, and then jump off.

9- 3 Tier Tower. It's a 3-story tower. You stand on the first floor, pull yourself up to the next floor, pull yourself up to the 3rd floor, and then climb down a cargo net on the backside.

10- Weaver- In the movie Full Metal Jacket, if you look in the background, you can see a roof like structure made out of logs.

That's it. You go under the first, over the second, under the third, over the fourth. You go all the way up and all the way back down in that fashion.

11- Balance Beam- This was a cakewalk. You walk up an 8-foot wide board and then right back down.

12- Arm Stretcher- Monkey bars that go up, down, up, down, up.

It's actually harder than you would think. Gunnery Sergeant Hartman said you had to negotiate this obstacle in 10 seconds in the movie.

13- Rope Wall- You grab the rope and climb up the wall. No big deal. Don't be the one to use the little girl steps. There are little pieces of wood nailed to the surface so you have a place to put your boot if you can't do it right.

14- Wire Bridge- It's 2 steel cables suspended over water.

You grab the top cable with your hands and step on the bottom cable. It takes a bit of balance but no big deal. The only way you can fall is if you just wig out and lose your grip.

That's it. Like I said, today was the introduction. The Drill Instructors demonstrated everything today. At a later date, we'll actually get to do all of it. We had another 5-minute lunch. 45 seconds for the sandwich. Cookies, raisins, and chips were mixed, crushed up, and swallowed in 45. Eggs were in 45. And the granola bar was in 30. We tore it up. This was the first time that the majority of the Platoon got everything down. Water helps out a lot. Take a bite, add some water, and swallow it all.

At the end of the day, I can remember thinking how glad I'll be to be back teaching at the school. Boot Camp life can be fun, but mindless repetition gets old really fast. I'm about done with rifle drill. Regular marching drill is cool, but we always end up paying for some idiot in rifle drill. Oh well. At least tomorrow usually come with new stuff to learn. I gotta keep swingin.

20071121 WEDNESDAY
The Games we Play

For some reason, I jumped out of the rack with a spring in my step. I felt good and I was ready to go. However, not everyone felt the same way. The recruits are moving slow and are having a hard time with the concept of freezing their bodies and not moving. In Boot Camp, you are counted down for everything and once the Drill Instructor gets to 1, you better be locked out. Otherwise, you're just going to play games, get smoked on the quarterdeck, or sent out to play in the sand box. No matter what, pain in your body will be the end result of moving too slow or when you're not supposed to. Not only that, but everyone talks when they're not supposed to. Some recruits always have to say something. Either they are trying to shut someone up or they just want to talk to their buddy next to them. Whatever the case, our Kill Hat aimed to put an end to it all.

The game he used for this was the "bull run". In this, he would order everyone to get their scuz brush on line. Then we would go to the back quarterdeck. We would be ordered to squat down and, when given the command, push our scuz brush to the front quarterdeck as fast as we possibly could without our knees ever touching. The time frame was 60 seconds. As soon as he said go, we looked like a bunch of bulls running for our lives to the front quarterdeck. Hence the name bull run. It was hard to make it because everyone is kicking everyone, bumping in to each other, and if you're in the back, you have to wait on the slow recruit in front of you. We did it... a lot! We would almost all get there and then our Kill Hat would say-

Nope, Nope, Nope. You didn't make it. You movin to slow. Get to the back hatch!

Over and over. If you talk or move slow, you can count on the Bull Run. We absolutely hated it. But true to fashion, it began to break us of talking or moving when we weren't supposed to knowing that at any moment, we would be bringing our scuz brush on line.

Breakfast was actually really good. I've learned how to pick the right foods and finish everything regardless of the 6-minute time frame. After that, we drilled for 2 hours. It was by far the longest drill session yet. Marching and marching and marching. I thought it would never end. But... it did. We went back to the house and got ready to go to the RTF. While everyone was getting ready, our Knowledge Hat killed me for everyone moving too slow. When we got to the RTF, he took me to the sand box outside the RTF. Sand boxes are everywhere on Parris Island. That's twice. Grrr! Finally, I was in class. I could have a break from getting smoked. The class got over and we had a 10-minute break. That's when I heard- *"Where you at Guide?!"*

Here we go again. Back out to the sand box for me. This time it was with our Heavy Hat. That guy's crazy. Every Hat smokes you a different way. You stay because either you are too slow going from one drill to the next, or you have no volume, or in the case of my Heavy Hat, you're just a pathetic recruit and you're gonna stay there until someone makes him stop.

Finally, classes were starting back up and he was instructed to get me back in class. As soon as we got back to the house, my Knowledge Hat smoked me again. It was at this time that I figured the Drill Instructors were trying to see if I had any quit in me. They kept telling me it wasn't worth being the Guide. They said I'd never keep control of the Platoon. I wasn't the right recruit for the job. This all fueled me. I never quit and I never slacked on volume. These are the two things they wanted to see. It worked. They pretty much left me alone after that.

If you are ever the Guide, NEVER under any circumstances let anyone except the Senior take the Guidon. If you do, you will pay. The Guidon serves as a learning tool to keep what you have earned. The Drill Instructors will do whatever it takes to get it from you. This is the one case where you can tell any Drill Instructor NO. Whenever they try to take it, simply say-

Sir! This recruit is not authorized to give the Guidon to anyone but this recruit's Senior Drill Instructor.

DO NOT let anyone take the Guidon. That also applies to the Brassard. I remember that night after we came back from evening chow, My Kill Hat tried to rip it off my arm and say I wasn't the Guide anymore. Our squad bay was on the 3rd Deck and I am always the last recruit up the stairwell. As the recruits make their way up, I unscrew the Guidon, remove the spearhead, and then hustle everyone up. My Kill Hat told me to hang back after all the recruits were up. He told me that they didn't make it all the way to the top and that I wasn't the Guide anymore. This was simply a test. No one but the Senior can fire me. He tried for the Brassard. The Brassard is a piece of Blue and White cloth bearing our Platoon number on it. There are two Velcro straps on the top and bottom used to keep it secured to your arm. Because it's velcroed and not tied, it can be easy to rip off with enough force. He got a hand on it and was about to rip it off but I grabbed it, ripped it away from him, and shoved him back into the steps away from me. In **ANY** other case he would have destroyed me for shoving him off me. You get absolutely destroyed for simply touching a Drill Instructor. NEVER, EVER touch a Drill Instructor. But since it was a test, he left me alone. It surprised him.

Our Kill Hat would always put us to the test. If someone does something wrong to a recruit, you have to inform the Senior about it. At chow, our Kill Hat sabotaged Moseley's food. He had a piece of chicken and when he went back to get his drink, our Kill Hat covered it with salt and through away the rest of his food. Sure enough, that night Moseley spoke up and informed our Senior what happened. True to his word, that stuff didn't happen again. If Moseley didn't say anything, it would have continued until we Graduated. Everything is a test to make you do the right thing.

Every single night consists of one final sweep before we hit the rack. Our Knowledge kicks it off with-

Scuzbrush online! **SCUZBRUSH ONLINE AYE SIR!**

Re-ady…MOVE! (With this command we dive into our footlockers as fast as we can. First we gotta get the combination lock off, flip the lid, get the scuzbrush out, close the lid, lock it back up, and then get back to the position of attention as fast as possible)

Depending on how fast we move will determine if we play games or keep going. If we move too slow, we played the bulkhead online game. That's where he says go, and we sprint to the bulkhead and back online as fast as possible. The problem is two recruits have to go between the racks and there is really only room for one. At first it seems impossible to do as fast as the requirement. But then you and your rackmate learn to work together and get it down. Once the games are done we carry on. He says-

Scruzbrush the bulkhead **SCUZBRUSH THE BULKHEAD AYE SIR!**

Re-ady…MOVE! (With that, we bolt to the bulkhead and then sweep everything from the bulkhead up to our position on line and into the highway.)

When we start getting close to the highway, he'll start counting down from 20.

7,6,5,4 (When he gets to 3 we scream **LOCKED** and would freeze our bodies in the crouched position

When he said 2, we would bang our scuzbrush on the deck 3 times)

When he says 1, we scream **DONE SIR!**

If we do a good job, he'll say Scuzbrush away! **SCUZBRUSH AWAY AYE SIR!**

We did this every single night until graduation. It was always interesting to see if it would be a short night or a long night. It just depended on if everyone wanted to play games or be done with.

Before we hit the rack, I got the single greatest thing anyone can ever receive in Boot Camp. I got mail. Let me just tell you right now, nothing matters to a recruit more than mail. It's better than food. A recruit feels so alone in Boot Camp. Mail is just the thing that reminds you that people are counting on you to make it. I got mail from my Dad. Up until this point, I thought I was lost. My address book was gone and I didn't know if word would get to back.

I sent mail to the Karate school. In the letter, I asked if someone could call my family and give them my address. It worked. Word got to them and they sent me mail right away. As it turns out, they had missed me just as much as I missed them. I found a place in the back of the squad bay and read it over and over. I never cry about anything. I cried.

But after, I was stronger than I had ever been. It was soul cleansing. All my fears didn't matter anymore. I knew that my family cared about me and that was good enough for me. It was all I needed. They were my secret weapon in making it through Boot Camp.

Making a calendar helps as well. Just don't be the one to get caught with it. It'll be over if you do. I kept mine hidden in my Bible. It would be safe there and I could mark off days and update it every Sunday during church. Counting down days is awesome. It helps a lot to know that you're almost done. In this game, it's all about the tricks of the trade that help you through.

20071123 FRIDAY
The Games We Play. Take 2.

Today, we made our first PX call. We got our original issue of gear when we arrived at the Island. Now, we were going to restock. The Marine Corps gives you 300 bucks on a card to use at the PX. However, do not be fooled. This is Marine Corps money and they're going to use all of it for training. They give you just enough to purchase everything you need throughout Boot Camp and just a bit more to get another pair of socks, stamps, or something cheap but important. The part that sucks is the fact that you really don't use everything you buy.

Anyway, the way it works is the Drill Instructors give you a list. You go in and get everything on the list as quickly as possible. Then you get right back out. But beware, Drill Instructors LOVE to play with recruits during PX calls. They form as a pack of wolves right near the exit so when you come out, you better say what your supposed to say super loud, the first time, and then bolt to your formation. Make one single mistake and a Drill Instructor from another Platoon will call you back and then the games begin. They'll make you run around, back and forth, screaming stupid junk as loud as you can (The PX is located between two facing buildings so it echoes really well) or they may take you and a few other recruits to the sand box that just so happens to be located right across from the PX.

Right after the PX call, we got another haircut. Yeehaw! While we were waiting for all the recruits in our Platoon to get out of the PX, Recruit Stahling pissed his pants. He asked to use the head and the Drill Instructors ignored him. After a while, he couldn't hold it anymore and pissed all over himself. Garbage. If you have to use the head and a Drill Instructor ignores you or says no, take off and use it anyway. Yeah, you'll get yelled at or quarterdecked for it, but then the Senior will blast the Drill Instructor for it. They have to let you use the head. Pissing on yourself is completely unsat.

Besides that, everything was going great. We started marching back to the house with all of our replenished gear. The bag of gear we were carrying weighed about 30 lbs. loaded and cinched close with a cord. We were only allowed to hold the bag by the cord and that was garbage. The cord digs intro your palm and since you're carrying your rifle strong side you can't switch because everyone has to keep their rifle over their right shoulder to be the same. It sucks but you just have to grit it out. Then, I don't know what happened but our Kill Hat wanted to play games with us while we were carrying all our new junk. We must have made 100 U-turns. We would be marching and then he would say- "U-turn left now!" Then we'd go back the way we came. Then we'd turn around again. We'd get a tiny bit farther then turn around again. It went on and on all the way back to the house. Grrr!

Finally, we got back. While we were unpacking, recruit Abbett, the Scribe, was caught standing in one place for too long. It looked like he wasn't doing anything. Guess what that means? *"Where you at Guide?!"* Crap! I ran up and hit the quarterdeck while Abbett was told to sit on a footlocker, read a newspaper given to him by our Knowledge Hat, and he had to tell me to go faster. It was garbage. A few minutes later, the 4-squad leaders were instructed to join me in the fun. After that, the Platoon was done unpacking and organizing everything so they could all join in. It was a never-ending smoke session. We just kept going. Finally, we cleared the quarterdeck and ran back to stand on line. When the Heavy Hat came on deck, he saw us flying back to our spots and asked what was going on. Our Kill Hat told him the deal. When he heard the whole story, he said- *"Where you at Guide?!"* Nooooo. Crap again! I ran up and it was just me and my Heavy Hat. He hit me with the Face/Feet game. He would say Face/ Feet and then count down from 10. In that time frame, I had to get on my face and spring back up to my feet before he got to 1. We played that for... awhile.

Here's the deal- Kill yourself and stay there for just a while. Don't put out, and even though it doesn't seem as hard, you'll be there forever. I'll take option 1. I tried to stay with him and sound off. Just then our Senior came in. He asked me why I was on the quarterdeck. I told him I didn't know. With that, he told me to get back on line. If you didn't know why you were up there, he would usually let you go if you are putting out and sounding off. Right when I got back on line, our Senior took us out and smoked us as a Platoon in the sand box. Awesome! Today was nuts. It was one smoke session after another. Apparently, when you have extra time before another event in the day, that's what happens. But this was only the beginning of our fun.

When we got back from the RTF, some garbage recruit wrote on the stall in the head. OH MY GOSH! You have got to be kidding me. After all the time we spent getting worked, some idiot recruit wanted to deface Government property.
My Heavy Hat said- *"Where you at Guide?!"*

I bolted up to where he was. He called for the Kill Hat. Great. He then quietly told us to go back to the RTF. I was to scrub off whatever was written on the wall and then report back. I got the cleaning supplies in my daypack and was ready to go. It was just me and my Kill Hat. I swear he was growling the whole way there. We stepped outside and my Kill Hat started making me yell diddy's so there wasn't that awkward silence. Very well. I belted it out even though it was just me and him-

Step it out.
Step it out aye Sir!
Step it out.

Step it out aye Sir!
Faster.
Faster aye Sir!
Faster.
Faster aye Sir!
Step it out.
Step it out aye Sir!
Stop.
Stop aye Sir good afternoon Sir!

We stopped at a street. He looked both ways, and then told me to bolt across and stand by. As soon as he got across, we kept up the same thing. This is what was said 3/4 of the way there. He would direct me on the correct side of the road, to speed up, slow down, or to stop. It may have sounded dumb but I sounded off to whatever he said. When he saw that, he said nothing more. That was fine with me. For the rest of the time, we just stepped to the RTF without saying a word. When we walked by some Drill Instructors and some Brass, he told me we didn't have time for games and to just salute when he said and keep moving. Within 10 feet and under his breath he said- *"Ready...Salute."* I followed as sharp as I could. Some of the Drill Instructors tried to play with me but he waved them off and said- *"Ignore 'em boy. We got a job to do."* Good to go. We walked into the head, looked on the wall, and there it was. It read-

I'M GOING CRAZY.
I CAN'T FUCKING TAKE THIS ANYMORE.
SOMEONE PLEASE HELP!
3014

My Kill Hat started to fume! He took my bleach, scuz brush, and my towel, and started working on finding the right combination. Once he figured it out, he instructed me in what to do to get it all off. I said- "Aye Sir!" and got cracking.

I figured if I did a good job, he might spare us. I got to work and he left to talk to the Brass. When he came back, I had gotten it completely off. It took HARD scrubbing but it came off. My Kill Hat was pleased with the job. He then informed the Brass we got it all off, and we were on our way back. He said nothing to me the whole way. No "step it out aye sir" or anything. He just told me when to stop or cross the street. When we got back, the Platoon was getting smoked. They stopped and got on line when we walked in. Our Drill Instructors talked and our Kill Hat said we got everything taken care of. That was the end of it. For today.

That night, our Heavy Hat told us-
Everyone has limits and it takes a man to ask for help. However, if you ask in the way of wanting attention by writing on a fuckin' stall, then you're a bitch and the Marine Corps doesn't want you say Aye Sir.
AYE SIR!
Whoever wrote that shit on the stall shoulda joined the fuckin Coast Guard.

20071124 Saturday
1st Conditioning march

My firewatch was from 2-3 and instead of getting up at 4, we got up at 3. Awesome. Today was an early start day because it was our first conditioning hike. 3rd Battalion met out on the grinder with our packs and got ready for the hike. With everything in Boot Camp comes challenge. 3 miles is a cakewalk. The problem was the weather. It was our first lesson in dealing with frigid cold weather. Oh my gosh. It was freezing cold. Normally, when it gets cold, you naturally put on warm layers, a hat, a pair of gloves, and you're able to put your hands in your pockets or do whatever you need to do to keep warm. We wore nothing but our cammies and our cover. No beanie or gloves. No warming layers. You're not aloud to put your hands in your pockets or under your arm. It was just us against the cold. That's when words of wisdom flashed in my mind-

The weakness of others will become your strength.

Clearly, the Drill Instructors were not cold. How could this be? I would later learn that they would have so much fun watching the recruits freeze that they wouldn't even be thinking about the weather. Seeing recruits weak made them feel invincible. I'm not gonna lie. I was cold. I remember closing my eyes standing there in formation and praying for some hope of comfort while we were just waiting. I knew once we got going we would all warm up. However, we were just standing still waiting for all the Platoons to get in formation. When I opened my eyes, I was looking into the eyes of my Knowledge Hat who was shining a moonbeam in my face to see if my eyes were closed. When my eyes opened all the way, he quietly smiled and said- *"Really Guide?"*

I don't know what it was but it pissed me off. He called me out. I couldn't show this kind of weakness. Sure, it's cold. But when it all comes down to it, you don't HAVE to show weakness. You can feel it all day long. But you don't have to show it. I never showed it again. No matter what, I was going to grit my teeth and fight through whenever something like that happened again. It actually worked.

The coolest part of the hike was being able to talk to the Senior because he stands right by me. He was asking me questions about what I did for a living outside the Marine Corps. He was interested in my Martial Arts background. I was then able to ask him some questions. I kept myself in check making sure to ask everything the right way. But today was the first day I had ever spoken to a Drill Instructor about non Marine Corps subjects. I asked him advice on how to control problem recruits in the Platoon. He told me what was acceptable and what was not. Since I was able to put my hands on recruits, he told me my limits and it helped out a lot. The biggest thing he told me was to *"Inspect what I Expect."* He told me to always follow up and make sure things got done the way I wanted them to be done. He told me to be the example and verbalize/ demonstrate what I needed done. It was great stuff.

As for the rest of the hike, we were constantly kicking knowledge. We were always having to scream louder and louder. The problem was that 30% of the Platoon had lost their voices all together. It's not that they didn't want to scream; it was just that screaming while you have no voice doesn't exactly project. But that's no excuse. Everyone that still had a voice just had to sound off even more. When we got back to the house, we got inspected. That's when the Company Commander comes on deck and you have to report your condition. When he steps in front

of you, you simply-
Drop your towel, Step out of your shower shoes, turn like a friggin ballerina and say-

Sir! This recruit has no medical, mental, or physical limitations to report at this time!

That's it. Once you're done, you get dressed and stand back at attention. No big deal. We did that after every single hike. Today, we had lunch with our First Sergeant. That was cool because he let us eat our box chow without rushing. We took our sweet time. We got to eat everything in the box without having to swallow anything whole. He told us some really funny stories about recruits and answered some questions for us. It was a good time. When we got done, we had some time before we had to step off to our next RTF class. Our Senior took this time to work on marching. What shocked me the most was that my Kill Hat took me to the side and showed me some Guidon techniques. It was great. For the first time ever, he did something besides put me on the quarterdeck. It seemed like it should be against the rules for him to do what he was doing. He's not supposed to teach anything. But he did. He showed me some good stuff. And he actually talked to me like he was trying to really convey the knowledge so I would get it right. I accidently made eye contact with him and he blasted me but then we just kept going so it was cool.

That night we had another Rifle Battle with 3010. It was a shirts and skins game. We were standing there in cammie bottoms and PT shirt. (AKA Boots and ute's) 3010 came on deck, locked out in front of us, and we were ready to go. All of the sudden, they pulled their shirts off. Weak. We kicked into the battle and it was fierce. 3010 had gotten a lot better. They actually scored a few points this time. But we held our own. We'll have to step it up if we're gonna stay ahead of them. This time, we had a trick up our sleeve that kept us on the up and up. When our Heavy Hat instructed us to put our rifles on kill, we bent over, flipped the switch, and with our heads down said-

Awww shit! Someone's gonna get smoked up in this...

Then we would all shoot upright together and yell-

BEE-YATCH!

Welcome to the world of Custom Diddy's! As a reward for winning the battle, our Senior had a workout with us. We did a few max sets of pull-ups, sit-ups, push-ups, and flutter kicks. He got right down there with us and hit it pretty hard. It was cool. The absolute BEST part of it was that he brought out a CD player and kicked some music. I don't care if you like Rap music or not. It was great. It served as a reminder that the world was still turning and someday, we would be out of here.

20071125 Sunday
Tricks of the Trade Continue

Wow! We made it to another Sunday. We started early as always, cleaned the house, and got ready to leave in our church groups for chow. I took my Senior's advice and started getting in some faces in order to get things done. It worked great if you had the authority to back it up. As the Guide, all I had to do was get within an inch of their face and scream to the top of my lungs. The real magic was the motivation behind it. I always told the recruits to do stuff that would keep us from getting killed. That worked the best. No one wanted to get killed if they didn't have to. Most of the time, you could get them to move without raising your voice. It was the knuckleheads that you needed to put under the spotlight that got yelled at. Once you yelled at someone, the Drill Instructors would think that recruit was garbage and get them on the quarterdeck. No one wanted to get yelled at.

So the way they saw it, if I wasn't yelling, then they wouldn't be quarterdecked by a Drill Instructor. So they were happy to do what I asked. They knew I was just trying to keep them out of trouble if I spoke to them quietly. They knew that if I raised my voice, they knew it would draw quarterdeck attention. For that reason, I made sure I didn't yell without reason. I tried to solve everything under the radar first. We worked good like that. The moment I abused that power, the trust would collapse and I would lose control. So I made sure I didn't yell at anyone unless it was legit.

The rules are the same as in the Karate school. Kids do what they are told because they don't want to get in trouble with their parents. Here, the recruits did what I told them because they didn't want to get in trouble by their new parents (Drill Instructors). That was my only angle of control. Because Boot Camp is such a hostile environment, you can't always count on mutual respect to be what keeps everyone loyal. Here, it's fear. Fear is what drives loyalty. Recruits are afraid to get quarterdecked, they are afraid to get recycled, shoot they are even afraid to ask a Drill Instructor a question. I cannot tell you how many times I was asked by a recruit to ask a Drill Instructor a question. But it was constant. I was always doing it. But since it kept the recruits loyal to me, I rode that wave. These are the kinds of lessons I have never learned in civilian life. Amazing.

Chow was phenomenal. Here's a little secret. When you go to chow on Sunday, the Drill Instructors are in charge of multiple Platoons and have to get all the recruits in the chow hall at one time. Meaning- you get enough time to eat a big breakfast. (If you can shovel fast enough that is.) Typically, I was able to eat just enough to keep from being malnourished. On this Sunday, I was able to down-

Peach Yogurt
2 Pancakes
Cocoa Krispies
Scrambled Eggs
PB+J Sandwich
Cinnoman Roll
Carton of Milk
Glass of PowerAde

Let me tell you something. In Boot Camp, this is huge! I quickly found that if you can eat fast, you can eat a lot. I eat FAST! For the past 7 days I had been feeling sick. I never get sick. Now I was starting to feel it. Luckily, all I had was congestion that came and went. It made physical training rough but it wasn't enough to cause a major issue. Yeah. Go ahead and go to Medical in Boot Camp. I promise you that you'll get recycled. Even if you have the tiniest thing, Medical will throw you back.

It's garbage. That's just the way Boot Camp is. You're going to feel like crap most of all the time. Get used to it by enjoying the silver lining wherever you can find it. In this case, it was definitely Sunday morning chow!!

During church, it's fun talking to the other recruits about what they are experiencing. Mostly all of it is the exact same but every recruit has a story about an infamous Drill Instructor that has walked them right up to Pain and Misery's door and kicked them through it. This is the first Sunday that I realize we are nowhere near as skittish as we were when we picked up. It's becoming easier to sing songs and we are really starting to bond. When we got to big church, I saw 3 rows of brand new recruits that just picked up. Their eyes were straight trauma and culture shock. So myself and some of the fellas made a point to tell them to hang in and keep digging. It would get better. I told them they might not understand how, but it would get better.

20071126 Monday
Come and Get It!

Wake up! Sunday's over and it's back to work. Morning chow could be described in 3 words- fast, fast, and fast! Oh my gosh! Our Knowledge Hat turned us into a racquetball and the chow hall was a brick wall. We flew in and flew right back out. Better luck next time.

After our chow experience, we hiked over to the "O" Course. Finally, I have been waiting for this. I remembered practicing making it through the "O" Course in Maryland and now it was time to see if it would pay off. 3 Platoons met out at the course. It was all of Follow Series. As soon as we got formed up, we were told that we would stay in our Platoons, rotate through 3 stations, and then run the "O" Course as a competition. Awesome.

Our first station was to hit some remedial MCMAP training. Our Knowledge Hat and Heavy Hat took turns going over techniques with us. It was no big deal. We went over all the combative strikes and that was it. Our next station was over at the pull-ups bars. We would do a max set of pull-ups, a max set of push-ups, and then wait in line for our next time through. Then it hit me. I gotta make a head call. Crap! I went up and asked my Heavy Hat-

Good morning Sir! This recruit requests permission to speak to Drill Instructor Staff Sergeant N!
What!
Sir! This recruit requests permission to make a head call!
Do you see a head out here?
No Sir!
Well then I guess you'll have to find one. Go in that squad bay and ask to use theirs.
Aye Sir! Good morning Sir!

So, me and another recruit took off to find a head to use. We went and banged on the first hatch we could find. When the recruit answered, I told him that we were two recruits from Platoon 3014 requesting to come on deck and use the head. The recruit told us there wasn't a Drill Instructor on deck but we could use it anyway. We just had to make it FAST! Good to go. We ran in the head and got to work. Luckily, it wasn't a sit down head call. About half way through, I heard the Drill Instructor come on deck and the recruit was reporting our situation. The Drill Instructor went through the roof. He was screaming at the recruit to get us off his deck. The recruit flew back in the head and started yelling at us to get out. There was no way I was going to stop. I was almost done. The recruit could see that and just did his job of yelling at us. As soon as I was done, I bolted off deck. We made it. What a relief.

When we got back, we were just about to rotate for the last time. We headed over to the "O" Course. For now, our job was simple. We were instructed to go through as many times as possible in 20 minutes. That's a LONG time. Oh well. I was in the first group to go and blew right through the course. BAM! Practice paid off Big Time! Wow. It was a cakewalk. I was already up the rope and tagging the log by the time the rest of my group had gotten to the triple jump. The best part was the fact that it was taking me less energy because I knew how to clear each obstacle without killing myself.

We kept going through nonstop. I finished it about 6 times when I saw my Heavy Hat walking towards me and Bell. He came over and asked us how we felt. We told him we were great. He told us to hang back and let the others stay on the course. He was putting a team of 4 of us together for a Series race. Awesome! The team consisted of myself, Bell, Jewski, and Larson. I was picked as the first to go. I can dig it. The other teams formed up, our Series Gunnery Sergeant told us the winning Platoon would win the Series rag (That's another Guidon that we get to carry whenever we march), and we took our positions. We were amped.

The whistle went off and it was on! My Heavy Hat stayed right next to me the whole way through the course off to the side. He was telling me where everyone was and how I was looking. Today was my day. I was blowing through the course. He was getting quieter and quieter as my lead began to lengthen. It was like he didn't want anyone to know he was excited that we were going to destroy the other Platoons. He kept telling me not to worry about looking back, just keep moving, hurry it up, I was way ahead. When I got to the rope and was making my way up, I could see how far back they were. That gave me a rush. I hit the log and slid/fell down the rope. I just wanted to get down as fast as possible. I sprinted back to the finish and tagged Bell. 3014 was in a frenzy! I finished the course in 48 seconds. Bell shot out like a rocket. He was a beast. If anyone could maintain the lead if not lengthen it, it would be my man Bell. Sure enough, he was on his way back by the time the other Platoon's 2nd teammate was getting to the wall. Jewski took off, flew through the course, and hustled back. The last one to go was Larson. He was our only questionable player. However, he was feeling the energy and made it happen. He did his job and it was in the bag. WE WON!

As soon as he crossed the finish line, 3014 lost its mind. Everyone was screaming. Our Kill Hat shut us up. From that point on, 3014 carried the Series Guidon as well as our 3014 Guidon. We were all jacked up on energy. Our Heavy Hat told us it was no big deal but inside, he was proud that his Platoon stepped up and made it happen. From there, we headed to the grinder to march. Bad news. Some of the recruits were showing signs of laziness and that got us sent to the sand box. It was messed up because we just came out of a victory and now we were getting smoked. Roberts spit in the pit and our Kill Hat made him eat it. That must have been crunchy. No one ever spit in the pit again.

When we got back to the house, our Knowledge Hat busted out the questions and answers that we needed to know for the test coming up. It was a lot of stuff. It's not hard if you kept it in your head all along. But if you were a slacker and didn't try to keep it in, you were in trouble.

When we went to chow, you always assign two hatch recruits to hold the door for everyone else. I got this recruit named Tuller to do it. As soon as I called him up, he started complaining because he thought that would mean he would have to go to the back of the line and eat last. Grrr! This pissed me right off-

1 I always eat dead last and you don't see me whining.
2 I was going to put him right back in his spot like we always do. I just needed someone to hold the door.

But since he wanted to have an attitude about it, he ate with me. I told him I would have let him go back to his spot and that next time he needed to learn to keep his mouth in check until he knows the full deal. He understood... until our Kill Hat made us get up and he was only half way through. Once he saw what it was like eating last, he never said another word.

That night, I got a huge surprise. Mrs. Benson, one of our Instructors from Davidsonville, wrote me a letter that included 5 Sudoku puzzles out of the local newspaper. Call me a geek, but I was excited. It was just a sweet touch of normality. Since I love Sudoku, it was the perfect thing to take my mind off the rigors of the day. For the first time in my Boot Camp experience, I clearly remember the days starting to go a bit faster. That could only mean that things were starting to find a rhythm and the days were becoming less chaotic. I can dig faster days. Before we hit the rack, our Heavy Hat came through and wrote our weight again on our hands. For some reason, he added 10 pounds to mine.

20071127 Tuesday
Lesson's Learned and Shadow Watch...Yeehaw!

Hooray! I finished morning chow again. I can't describe to you how great that is. Finishing chow is fantastic. We did some MCMAP as always and it's not that bad. It's really really basic but it's good for someone who's never thrown a punch. Everything is broken down Barney style. It reminds me a lot of Krav Maga. After we got done with MCMAP, it was Pugil Sticks II. Awesome.

This time, however, it wasn't in a ring, it wasn't against our own Platoon, and we weren't going to be trying to hold back. Today, the fight was going to take place on the bridge. It's wood construction, 5 feet wide, and about 60 feet long including the up and down ramps. And it's set about 3 feet off the ground giving you the chance to knock your opposition off! Sweet!

Most of the fights were fun to watch. Everyone had learned that shoving doesn't work and it's better to swing away. When my turn came up, I had my game plan set. As it was, everyone was running in and swinging for the head. I adjusted my attack in anticipation. As soon as my opponent charged in, I stuck my Pugil Stick straight up and caught my opponent under the chin. The result was his feet flying up in front of him and landing on his back. It was beautiful. However, the next time he charged he was ready for it so he settled down a bit. It was like a magic trick that you can only use once. I didn't get my opponent off the bridge, but I did manage to get another foot on his chest and smash him in the face. Pugil Sticks was definitely one of my things. I was lucky.

After my fight, our Drill Instructors informed us that if we knocked our opponents helmet off, or knocked their mouthpiece out, the whole Platoon would get a powerbar when we got back to the house! Good to go!! From that point, 2 recruits had their helmets knocked clean off and 3 recruits lost their mouthpieces. It was good training.

After Pugil Sticks, we went to chow. Yeehaw! I finished again. That's two in 1 day. I couldn't believe it. That had never happened before. Finally, I was starting to eat the right foods that would allow me to fill myself totally up. When we were about ready to go, we were put on stand-by. That means we wait till the Drill Instructors are ready to go. As I was waiting, I noticed how Guides from other Platoons were talking to their recruits. It was messed up. At that moment, I learned that there is a huge difference between speaking with authority and just being a dick. All the Guides that were being dicks got absolutely no respect or support from their Platoons. There is absolute zero tolerance when someone is being sarcastic. Everyhting is better when it's straight black and white.

All the Guides that led their Platoons based on simple authority and who actually cared about their team worked very well. I was once criticized by another Guide for not being more of a dick and now, we could all see who had better cooperation and more control. It was the Guides who led by example. Whenever you're just a straight up dick to someone, I promise you it'll just be a fight. That's no way to lead.

Our Heavy Hat was cool in the things he would say. One of his big expressions was-

Shut your mouth and save your teeth!

He repeated stuff twice, stammered, and said- "fuckin" ALOT.
He would say something like-

So tomorrow, yoooooou're gonna fuckin run for morning PT and you bitches better fuckin hustle ooooooooor it's gonna be fuckin over you understand? It's gonna be fuckin over!

Everything was going great. Before we left for chow, our Heavy Hat told us we could finally have dessert when we are at the chow hall. Since we picked up our Drill Instructors, no one ate dessert because if they did, they would get quarterdecked immediately once we got home. We were happy.

However, as soon as our Kill Hat and Knowledge Hat heard that, they were seething. But they knew their place, they didn't say anything to anyone in the chow hall and they let anyone get dessert. I wasn't stupid. I knew what was coming. Sure enough, as soon as we got out of the chow hall, our Kill Hat split out everyone that got dessert. (Except me because I hid my cookies in between my bread!)

Those recruits became road guards. They would have to sprint from one intersection to the next all the way back to the house. As for us, we weren't out of the woods either. We just ran in circles all the way back. Everyone paid. Our running cadence was-
LEFT FOOT... **LEFT FOOT**
LEFT FOOT... **LEFT FOOT**

I LOVE COOKIES... **I LOVE COOKIES**
I LOVE CA-AKE... **I LOVE CA-AKE**
WATCH ME SHOVEL THEM... **WATCH ME SHOVEL THEM**
IN MY FA-ACE... **IN MY FA-ACE**

We sang that junk all the way home. GARBAGE! Everyone was pissed off and they asked if I would bring it up to the Senior during SDI time. So I told the Senior what happened, he taught us a very important lesson-

Good evening Sir, this recruit requests permission to speak to Senior Drill Instructor Staff Sergeant B?

Ok. What's up Guide?

Sir, these recruits were informed by their Senior Drill Instructor that these recruits could have dessert at the chow hall.

Yes, that's correct. I did tell you that. Did someone tell you that you couldn't?

No Sir! These recruits did get dessert. But after these recruits left the chow hall, these recruits had to play games all the way back to the house.

Very well. So what the fuck are you complaining about?

Sir, These recruits got punished for getting what the Senior Drill Instructor said it was ok to have.

Well, did you get your dessert?

Yes sir.

Well, you got yours right? What's the fuckin problem? So you got some extra PT out of it. You still got what you wanted didn't you?

Yes Sir.

I had nothing to say to that. We all understood right away. The point was, who cares what happens after you get what you want. The point is you got exactly what you wanted. So we had to run home after chow and play games. We got what we wanted. In a way, we won.

That night during firewatch, another stupid recruit from the Platoon below us tried to kill himself. He stole a fork from the chow hall and went at his wrists with it. Luckily, a Drill Instructor caught him in the act and he was simply sent away. But before he left, he was stripped of everything that could be used as a weapon. No belts, shoelaces, or foreign objects. While he's being out-processed, we had to stand watch over him. It's called "shadow watch".

Shadow watch requires two recruits shining a blue lens moonbeam at him while he stares at a wall for 2 hours. Boring. Shadow watch sucks! To top it all off, the idiot we had to watch isn't even suicidal. He just puss'd out and wanted to escape the Marine Corps. To amuse ourselves, we would make a point of reminding him how stupid he was. We told him what would happen to him and that he'd never get home. Now he's all upset. We prayed he'd swing on one of us but he never did. That would have been fun. Oh well.

20071128 Wednesday
That's some Nasty junk!

Morning chow Finished. I'm on a role. After chow, we headed to the PT field. We did the Strength/ Endurance course 2 times through. I don't care how many times you do that course: You just can't get used to it. You'll make it, but it breaks you off and laughs in your face during the process. Good stuff. After that, we did a max set of pull-ups 2 times through and then hit the sit-ups. For sit-ups, I'm up to 109 in 2 minutes. That's good to go. Sit-ups have been kicking my butt for the last couple of PT sessions but not today. They've really improved.

Following PT, we did some MCMAP. Today's class was fun because we did rear naked chokes. I love this stuff! My Heavy Hat was impressed with my technique and got some other Drill Instructors to have a look. My partner was finishing up so they asked who I wanted to choke out in a race. A race is where you try to wrap up your partner as fast as you can from a dead stand still. You don't really choke your partner out: you simply stop when your partner confirms the technique is locked on and employed correctly. The fun thing is you get a chance to try to be faster than someone in another platoon. The potential bad thing is that your partner has to be tough. You're grabbing a hold of their throat pretty hard and it's easy to get cross-faced. Again, You're not putting your partner unconscious by any means but it's a rough game. And once the Drill Instructor sees you're too slow or your partner is whining, you start going more rounds.

I picked recruit Becker. He's the only one I knew of that I felt could take it. I think anyone else would have been bad news. Becker is a super tuff guy. Sure enough, he came over, I raced a few times against a few recruits, and Becker was totally fine. In fact, we was talking trash to the other recruits we were racing against. He was just as good at it and we made a great team. When we got back to the house, Becker came up to me and was pissed off because someone said I picked him on purpose to make him look bad. Apparently, Boyd was spreading that garbage. That was not the case at all. He was trying to cause some static between us. So during chow that afternoon, I sent Becker to the front of the line and Boyd to the back of the line. Boyd never interfered again. While Becker was up there, I clarified my reason and that I didn't pick him to do anything but win and we did. In my opinion, he had it down the best and was one of the toughest recruits in the platoon. I was sincere and he knew it.

As soon as we got back, our Knowledge Hat said we looked dehydrated. No one was dehydrated, we just ate. But he made us get a canteen on line and drink the whole thing. As soon as you finished it, you had to tip it over your head to show it was empty. He told us to fill 'em back up. We did and got back on line. He told us to down it. I knew what was coming. I stopped drinking it. My Kill Hat ordered me to drink it. I said- *Aye Sir!* But I didn't move a muscle. He repeated his order and I said- *Aye Sir!* Just then, 2 recruits threw up everywhere. After seeing that, 3 more threw up. It was a nasty chain reaction. 9 recruits threw up total. Not me. I refused to drink anymore. It was a bogus order. Our Knowledge Hat was just playing with us. That was some nasty junk. Our

Heavy Hat suddenly came on deck. He saved the day. Who knows what they would have tried to make us do next. Our Heavy Hat was infuriated and threw the two Drill Instructors out of the squad bay. Our Heavy Hat was mean, but some games he just didn't play. Blowing chow is not one of them! And since he's the highest rank besides our Senior, whatever he says goes.

From there, we went out and marched for 3 hours. It seemed like forever, but it was better than being in the squad bay and playing games. When we came back, we found our hygiene bags were totally filled with shaving cream. It appeared to us that our Kill Hat was pissed off that our Heavy Hat stopped their fun. I picked up my hygiene bag and took it up to show our Senior. At first he didn't care. He assumed that another recruit was jacking with me. I then informed him that all the bags looked like that. He informed all recruits with shaving cream in their hygiene bags to bring them to the quarterdeck. All of them came up and were put in a row. We were standing on line when our Senior called our Kill Hat out from the office. He ran out (He NEVER walked!) and posted himself by our Senior. When he saw the bags, he clenched his teeth. Our Senior said something to him inaudibly and the next thing we knew, he was taking them into the head. Our Senior gave us a head call and when we ran in, we saw our Kill Hat cleaning them out one by one. Steam was coming off his entire body. I have never seen him so furious! We all stayed well clear of him. Far beyond arms reach. However, inside I was thinking cha-ching. One point for us!

After evening chow, our Senior left. That meant it was just us and our Knowledge Hat. However, the Senior told him not to do anything crazy. One thing is for sure, our Drill Instructors never disobeyed an order. They were awesome Marines! Our Knowledge Hat got us on line and taught us a new diddy.
He taught us-

Quarterdeck!
Sir! The purpose of the quarterdeck is Keyword PEP-
P- Pull off blouse!
E- Empty pockets!
P- Push Bitch!

We said that one a lot. It was definitely a Platoon favorite for us! Not too many platoons pride themselves on a quarterdeck diddy. Most platoons fear the quarterdeck. From this day forward, we looked at it a bit differently. We were starting to last through entire quarterdeck sessions. Not all the time. But we started making it through here and there. We also jumped in if someone was getting smoked. Myself or one of the squad-leaders would stop whatever we were doing and jump on the quarterdeck if we saw someone working. It wasn't because we were bad or it wasn't that hard. We jumped in to build spirit within the team. It's a lot easier to make it through a smoke session when you're with someone else. Sometimes we would jump in and the Drill Instructor would tell us to go away and we did. Otherwise, you just jumped in screamed your head off. There was no chitchat like "come on recruit, you can make it." One word of that and the entire Platoon would get murdered outside in the sand pit. If they asked why you were jumping in, you'd just say- *"Sir, Spirit and Discipline Sir!"* That's the 3rd Battalion motto.

When we went to evening chow, we ALL got dessert. We figured that recruits threw up when we didn't get dessert so what's the worse they can do if we do get dessert. It's not going to matter. No matter what, we got ours!

I learned a valuable lesson today when it comes to physical conditioning. I used to base my ability on when I was starting a workout. That's garbage. People can do incredible things when they are fresh. But what are you able to do when you are cashed? For the past couple weeks, I have been working in a constant state of smoked. I'm getting to the point where I can still push hard even though my body feels dead. I haven't felt 100% since we picked up on the 10th. There is no such thing as an "off" day. We are constantly working out. But even though I don't feel 100%, I feel my recovery time skyrocketing. That's awesome. It's taking me half the time to get ready for another round of hard work. And it's not just me. I'm speaking for my platoon. We are becoming machines. No one has hyperventilated, thrown up, or fallen out of a PT workout in the past week. That's awesome. There was ALWAYS 1 or 2 that would gas out. Not now. We're entering into a whole new world of physical ability.

20071129 Thursday
Ready, Set, Fight!!!

Morning chow is in the bag. I got it figured out. It only took a couple weeks. But now I can consistently finish everything and be leaving the chow hall filled up. We headed for the PT field to take part in the infamous MCMAP Endurance Course. When we got there, Boyd wigged out because he chipped a tooth when we were forming up. He refused to form up. He wanted to sit this training session out until he could go to medical and get it fixed. What world does he think he is in? There is no such thing. That is impossible. There is no sitting out of anything, anytime, anywhere. You always work. I don't know where he got the idea that he wouldn't do anything. This isn't a high school football game where you sit out if you are injured. It's simple, you go straight to medical or jump back in the mix. Since medical isn't open yet, that narrows it right down.

So our Heavy Hat made us play games until he changed his mind. We ran all over the place. Out and back, out and back, out and back! Finally, I got the squad leaders together and we attempted to "persuade" Boyd to come back. He wasn't going to cooperate by being asked. The corpsman showed up just when it was about to turn into a fistfight and took him away. I'm glad that's over. The squad leaders were about to beat the piss out of him themselves for not following orders and having to play games because of him. The squad leaders are turning into straight pit bulls. It's getting to the point where you never just deal with one if there is an issue. They go from motivating to wolf pack in a snap. Good junk.

The MCMAP Endurance Course. That's where you have stations all along the track. You punch targets, then elbow targets, then knee targets, then kick targets, then do buddy carries, then do push-ups, then you do buddy drags, then you do bear crawls, and then you do sprints. And between every station, you do a 1/3 mile run. So it's work/ run/ work/ run/ work etc.

It was no joke. We were dead after that. It was GREAT! While we were finishing up our last run, a recruit from another Platoon fell out and there it was. The safety Officer did exactly what we heard he would do. He rolled him over, whipped down his trousers, and shoved the thermometer right up his backside. The recruit didn't even flinch. He was OUT! The Drill Instructors huddled around him to make sure if he needed to be rushed to medical they would get him there. Once the recruit came around, they got him to his feet with a canteen of water and the threats from the Drill Instructors started reigning in.

OH you're getting dropped bitch! Say Aye Sir!

You're out of this platoon you nasty, no running, no heart, garbage, piece of shit mu-fucker! Say aye sir!

See that? You can't even die right you stupid shit! The doc had to wake you back the fuck up! Say aye sir!

It was crazy! To top it off, McKool and Kimble got into a fight on the track. The Drill Instructors let it go for a bit and when they were slowing down, they broke them up. Nothing happened to them. They were just told to get back into formation. It was an exciting break. Great way to end the workout.

After PT, we had a leadership class with the Senior Drill Instructor from a deck below ours. Wow! That Marine is HUGE! He reminds me of the Michilin Man. He's also a great Senior. Our Senior was really bad at giving leadership classes. He would typically close the book back up after looking at what the topic was and then just talk to us about bangin' female Drill Instructors. It was usually a huge waste of time. However, this Senior actually taught us a lot of stuff. He taught us how leadership works in the Marine Corps and what to expect when we get out. He also talked about land warfare: such as who to shoot. When it's ok to shoot someone and when it's not. He was a fantastic motivator when it came to leadership classes.

Once leadership class was done, we headed out for some more motivated drill. I've had about enough of drill. March, march, march, ...march, march, and march. And then, march some more. Luckily, nothing lasts forever in Boot Camp. There comes a point when you have to go to the next event in the day. Thank goodness. The only good thing sometimes is the stuff the Drill Instructors say while you're out there marching. Like I had mentioned, our Heavy Hat was known for choice phrases that made him our Heavy Hat. In Drill, his top 3 phrases were-

Garbage as Hell- Ask anyone from Platoon 3014. This was used to describe an action that was less than satisfactory. It's important to drag out the "Gar" part of garbage too for effect. So it's actually heard as, "Gaaaaaarbage as Hell! We heard this a lot.

Get it Back- This was said whenever we had to do something again. Start position, execution, "GET IT BACK!" repeat. This applied to marching and rifle manual.

So you wanna play games?- This is something that told us life was about to suck! If we were asked this question, it was already too late. It meant our Heavy Hat was already fed up and pain was now inevitable.

The last thing I was thinking that night was that I was going to have to look out for Boyd. He was a good guy. He just let things get to him too easily. He got flustered and frustrated at the flip of a switch. At least if I kept an eye on him, he might know that he wasn't alone and things would get better. It seems that if the entire Platoon hates your guts but someone in authority likes you, you can care less about everyone else and keep pushing forward. It may seem odd, but that's the truth.

20071130 Friday
Staff Sergeant Assassin is born!

Field day in the house was important today because tomorrow we have the Senior Drill Instructor's Inspection. That's when some Brass comes through and checks to see if the recruits are taking care of business. It's our very first Inspection. We wanted to make it happen for our Senior. After a heavy field day session, we headed out for the Confidence Course. Last time, we just got a demonstration. Now it was show time. We were put into 4 man teams and then got cracking. I was proud of my team. We finished first and got to watch everyone else.

Interestingly enough, our Scribe (Abbett) wigged out on the A-Frame obstacle and outright refused to do it once he got to the top. He was afraid of heights. Everyone has their weakness. Heights was his. When he climbed back down the way he came, our Heavy Hat told him he was getting washed back to Kilo Company. That sucks! Getting sent back would mean he would add 3-4 more weeks in training because he's scared of heights. A new Scribe was immediately appointed and he didn't hear the end of it from the Drill Instructors for the rest of the day. I truly felt bad for him. That sucks man!

Things are getting better though. The Platoon is really coming together and everyone actually listens when myself and the squad leaders are passing word. That's really important in a world of alpha males. Everybody in the Marine Corps wants to either be the boss or a complete individual. Neither of which is possible. You may be the boss, but there is always a bigger boss above you. An individual in the Marine Corps?
No such thing. In Boot Camp, everyone does the same thing, the same way, all the time.

I thought about a lot of stuff today. That's a first because typically, your mind is pretty occupied. But I remember how much I couldn't wait to have Mountain Dew. I have been living on water, milk, and Red PowerAde long enough. That's all we've had up to this very day. We once had Blue PowerAde, but our Heavy Hat ended that. He said we didn't rate 3rd Battalion Blue PowerAde. (We wouldn't be able to drink that until the week we Graduated) Our Heavy Hat would personally jack with you if you tried. That would be way worse than getting quarterdecked for dessert. Don't mess with 3rd Battalion Blue PowerAde. It's not worth it.

It's tough with Boggs in the Platoon because on one hand, he's a good friend of mine, but on the other hand, I have to keep him in line and out of trouble. That can be tricky sometimes. It's easy to take things personal when it's really just business.

For the past 2 weeks, my right heel and ankle has been killing me. It all started when we were doing rolls in MCMAP. I came down one time too hard on my heel and it has been sore ever since. Compound that with marching everyday and the way we have to drive our heels, and I got a bit of a problem. My solution- wear 2 socks instead of one. I thought the socks we have are a bit thicker and so maybe the extra cushion will do the trick. I was right. After a couple days, the extra cushion worked like a charm. My heel is almost back to normal! It sucks to be injured in Boot Camp because you can't tell anyone and you really can't manage how well or fast it will heal. You just have to pray it'll heal up even though you're going to continue pounding on it.

Tonight was a special night. We had an event called the recruit wrap. That's where we were marched into the civilian part of the Island to this department store (Like a JC Penney). We were instructed to purchase a couple gifts for our families. The minimum you had to get was a card. If you bought anything big, you immediately took it across the street and had it shipped right then and there. Any cards could be sent later at your own discretion. That was a trip.

On our way there, we were marching along and all of the sudden we crossed this invisible boundary that is no longer Boot Camp world. There are normal cars and civilians everywhere. However, the rules still applied to us. We were not allowed to talk to anyone except the cashier and it better be "Yes ma'am" or "no ma'am". Nothing else could be said. No "thank you very much" or "I appreciate it" was aloud. We were being watched through a scope and our Kill Hat was looking for any reason to smoke one of us. The Brass were the only ones allowed inside the department store. I made the mistake of saying "Thanks, I appreciate it" to the cashier lady and the Captain happened to be right behind me watching me and when he heard that he ripped into me. This recruit should have known better than to say "thank you" and "I". Oh well.

We were given a time limit of 45 minutes and had to be back outside ready to go. Sweet! It was awesome. I bought 2 Christmas cards for my parents. I got one funny card and one serious card. I figured I would write stuff in them on Sunday and so that was it for me. When we were all done, we formed back up, crossed the invisible line back into Boot Camp world, and went home.

Before we hit the rack, our Senior told us that Abbett was going to keep his job as the Scribe and not be sent back to Kilo Company. That was just a game the Drill Instructors were playing with us. As it turns out, the Drill Instructors have a say in who stays and who doesn't and apparently, the Scribe will live to see another day with Platoon 3014. Good to go. He's a good guy and I would miss him if he wasn't here.

I told you that our Heavy Hat had some unique phrases that made him who he is. Well, so does our Knowledge Hat. Here are a couple of his-

Bitch! Have you lost your fuckin mind?!- This is what was said to any recruit that did something wrong/ stupid. Moving in formation, not answering loud enough, saying the wrong thing, or doing something wrong in practical application training. Anytime you jacked something up, that's what you would hear.

No Volume!- This was said ALL throughout Boot Camp. We were NEVER loud enough. Even though we smoked every other Platoon in volume, we were never loud enough for our Knowledge Hat.

Staff Sergeant Assassin- This is what he wanted us to call him because of how he smoked recruits, other Platoons in knowledge battles, or during combat training. It was actually fun. We greeted him by saying-

Good Morning Sir! This recruit requests permission to speak to Drill Instructor Staff Sergeant Assassin!
This always put a smile on his face. Especially when we did it in front of other Drill Instructors.

You shut your face!... Now open your face!- This was said when we talked when we weren't supposed to or asked a dumb question. He followed that up with the next line because you didn't say, **"Aye Sir"** loud enough. Open your face means No volume! Say it again!... LOUDER!

I'm gonna kill you!- This was said any time you did something stupid and he couldn't quarterdeck you on the spot. You were going to get it bad later. And he never forgot. If he said you were going to die, he would write that junk down on his little pad and you could count on it. Sometime he wouldn't write it down. He would just walk up and down the line, look you in the eye, and if you owed him, he'd remember and say- *"You owe me."*

I own you!- This was a mental game he played with you to let you know there was no escape. You were going to do anything and everything he said.

Oooo you fuckin little bitch you!- This was my favorite. He would point his first finger and thumb at you in such a way that he would cock his wrist back so they were the same length. It was like he was squishing a grape. He would say that when you had made him so mad that he couldn't say anything else. He would say it through clenched teeth and put his finger an inch from your eyeball. I smile to this day when I think about it.

20071201 Saturday
Senior Drill Instructor's Inspection

Big surprise this morning. They closed down the 3rd Battalion chow hall for renovation. So we had to hike all over to find another chow hall. There was some miscommunication as to which one was available between the 1st Battalion and 2nd Battalion chow halls and the only way to find out was to hike over and see. We finally got in to the 2nd Battalion chow hall and had to eat fast. We were doing a 5-mile hike this morning so even though we had to eat fast, our Drill Instructors made sure we got enough. Believe it or not, as crazy as they can be, they made sure we were prepared. You can't hike if you don't have fuel. Does that mean you can take your sweet time? Negative. Their job is to get you to the chow hall. Your job is to show your appreciation by shoveling as fast as possible.

After chow, we stepped off for the hike. We kicked knowledge the whole way. Yeehaw! Let me tell you one thing. I can take the quarterdeck, and not eating enough, and not sleeping enough, and playing stupid games. I can take that no problem. The one thing I hate is being on a 3rd Battalion hike and having to make a head call. You can't just stop and go. You're on a friggin hike. You're stuck! And every step you take makes you have to go more and more. It's a helpless feeling. I was just about to break formation and run for the tree line when our Senior announced the halfway point. This is where we can make head calls. OH MY GOSH! When we were asked who had to make a head call, my hand fired up to go. I was the first in line, and I didn't mind double timing to the head. Good to go! If we hadn't of stopped then, I was just going to have to get quarterdecked for breaking formation. But luckily I was saved for today. When we got back to the house, we had to hustle to get ready for the Senior Drill Instructor's Inspection. It seemed odd because as important as our Senior made it sound, we didn't do a whole lot to make sure everything was perfect. We cleaned up everything really well but we didn't practice the grill session at all.

The grill session works like this- Supposedly, other Drill Instructors are supposed to come on deck, we stand at parade rest, they step in front of us, we snap to attention, perform Inspection Arms, hand our Rifle off, introduce ourselves with the proper greeting of the day and identify where we live, they ask us questions, we answer the questions, they hand our Rifle back, and they move on. That's it. We didn't practice that at all. But it's ok because our Senior said it wasn't going to be that big of a deal. We had the answers so it'll be a cakewalk. Finally the time had come. We were standing on line in parade rest and perfectly motionless. We were ready.

Our Heavy Hat walked to the hatch and opened it. 6 Drill Instructors marched on deck in perfect step. And they didn't march nice and easy, they stepped with a purpose. As soon as they crossed the office door to the Drill Instructor's office hatch everything went nuts. Someone was turning the lights off and on like a strobe light. The Drill Instructors split up along the line and started in on the recruits. I was the Guide, so I was one of the first to get hammered. A Drill Instructor stepped in front of me, I snapped to attention, performed Inspection Arms, handed my Rifle off, introduced myself, and gave him the proper greeting of the day-

Good Morning Sir! Recruit Killian, Annapolis Maryland!

Fuckin Maryland huh? I guess this Platoon's got no fuckin volume! I guess you don't give a fuck about your fuckin Senior Drill Instructor do ya you piece of fuckin recruit shit!

Yes Sir! (It's Yes Sir, No Sir, or Aye Sir unless they want you to explain something. It's a good thing cause I didn't know what to say to that.)

By the way, that was the worst fuckin Inspection Arms I've ever seen. At least you found a way to get all the fuckin steps in. What's the serial number on this Rifle?

Sir! This recruit's Rifle serial number is 10242754 Sir!

What's your 2nd General Order?

Sir! This recruit's 2nd General Order is to walk my post in a military manner, keeping always on the alert, and observe everything that takes place within sight and hearing Sir!

What's your Senior Drill Instructor's name?
Sir! This recruit's Senior Drill Instructor's name is Senior Drill Instructor Staff Sergeant B Sir!

At this point he gave the Rifle back to me and told me that the crack on my Order Arms sucked. I said- *"Aye Sir!* This was a huge mistake because you NEVER speak during a movement with a Rifle. He said-

Oh! So I guess we open our fuckin face during Order Arms! I guess your fuckin Senior Drill Instructor didn't teach you shit. You fuckin fail! Get on the fuckin quarterdeck bitch. You're gonna fuckin die!!

I put my Rifle away and formed up on the quarterdeck along with everyone else that failed. (Which was just about everyone by this point.) My Heavy Hat asked me what I failed for and I told him it was because I spoke during Order Arms. Just as fast as the Drill Instructors came on deck, they marched right back off in formation. The pit bulls had left the building. The lights stopped blinking. The chaos had ended. Everyone was on the quarterdeck. Our Senior stepped in front of us and said-

Fuckin recruits! I go way out of my way every fuckin day to help you bitches out and this is how you repay me. I guess you just don't care. I told you everything you had to do. I showed you everything you had to do. But you all want to fuck me. Well, fuck you too!

He turned to our Kill Hat and instructed him to get us out to the pit. Once we were there, it was on. When we got out there, there was another Platoon already playing games. I guess they failed too because they were getting the same deal. So there were now two Platoons in the pit. About 5 minutes later, another Platoon came out. No big deal. 2 Platoons played in the pit and the other just ran around until they wanted to rotate. Soon, every platoon was out to pay. It appeared that we weren't the only platoon to fail. Every platoon had failed.

Finally, we were the only ones left still working in the pit. Our Senior would talk to us and tell us how pissed off he was and then put us back to work. Then he would stop us, tell us some more and then work us again. All the while, the other 3 Drill Instructors were swarming us making sure we were putting out and telling the Senior if we weren't. It was crazy. The work wasn't that bad but not knowing when it would all end was making it go on and on. But just like everything in Boot Camp, it finally came to an end.

I believe it was a set up. We were set up to fail. Looking back, we were not prepared for what was going to happen and I believe that was done on purpose. Failing so terribly and then having to pay for it made us harder because we were pissed off. We hated the fact that we were playing games because we messed up on the inspection. In a weird way, it made us care more about being perfect. If we had passed, it wouldn't have been anything but another day. But since we failed and got killed for it, it made us work much harder. That's Boot Camp for you. It's all a trick or a test. There's a lesson and a reason in everything.

We popped sticks with the Heavy Hat and since we were all still pissed off, we smashed it. He saw the aggression and intensity in our faces and knew we were mad. We fed off it and it was a great Rifle session. He was happy. That's rare. And by happy, I don't mean smiling. When he's happy, he won't make recruits play with the Kill Hat if they make a mistake. He'll just yell at you and that will be that. When he's pissed off at us, you play a lot of games for little mistakes.

When we went to chow, I got an extra fudge cake for being the Guide. I didn't even ask for it. The lady just put it on my tray. Sweet. I'll take whatever you give me. I stacked one on the other so it just looked like 1 piece of cake. If I had separated them and you could see I had two, I would have been screwed. But tonight, I was screwed anyway so it didn't matter. Recruit Comano was caught talking in the chow hall by our Heavy Hat and it was over. We got up right then and there, stacked trays, formed up outside, and ran back to the house. Great! We crunched the house 4 times. That sucks! It's where you move every rack to the back of the squad bay under a given time limit. Then you put everything back in its place. That means every time you crunch the house, all the footlockers come off the floor, all the sea bags come off the floor, shoe displays come up, and all the racks are crunched. Then, you gotta put everything back perfectly. Good times. Oh well.

Today started easy and ended hard. However, today was the last official training day of Phase I. We made it. We lost about 9 recruits but the ones left were holding on for dear life. We were going to make it. Monday starts Phase II. Bring it!

20071202 Sunday
The choice is ours.

Early morning wake up as always. But hey, it's Sunday! What does that mean- Super Breakfast chow! This morning, it was scrambled eggs, Cheerios, 2 pancakes, hash browns, banana nut cake, blueberry yogurt, PB+J sandwich, and a glass of Red PowerAde. It was awesome! I LOVE SUNDAY MORNING CHOW! You starve during the week... but then Sunday comes. Ahhh Sunday.

When we got to church, I was able to write to Mr. Palmer, Amelia, my Dad, and the school before church started. You can't write during the actual church service so knocking this out was fantastic. I found out the hard way that you can't write after lights out at night. I tried that the other night and my Kill Hat caught me and took the letter I had been writing and threw it away. Grrr!

Today, I started to notice that my platoon wasn't looking anything like the new recruits that had just started 1st Phase. We were relaxed and smiling while they were looking horrified. I know exactly how they feel. I would always go over and talk to them as much as I could and let them know everything would turn out great and to just hang in. I really wish someone would have done that for me when I was a 1st Phase recruit but no one did. So this was my chance to help out a bit.

When we got back from church, we headed out to the "O" Course to work on climbing the ropes.

There were still a few recruits that just couldn't get up there. Some try to climb the rope with brute strength, but that's not it. The magic is in the technique. If you use the correct technique, you can go up and down that rope as many times as you want and it will never gas you out. Since I was the Guide, our Senior didn't mind me staying by the ropes and helping out some of the struggling recruits. My buddy Conrad was having a hard time. We worked on the technique for a bit and then BAM he had it. No problem. Unfortunately for Stahling, he didn't get it. Our Senior was PISSED. Not because he couldn't do it, but because he just wasn't trying. Stahling was the type of recruit that tried to get through Boot Camp on the bare minimum. He was garbage and just didn't care. So while we went to the grinder to march, he went back to the house with our Senior and our Senior had a special heart to heart kill session with Stahling. When we got back to the house, he was screaming for his life. We smiled.

After the ropes session, we changed over and got ready to leave again. This time it was our Heavy Hat's turn to take us to drill on the grinder. But it was bad news for us. The sand fleas were coming with a vengeance and everyone kept losing bearing by swatting at them. Yes, they suck to deal with, but it's not actually that bad once you get used to them. They land on you, bite you, then fly away and the pain eventually goes away. You learn to deal with that and by the time Final Drill rolls around, you can march straight through a storm of them without losing any bearing. You just have to get used to it. However, today we lost the battle and our Heavy Hat just gave up on us. He marched us back to the house and told us-

You bitches suck! We'll be performing this shit in a few days and you bitches are worried about fuckin bugs. See what happens to you if you lose your fuckin bearing on Drill day! See what happens! I'm done with you. Go do whatever you want!

Well this is no good. Anytime he says- *"go do what you want"* it's so that he can call the Senior and ask permission to really jack us up. He'll tell the Senior what he has planned, why he's doing it, and then he comes back out and it's on! I knew we were in trouble so instead of doing what he said to do, I split everyone into working parties and we cleaned the house. After that, we split into new groups and half of the recruits studied for the upcoming test and the others did PT. Since we have a pull-up bar in the squad bay, we hit that pretty hard. We did that for a while and then switched groups so that everyone got to study and PT. it was good to go. Our Heavy Hat saw what we were doing and it seemed to take the fire out of him. We wanted to work. We didn't want to just sit around and wait for him to kill us. So we stayed busy being productive and he let it go.

At the end of the day, two incredible pieces of knowledge were tattooed into my memory. These two things stood with me all through Boot Camp and I repeated them over and over to myself when things got crazy. They are-

1- **This too shall pass**. That's actually from the Bible. It reminds me that whenever things are really bad, it's ok because it will pass eventually. It may seem like it's the end of the world and you have nowhere else to go, but you know what? It'll pass and soon it'll be just a memory.

2 **Nothing lasts forever**. This goes along with the above but it's a little bit different. On one hand, nothing lasts forever in the sense of being on the quarterdeck or playing games. It won't last forever. It'll end at some

point. On the other hand, I'm reminding myself to enjoy the moment because it won't last forever. Not everything in Boot Camp sucks. Some things in Boot Camp are simply awesome and you get to do things you'll never get to do again. So stop complaining and remember the good times. This trip won't last forever.

Parris Island runs by the clock. It runs by the strictest of most severely disciplined schedules. It occurred to me that this "Who Cares" time wasn't a punishment or a case where our Heavy Hat gave up on us and didn't want to do anything with us. It was 2 hours of actual free time because we made it to Phase 2. There was actually supposed to be a PT session that went along with it, but since we PT'd on our own, that box was checked. So it was actually a great move that we stayed motivated.

That night, recruit Graham came up and asked me why I hated him. He asked why I was always yelling at him and blowing up on him for talking in line but not at anyone else around him. I told him I didn't hate him at all. Then he asked me why in the world I was always going off on him. I told him that I was pissed off because he's got the most potential out of any recruit here and he's blowing it. He's smart, physically talented, and picks stuff up really quick. Yet, all he does is talk in line and get in trouble with the idiots that truly don't care. Those recruits are worthless. I told him he could be great. And I told him he's way better than how he sees himself. This actually surprised him. But from that point on, I never had to get onto him again. He squared himself away and became a heavy hitter in the Platoon.

PHASE II

*If **size** truly mattered, **Elephants** would be **King** of the Jungle.*
-Rickson Gracie

20071203 Monday
Food for thought.

This morning, we took the bus to chow. Since our chow hall was closed down, we are always going here or there for chow. If we go to the Weapons Chow Hall, it's on a bus. That means we pile in while being counted down. My job is to stand at the door of the bus. I get the count of all recruits on the bus and report (If it's not right I get smoked.) Another Platoon has to fit on so we crunch 80+ recruits on 1 bus. We put our heads down and everyone is silent the entire way. We get to the chow hall and fly off the bus and straight into our formation to go into the chow hall. We did that a lot. Crunching on the bus was nuts, but we had a diddy for that! It goes-

*1,2,3 **CRUNCH!!!** 1,2,3 **CRUNCH!!!***

Yeah, it was tight! There was a common joke among us that was-
How many recruits can fit on a Parris island Bus? Answer- One more.
When we got back to the house, Boggs and Kimble got into a fight in the head. Kimble's a little hot head and started it so we let them go a little bit before we broke it up. When I reported to my Kill Hat there was a fight, he told me to smoke Kimble. What? Sure enough, he told me to put Kimble on the quarterdeck. Good to go. It's a VERY rare thing for a recruit to quarterdeck another recruit. Usually that duty is reserved to no one but a Drill Instructor. For just a moment, I felt the rush of putting pain in someone's body without regard to their well-being.
However, the actual lesson learned was about being a "Billet Holder". A learned that a Billet is a Job or Duty you have to perform. When you are on duty, it may warrant the responsibilities of a higher rank than you actually are. And even though the responsibilities are above your pay grade, you still have to perform them to the required standard. Just make sure you know the consequences for that rank because you are ultimately responsible for the success or failure of your job.
When we went to the RTF for classes, we got a few memorable quotes from President Bush. I thought they were great so I had to write

them down so I wouldn't forget.

"Hand the terrorists over, or share in their fate." That's the best ultimatum I've ever heard. It's simple. Hand over the bad guys that are responsible, or we'll kill you too. That's good to go.

"The Marine Corps represents a worldwide threat to the enemies of America." We are a threat to the enemies of America. If you are an enemy to America, we're going to kill you.

It doesn't matter where in the world you are. If you're a bad guy, we'll find you. But what about Osama? We haven't found him. That may be true. But until we do, he knows we're coming after him and that will ensure that he will never have a peaceful night's sleep. He'll ALWAYS be running. We'll never stop. We will be relentless until we find him. Someday, America will have its justice. Marines will ensure it.

That night, our Senior and Heavy Hat got us online just before mail. They looked like they were working out a game plan but we couldn't hear what they were saying and didn't dare look over. We stood their just waiting for the unknown. Our Senior left and our Heavy came over and asked-

Ears! **OPEN SIR!!!**
Ok, raise your hand if you can't fuckin swim. (5 hands went up)
What the fuck. Really? Those recruits with your hand in the air take one step forward. (The 5 step forward) Tomorrow is fuckin swim qual. We're gonna form up in the morning and step to the pool. You're gonna get some instruction and then you're gonna fuckin swim in your cammies, you're gonna fuckin jump off the high deck and swim to the side, and then you're gonna swim with a pack and some gear. It's easy, but if you fuck up you're gonna get dropped. Who thinks they'll have a problem with that? (3 more raised their hands)
No fuckin shit. All of you recruits come up to the quarterdeck. Everyone else turn to hygiene. Guide and squad leaders, you got 'em. **AYE SIR!**

He informed those recruits they would be referred to as "Iron Ducks". They were going to leave early to the pool to get some extra help first, help the Platoon get through training with moving gear here and there, get some more practice, and then they would be tested afterwards. As hard as everything is, I have to say the Marine Corps does make an effort to stack the deck in your favor. It's up to you to get the job done.

20071204 Tuesday
Swim Day 1

Today is a big day. We were told again that this is another one of those events that if you don't pass, you get recycled. That morning, our Senior asked us who the "Iron Ducks" were. They raised their hands and were separated from the group. Our Senior asked if they got the word last night from our Heavy and the recruits confirmed it. They got their stuff together and left. After chow, we headed to the pool. We showed up outside the pool while it was still dark. 3 Platoons were present and ready to go. Before the Instructors came up, we kicked knowledge like always. It was interesting hearing another Drill Instructor kick knowledge for us. They didn't always ask the questions the same way, but we got it all together and screamed regardless of who was asking.

Finally, the Instructors came out and gave us our safety brief. They gave us the directions about going into the building and where we had to go. They didn't play around. We got in, changed over into issued swim cammies, and headed to the pre-rinse showers. We didn't wear our own cammies because the chlorine would have destroyed them. After we pre-rinsed, we walked around the edge of the pool all the way down to the staging area. The instructors came down, gave us our indoor safety brief, demonstrated what was required to pass Swim Qual 4, and got us on our way. Today, we had to climb a 10-foot tower, jump off, swim 25 meters, and tread water for 5 minutes. Let's go!
When I approached the tower, I noticed 7 chickens stamped on the side. On top of the chickens read-

THEY CLIMBED.
THEY CRIED.
THEY CLIMBED BACK DOWN.

The chicken stamps represented the number of recruits that climbed up and failed Swim Qual 4 because they refused to jump and the Instructors were keeping track. Garbage. It was fun. I walked to the edge, got the go ahead, gave my head nod, and made the jump. It's too easy.

Everyone was thinking the same exact thing before taking that first jump. How cold is the water going to be? It is Boot Camp after all and this is a huge pool. As it turns out, the water was awesome. It was actually really warm. I came up and swam my 25 meters. It's a bit more challenging swimming with cammies and boots on, but it's not that big of a deal. As soon as I got to the 25-meter mark, you swim to the side and then head back along the side of the pool. I did my hand shimmy down the side and prepared to tread water. You could tread water normally by kicking, by blowing up your blouse, or by blowing up your sleeves. I blew up my blouse because I had never done that and then finished my last minute by kicking. It was way harder treading in boots by kicking! Wow. Now I see why they blow up their blouse. It's much easier. By completing that, we successfully passed Swim Qual 4. Tomorrow we start Swim Qual 3.

I'm excited to see what they make us do next. To be honest, swimming is my greatest weakness. I can swim great in shorts, but based on what we did today, swimming with gear is way harder. After we got done, I got to march 9 recruits back to the house. That was cool. Even though there were Drill Instructors all along the way, hiding to see if we'd mess around, I had fun with my group. We looked sharp. Calling cadence was tough at first, but then you get the hang of it.

When all the groups got back, we were put on line. It turns out that there is this new thing called the VGE virus. It's nasty junk. The problem is the fact that it's an airborne virus. So if a recruit throws up 5 feet from you, you'll get it. We started noticing when recruits started throwing up after chow and it was spreading wicked fast. Out of the 3 decks in our building, 38 recruits got the virus. 15 came just from our deck. It was jacked up. Luckily, I didn't get that crap. I was really lucky.

To make matters more interesting, lunch chow was turbo style with no water. That was crazy hard. It's easy with fluid to wash it down. This time, we didn't have any water while we ate. We had to drink after we got done eating. Nobody finished the box chow. The bread and cheese was murder to swallow without water. It was like trying to eat Styrofoam and cotton. But it got better.

We went out to march and were doing really well. 3010 was also out there. My Knowledge Hat rolled us up right next to them and we had a knowledge battle. Of course, we killed them in volume. My Knowledge Hat smelled blood. After that, we marched forward, did a to the rear march, split in two, and oreo'd their Platoon. With that, we kicked knowledge and murdered them. Our Knowledge Hat was happy. As a reward, we got back to the house and our Heavy Hat had a surprise. Today we got our Desert cammies with our Last name stitched on them. The only rule was that we were not allowed to stare at our name or make it a big deal. Of course, one stupid recruit did. *"Where you at Guide?"* Yeah. I know the drill. We paid together. Grrr!

That night, I got out of the rack with my moonbeam and had a look at my cammies. Up until now, we didn't have name tapes and didn't even think anything of it. Now we have cammies with our name on them. I started to wonder if anyone in my family did the same thing I was doing. My Uncles were in the Army and so KILLIAN would have been on their uniform. My dad was in the Air Force and I saw a picture of KILLIAN on his BDU's. My Cousin was in the Navy and KILLIAN was on his uniform. Now, KILLIAN has made its way to the USMC. The KILLIAN name has been in every branch of service. I felt mighty proud to be a part of it.

KILLIAN never looked so good.

20071205 Wednesday
Swim Qual Day 2

It's back to the pool for these recruits. Yesterday was pretty fun so we'll see what we get to do today. We did our arrival routine and headed to the staging area. The Instructors showed us what we were doing today. Good to go. We walked in line to the start in the shallow end and got ready to go.

The first step was to jump in the shallow end and wade 25 meters in cammies with a Rifle, Kevlar, pack, and boots to the other side of the pool. I jumped in and made my way to the other side. No problem. Then we were to turn around, sling our Rifle another way, and wade to the other side. Again, this was a cakewalk. After that, we had to paddle/ float to the other side of the pool with all our gear. It's actually easier than you might think. There seems to be air pockets in the pack so by design it actually floats pretty well. Then you do this whole knuckle to knuckle over the buckle swim stroke to propel you forward and you're good. Just make sure you keep your head back and your eyes on the ceiling. Once you put your chin down, you'll rock forward and sink. It's cool. Once that is complete, you have to repeat that stroke over twice the distance and it's in the deep end so you can't put your feet down if you screw up. That's when a lot of recruits wigged out. They would put their chin down to see how much further it was, start to sink, and it was over. The Instructors had no time for it. They would jerk you up out of that water quick, fast, and in a hurry.

The truth is, you are only required to pass Swim Qual 4. There's always some idiot in the Platoon that says you have to pass a certain swim qual level for your MOS. That's horse crap. If you need a higher swim qual, you'll get that at your MOS school. Just get through swim qual 4 and do your best on everything else. Everything else is like a gift to try and pass. If you don't, screw it, you're gone. Better luck tomorrow.

The last part of Qual 3 was to jump off the 5 foot deck, unstrap one side of your pack, and do a side stroke 25 meters to the ladder. I climbed up, jumped off, did my knuckle to knuckle over the buckle swim to the side, unstrapped my pack, started my side stroke, and it was over for me. I got something wrong and my feet sank below my body. When that happens, you can't recover. I sank. I got the whole enjoy the ride to the side treatment and had Instructors screaming at me for screwing it up. This was the first time I had unsuccessfully negotiated a challenge. I would get another try tomorrow, but I would have to chalk it up as a learning experience for today. Later, I found my problem was that I put my pack on the wrong hip. A lot of recruits failed the same way so we were ready for tomorrow.

We left and I called cadence again and this time it was a lot better. Everyone looked sharp and so the Drill Instructors didn't mess with us. We had another 2-hour Drill session on the grinder. We're starting to get the column left and right down a lot better. In Drill, that is one of the most penalized movements for a Platoon. It will make or break your score. If one recruit misses a single step, recovery is next to impossible. The Platoon will either bunch up or spread way out. It'll be a garbage fest in full effect. However, today was our day. As a reward, our Heavy Hat took us back to the house and let us watch Final Drill footage from previous Platoons. It was amazing. We got to see the final product of all the hard work we were putting in. It looked great and we all wanted to be like that. From that point on, Drill sessions got a lot better now that we saw what we were trying to achieve.

Boot Camp is like a rollercoaster. Up and down, up and down. We'd been up all day. Right after that, Davidson wanted to move slow getting on line. When the Drill Instructors tried to hurry him up and he didn't pick it up. I knew where this was going. *"Where you at Guide?"*

I guess it's time to play on the quarterdeck because friggin Davidson didn't want to open his face and move fast. How hard is it? Just scream at the Drill Instructor and they'll leave you alone. Oh well. At least that night I finished all my box chow. You take a win wherever you can get it.

20071206 Thursday
Swim Qual Day 3

Box chow again. It's not the way I like to start the day, but whatever. At least our Heavy Hat let us finish it all before taking off for PT. Today we did Diablo's Triangle. It was the same thing as the other day when we rotated MCMAP review, pull-ups, and the "O" Course. But today, it was wicked hard. It was like the Drill Instructors wanted to make it as hard as possible. In MCMAP, when you perform an uppercut you drop your body down a bit and then shoot up. When we dropped our body a bit, we held it until our legs started to shake.

We had 20 minutes in each group so you could do that move a lot and hold it for a looong time. When we did the pull-ups, no one got to wait around in line. As soon as you were done, you went over and did push-ups until our Knowledge Hat and Kill Hat wanted to let you go. Some of the recruits did A LOT of push-ups. After that, our Senior made us "Watch TV" for what seemed like forever. Watching TV is this Pilates looking move where you hold your body up using only your forearm and side of your foot. It's nothing more than a side plank. Bell is the strongest guy in our Platoon and when he's shaking, you know it's friggin hard. After that, we did the "O" Course for the entire 20 minutes. Our Drill Instructors made sure we were constantly moving through the obstacles. There was no waiting in line when you got done. It was crazy hard but I liked it. I'd rather do that then watch TV or basic MCMAP any day.

Finally, we headed to the pool. It was time to go toe to toe again with this challenge. We had to do all the earlier stuff again before we could get to the 5-foot ledge. When I got to that, I remembered what I did wrong and this time I killed it. I had no problem what so ever. My technique was all wrong last time. This time, I relaxed, concentrated on the steps, put the pack on the correct hip and not under, and it was a done deal. Score!

Swim Qual 3 was in the bag. Swim Qual 2 should be fun... maybe. I guess I'll have to find out next time. You could only pass one Qual level at a time. I was really happy I got through Qual 3. I really didn't want to have a challenge that got the best of me during Boot Camp.

When we got back, we popped sticks with our Senior. It was awesome because he brought out the CD player and we listened to one of my favorite bands of all time- **RAGE AGAINST THE MACHINE**. Awwyeah! We listened to the Battle of Los Angeles CD and everyone was into it. It was a little taste of the real world.

It's funny how by doing something that might not make sense works out in the end. We got this recruit named Bryan. He's a good guy. But he talks ALL the time. He's always got something to say. The main problem is that he opens his mouth when it's not the right time. He was a squad leader and a pretty good one at that. He was squared away. Unfortunately, he got canned from that position early in the cycle. After that, he just didn't care anymore. He put so much effort into doing the right thing that when he got fired for something petty, he just didn't see the point anymore. I saw this in him. I know he's a good guy. He just got kicked in the balls really hard. So when we got the Series Guidon, I appointed him to take charge of it and march up front with me. Everyone was pissed off because he had been getting in so much trouble for doing dumb stuff and I was giving him the rag. But it didn't matter. I did it anyway. And sure enough, it put some fire in him and he squared himself away. He stopped doing dumb stuff all together and worked on helping the team. No one said anything after that. Platoon 3014 was coming together.

20071207 Friday
Game Day

Eurika moment! I had finally found out the 3 laws of finishing chow. I had played around with a lot of stuff and now, I got it. It was a given that I had 6 minutes to eat and there was no way around that. So here was my final game plan-

1- Use a spoon for ALL food. Never use a fork.
2- Drink a little fluid with every single bite. No matter what, it'll help to get it down no matter what you are eating. Plus, if the food is unexpectedly hot, it will instantly cool it down.
3- Choose only the food that doesn't require chewing or at least very very little. For example, if you get a salad, never get lettuce. It requires too much chewing. However, the olives, little chunks of ham, bacon bits, and shredded eggs can be downed without a problem especially if you glob some dressing on it. It works great.

From that point on, I didn't have a problem stuffing myself on limited time. Well, today was our last day at the pool. We did the requirements of Swim Qual 2 and hardly anyone passed it. It was nuts. It required swimming with a flak jacket on along with a few other things thrown in. My buddy McGill made it. I was so impressed. That guy is a beast in the water. I think if we had more time working on it we would eventually make it, but not today. Swimming is done. Thanks for the fun.

After that, we came back to the house to get ready for our MCMAP Tan Belt test. We had to know all 44 techniques in and out. My Kill Hat let me demonstrate in review and that was cool. It's rare to be able to work within 1 foot of any Drill Instructor let alone a Kill Hat.

Normally, they don't let you get that close. After the review, we left for the MCMAP pits and it was on. The 3 Platoons were split up and we got tested. It wasn't too hard at all. It was just like at my school. They tell you what they want to see, they show you what they want to see, and all you have to do is execute it right the first time. No big deal. And you have to show it right otherwise you fail.

To be honest, you have to be a total idiot to screw up this test. Everyone in 3014 the first time.

When we got back, we went out with our Heavy Hat and drilled. That was bad. We pissed him off because some recruits were getting lazy and so we came back to the house and he smoked the Platoon. Zanis lied about something and I thought our Heavy Hat was going to rip his throat out. Instead, he put pain in his body. Tuller was up there with him. Tuller got in trouble for being a girl about being smoked and so Zanis and Tuller got slayed. They ran the highway Indy500 style far beyond collapse. Zanis took it pretty well. However, Tuller was screaming for his life and begging for mercy. The Drill Instructors were pouring water on them and making them fall over, get back up, and then kept them running nonstop. I bet they won't forget that day. I thought Tuller was going to die. But he didn't. He made it through.

The rest of us had to hold out our Rifle for 20 minutes. I know because the Senior has a little digital clock just inside his window and since I was over there, I could keep an under the radar eye on it. And I'll tell you, after 20 minutes, that joker gets heavy pretty quick.

It sucks but I learned something. When someone screws up, I know I'm going to pay. I've come to terms with that. The person that screwed up is weak. Knowing that they are paying for being stupid actually gave me strength to make it through the games. It's not personal to me because it wasn't my fault. It's extra training for the weak ones and it will only make the strong stronger. Machines were beginning to immerge. The squad leaders were becoming animals because we were always on the quarterdeck with other recruits. The Drill Instructors were having to keep us up longer and longer to get the same smoked effect out of us. We started to realize this and it was energizing. Stupid recruits were taking us to a whole new level.

Speaking of people being stupid, I almost killed the Scribe today. Everyone was yelling about the Guidon because no one is allowed to touch it except for the Guide, the Senior, and the Heavy Hat. This is the part they didn't know. The Heavy Hat can do whatever he likes with it because he is in charge of all of our Drill. When the Heavy Hat grabbed it, the recruits that didn't know that went crazy. I told them to shut their holes and told them the deal. Everyone but the Scribe shut up. I told him to shut his face. He got pissed off and gave me attitude. I walked up to him to tell him the deal so he would understand the rules of the Guidon. He tried to shrug me off and give me attitude. I told him to chill out because I just wanted to explain the deal. I wasn't mad at him. He just needed to understand why I told him to shut his face.

He threatened me for getting in his way. I forget what he said but it pissed me right off. I grabbed him by his collar, threw him between the racks, and started choking the piss out of him. Everyone jumped in and pulled me off of him. I told him that he had no reason for giving me attitude. I told him the next time he said that to me, he better pray there's someone around because I'd choke him out and then beat the piss out of his unconscious body. To be honest, I didn't mean it. I liked the Scribe. He meant well. But a Guide that's crazy enough to choke someone out for being stupid works wonders in Boot Camp. Ever since that moment, he always listened to me and we were good to go.

20071208 Saturday
14 and Quarantine

Early morning PT. I must say though that it was a great morning for PT. The sun was up but it was cool out. Our PT session consisted of a 2.5 mile run. Awesome. We took off and I felt really good. It's a lot harder to run on our track than a normal track. Like I mentioned, ours is loose sand. It takes a bit more leg power to get you around it. The track is a mile long and sense we're doing 2.5, we got to break off onto a woods trail to get to the halfway point. There is no greater feeling then being in the top 5 and coming back and your Platoon seeing who's in front.

I got a lot of motivation from my Platoon. They were saying **"Way to go Guide!"** and **"Go get 'em Guide!"** It's a great feeling. I passed my Kill Hat and that was even better. I know he was pacing himself to motivate recruits, but knowing I was pushing myself faster than his pace was an accomplishment in my world. He always ran at a pace I couldn't catch. Over the weeks, it went from not seeing him at all on a run, to seeing him way ahead finishing, to being a 100 yards behind him, and now I passed him. And it's not just me. We are all getting faster. Before I knew it, it was over. I finished 2.5 miles in 14:57. I came 4th out of the Battalion, and 1st out of 3014. That was a great day for me.

When we got back to the house, we had a huge problem. 13 more recruits got the VGE virus out of 3rd Battalion. That means that we were going to be put on 48-hour quarantine for the weekend. Grrr! That sucks bad!

What does that mean?

No hot chow: only box chow.

Marching in the squad bay.

Popping sticks in the squad bay.

Everything in the squad bay.

No going to regular church on Sunday.

No Sunday morning super breakfast! Ahhh!

This sucks. I'm not even sick. 48-hour lockdown. On the other hand, at least we wouldn't be taken to the sand box. Oh well. So even though it wasn't what we were used to, it worked out great. It really hit home with me that you just don't get what you want and you gotta roll with the punches when it doesn't. Just when you get used to something, Parris Island finds a way to shuffle the deck. Improvise, adapt, and overcome.

That's no joke.

20071209 Sunday
Think Fast!

It's Sunday and we're still locked down. A part of me was praying we would wake up and the Drill Instructors would inform us that everything was good and we could carry on as normal. That didn't happen. We weren't allowed to leave the squadbay. We weren't even allowed to go to regular church service. We were instructed to go across the grinder to the 3rd Battalion building and we would have church service in there. The hits just keep coming. HOWEVER- Church service was led by Captain Myhand and he was awesome. We hadn't had him as a preacher but he was really good.

Eureka moment #2. In Boot Camp, you're going to hit the rack the vast majority of the nights hungry. Until you figure out how to shovel chow, you'll be hungry all the time. Hunger pains suck. My solution- All you have to do is take a shot of Scope when it's time to hygiene. You're issued a bottle of Scope. Put a quarter inch in the bottom and down it. It'll make you nauseous at first, but then after that you're good to go. No more hunger pains.

The problem with box chow is I crush the whole box and I'm still hungry. We are burning a sick amount of calories and so fueling up in the morning is paramount. That's one of the biggest reasons I love Sunday morning super chow. However, for some reason, no one wanted their eggs. They all passed them to me and I must have gotten 7 bags of eggs. That's 14 extra eggs that I didn't even ask for. They just passed them to me without saying a word. I even got an extra box of raisins on top of that. Man, I love 3014. They know how to hook a Guide up. I was good to go. I was so pissed off because I couldn't get chow hall chow, but God works in mysterious ways. I was totally full that morning!

Here's another rule in Boot Camp. If you're going to break the law, do it with a friend. That way, no one can squeal. If you get caught, at least you share the quarterdeck with someone. One thing you will find out right away is that Drill Instructors scalp the box chows ALL the time. The box chows are left downstairs for the recruits to come and get so Drill Instructors can walk by and grab eggs, or raisins, or cookies whenever they like. I cannot count the times I got a full box chow. Something was always missing. One time, I just got a sandwich. Everything else was gone. Grrr! I tried to show Staff Sergeant Assassin and he replied-

Looks like your bitch ass is on a diet. Get the fuck away from me!

Get used to not getting everything in a box chow. Getting back to my point, I learned from the Drill Instructors. The recruits never finish a whole box chow anyway, so when myself and a squad leader take the trash out, we always scalped raisins or cookies from the used box chows and ate it turbo speed while we were throwing the garbage in the dumpster. Just make sure you do it with your buddy. If you eat something and your buddy doesn't, it's bad news. He can rat you out. In that case you'll have to pass on the free chow. But for the vast majority of the time, he'll always jump in with you so it's good to go. Did I mention not to get caught in the process? Well, don't get caught. They still haven't found the recruit that was caught scalping in the 2nd Battalion dumpster. Who knows?

Get used to things running hot and cold. Just when you think everything is great, something always happens. We were popping sticks in the squad bay and our Heavy Hat was happy with us. So, he played some new songs on the radio that had just come out. It was great. Popping sticks and listening to music is something you cherish. Right after that, a recruit kept screwing up. Our Heavy Hat turned off the radio, and we then crunched the house a few times.

Just when we were having a good time, someone has to screw it up. Crunching the house sucks! At least we're getting better at it. It only took us two times tonight to get it in the time given.

My firewatch plan had worked. I was one of the first recruits to have the entire Rifle Creed memorized. Every other night I had firewatch. During that time, I worked on the Rifle Creed. It was a done deal. Firewatch is AWESOME for memorizing stuff!

That night, my buddy Larson told me a funny joke. Now you must understand that Boot Camp is no place to be telling jokes. 3 weeks ago, telling jokes would have been the very last thing on our minds. But Boot Camp was getting better. This is what he told me-

A guy walks into a bar. He goes up to the 3rd floor VIP section. He looks around and sees a VIP have a drink, jump out the window, and moments later come back through the front door completely unharmed. The guy walks up and asks what he had. The VIP responds "The Special." The guy asks why he doesn't die. The VIP responds by saying- "It's because of the combination between the drink making you lighter and the terrific updraft outside the window." The guy immediately turns to the bartender and demands The Special. The bartender asks, "Are you sure?" The guy replies, "Yes." He then drinks The Special, jumps out the window, and falls to his death. The bartender

turns to the VIP and says- "You know Superman? You're a dick when you drink!"
I love that joke.

20071210 Monday
KNOWLEDGE TEST/ GAS CHAMBER/ TOWER

Today's a huge day. It starts with going to the RTF and taking our first Knowledge Test. You would think making a bad grade would be depressing. That's civilian world thinking. Who cares about depressing? If we make a bad grade, we get to play with Staff Sergeant Assassin and our Kill Hat on the quarterdeck. He vowed that he would make sure we were out of the Platoon if we failed. So, that's our motivation. To be honest, it was actually pretty tough. We had the knowledge, but the way it was worded made it difficult. Luckily, he told us before we went in to NOT over think the question. He said-

It's fuckin easy. Just read the fuckin question, and whichever answer jumps out at you, that's the shit you choose. It's fuckin easy!

It worked out great. No one got killed. It was funny though because whatever Platoon has the highest average on that specific day gets to be known as the Knowledge Platoon. If you have a diddy-disabled recruit in the Platoon, he magically goes to medical that morning and retests on a later date so it doesn't affect the Platoon's average on Test day. I don't know how, but Jons slipped through the cracks and made it to the RTF. Instead of going to medical, Jons took the test with us. Staff Sergeant Assassin didn't know that until the very end because our Kill Hat marched us to the RTF ahead of Staff Sergeant assassin and Drill Instructors aren't allowed in the RTF once testing begins. When I got done, I went outside and joined everyone in formation. After a bit, he told me to go back in and see who's left. When I got back out, he said-

Hey Guide! Who is still in there taking the test?

Sir, Recruit Harmon, Betze, *and* Jons *are still testing Sir!*

Harmon, Betze, and Jons... *JONS?!! WHAT THE FUCK IS HE DOING HERE?
I SENT HIS ASS TO MEDICAL! MOTHER FUCKIN SHIT!!!*

He wasn't happy about that. When Jons came out, Staff Sergeant
Assassin grilled him-
Well? How did you do Jons?!
This recruit don't know sir.
*What the fuck you mean you don't know? How many do you think you
might have missed?!!*
Well…. this recruit got a couple sir.
How the fuck do you mean a couple?!
This recruit got a couple right sir.
MOTHERFUCKIN SHIT!!!

Oh well. After that, all 3 Platoons were loaded onto buses and we
were on our way to the Gas Chamber. That's right ladies and Gents. We
are now off to the single most feared and talked about event in Boot
Camp.

Upon arrival, we headed inside and had our class. We learned all
about the M240 Gas Mask and most importantly, how to put that joker
on in under 9 seconds. As soon as the Instructor says- *"GAS GAS GAS!"*
you have 9 seconds to don and clear your mask and then signal to
everyone else gas is present. It's tough at first, but then you get the
hang of the straps. After that, we headed outside.

All 3 Platoons formed up outside the actual gas chamber. It's
nothing but a 25-foot by 25-foot brick building covered in camouflage
paint. We were put in sticks of 20 and stood by ready to wait our turn. I
was in the 3rd stick. Everyone's heard the horror stories. Now it's time
to see what's up. The first group went in and all was quiet at first. The
Drill Instructors could look through a window on the side and they were
pretty much giving the play by play. They would announce what was
going on, who was freaking out, who was trying to run out, and who
was turning into a volcano. The fun part about the Gas is that it sucks
every particle of mucous out of your body in a hurry. So, if you have
been congested for the past few days or weeks, that junks coming out

NOW. It kills Benadryl. Finally, the first stick came out. Recruits were hacking, crying, and coughing like crazy. One recruit had mucous forcing its way out of the sides of the mask (Volcano). It was ugly. However, I didn't see anyone dead so that was good.

While the next group went in, we started to get the bonus features in this training. There is always a little bit of Gas on the straps of the mask. We all have bald heads. Those straps were tight to create the right seal so they dig into your head. While they are digging in, the gas is irritating the piss out of your head. It's garbage. Everyone knows in Boot Camp that you don't move unless you're told to. So you can't touch your head or reposition your mask so the straps can bite into a different part of your head. Zanis moved and so our Heavy Hat came and took the filter valve out of his mask. That means that he won't be able to breathe clean air. He'll have to stomach the gas. Zanis was horrified. He thought he was going to die. I've never seen anyone so scared.

Eventually, it was our turn. We filed in just as we were instructed and put our backs to the walls. You can't help but think about what it must have been like in Concentration Camps. 100% of everyone who goes through the gas chamber has that thought cross their mind. It's a horrible feeling. It's the elephant in the room that everyone has enough respect to not discuss or compare but the thought is all consuming. I can't even imagine. I'm thankful this was NOTHING like that. With that in mind, I was determined to come out without making it a big deal just like some of the others had been able to do. After the door closed, we did our jumping jacks to get our breathing and heart rate up. We did our head shakes to make sure we still had a good seal. And then we received our final review of instructions. The chef started making the magic and we could see the room start to fill up. Just remember- Close your eyes, break the seal, breath normal, listen for the instructions, secure the seal, clear the mask correctly, and return to breathing normal. Sounds easy. To be honest, it wasn't bad at all. We closed our eyes, we broke the seal, the Drill Instructors waited for everyone who was holding their breathe to run out and eventually breath in the fumes, we received the instruction to secure the mask, clear it, and return to breathing normal. It was easy to panic because it was new to our lungs but you just have to stay calm. We only had one recruit wig out. Gibson was doing great but he started to freak out when his mask wasn't clearing. He ran for the door and got clothes lined by a Chamber Instructor. He started to fight him off, but then the other 3 jumped on him, threw him to the deck, and they made him work the mask properly so he could see that he could regain control. Sure enough, it worked out fine and he got the hang of it. Once he was calm, they actually helped to pick him back up, brushed him off, and put him back against the wall without saying another word.

Our stick came out and we all looked a lot better than the other groups. Just make sure that you remember the eye trick. Once you take the mask off, DO NOT wipe your eyes. That'll grind that stuff right into your skin. Instead, let the tears dry from the air and then once the gas has crystallized on your face, you can then wipe it off no problem. It takes about 15 minutes. I wish I would have known that trick then. By the way, my Heavy Hat just played a trick on Zanis. That piece he got off his mask was nothing special to his breathing function. He was just messing with his head. It worked!

After everyone was done, we changed over into a fresh set of cammies and headed over to The Tower. The repel tower was awesome! The tower is 50 or 60 feet high and it has 4 different areas to come off. Two sides are standard flat walls that you fast foot down. The other two have mounted helicopter type skids that you jump off of. After we got our repelling helmet and gloves, we were set to go.

First we got to learn how to "Fast Rope". It's really cool. You just grab the rope, lock your feet and knees to it, and fly right down. Just make sure you get out of the way because right when your feet hit the deck, you can best believe the next recruit is already on his way down. After that, we learned how to make a repelling harness out of a single piece of rope. Holy Crap! The harness sucks. You have to make sure it's tight. Once you've made sure it's tight, the Rope Instructors make sure it's extra tight. If you talk when you're not supposed to, the Rope Instructors will make sure the next 3 generations of your kids will feel it. It's no joke. You'll want to secure your mouth during this evolution of training!

Once we were all ready, we headed to the top. The Guides got to go first because after that we were tasked with getting recruits in the line they needed to be in and clicking a button every time a recruit went down. When it was my turn, I headed straight for the skid. I've repelled before, but this was something else. You had to jump out from the skid, let some line go, and as you swung back in, you prayed that you would swing under the skid and be able to continue on down from there. It was great! I did everything just as I was instructed and flew down the tower. Good times!

When I headed back to the top, it occurred to me. What happens if you don't let enough rope go when you jump out from the skid? Answer- As a few recruits found out, they swung right back in and smashed their face into the skid. It was ugly. My Heavy Hat could see it coming and as soon as they hit the skid he would yell- *"YEAHHHH!"* That was his notorious line for whenever a recruit was getting jacked up. It didn't happen too many times but if you did hit the skid, you got to try it again once you got to the bottom. The tower Instructors made sure that everyone went. There is no time for any recruits being scared of heights by now. As long as they have the line secured so you won't fall, they'll kick you right off the tower. Or at least make you think they will.

When we got back to the house, we went out for our last practice for Initial Drill. We did really well. We could tell that our Heavy Hat was pleased with us. He took us to weapons Battalion parade deck, which is one of the most sand flea infested decks on Parris Island. He marched us right into a huge swarm of them and we just stood there at the position of attention. They were ALL over us. They were crawling on our face, on our necks, going down our cammie tops and bottoms, up our noses, and in our ears. We couldn't move. It didn't really bother anyone to have bugs on us, but they were biting the piss out of us everywhere they went. Your natural response to being bit is to swat at it and hope to kill it. That was out of the question. No one was allowed to move. You just had to stand there and let it be. Our Heavy Hat kept saying-

Let 'em eat. It don't fuckin matter.

And this time, we didn't move. No one swatted at anything. We were just frozen at attention and dead set on the task at hand. We did our job and no one moved a muscle. We were learning. The sand fleas were all over us eating away at our skin. Hundreds of thousands of them everywhere. Then we started to march. You would thank that we would march ourselves right out of the swarm but they kept with us as we marched. They were on our face, down our shirts, up our arms. They were biting us everywhere. We kept marching, slamming heels, entirely focused.

Our Heavy Hat smiled.

20071211 TUESDAY
INITIAL DRILL

Today is Initial Drill. It's our chance to go out on the grinder and show the big dogs what we've learned so far. Lights came as always but this time there wasn't such a sense of urgency like always from the Drill Instructors. We got online without the normal screaming fits that start our day. We got our stuff together and stepped to chow. The whole way, we were discussing our game plan for Initial Drill. Our Heavy Hat was going over everything step by step to make sure we all knew what came next on the Drill Card. We had to have the order memorized that way after something was called, we were already thinking about what was coming next. Once in the Chow Hall, we got extra time to eat. Awesome! We weren't in and out like usual. When we got done eating and formed back up outside, we didn't have to double time back to the house. Had I woken up on a different Island? This didn't seem like the place I was used to.

When we got back to the house, our Heavy Hat put on some Rage Against the Machine and Godsmack as we kicked through the Drill Card a few times. This time it was relaxed. No consequences and repercussions for making a mistake. It was more like a-

Hey idiot, make sure you don't fuck it up!

And that was it. After we practiced, we put on our "Drill Cammies", gave each other a once over, and got ready to go. We stepped out to the waiting area and started getting it from the other Platoon's Drill Instructor. He was telling us that we didn't have a prayer no matter how great our Heavy Hat was. Our Heavy Hat stayed cool. He told us that the more the others say; the more scared they were of us winning. Our Heavy Hat was behind us. We agreed and stayed focused on the task at hand.

We fell into Drill Formation and got the party started. Our Inspection Arms was incredible. One crack, one bolt, one click-pop. It was fantastic. That's the move that will make you or break you. We kicked it in the face! After the rifle manual, it was time to march. We started our rounds and even though it was our Knowledge Hat who was calling cadence, we did great. Why our Heavy Hat was not permitted to call cadence was beyond me. But no matter. We were more than happy to step for Staff Sergeant Assassin. When we were done, we simply fell out and headed back to the house to await the results. After about an hour and a half of cleaning and organizing gear, the results were in. our Senior came in and got us all on the quarterdeck. He wrote the scores on the board and told us we got second. Just when we thought this would turn into a slaughter-fest, he told us that he was proud of us and that he didn't believe we deserved second. (Big sigh of relief) As a reward, he busted out some oatmeal cookies and gave us one. This was unheard of. Sweets in the house? Whatever. I'll take it. We were proud of ourselves.

After that, we went out to the grinder and started our new material. Our Senior was making this our statement that coming in 2nd simply means learning new stuff relaxed and enjoying it instead of lecture time or getting smoked in the house like all the other Platoons. The new material incorporated popping sticks and marching at the same time. It was really cool. To let us know the Rifle Manual commands were coming, our Senior used a cadence call from Full Metal Jacket. It was actually fun because we all recognized it immediately and our Senior had fun doing it.

The only thing left on the schedule was going to the "House of Knowledge" and learning about personal grooming standards for the USMC. I have to say that today was an "easy day." It had a bit of stress in it because we didn't want to let our Heavy Hat down, but for the most part, it was actually a great day. It was absolutely nothing like normal days. For that reason, we tried to enjoy it as much as we possibly could by not trying to screw it up.

20071212 WEDNESDAY
CLOTHING ISSUE

After early morning chow, we marched down to clothing issue. Today was the day that we were going to get sized up for our uniforms. We got a lot of stuff-

Greens- Charlie Blouse (long sleeve and short sleeve), Alpha Blouse, Alpha Trousers (2), Alpha Belt, Piss Cover, Wooly Pully, All Weather Coat (We look like Inspector Gadget), Black Leather Gloves, Green Barracks Cover, Shirt Stays, Edge Dressing, and Dress Socks and Shoes.

Blues- This was the magic. Blues Coat, Blues Trousers, White Belt with Brass Buckle, White Gloves, and a White Barracks Cover.

Staff Sergeant Assassin said-
Even Jons could get some pussy wearin this shit.

We had this guy in clothing that would size you up and square you away. There were of course other tailors there but I had the same guy for all my rounds. I was glad too because the other tailors were dickheads. They were trying to act like wanna be Drill Instructors. That just doesn't fly. There is no way we'll snap and pop for a garbage civilian being disrespectful. We were assuredly respectful and courteous because our Drill Instructors were keeping their eyes on us, but we weren't going to be jumping through any hoops for dickhead tailors.

My tailor was this big huge Black Guy that had been on the Island forever. He loved his job. I think he just loved being able to help new recruits. We nicknamed him Jabba because he reminded us a lot of Jabba the Hut. When we were waiting in line for Jabba to have a final look at us, one recruit slipped up and forgot to say "Yes Sir". Jabba isn't the type to yell and scream or put a Drill Instructor on you. He'll just make his eyes real big, lower his voice so it cuts right into you, speak just a tad slower so you can feel every word he says, and he'll set you straight. Jabba said-

Look here son. You always gotta say Yes... Sir.
The world... needs it.
The world needs young, strong, disciplined men to show them what's still right... and good.
You have to stand up and be that man. You feel me?

That's all he had to say. No yelling. No screaming. No 3-hour lecture. He wasn't a dick or condescending. He just dropped the bottom line. We simply have to show the world what's STILL right and good. How much simpler does it get? Jabba was great. He's been there at Parris Island for some 35-40 years and has seen all kinds of recruits stand in front of him. I felt fortunate to cross paths with him.

Staff Sergeant Assassin smoked the Platoon that night. We had had two easy days and we were getting a bit too relaxed and he had enough of that. He wanted to make sure we didn't lose our edge. It all started by us not sounding off the way he expected. When he heard what we were trying to get away with, he put us on line and we knew it was coming. We did the hatch run A LOT!-

Run to the front hatch! **(Aye SIR!)** Run to the back hatch! **(Aye SIR!)** Scream Louder! **(Aye SIR!)** No Volume! **(Aye SIR!)** No Volume! **(Aye**

SIR!) Run to the front hatch! **(Aye SIR!)** You bitches are gonna die! **(Aye SIR!)** Louder! **(Aye SIR!)** No Volume! **(Aye SIR!)** Run to the back hatch! **(Aye SIR!)** Run to the front hatch! **(Aye SIR!)** Run to the back hatch! **(Aye SIR!)** Run to the front hatch! **(Aye SIR!)** Run to the back hatch! **(Aye SIR!)** Louder! **(Aye SIR!)** Scream Louder! **(Aye SIR!)** No Volume! **(Aye SIR!)** Louder! **(Aye SIR!)** Scream Louder! **(Aye SIR!)** No Volume! **(Aye SIR!)** Run to the front hatch! **(Aye SIR!)** Run to the back hatch! **(Aye SIR!)** Run to the front hatch! **(Aye SIR!)** Run to the back hatch! **(Aye SIR!)**

It went on for a long time. We just kept running and running. He always gave us a time limit that we just couldn't make. Most of us did but there were always those few recruits that just couldn't get there. It wouldn't have mattered even if they did make it. Staff Sergeant Assassin would have just come up with another reason we deserved to spend the night running. When all was said and done, we were exhausted, pissed off, and miserable, just like we needed to be in Boot Camp.
For some reason, it felt better that way.

20071213 THURSDAY
TRIAL PFT

Woke up to Lights, Lights, Lights, and we were online. As for myself and the squad leaders, Staff Sergeant Assassin wasn't done with us. He wanted to reinforce the lesson learned the night before. While everyone else was getting dressed and field daying the house, we were getting smoked on the quarterdeck. Push Ups, Crunches, V-Ups, Arm Circles, over and over and over. On your face, on your feet, on your face, on your feet, Arm Circles, Crunches, on and on until we heard ...*ZERO!*

A Drill Instructor will yell *STOP!* However *"ZERO"* comes from the Senior. All you do is freeze and scream, **"Freeze Recruit Freeze!"** If you're not loud enough, he'll say *"Carry ON!"* and you're DEAD because the Drill Instructor knows the Senior could have saved you and he didn't. However, if you're loud enough, he'll ask you the next 50/50 question-

Why are you on my quarterdeck?

Whatever the reason, you have to explain yourself. If you deserve to be there, then it's *"Carry ON!"* and you're DEAD. Once the Drill Instructors know the Senior isn't going to save you, it gets bad in a hurry.

In this case-

Sir! These Recruits don't know Sir!

Salvation came in two words- *Go Away!* With that, you better RUN away as fast as you can because if you don't, he'll pull you right back and you'll be stuck on the quarterdeck for who knows how long. Once we were back on line, we grabbed our gear and we were out. Today, we're kicking a trial PFT to see how we do.

The PFT stands for Physical Fitness Test. You have to pass it in order to get off the Island. Requirements are-

- 3-mile run- <26 minutes. (Best is 18 minutes)
- Pull-Ups- >3. (Max is 20)
- Sit-Ups- >40 in 2 minutes. (Max is 100)

You're scored on each event and then the total score will give you a 1st, 2nd, or 3rd Class PFT. You want that 1st Class PFT. A perfect score is a 300. 1st class starts at anything at or over 225. Since it's a big deal, today we are running a trial PFT to see how much work we need in order to snatch that 1st Class PFT score when it counts.

We started with the 3-mile run. The course was set and we were off. Drill Instructors are required to run at a certain pace, which will allow you to try to stick to one that has a time you want to shoot for. Since I'm shooting for 18 minutes, I stuck with the 6 minute Drill Instructor. We were good for the first 2/3 of the run but then he started to pull away. The next Drill Instructor behind me was finishing in 19 minutes. As long as I stayed in front of him, I would still improve my score. He passed me just at the end of the run and I finished with a time of 19:15, which was still a tremendous improvement from my last run. A 19:15 run gives me 92 points so far. Not too bad of a start.

Next came the Pull-Ups. I stepped up to the bar and knocked out

13. Once your form goes to crap you're done. The Drill Instructors simply won't count any more. 13 Pull-Ups gave me 65 more points. That gives me a total of 157. Pull-ups is where you make your money. My Pull-Ups are garbage. That's definitely something I have to work on.

Time to do some Sit-Ups. We got in place and I was still feeling strong. This is a first. Usually by now I'm smoked. Let's see what happens. We got the go and I fired into my tempo. I didn't even think about the numbers. I just wanted to do as many as I could until they said stop. All the sudden I started to feel gassed.

When I started paying attention, my partner was on 106! Awesome! My final number was 111. Even though 100 is the max, there's no way you're allowed to stop so you just have to keep on going. A max Sit-Up gives me 100 more points. That puts me at a 257! A 1st Class is a 225 or more so I was good to go. This was a big day in the world of Recruit Killian.

When we were done with that, we went back to the house, cleaned up, and then headed out again. By the sounds of it, it looked like we were going to get smoked for the recruits that didn't pass. But truth be told, today was the day we were allowed to order our USMC Graduation Rings and take our Individual Photo. It was cool. A nice young lady came out and showed us all the options and we got to pick what we liked. Then it was time to take our picture. You get to take it in a mock Blues Top and a white Barracks cover. The Blues top simply covers you in the front from neck to chest. There is nothing else to it. The Barracks covers are all lined up by size. You tell the recruit your size and he gives you what you need. It was a pretty sweet system.

The Drill Instructors allowed the Guides to move everyone through the system and that was new. Normally, they are controlling every step you take. This time, they left us alone and only came in if absolutely needed. There were 2 other Platoons in the room so we all had to work together to get everyone through.

It was cool rubbing elbows with the other Guides, Squad leaders, and recruits. Things have really calmed down. Before, I noticed some of the Guides being dicks to their Platoon. They had either gotten fired and replaced by a new one or adjusted their attitude. I noticed a lot of similarities in how we kept the order and discipline with the recruits and squad leaders. Some of the other squad leaders would respond in the same respectful manner to me when I asked them to do something and I'm not even their Guide. If a recruit from another Platoon was disrespectful to me, his Guide would get all up in his koolade and I in turn did the same if one of mine got our of line. It was teamwork at its best.

When we got back to the house, our Senior put on some music and we got to work out with him. He did everything right along with us so it wasn't like some sort of smoke session. He took us through a workout that Marines do when they can't go outside. It mainly consisted of Pull-Ups (since we have a pull up bar in our squad bay) Sit-Ups, and Push-Ups. It was relaxed but definitely a hard workout. As a bonus, our Senior had a CD of one of his Marine buddies that produced a hip-hop CD. All the lyrics are about being in the Corps. It was actually really good. Not a bad day in my book.

20071214 FRIDAY
My BBQ Day

The morning started with a bang. The head closes 15 minutes before lights come on. Everyone knows this. I heard a couple recruits arguing. The firewatch was telling Kimble he couldn't go into the head. I told the firewatch to go back to his post and turned to deal with Kimble. I started after him and started telling him he had to go back to his rack. He tried to ignore me as he continued on to the head so I pushed him to get his attention. He whirled around and pushed me back. With that, I punched him in the mouth. It got his attention and he turned and went back to his rack without saying another word.

After chow, we had to get shots. Notice that's plural. You never get one shot at Parris Island. You always get 4-5 at a time. It was my job to stand at a desk and record recruits from 3 Platoons off a checklist and tell them where to go. When the lines were almost done, I got introduced to a "Code Red". I was asked by one of the medical staff if that was the last person and when I said yes, he nodded and said I was last. As I checked off the last name, 4 needles went into me at the same time. The corpsmen snuck up on me and each took a place to shoot the needle. 4 needles at once. I became the pincushion kid. I was stunned. I tried to holler but couldn't. And just like that, they smiled and told me to take off. I didn't know what to say... thanks? So I just smiled and rolled out. Good times.

We headed out to the grinder to continue on with yesterday's lesson. We're really picking it up fast. We just have to remember that "port arms" comes really fast right after "right shoulder arms" and we have to stay awake and sharp. Our Senior is patient with us right now and he's letting little things go. That will only last for so long. Then he'll know we've had enough time to get the mistakes out of our system and everything else will just turn into a smoke-fest.

When we formed up for Chow at Weapon's Battalion, I made one of the biggest mistakes **EVER**. As the Guide, you are responsible for paying attention to the lines inside the chow hall so you know when to bring the Platoon in. Since we form up and wait outside until it's ready, I'm constantly poking my head inside the door, keeping the Platoon quiet and studying knowledge, and talking to the lady that gives us the go ahead. The lady had just asked me if we were ready- I said- Yes Ma'am. Then Staff Sergeant Assassin asked if we were ready- I whipped around to face him and said Yes Ma'am.
AHHHHHHHHH!!!!!!

I just told my Knowledge Hat **YES MA'AM!** I immediately corrected myself but the damage had been done. The whole Platoon went- **OOOOOOOOOOOOO!** Thanks a lot guys! Staff Sergeant Assassin looked at me and said those magic words real cool-

Ma'am? So I'm a fuckin bitch? OOO you fuckin little bitch you. You're gonna die when we get back to the house.

Great! I didn't know what to do. Go easy on chow so I don't throw it back up, or eat as much as I can because it'll be my last meal. Whatever. I'll eat as much as I can. I'm going to get smoked. What else is new? All throughout chow, Staff Sergeant Assassin was over my shoulder reminding me how I was going to get it. Luckily for me, the more he threatened me, the less I cared. It's going to happen no matter what he says to me. There's no use thinking anything more about it.

When we got back to the house, Staff Sergeant Assassin held me back from going in the house and took me to the pit. Here we go-

SAND PIT!

SIR! Purpose of the sand pit is keyword PEP!
P- Pull off blouse.
E- Empty pockets.
P- Push recruit!

PUSH RECRUIT? WHAT THE FUCK IS THAT? THE DIDDY IS PUSH BITCH! SAY PUSH BITCH!

SIR! This recruit doesn't swear Sir!

WHAT? YOU'LL SAY WHATEVER THE FUCK I TELL YOU TO SAY. WHAT'S THE FUCKIN DIDDY FOR DISCIPLINE?

SIR! Discipline is instant and willing obedience to all orders and instructions SIR!

WELL HOW BOUT THAT SHIT! IF I TELL YOU TO SAY "BITCH" THEN YOU BETTER SAY BITCH THEN RIGHT?

SIR negative SIR!

WHY THE FUCK NOT?

SIR! Moral courage is defined as doing what is morally right in the face of adversity SIR!

As soon as I said that, he got right up in my face and stared at me. I just kept staring dead ahead so I didn't accidently make eye contact. This was the moment of truth. After what seemed like an eternity, he told me to empty my pockets and get in his pit. That was that. I did everything as fast as I could and as loud as I could. He could tell that I was going to work to make up for my mistake. It went on for about 10 minutes and then he cleared me out of the pit. I'm glad too because I was smoked. My whole body was shaking from exhaustion. But, and this is a big but, I made it. I did everything he asked of me and didn't show any signs of slowing down.

We were getting stronger and getting smoked started to take more time because we could go a lot longer than at first. Staff Sergeant Assassin made his point for me to watch what I say and that was that. When I got back on deck, it turns out that I wasn't the only one screwing up. The Platoon had gotten in trouble for moving slow. My Kill Hat screamed at me to hurry up and pick up my footlocker. Ahh, the almighty pick it up and put it down game. Great. Well, it sucks. That footlocker is packed with your crap and it doesn't get any lighter unless a Drill Instructor empties it for you. We picked it up and put it back down A LOT. Everybody's arms and legs were shaking. By the end of it, a few more recruits threw in the towel and we were down to 53 recruits in our Platoon.

Later that night, we found out Jons failed the knowledge test. Staff Sergeant Assassin was passing out mail and he remembered. He walked up to Jons and started lightly tapping the sides of his face with the mail.

You stupid fuckin bitch. How you gonna fail the shit?

(No answer from Jons. Just a glazed stare)

Well?!

This recruit don't know sir.

We went over the shit. I gave you the fuckin answers and told you to memorize the shit. Then, when you see the shit on the test, you fuckin answer the shit with the fuckin answer that pops the fuck out at you on the test. Right?

Yes sir!

Then how could you fail the shit?

This recruit don't know sir.

Stupid fuckin bitch! You're hopeless. Where you at Guide?

20071215 SATURDAY
Staring Death in the Eye!

We woke up and got ready to jump on a bus to go to Weapons Battalion Chow Hall. I was considerably irritable from the previous day and this day wasn't looking any better. We formed up outside with 3 other Platoons. Our Platoon was making too much noise and so our Kill Hat just made us run in big circles around the sand pit until it was time to get going. We must've run for a good 10 minutes. However, it was really cold out so it kept us warm. When we got the go ahead to load the buses, we formed up behind another platoon in a single line. I was watching everyone in my Platoon to make sure they didn't do anything stupid.

All of the sudden, I looked up and noticed that either the Guide or one of the Squad Leaders from the Platoon in front of us was yelling and screaming at the recruits in the front of my line.
Oh it's on now! I was pissed.

Yell at your own Platoon all you want but stay away from 3014! I flew up, got nose to nose right in his face, and started screaming at the top of my lungs-

GET AWAY FROM MY PLATOON!!! GET AWAY FROM MY PLATOON!!! GET AWAY FROM MY PLATOON!!!

He froze all together and started easing back away while I was in his face and when I stopped, I got a bad feeling. He looked at me real careful and he realized I was a recruit. When he saw that, he blew up on me. As it turns out, he was a Drill Instructor that just graduated Drill Instructor school and was here to help out a Platoon in order to get himself ready for his first full cycle. Yup. I just screamed at a Drill Instructor!
I'm gonna die!
After his initial tirade of telling me over and over –
You're gonna fuckin die you fuckin recruit

Drill Instructor Staff Sergeant H heard the commotion and came over to see what was up. At this point I was still locked out, eyes forward, and saying "Aye Sir!" when I was supposed to. The new Drill Instructor told Staff Sergeant H what the deal was and why he was going off on me. Real cool and calm, Staff Sergeant H looked over at me and said-

Is that right Guide? You yelling shit at this Drill Instructor?

Sir, this recruit thought he was another recruit Sir!

In boot Camp, NEVER ever under any circumstances answer a question with YES or NO when you are in trouble or trying to defend yourself. Always give a brief explanation of what you did or failed to do. Otherwise, the Drill Instructors will screw with you to no end. For example- If I said NO in this case, he would say-

So he's a liar and made it all up. Very well. You're gonna die now.

If I said YES, he would say-

Very well, you're gonna die now!

However Staff Sergeant H looked at him and understood why. The new Drill Instructor was wearing an 8-point cover instead of a Drill cover, no Green Belt, and he was wearing a glow strap. That sealed the deal right there. He shook his head and said-

Very well, get on the bus Guide.

With that, he turned and walked away. However, the new Drill Instructor said that he was going to tell my Senior and that I was still going to die. Great. I didn't feel like eating chow but I forced myself to anyway. I knew I was going to throw it all right back up when I got back to the house. But, it's better to get quarterdecked with some fuel in you than without. It was a long bus ride home. What was I going to say? I remember staring at the floor knowing what was coming as far as being quarterdecked, but I didn't know if I would get fired too. You just don't yell and scream at a Drill Instructor. As soon as I took one step through the door, I heard from the Drill Instructor's house-

Guiiiiiiiiiiiiide!

Here we go. I stepped on the footprints, banged on the hatch, and spoke my last words-

Good morning Sir, Recruit Killian reports to Senior Drill Instructor Staff Sergeant B as ordered Sir!

Get in here Guide! I just got off the phone with a Drill Instructor that said you were giving him attitude and yelling at him. What makes you think you can fuckin yell at a Drill Instructor?

Sir, this recruit didn't know he was a Drill Instructor Sir?

Oh so you're fuckin stupid, you don't know what a fuckin Drill Instructor looks like?

Sir, the Drill Instructor was wearing an 8-point cover and a glow strap. This recruit thought that he was another recruit Sir. (Notice how I didn't say yes or no.)

He said you told him to get the fuck back, get the fuck back, get the fuck back! Is that true?

Sir, this recruit told the Drill instructor to get away from his Platoon. The Drill Instructor was yelling at a 3014 recruit and this recruit wasn't going to let that go Sir.

What did he do after you said that?

Sir, the Drill Instructor froze and stepped away from the Platoon. When the Drill Instructor saw he was looking at a recruit, he went off Sir.

So he was yelling at one of my recruits and you shut him down?

Sir, this recruit meant no disrespect. This recruit was just standing up for the Senior Drill Instructors Platoon Sir.

Very well, go away.

That's it? How could that be it? What? I'm not going to die? I'm not going to get quarterdecked? Not even just a little? All this flew through my mind in a split second. The second half of that split second was me flying away before he changed his mind. I couldn't believe it. I had been killing myself worrying what was going to happen and now, nothing. Awesome.

What saved me was the fact that my Senior was extremely arrogant. He took pride in his recruits fighting in the name of 3014. Anything you did to show that 3014 was the craziest, the meanest, the most loyal to our Senior Platoon without being outright disrespectful would slip under the radar any day. If only I knew that when it was taking place!

After chow, we went on a 6-mile hike. And we were screaming all the way. We were kicking knowledge the entire time. Even though it kinda sucks, we are definitely getting a lot more volume, which is helping us stomp other Platoons in battles. So it's worth it.

We were rewarded with a 4-minute box chow for lunch. That was long enough to finish the meat from the sandwich, chips, and an egg. The killer was that we had to do it without water. Normally we take some water with the food so it goes down fast. Not this time. We were given time limits for food only and then when everyone was done, we hit the canteens. GARBAGE. It pissed us all off. My buddy Allen choked because he got a piece of cheese stuck in the back of his throat. A strong thump on his back sent it flying out of his throat and across the squad bay.

We hit the grinder for some drill and got killed by our Senior for screwing up "Stack Arms". After we got out of the pit, he sat us down and gave us a talk. He said-

Listen up recruits, I know you're getting sick of paying for someone else. But you know what? If you don't stand up and do what's right, you're the dumb shit. You gotta fight for what's right. That's what makes Marines different. It's our job to do what's right because we can. Everyone else has an excuse. Not us. We are the best. If a recruit to your right or left fucks up, it's your fault. You had a chance to make sure he did what was right and you let him go. That's how Marines work together. We look out for our own.

He then told us about one of his last Platoons. He said the recruits had enough one day and chased a Drill Instructor into the house because the Drill Instructor was going against the Senior's instructions and the recruits knew it.

That's loyalty to what's right. To look the devil in the face and look to throw down. That's loyalty.

It's on! That's all I could think from that pep talk. From that point on, myself and the Squad Leaders started getting more "hands on" with the stupid recruits. I would throw them down on their footlockers for doing something stupid and the rest of the Platoon wouldn't so much as bat an eye. Welcome to the new 3014. We had a great dinner chow and wrapped up the day. That night, we got a protein bar from our Senior. Finally. I stashed mine and saved it because I was full from chow. Pretty good day in my book.

20071216 SUNDAY
Questions= Answers

Great morning chow. When we got back, we loaded the trailer with all our gear and it was moving day. Before we stepped to church, I got a gift. This one freakin "beverly hills" recruit always pisses me off doing stupid junk. Bottom line- he's lazy. I told him to get to work, and when I walked away, he started talking about me to another recruit. With that, I walked up behind him, whirled him around, and threw him up against a wall and started screaming at him to say that junk to my face! He started wigging out and said "ok, ok, ok, I'm going." I just liked throwing him into a wall. I prayed he would swing at me but he didn't. Oh well. He deserved it.

When we stepped to church, you could tell we stepped with a sense of pride for each other. It was clear. We were becoming a family. You can't force that bond or expect it. You have to grow together through suffering. That's the strongest bond. We felt invincible together.

During church, I got to talk to a lot of newbie recruits. Instead of getting a power trip and mess with them, I took the other route and wanted to help and encourage them. They asked all kinds of questions. The questions I tried to ask but no one would explain when I was going through. For example-

Does it get easier? That's the number one question ALL recruits ask. YOU BET: But it only gets easier in the sense that you become conditioned to dealing with it. Once you adjust to life at Parris Island, it becomes something you can handle/ tolerate/ and at times, survive. It's still very hard training but that sense of hopelessness fades into sheer strength. You just have to make it to week 5. That's when you start getting used to things.

How do I get out of here? This is the second question most recruits ask. Graduation or a body bag- Don't fight it. You'll NEVER win. It's supposed to be hard. It's supposed to make you think you can't make it. It's supposed to make you want to try and escape. It's called Marine Corps Boot Camp. Suicide and injuries won't get you out of here. You'll stay forever. Adapt and overcome. You came here to be a Marine and there are people counting on you to make it. You'll make it.

I told them that working together is everything. Even if you can't stand anyone in your Platoon, put that aside and work together. Never give up. It seems cliché but in truth, you are given a choice to give up or keep going on a daily, sometimes minute by minute, basis. Nothing will get you off the quarterdeck faster than gritting your teeth and throwing down with everything you got.

What happens to the weak ones? They go away. They don't always go home. They just go away.

When we got back from church, we loaded up and moved to the new house. Weapon's Battalion. When we got there, the other Platoon was still moving out and we had about 45 minutes. We hit the grinder and marched for "fun". As soon as they were out, we went to work getting the new house set up.
Boot Camp works like this-

Phase 1- Start in your original Squad Bay.
Phase 2- Move to Weapon's Battalion for the rifle range.
Phase 3A- Move to a bigger house for A-line and BWT.
Phase 3B- Move back to the original house for the Crucible and Graduation.

There was a lot of work to do to get the house ready. Cleaning, setting up, and cleaning some more. It was busy work. I noticed a whole bunch of nickel-sized dots on the walls about waist level height. They were everywhere. It was strange. After that, we met our official Range Coach. Her name was Corporal King and she was going to teach us how to shoot. She was great. Corporal King is a short little dark green Marine.
(Like I said, there is no such thing as a black person in the Marine Corps.

You're either Tan- Caucasian, Brown- Mexican, Dark Green- Black)

She cracked jokes and had a Cheshire cat smile. Most importantly, she knew her stuff. I was totally impressed. She taught us how to make the loop sling and then told us about starting tomorrow. We were psyched.

I got to kick knowledge during afternoon chow. That was great! Typically, only Staff Sergeant Assassin leads in kicking knowledge. So it was cool that he let me lead it. While we were waiting to go into the chow hall, a 3rd Phase Platoon rolled up. We kicked a volume battle as a bet to see who would go into the chow hall first. Usually a 3rd Phase Battalion has seniority but our Knowledge Hat that was dumb. So we made a bet with them and we blew them out. Our Heavy Hat was impressed and tried to hide a satisfied smile. We were coming along.

Back at the house, a recruit gave my squad leader some attitude, and instead of saying anything, he jumped on him and threw him into his rack. My Squad Leader told him if he said another word, we were going to break him in half. He was scared. My squad leader wanted to hit him but when the recruit chilled out, he let him go. I told everyone that had run over to watch that 2nd Phase was going to be different. I said-

We're not arguing with anyone anymore. I don't care who it is. Go ahead and say something. See what happens. Please say something. I'd rather get fired from breaking some recruit then to always pay for stupidity!

The Platoon was good to go with that. Later, that recruit apologized and they worked great together all the way to Graduation. He was a good guy. My squad leader said he didn't really want to hit him and he knew it. We all have our moments.

During "free time", I led a pull up workout for the recruits still struggling. They improved. The best part was that when I got pulled away to deal with a problem, some other recruits stepped up and kept everyone going. It was great to see everyone pulling together.

20071217 MONDAY
1ST DAY OF GRASS WEEK

Out of bed and dressed before lights. Sometimes we would be woken up and told to get dressed before lights came on. We usually had 2 minutes. It was a flurry in the dark. If you're not completely dressed and the lights come on, you're on the quarterdeck.

Had a great morning chow and then we were off to PT. It was a simple circuit. You run 3 laps, which equals 2.5 miles. In between each lap, you stop off and do-

50 push-ups
60 air squats
70 crunches,

Then you go on to your next lap. I finished in the top 4 so I felt great. After that, we headed back to the house. Corporal K was our CMI (Combat Marksmanship Instructor) She talked a bit more about the loop sling, shooting fundamentals, and her retention average as far as making sure recruits can pass the Rifle Qual.

Then she talked about snapping in. That's when you practice dry firing. That's all Grass week is. You dry fire all day long.

Today we practiced in the prone. We went outside and formed up on the range. Everyone makes an L shape and snaps in on a barrel with a whole bunch of nickel-sized dots. You just pick one and practice your dry firing on it. It was cold cold cold. The ground had frost on it and we laid there for a good solid hour. When we got back up, the ground showed a whole bunch of green spots where we were laying and the rest was frost. Your arm falls asleep a lot when snapping in. Get used to it. That sling has to be tight.

The diddy for that is-

LOOP SLING
Sir, Loop Sling is, If it hurts, it works Sir!

CHRISTMAS IS NEXT TUESDAY!!!

20071218 TUESDAY
ISMT

Chow was better but man is it cold out. I don't care who you are. Parris Island has the craziest weather I have ever experienced. You would think there is an enormous dome over Parris Island and the Drill Instructors controlled the thermostat. It doesn't make sense. Anyway. It's cold.

Today, we're off to the ISMT. ISMT stands for Indoor Simulated Marksmanship Training. From the exterior, it's just another unique-less building. But the inside, well that's something else all together. It's where recruits get to play "video games". You walk into a room that's nothing more than a concrete floor, 4 mats on the ground, a huge screen about 16 feet away, and very low lighting. A computer operated by Corporal K runs everything. You shoot an m-16 a2 that is specifically modified with the look, feel, and weight of a stock m-16a2. But it doesn't shoot anything but a laser, and the magazine doesn't hold any rounds. It's just for training purposes for loading and unloading.

It took the whole morning. Boyd did really good. The Captain said he was the Forrest Gump of the Platoon. The rest of us just did ok. It was a good way to see what Corporal K needed to do with us when it came to game time.

At one point, Corporal K had to recalibrate a rifle. She sat down, shouldered the rifle, and took 10 shots. When you aim at the screen during testing, you can see the laser point on the screen. When we tested the Rifles, the point was all over the place. With Corporal K, she could keep it practically right on a dime-sized spot, and when she actually fired, she always hit the bull's eye. It was staggering. All 10 shots could easily fit inside a dime. In fact, she "key holed" 4 of the shots. That's no joke. The target was simulated to be 200 yards away. It was crazy good skill.

While I was there, a Marine asked me about my Martial Arts background. I couldn't figure it out. How did everyone know? As it turns out, he told me that the Drill Instructors constantly talk about the recruits in their Platoon and I came up a few times. He knew about stuff I had done in Boot Camp and I had never met him. Parris Island is like small town living. Everybody knows everything I guess.

After the ISMT, we headed outside for box chow with the Series Gunnery Sergeant. The Series Gunnery Sergeant was great to talk to. He put us in a circle around himself and ate right along with us. He talked to us about life outside Boot Camp, making money in the Corps, and his infamous car buying strategy. He talked to us like he was our big brother. He wanted to make sure everyone was being taken care of. Even though our Senior hated him with a passion, I thought he was great.

After chow, we finally got to fire our weapon. We carried it everywhere we went, we cleaned it every night whether we shot it or not, and we memorized every feature including nomenclature, components, serial number, and specs. We knew it in and out and now we got to FINALLY fire it.

I was put in Lane 26. My immediate line coach was Sergeant D. Awesome. Everything is really relaxed on the line. The coaches put you at ease so you can focus and the Drill Instructors aren't there messing with you. We loaded 5 magazines with 3 rounds in each. 15 rounds total.

Earplugs in? Check. Loop sling ready? Check. Rounds in magazine? Check. Target acquired? Check. Here we go.

I was in the first stick to go. We all took our place. I followed the instructions from the tower. I took my position in the prone, snapped in, loaded a magazine, did a small brass check, tapped the forward assist, and took my weapon OFF safe. Game on. This is the moment we have ALL been waiting for.

When the tower said TARGET, we were free to fire our first three rounds. I took a small relaxing breath, started to squeeze the trigger, and then BAM! The guy in the lane next to me fired. To be honest, it startled me. I was in my own little world and then realized I'm not alone. All right. Back to business. I sighted back in, squeezed the trigger, and then this time it was my shot and my recoil I felt. There's hardly any recoil from an m-16a2. A sudden jolt, a loud bang, and the smell of fresh gunpowder is what you get. The result- a testosterone rush that is simply second to none. All I could do was look back to my line, grit my teeth, and give them that 2 finger "Rock on" hand sign to signal my exhilaration. To say it was awesome fails to bare any justice to how firing that rifle feels. I'm struggling now to put those feelings into words to express to you now. It was what we were waiting for and it delivered. A buddy of mine said-

There was uninhibited sex on the range that day. We were fucking the shit out of those targets!

I had fire watch that night and for the first time since I got to Parris Island, I started thinking about the Martial Arts School. I started thinking about the drills I could bring back to share with the students. If I would be too different when I got back. If people would still like me. I had to make a conscience decision right then to make sure I came back a new and improved Matt Killian. I had to make sure I never lost my ability to smile and enjoy the little things in life. Boot Camp can make you very mean. You hate everything you don't like with a newfound intensity. I had to be careful.

When my shift was over, I laid down in my rack. 3 minutes later, the fire alarm went off. Great. Time on deck was 0207. All 3 Platoons had to run out with no jackets, no warm clothes, or anything else for that matter. Some recruits in our Platoon had managed to get their cammie bottoms and boots or sweat bottoms on before getting out. All that practice getting dressed at light speed paid off. I hadn't changed completely out of my cammies and boots so I was good to go. We formed up and huddled tight together. It was frigid outside. I took my blouse off and gave it to a recruit. I told the barefooted recruits to stand on the feet of those wearing boots so they weren't on the cold ground. Then I got everyone wearing the most clothes to be on the outside of the huddle and put the ones wearing the least in the center of the huddle. We were good. We stayed out there for an hour and 15 minutes before we got the go ahead to get back in. It was just a drill.

20071219 WEDNESDAY
Range Diddy.

Our Kill Hat woke us up. All that means is move fast and scream loud for everything. Easy. Our Senior took us to chow and taught us an AWESOME new step diddy. Let's see if I can describe this-

We march along and he says Mark time... March!
We stop forward movement and start marching in place.
Then he says in cadence to our half steps- Close it up while marking time!
Everyone brings their forearm up to cover their face while their head shoots down. The front row marches in place while the rest of the Platoon half step marches forward to close up. We started 40 inches back to chest and now it's 12 inches back to chest. While they are marching forward, we say a word or two and every time we speak, our head shoots up from being covered, we say the words, and then we shoot our heads back down. It's like Marine Corps peek a boo while shouting cadence. The words that we shout are-
Through... the pain... comes discipline.
When the formation is closed up we wait for the halt. When we halt, we stop marching, pop our heads straight forward, hands to our sides, and scream the last part of the diddy. Our Senior asked us to come up with the diddy. The squad leaders came up with **ONE SHOT, ONE KILL** from the "Sniper" movie. Original I know. But we liked it, so whatever. It seemed appropriate because we were at the rifle range. But it still needed something at the end. So I took the line from "The

Karate Kid" where the Kobra Kai Instructor says- **NO MERCY!** And that was that. It was perfect for us. The full diddy goes like this-

Close it while marking time!
THROUGH (step, step, step) **THE PAIN** (step, step, step) **COMES DISCIPLINE** (step, step, step)
Platoon...HALT!
PLATOON 3014! SENIOR DRILL INSTRUCTOR STAFF SERGEANT B!
ONE SHOT, ONE KILL, NO MERCY!

It scored huge among the other Platoons. They really liked our diddy for closing up. We did that every time we went to the chow hall. The only exception was if we were with our Kill Hat. He said-

It's fuckin stupid! Say that shit when you're with me. Go ahead. I'll see your stupid ass on my fuckin quarterdeck!

But, we liked it. When we got back to the house, our Senior left us with our Kill Hat and he played games with us. Today, it was the footlocker game. We picked up our footlockers and in 60 seconds moved them here, then over here, then over there, then back to here, *too slow!* Now back to here, *too slow!* Now over there! Now over here. It went on for a while.

Then it was the shoe game. You take your go fasters down to the end of the squad bay, then on the count of *NOW!* You threw them down the highway. Then, you run around and kick them to get them all mixed up. Then you have so many seconds to find yours and get them back under your rack. Good times. Luckily, we got a tip from another recruit and "Marked" our shoes with a sharpie. That way, they were much easier to locate. It sucks no matter what.

Then we went to the range to snap in. Today's position was kneeling. The trick is finding the position that works best for you. There is high kneeling, low kneeling, and a variation that is acceptable. You gotta try them all out to see what works. We then snapped in and a 5-minute snap in drill stretched to 10 minutes, and then found its way to 25 minutes. That's a long time to be kneeling without moving. When we were done, our Senior told us to stand up. We stood up really slow.

Then he said we had 30 seconds to horseshoe around the barrel...*GO!* Welcome to the "retard two step". Recruits were falling over, standing up, taking a step, and then falling over again. It was ugly. One leg was good to go, but the other was in a coma. We were good at first while we were kneeling. Then our foot started to burn, then it got numb, then it went away. We thought we were good. O contraire. It teaches you that circulation is muy importante. Find the position that works. Or else you fall prey to the retard two-step.

As a reward, we met back up in the shack on the range and got introduced to a Marine Corps sniper. He didn't look anything like I thought he would. I was expecting some clean cut high-speed muscle head that you see in the movies. This guy was in his own world. However, he carried a fully packed Wikipedia level of knowledge on marksmanship. He was about 6'1, thin by Marine standards, unshaven, and a fine mix of redneck hysteria. He had everyone rolling. He said great marksmanship is all about sight alignment and trigger control. That's it. If you really pound on those two elements, you'll be unstoppable.

He showed us how to squeeze slow and feel every millimeter of the pull. It all made sense. No Kentucky windage tricks. Sight alignment and trigger control. It worked GREAT!

I'll never forget that Marine Sniper. Corporal K made us memorize the definition verbatim for sight alignment. It goes like this-

Sight alignment- is when the clear tip of the front sight post is centered both vertically and horizontally through the rear sight aperture.

His definition was-
Looky here boys. You gotta fuckin align that shit by the fuckin numbers. It goes- Eyeball through the fuckin rear sight fuckin aperture, down to the fuckin post, all the way to the mud fuckin target. You gotta line that fuckin shit up perfect boys. Make sure that front sight post is clear as shit and then fire away. Slow and steady pressure on that trigger equals dead fuckers

After that, he told us some of his stories and what it takes to be a Marine Corps Sniper. One time he was in a training exercise and him

and his buddy were tasked with finding snipers that were learning concealment. They were walking around talking and he suddenly stopped and slowly turned around. His buddy asked what was up. He said-

Hey bush! Did you just move? (nothing)
Hey BUSH! I'm fuckin talkin to you. Did you just move?!
The bush stood up and said "Yes, Sergeant."
Way to fuck dat shit up Bush!!
Wow, did he have some stories.

20071220 THURSDAY
MCMAP Endurance Course V2.

After chow, we did the MCMAP Endurance course version 2. It was no joke. We had 6 stations total. The stations were PUNCHES, KICKS, ELBOWS, SWEEPS, BUDDY DRAG, and LOW CRAWL. In between each station, we ran a quarter mile. The first couple stations weren't that bad at all. But then you get to the buddy drags and your partner feels like they gained weight on you. Now, I officially know the meaning of "Broke Off." We were smoked after that. However, it was a great lesson. Anyone can do anything when they are totally fresh. However, if you can still get the job done when your smoked, that's when you know you've reached a new level.

On the Rifle Range, our Kill Hat got pissed off because he told us to run, and we told him we weren't allowed to because no one is allowed to run on the range. So he marched us to the part of the range you could run and took us for an impromptu run. We got about 4 ranges away when our Senior found out and chased us down. Wow was he pissed!

He fired into the Kill Hat and we were just frozen stiff. We didn't want that rage turned on us. As a disciplinary action, our Senior made our Kill Hat run the distance he took us 10 times and then sent him back to the house. Our Kill Hat didn't argue or show any sign of disrespect. He simply said "Aye Senor Drill Instructor" and got right to it.

When we got back, we learned how to fill out our Data Book.

277

It's what we use to record every shot we fire. We snapped in for the standing position and that's no joke. It's much harder than one would think. It feels like your front sight post is all over the place after you've been in the prone and sitting position. Speaking of, my sitting position is much more stable. Now I just have to dial in my kneeling and standing. I just want to Qualify. I could care less about anything else.

I found out today that if you UNQ (pronounced unk) you go back to the next Platoon starting at Grass Week Day 1. All I want to do is qualify. I'm ready to Graduate. I can't wait to get out of here. However, today I had some victories. My heel finally stopped hurting completely. I injured it in the MCMAP pit when we did rolls. I didn't say a word about it or let it slow me down. But it bothered the piss out of me. Finally it went away and I was back to 100%.

I can't imagine going to medical and getting washed back if my Drill Instructors found out. For the first time, I was getting smoked on the quarterdeck by Staff Sergeant Assassin and my Kill Hat and made it all the way through both sessions. Normally when they tag team you, the first breaks you off and the second hammers you deep into submission. That's a BIG deal. It was hard and not too pretty but it was the first time I made it through a back-to-back kill session without dropping a knee. Our Drill Instructors were finding that one session wouldn't break us. Now it's getting crazy!

20071221 FRIDAY
ISMT -Take 2.

Firewatch. Yeehaw! I had rover duty so I marched up and down the highway for an hour. I came up with my own cadence so if I ever have to lead a detail, I'll be able to say something with confidence. After my Firewatch was over, it was time to get everyone up. 0400 comes quick.

I got smoked by my Kill Hat. He found out about the card I got in the mail and wanted to see it. When I showed him, he started to smirk and then threw me on the quarterdeck. However, I made it through again. No knee drops. I was moving fast and screaming to the top of my lungs. Good times.

After morning chow, we headed to the ISMT. It was raining hard. While most Platoons get a bus for when it rains, 3rd Battalion marches. My Heavy Hat always says-

If it ain't rainin, we ain't trainin.

We practiced snapping in and we're getting better at finding our position right away. Before, we would get in position, then adjust, check our aim, and then adjust again. Our Kill Hat showed us how to get right to it and we were better off ever since. We would sit right down and BAM, ready to fire. Our scores went from 42's to 50's just like that.

It's funny how some recruits are always trying to tell us (Guide and Squad Leaders) how to do our job. They always say what they would do and what we should do differently. My dad always told me to listen to other people and take what I could use and drop what I couldn't. So, I listened. But after a while, it got out of hand. I finally snapped one day and addressed them all.

I told them that they had their chance to step up and get picked for the position and they didn't. If they were so good and knew how to do everything, they would be the leaders and we would be the ones following directions. But they didn't. It was up to myself and the squad leaders to work and make decisions as a team. And that's what we did. We would come up with an idea, present it to the team, and find a way to compromise or agree together. The recruits that always talked junk shut up after that. They got it.

We also got to start on the Range Flag. We have our 3014 Guidon. But when you get to the Range, you get to make up another Flag to hang right underneath the 3014 Guidon Flag. One side of the Flag is supposed to have something to do with your Drill Instructors. The other side is supposed to have something to do with the Range. Our Heavy Hat came out and addressed the Platoon. He said-

Alright. The Platoon needs a Range Flag. Where's my recruits that think they can draw?

A few of us put our hands up.

Very well. Get out a piece of paper and draw something fast so I can see what we have to work with. You got 5 minutes. When you're done, give it to the Guide. Guide; bring them to the hatch when you have 'em all. Go!

I got the sheets of paper and took them to our Heavy Hat. He took a look at them. We then got on line, and he picked the Artist Recruits and that was that. I was in the mix too so that was cool to be a part of that. As for our job, it's simple. Artist recruits work on the Range Flag during chow. The Scribe brings back chow from the chow hall and you eat it right then when they all get back. It's a sweet gig and gets you out of the scope of the Drill Instructors for 45 minutes. Just don't be the one to be stupid while they're gone because someone's ALWAYS watching. ALWAYS.

20071222 SATURDAY
Initial PFT

Chow was great. Today is Initial PFT day. It will stand to show us how far we've come and how much work we may need to do. You know the drill by now.
Max Pull-ups- Max Sit-ups- 3 mile run

I did 13 pull-ups. Not my best. But I figured out what my problem was. I was taking way too long between each Pull-Up. I should just focus on the rhythm of going up, coming straight back down, and then heading right back up. I found today that I was pausing too long at the bottom and it was taxing me. I just wish I had figured that out before today!!! I'll have to work on it. I did 100 Sit-Ups in 2 minutes. I felt great about it. You're not supposed to stop even after you've hit 100 so I made it so I took my sweet time on the last 5 so that I finished 100 on the dot with 3 seconds left. There's really no point in doing more than 100 because it's a waste of energy. For the run, I got it in 19:50. Not bad. That's a 6.5-minute mile. Not bad.

That gave me a score of 255, which gives me a First Class PFT. Good to go. When we got back to the house, our Senior was happy with our performance except for Zanis, Jons, and Richter. (Why do I put their names in here? Because they all passed the Final PFT in our Platoon with flying colors. That's a true victory for them!) While a lot of recruits failed the Initial PFT and got washed back, these recruits stepped up and made it happen.

For our efforts, we hit the grinder to learn "Column of Files". It's not that hard but someone always jacks it up. 4 recruits kept messing up. Grrr! Our Senior was pissed! He humiliated us because of it too. He rolled up the Guidon, made us unblouse our boots, wear our covers wrong, and made us walk with our heads down. He then told us he was leaving us with the Drill Instructors when we got back to the house. That's bad...very very bad. When we got back to the house, our Senior left and when we walked into the Squad Bay, we had been BOMBED! The whole house was upside down. Our Kill Hat had left the grinder with Staff Sergeant Assassin as soon as they heard the Senior was leaving us with them, and the two of them destroyed the house. Everything was everywhere.

Get your daypacks on line. Empty dat shit. Now get your LV pack on line. Empty it. Footlockers on line. Empty it. Now wagon wheel!

That means walk around and kick everything so it makes a bigger mess. We were then instructed to grab our scuz brush and scuz brush all of our stuff to the front quarterdeck. So now all of our stuff, let me say that again, **ALL of our stuff,** was on the front quarterdeck. Everything we owned. Everything! We made a huge pile and then Staff Sergeant Assassin took the Series Guidon and stuck it on top. It was Mount Sarabachi on Iwo Jima. There's only one thing missing. Iwo Jima is an Island. We're missing water. So Staff Sergeant Assassin took the two igloos and dumped the PowerAde all over the floor. *Now roll in it!*

So we all rolled in the PowerAde. Luckily it was orange instead of red. Red PowerAde doesn't come out of cammies too well. After that, we were instructed to stack the footlockers in front of the hatches so no one could come in the squad bay.

I guarded the Platoon Guidon. The Drill Instructors tried to find it but I hid it while we were dumping everything on the deck. When I was ordered to get it, I did, but when they grabbed for it, I snatched it away. I was pissed so they could try but I wasn't giving it up after what happened last time. After the Senior's story, 3014 was prepared to fight the Drill Instructors if they tried to take the Guidon. They could see the Guidon. I did what I was instructed and brought it out. But I didn't let them touch it.

When the Senior came back, he saw we were getting smoked and told the Platoon to stop, clean up the house, and get everything back in order. He just looked at the Drill Instructors and shook his head. Barricading the hatches is a no no. They knew better. But since he was pissed at us, he didn't care really.

When the house was back to "normal" as far as racks being in their place and footlockers in their place, we went outside and snapped in for some evening practice with Staff Sergeant Assassin. He was actually really cool with us. He didn't mess with us or make us do stupid junk. We didn't know whether to be thankful or nervous. He then took us to the Range Pits because we would be working them in the next few days. It was cool. When we got back, I blasted two recruits for being stupid. When another tried to jump in I threw him over a footlocker and that's when the Squad Leaders jumped in the mix. We were becoming pack hunters. That was that.

Today was the first day I didn't care what games the Drill Instructors tried to play with me. No matter what, it's wasting down time and I'm usually getting stronger because of it. Whatever.

That night, Staff Sergeant Assassin made us all strip down to our towels before we hit the showers. Then he tried to make everyone drop their towels and stand their wearing nothing but our shower shoes. I didn't do it. Our Senior told us not to do anything stupid. That was stupid. I stood there with my towel. I told the Squad Leaders to do the same. No matter what, do what's right. Our Senior had just gotten done telling us to only follow appropriate orders. This was a game.

Staff Sergeant Assassin told us he was going to take our "manhood" away. When he saw that the Squad Leaders and myself were having none of it, it pissed him off. He called me on it. He said-

Drop the towel Guide!

Sir, this recruit is not authorized to comply with that order Sir!

What? What the fuck is that shit 'sposed to mean? I gave you a fuckin order. You better drop that shit or you'll all pay!

Sir, this recruit was ordered by the Senior Drill Instructor, Senior Drill Instructor Staff Sergeant B not to follow any order that violates the standards he set for the Platoon Sir!

With that, he got right in my face and stared hard into my eyes. I was looking straight ahead and knew not to make eye contact. After a moment, he said- *Very Fuckin well Guide"* real low and almost under his breath. Without taking his eyes off me, he hollered for everyone to get in the head for hygiene time. He turned and walked away. I sighed in relief. However, this would probably be coming back to haunt me in my next smoke session. Oh well.

Being a Drill Instructor is as close to playing God as anything I have ever witnessed. They can send you to Medical, make you have an "accident", or turn you into the fiercest weapon the Unites States Military can offer. They can save you from pain, or put you in a world of it. They can leave you alone for 2 weeks straight and then make the world revolve around you for the next 3. One thing is for sure- there is no escape. Learn to play their games by the rules that they are governed by and you'll be OK. Otherwise, you'll pay.

That night we got mail. Heaven forbid you get a singing card or one that plays a song like myself and a few of my buddies did. And you better pray you never ever get one with any kind of Marine Corps insignia on it. The rules are simple: get any one of these cards and you're doing push-ups for a while. No big deal. That's just the rules. No one will scream over you to go faster or harder. They'll just put the card under your face and make you push until everyone is done.

It was going fine and dandy. I was pushing for the card my sister got me, and then Frey opened his. Frey (pronounced Fry) was this frail looking kid packed with an iron heart. The kid never quit regardless of his size. He opened the card and the tune was "Grandma got ran over by a reindeer." Frey started pushing on the quarterdeck without anyone telling him too. Then, Staff Sergeant Assassin told him to sing along with the song. So there he was, pushing along and singing Grandma got ran over by a reindeer. It was hysterical. Even Staff Sergeant Assassin was holding back trying not to laugh. Frey's voice would always crack on reindeer. You could bank on it. Every time it did, you couldn't help but laugh.

We finished that up and I worked with the guys that needed to work on their pull-ups and sit-ups. Every once in a while, Staff Sergeant Assassin would holler outside his hatch- *Sing Frey!* And he would. Frey learned the whole song from the card. He must have sung it 15 times that night. When we hit the rack, we were instructed to do 100 sit-ups in our rack before we were allowed to fall asleep. We all got done and settled in. Just about the time we were about to fall asleep, we heard footsteps walking out. They stopped about half way down the squad bay. The footsteps stepped up onto a footlocker. And in a real low voice that everyone could hear, we heard the voice say- *Sing Frey*.

Here are 2 more of Staff Sergeant Assassin's most famous words/phrases of choice.

1-   *Anytime to-fuckin-day.* He said this a lot when he wanted someone to hurry up. You'd be working as fast as you could putting your rifle together, scuzzing the floor, or making your rack. If he said that once, you were OK. You just needed to hurry up. If he said it twice, you could count on your name going in the Kill Book. A log he kept in his head of anyone that needed to be sent to the quarterdeck.

2-   *Shits.* Staff Sergeant Assassin is the only person I have ever met that pluralizes the word "Shit" and he has the ability to turn it into a useful noun, and uses it in every day speech. Such as,
You're gonna fuckin put those shits side by side nice and fuckin neat. Well? Anytime to fuckin day!

20071223 SUNDAY
Lesson's Learned

After chow, our Senior told us a story about stupid recruits. He told us that a 3rd Phase recruit was caught smoking in the Squad Bay when they were pulling firewatch. Our Senior happened to be walking by outside and saw grey smoke coming out of the head. He knew what it was. He ran up and as he turned into the head, the recruit was coming out. He asked the recruit what he had been doing. The recruit said nothing. He asked again, but this time, he looked at him real matter of fact like as if to say, just tell me the truth and I'll let it slide. But the recruit lied and said nothing. The recruit was charged as an integrity violator.
His crime- smoking.
His punishment- he was sent back to 2nd Phase DAY 1!
The moral of the story is this, just be honest. No matter what, be honest. That day I came up with a new Killian quote-

It is better to be honest and find discipline, then to be dishonest and find punishment.

Wow that would suck! Our Senior then told us some stories of things he did to recruits that were stupid. He said we all have our days. Bottom line- starting right now: do the right thing no matter what. Sounds easy. But seriously, you have to be the one to do the right thing.
We cleaned house a lot. It took us a while to get the new house in order. Especially being that tomorrow is the Battalion Commander's Inspection. That means nothing more than cleaning the house far

beyond OCD and then getting pitted for not doing it well enough and embarrassing the Senior Drill Instructor. We know that. It's no surprise. After that, we spent time snapping in in the prone, kneeling, sitting, and standing position. I'm getting a lot better.

There were 2 fights in the squad bay. Tuller is your every day momma's boy that decided to join the Marine Corps because he thought the title of Marine might make up for his deficiencies as a man. Everybody picked on him because it was amusing. He was as ferocious as Puss n Boots.

Luckily, he turned out really well. The Marine Corps did in fact turn him into a man. I gotta give him that. He didn't quit and he learned some valuable lessons that made him easy to depend on. But today, well today he got hammered. He was introduced to the school of hard knocks in full effect. Speaking of hard knocks, Boyer got thrown over the footlockers again. You know, that actually does more than straight out punching someone in the face. But I can't say anything because I got served too. Staff Sergeant Assassin smoked me twice. The first time I got it on the quarterdeck in usual fashion. The next time was up and down the highway. That sucks worse because it's always some scuz towel game. I didn't even do anything. Staff Sergeant Assassin just came in, told everyone to clean the house, and then said- *Where you at Guide?* And from that point it was on.

Later that night, Staff Sergeant Assassin played with me at chow. I sat down last as always and right when I started to chow down, he made me stop, then start, then stop, then start, then stop, then wait, then start and hurry up because by this time I had 2 minutes left. I finished but it sure wasn't pretty. I Hoover'd everything.

20071224 MONDAY
Christmas Eve

Today is the Battalion Commander's Inspection. The Battalion Commander is coming in at 12 to check out our Squad Bay, tell our Senior it sucks, and then that should leave plenty of time for us to get smoked before evening chow. Or at least that's what we thought the plan was. Yeah. The Battalion Commander decided to pay us a surprise

286

visit right before lights came on. Our Drill Instructors had gotten us out of the rack early to start the day and all the sudden, in strolls the Captain. We were dead. We got blasted for three things-

1-   The Hog board was still up. The Hog board is where we were able to post all the pictures we got of the girls back home. Not that they are hogs by any means, but because you always get some uber-sheltered recruit that just stands in front of it all day in wonder. That was supposed to come down. It was still up.

2-   Strike two came from one of the recruits screwing up the report. It's easy, the Battalion Commander stands in front of you, you snap to attention and in this case, I would say- *Good morning Sir! Recruit Killian, Annapolis Maryland, 7051 (MOS number)* How hard is that? Well obviously hard enough because that recruit blew it.

3-   Strike three was a hit on the Drill Instructors. They had us up before lights and that's a no no. We were supposed to be asleep when he came in, not scuzzing the floor and fixing racks.

        Oh well. Today we had PT after morning chow so we'll get served later I guess. We got out to the PT fields and today was an individual effort out and back with some work in the middle. The course was set up-
- 1.5 mile run
- 50 Push-ups in front of a Drill Instructor (That in itself can stretch out to 200 if you're lazy)
- 75 Crunches
- 100 Air Squats
- 1.5 miles run back
- 50 Push-Ups
- 75 Crunches
- 100 Air Squats

        Done. This was no joke. The Run spreads everyone out. But even if you're in the back, you can catch almost anybody if you're fast on the work. That is the part where most recruits slowed down a bit. That's where I made my money. You definitely want to set a goal to always finish in the top 5-10 whenever you're doing Physical work in front of the Drill Instructors. If they see you're in shape and you're hungry to win, they'll leave you alone. If you're slow and lazy, they'll put even more pain in your body.

And don't think the 1.5-mile run was a leisurely jog. Since it was less than 3 miles at one time, we were expected to sprint it full throttle. When I got done, I was able to watch recruits coming in to the finish and they were grinding it out with everything they had in order to finish strong. One recruit had a Drill Instructor pushing him along. He was gassed out, whiny, and looking like he was trying to die. The Drill Instructor was having none of it. It got to the point that the Drill Instructor had him by the arm in order to keep the recruit on his feet. When they got closer, I recognized the recruit. He was from another Platoon and he was known for doing whatever he could to get out of hard training. Faking injuries, trying to get excused due to no water, and other stupid junk. The recruit gave up and fell to the ground about 200 yards from the finish. He was just sitting on the ground moaning. The Drill instructor had enough. Instead of snatching him up, he called for the Safety Officer and told him to give him the silver bullet. With that, the recruit jumped to his feet but was tackled by the Drill Instructor. 3 other Drill Instructors ran over and pinned the recruit to the ground. The Safety Officer shoved in the thermometer and that recruit flipped out! With 4 Drill Instructors, he jumped to his feet. The Drill Instructors flew off as if a grenade hit them. The recruit grabbed his trousers, pulled them up, and FLEW to the finish. That recruit NEVER fell out of a run from that day all the way to Graduation.

After PT, we had some SDI time with Drill Instructor Staff Sergeant G. He's a Mexican terror. He's a short little guy with Pit Bull teeth. He talked to us about some things and even though you could hardly understand him, he knew his stuff and managed to get us all on his page. He didn't play around. He got Bell to stand up and smack Albert for falling asleep during his talk because Bell was the biggest guy in our Platoon.

Unfortunately, Bell is also the nicest guy. He doesn't like to mess with recruits and everyone was cool with him. Then Staff Sergeant G made me slap him because Bell didn't do it hard enough. Crap! So I walked over and slapped the piss out of Albert. I made sure I did it right the first time so that I wouldn't be told to do it again.

After the class, I apologized to Albert because he knew I didn't want to hurt him. He was actually totally cool about it. He knew what was going to happen if I didn't so he took it like a champ. At lunch chow, Gamble and Kimble got into it. I told them to knock it off because the Platoon didn't want to pay for them being stupid in "public". Luckily, they stopped. But when we got back to the house, they headed straight for the head to mix it up. I told them to knock it off because it was done. They had no reason to keep at each other. Kimble was actually trying to walk away and Gamble kept after him. I told Gamble if he took another step toward Kimble that I was stepping in.

When he stepped past me to get to Kimble, I snatched him around his neck and locked him in a choke. He started to flail but it was going nowhere. He started to relax and so I let him go. When he turned to me, his lips were blue and his face was white. Considering he's a dark green recruit, that said enough. It was over and so he let it go. Gamble is a good guy, a hot head, but nevertheless, he's cool.

We screwed up the inspection so we were told to clean until dinner chow. Somewhere in the middle of that, we were allowed to snap-in and practice a bit so that was really good. Qual is this week. After dinner chow, we got some "free" time and were instructed to make a Christmas tree. A few recruits were allowed to run outside and grab some branches from a tree. Some other recruits made some m-16a2 ornaments out of cardboard, and one recruit got a Glass boot in the mail so we used that as the stand. To finish it off, we took our moonbeams, put in different lenses and made red, blue, and white lights at the base of the tree. Good times.

20071225 TUESDAY
CHRISTMAS ON PARRIS ISLAND

From 2-3 AM I was on firewatch. It was great because I got to memorize a lot of stuff. There are always new diddies to learn and you have to stay on top of it. After firewatch, I got to go back to sleep until 0600 so that was great! Especially since we always get up at 0400.

Morning chow was awesome. Our Senior gave us a little more time than usual so we stuffed ourselves. He sent the other Drill Instructors home for the day so it was just the Platoon and our Senior.

1st present- Free Time. Full on, no joke, free time. As long as we stayed in the squad bay and didn't get too loud or draw attention, we could do whatever we wanted without anyone messing with us.

2nd Present- Our Senior brought out all the stuff that they took away from us that we had gotten in the mail and let us have at it.

Finally, I got to dive into those Oreos and beef jerky my family had sent me. I didn't mind sharing either. Our Senior then brought out some DVD's and we got to watch The Bourne Ultimatum. During the movie, we got to make a 2 minute phone call to anyone we wanted. We hadn't had junk food since we got on the bus to the Island or been able to watch TV. Both of those were things that we missed. But all that and anything else couldn't match the thought of being able to talk to your family for 120 seconds. We missed them the most! Junk food and TV became "whatever". We had to go in alphabetical order and the Scribe made sure we attempted to make a call and that we got no more than 2 minutes. He would hammer the receiver button if anyone tried to continue talking and end it right there. You really couldn't complain because the guy next in line was just as anxious to get on the phone.

When it was my turn, I frantically dialed the number to my mom and dad. The line was busy...CRAP!!! I hung up fast and tried again. Everyone is always calling them in the morning. I had a minute and a half left. My mom picked up the phone. I said- *"Hi ma"* and she told my dad to get on the other line. They were so happy to hear from me. I was so happy to hear their voices. We could say nothing but jibberish and it would have been the best 60 seconds in the world. It was the hardest call to make because my mom started crying and couldn't say anything and so it was just me and my dad with my mom sprinkled in. He told me he was proud of me and I told them I was fine, I was doing well, and not to worry about me. I fought my way through the call the best I could. It was GREAT to hear their voice. Then it was over. I had to go.

It really helps to tell them right away that you have only a minute and a half to talk. Otherwise, they won't know how much every moment counts. You only get one shot. There were a lot of recruits that didn't get that across and before they could say a word, they had to hang up.

It's wild because from the pansy-est, weakest, most garbage recruit in the Platoon all the way to the meanest, coldest, hardest recruit, there was very little if any differences in their inner strength. They cried like a baby when they got off the phone. They would be rock solid talking on the phone and being the strength in the conversation. They would assure their families that everything was just fine and they were pulling through no problem, and that it wasn't that bad after all. Then they would hang up, step away from the phone, walk over to some corner of the Squad Bay, and have it out for a couple minutes. No need to go over and put a hand on their shoulder or any of that crap. And it wasn't like some production that drew attention. For the most part, most recruits would play it off by doing some push-ups or pull-ups.

There was nothing you could say or do or what could be done. We ALL just had to get it out of our system. As soon as they got it out, they would square themselves away and rejoin the Platoon and no one would say a word about it. There was no shame in missing the people you lived for. It's true; the Marine Corps does make you harder. But your family keeps you human.

After the movie, we got to go to a special church service. It was Fantastic! I got to call cadence for the detail and we had some fun with it. We did karaoke cadence so that we could do all the moves that everyone liked. We did To the Rear/ 2 Little Horseman/ Right Oblique/ Left Oblique/ and a few others. When we got to the chapel, we walked in and immediately heard familiar Christmas songs being played. When the service started, we sang Christmas songs and heard the Christmas story. It was just like home. Not only that but for the first time in forever, we saw female recruits at he service. Normally, they go to their own service and you never see them. But since it was a special, they were there as well. We weren't allowed to talk to them much less look in their direction, but it was a change we didn't expect.

When we got back to the house, it was time to step for chow. Lunch chow was AWESOME! Turkey, sweet potatoes, and Pecan Pie. I don't even like Sweet potatoes, but I do now. Boot Camp will make you love anything. When we got back to the house, we had a quick clean up and then watched "Shooter". The movie was great until some of the recruits got a little too rambunctious. Our Senior told everyone to chill out or else and I guess they just wanted to push it. As a result, we were given "No movement" free time and our Senior jumped on the phone. Who knows whom he's calling. By the way, no movement free time means you sit on your footlocker frozen. It's free time because no one is yelling at you or telling you what to do. But it sucks because you can't talk or move.

This was the calm before the storm. The answer to whom he called was revealed. All of the sudden, our Kill Hat and Staff Sergeant Assassin showed up. Playtime was over and we knew it. The recruits that got us in trouble knew it more than anyone else. From this point on, anything that happened to us could be tied straight back to those two idiots. Our Drill Instructors knew for a fact that we did nothing all day and now it was on. But first, we had to go to chow. Based on how we acted at chow would determine what types of games they played with us.

When we got back, we played the "Incoming" game. That's when you stand on line, a Drill Instructor says- *INCOMING* and you drop to your face as quickly as possible. Then the Drill Instructor says- *ALL CLEAR* and you stand back up as fast as you can. We just did it over and over and over... and over. Oh well. It was new and it killed time. We played a few more games after that, cleaned Rifles and kicked knowledge, and then before we knew it, it was time for chow again.

Drill Instructor Staff Sergeant Assassin cleared the house for chow. He kicked the Squad Leaders out first, followed by the Platoon, and then he followed me while I checked to make sure everyone had locked up their Rifles like always. And there it was. Someone had left a Rifle unlocked. He brought the lock over to me and gave it to me to hold on to. He hooked it to my belt loop and when I looked back up, he said-

Very well Guide, let the Platoon forget to lock they shits up. You'll pay!

Great. But this time, I didn't look to see if it was mine like last time. Last time he tricked me. He came down when we were formed up and told me I had left mine unlocked and that I would pay when I came back to the house. In the meantime, I better not jack with the lock. I tried to unlock it because I knew for a fact that I didn't leave my rifle unlocked and I wanted to prove to him that it wasn't my lock. It was a simple lesson in following instructions. If I would have left it alone, he would have just taken it back and left me alone. So this time, I kept it on "O" and didn't touch it. When we got back. Staff Sergeant Assassin asked for it, and when I gave it to him, he checked to see if I had messed with it. When he saw that I didn't, he found Stratton and made him pay for it.

To end the night right, we did lots and lots of pull-ups. Staff Sergeant Assassin told us we had to work off all the junk food that we killed that morning. We just kept going through the lines until it was SDI time. Good day I must say.
Happy Birthday Jesus!

20071226 Wednesday
FIRE DAY 1

We woke up again before lights came on because we had to get to the chow hall before everyone else. Today was Fire Day 1. This would be the first time we got to actually shoot in the positions we had been training in. It was frigid! And to add to the fun and adventure we weren't allowed to wear our Polypro or sweatshirt. Grr!

We left the chow hall and formed up under these huge wall-less structures. All you get is a concrete floor and a roof. And they are enormous. All 3 Platoons could easily fit underneath. We nicknamed it the "thunder dome". This is where we staged most of our gear, got our last minute instruction from our Drill Instructors, and then met up with our shooting coaches to finalize the shooting game plan. Everyone was excited and in a pretty good mood. As soon as we were formed up into our shooting relays and had our coaches, we headed out to the firing line. I was in the 1st Relay. That was cool because we had never shot from the positions we had been practicing for the last few days. All we had been doing was snapping in. Now we got to shoot live rounds and see what needed to be done before Qual. Before we shoot, we had to get our safety brief from the tower and go over the safety rules.

The tower cracks me up. The tower guy has this crazy hillbilly accent that makes you think you're at some Tennessee State Fair. He'd say-

Gooooood Mornin' R'cruits!

GOODMORNING SIR!

Welcome to the Starlight Range. R'CRUITS! What is my number 1 rule on my range?

SAFETY SIR!

Dats right! Now, repeat after me as we review the 4-safety rules- Treeeeeat every weapon as if it was loaded! **(We'd repeat)**

Neeeeever point your weapon at anything you don't intend to shoot! **(We'd repeat)**

Keep your finger straight and off the trigger until you're ready to fire! **(We'd repeat)**

Keep the weapon on safe until you intend to fire! **(We'd repeat)**

COACHES! Git dat Relay 1 into position.

For the first time firing, I thought I did pretty good. We started with the-
200-yard
SITTING- This is where you can really make a lot of money!!! Every shot should be in the 5's! Every shot! Beside the Prone, this is one of the most stable positions to fire from.

KNEELING- There is HIGH Kneeling and LOW Kneeling. It's up to you to decide what feels best. I'm all about the Low Kneeling myself. It felt really solid and I felt like I could really dig in.

STANDING- This position is the most difficult to fire from. This is different from the "Combat Ready" standing position you find in Table II. Here, you stand sideways and aim to keep that barrel steady.

RAPID fire- 10 well executed shots in a given timeframe. Again, a ton of money to be made here!!

We then hiked back to the 300-yard line and did our sets there.

And then finished with the 500 yard PRONE. That 500-yard prone is no joke.

I never thought I'd be able to score a head shot at 500 yards without a scope. I was totally impressed. The coaches helped out a lot and we didn't have to worry about our Drill Instructors messing with us.

After we got done firing, we switched places and became the PIT Crew. As we walked down, it was wild to see how far the targets are away from the corresponding numbers that you fire on. You'd swear that the numbers are just a few feet away. That is not the case.

As you can see from the picture above, the Lane Marker is to the left and the Targets you fire on come up from the far right. Running the PITS is OK. It's not as much fun as firing obviously, but it was cool in its own way. You're standing there on this 4-foot walkway. You're looking up at the face of the target. All of the sudden WHAP! You see the shot appear on the target. You pull it down, mark it, score it, and send it right back up as quickly as you can.

And don't be the one to be the slow crew. Let's say that you're running PIT 25 and you're moving slow. The PIT tower will say-

Let's go r'cruits! Git dat "Dog" target back high in the sky!
OK 25. Let's move it. Git dat "Dog" target up dere. 25!
I'm talkin to you 25! You're moving slow 25!!!
Hustle it up 25!!!!!
Well congratulations Pit 25 you are today's slowest crew.
Drill Instructors!!!! Can I get a Drill Instructor to Pit 25!

When you hear that, stand by. It's crazy how a couple of Drill Instructors can simply appear out of nowhere on Parris Island. Just when you think it's just you and the fellas and you're safe away from the sharks, all of the sudden they magically poof from out of nowhere and pounce on you.

You know it was coming because they'd be running straight for you. If they come in 2 or more, there is a process to work through to limit how long you are getting verbally assaulted. One Drill Instructor will be the one that you actually need to respond to. The other Drill Instructors will be screaming at you, but your focus must stay on the primary and respond to only his questions. All you can do is stand by and wait when they are coming for you. The one that speaks first is usually the primary. So don't look him in the eyes but pay attention to what he is yelling, answer in a volume above and beyond his, and whether the storm. Don't stutter or stammer because that'll just tack on two more minutes because you're stupid.

To be honest, they don't want to waste any more energy on you than what's necessary, so stay sharp, take your licks, and give them the sense that you're squared away and they'll disappear just as fast as they appeared.

20071227 Thursday
"Play" Guide and Squad Leaders

Well, the Squad Leaders and myself got fired. The Platoon was screwing up and our Senior decided to make a point. He fired us and put the absolute worst recruits in charge of the Platoon. As Doctor Evil would say- Rrrrrrrright.

There are good and bad things that come with firing the Guide and Squad Leaders. One bad thing is having to pay for the stupid junk that the "play Guide and Squad Leaders" are doing. They don't know how to do things. So when they screw up, we get smoked for it. The good thing is that they finally understand what we were dealing with before and what it takes to hold those positions. But most important of all, we finally got to take our time eating chow. Normally, we were always last when it came to chow time. We sat down last, got started last, and still had to finish within the given time.

When we fell into formation, we made sure we were right behind the play Squad Leaders so that we would be first into the chow hall. We all sat down relaxed and ready to finally enjoy what we ate. I was the first to sit down. I started in and when I was almost done, I noticed I was being watched. When I looked up, I saw my Kill Hat was standing right in front of me. I made eye contact with him, then looked over to see the play Guide and Squad Leaders were still running around trying to keep order. They were taking their time getting their chow and sitting down. By now, I would have been 3/4th done and ready to go. My Kill Hat looked at me and said-

They don't even know do they Guide?

Keeping my bearing I stopped eating, looked straight ahead, and said- *"No Sir!"* Just then, something strange happened. My Kill Hat realized he was talking to me too casually and recovered by turning his attention back to hurrying the play Guide and Squad Leaders up. It was so weird because for the first time since I met my Kill Hat, I never ever heard him talk in a normal every day voice. He was always yelling, screaming, or snarling mad. It was the craziest moment in time.

The play Guide and Squad Leaders finally sat down, took three bites of their scrambled eggs, and then our Kill Hat ran over, got them right back up, and kicked us out of the chow hall. Welcome to my world. I was laughing so hard on the inside. It's totally jacked up to sit down and get right back up but that's how it is. My Squad leaders felt the same way. You think you know how it is until you march in those boots.

When we got back to the house, we got killed because the play Guide and Squad Leaders wouldn't shut up about not being able to eat. Tuller was annoying everyone. He was whining about not being able to eat, he would tell you to shut up and act all pissed off and mean, and then 2 minutes later, he would ask you for help because someone was talking and he couldn't shut them up. I called him on it and he got all up in my face.

I told him if he didn't walk away from me I would put him in EHP. That's the get well soon Platoon for anyone who has been broken. Tuller was hooked on a power trip. He honestly believed he was a Squad Leader because of his status as a worthy candidate, not as a punishment and learning lesson that we all understood it to be.

Jewski, my Squad Leader, was just about to kill Tuller when we got hustled out of the squad bay.

Today was MONSTER "O" Course day. That's the "O" Course just super sized. It's awesome. We were put into teams of 4 and sent through. All 4 team members had to stay together from one obstacle to the next. No one could continue unless your whole team was through the previous obstacle. I was with my Squad Leaders and we flew through the course. We started about 5 teams back and finished first. Good work in my book. I was with Jewski, Bell, and Betze. It was over. We hustled back to where we were supposed to form back up and just watched everyone else in our Platoon.

The tables turned bad on the play Guide and Squad Leaders. They were the first team to go and they were still on the course. Our Drill Instructors cared about no one else except for them. Even Drill instructors from other Platoons were jumping in the mix and giving them static. They finished dead last. Since we were right by standing water, the sand fleas ate well that day. None of us cared.

There is nothing worse than being on the bad side of your Senior Drill instructor. If last time I described what the Drill Instructors did to us was being bombed, this time we got nuked! When we got back to the house, everything came out. We dumped our footlockers, our racks came apart, mattresses were all over the place, the big gear and little gear locker was even bombed. Everything was... everywhere. Locks to our footlockers were chunked. It was a nightmare. Luckily, we marked our locks so we were able to find them. We got used to the Drill Instructors ripping our stuff apart so we found ways to mark everything we had so we could find it or return it quickly. Everyone was used to the game. The first time we played it, we were horrified because we thought we would never get all our stuff back. By now, they could do whatever they wanted and we would get all our stuff. It may take time but we had it worked out. After that, our Heavy Hat made us hold our Daypacks out for what seemed like forever. Pain baby! Yeehaw!

After we got everything back to wear it belonged, the play Guide and Squad Leaders were fired and my Squad Leaders and myself were reinstated. Everyone was glad we were back. Some were happy to give it up. Tuller was heartbroken.

20071228 Friday
PreQual

We got everyone up at 0300 to fix the mess that was made yesterday. We were told to just shove anything and everything in anyone's footlocker. So we had stuff, it just wasn't ours. We had to have all of our own stuff and everyone knew it so we all agreed to get up early and fix it. My Kill Hat blew a gasket when he came out and saw what we were doing. But when I reported to him what we were doing, he just said-
Very well, keep it down. And that was that.

When we got out to the Range, there was a bit of excitement in the air to see what we could do. This was our first real test with our Rifles. Every shot would count today. If weather was so bad tomorrow that we couldn't shoot, today's score would be our Qual score. If you UNQ'd, you would have 1 more chance to fire and then be sent back to the next Platoon.

I was in the 3rd Relay. I would score for my shooting partner, and then I would fire and he would score for me. The PIT Crew keeps score for you too and those numbers BETTER match! Otherwise they'll blast you as an integrity violator. I scored a 170. That's an UNQ. I wish I could blame the PIT's or something but I can't. I'm just not a really strong shooter. I'm OK but I'm not making the score I need. However, on the 500 yard round, I had slow PIT service and when the time was up, I had 7 shots outstanding. My coach called down to the PIT's to explain the deal to the tower. No more than 5 minutes later, out comes a recruit to stand on the Range's Yellow Footprints. That's where you NEVER want to be. That means you did something really dumb. You stand behind the Range Tower on the Yellow Footprints and the Drill Instructors line up and sink their teeth into you one at a time. Luckily, today is only PreQual and my coach said that if weather was bad, I would still get a chance to fire with my Platoon. Good to go.

When my Kill Hat found out I UNQ'd, he grabbed my gear and threw it all out during the shakedown. He didn't care about the circumstances. He just grabbed my junk and BAM! Yard sale!

That night, we had an awesome chow. Our Drill Instructors gave us plenty of time to eat and everything was actually relaxed. We got back to the house and snapped in for about 30 minutes. This time, our Drill Instructors worked with us quietly and showed us some last minute pointers. It seemed odd at the time. Usually they are hard bent to kill us. Right at this moment, they were explaining things that really made sense to me and it was a tremendous help. My Kill Hat helped me the most. He explained my mistakes I was making and gave me exactly what I needed to fix the errors.

Just before lights out, the Chaplain came on deck. He got us all in a school circle to talk with us. It was actually really cool. He said-

Good evenin' boys.

Good evening Sir!

I hope you boys don't mind but I'd like to have a word with you. Tomorrow is perhaps the most important day in your training. Tomorrow, you're going to go out to that Rifle Range, and you're going to qualify. From this moment on, don't even worry about whether you will or won't. It's already been decided. You will qualify tomorrow morning. How do I know that? Well, you've done your part by putting to work everything you've been taught. I'm sure your Drill Instructors have made sure of it. They've set you up for success, and tomorrow, that preparation is going to pay off.

After that, he gave us all a card called the Rifleman's Prayer, and he read it for us.
Good stuff.

20071229 Saturday
Rifle Qualification

I would have to say that today was the MOST important day in Recruit Training. The day when you have to prove you can shoot your Rifle anywhere from 200- 500 yards and score a head shot. (And not just once. A bunch of times.)

Every Marine is a Rifleman. Period. The morning of qualification is the BLUE Morning. I don't know why but it is. Everything is cool. You get up without being in a state of shock, you eat a big breakfast, the Drill Instructors don't quarterdeck you, you clean the house relaxed, it's a really laid back morning. The Drill Instructors ease back on the pressure so you're relaxed going to the range. They want to make sure that recruits don't have any excuse for bombing on the Range. It's like all the frenzy of the Island goes away and everything shuts down just so you can shoot. I felt like I stepped into another world. When we marched to the Range, I understood why.

I have fought in the State, National, and World Championships in Martial Arts and it paled in comparison to how nervous I was for this event. I was feeling great the entire morning until I crossed the road and took my first step on the grass. All of the sudden it hit me. I realized that it's all about the consequence. If you fail on the Range, you drop back 3 weeks in training, you pick up with a whole new Platoon, all new Drill Instructors, you lose your position if you're a Guide or a Squad Leader, it prolongs your Graduation Date, it would be really bad. After I snapped out of it, I tried to focus on what I needed to do to succeed. I knew what I had to do. All I have to do is take my time, make every shot count, stay cool for the bad shots, stay cooler for the good shots, and remember sight alignment and trigger control. It was just like being totally dry and warm from the sun and then jumping into a spring. It shocks you at first, but then when you realize where you are, you get used to it and you're fine. I'm ready.

We went over the rules with the tower and were waiting in our lanes for the sun to come up. Then, Tuller started piping up. He started PMS'ing about every little thing. I told him to lock it up. He started talking back so I slapped the piss out of him. Twice. Once for talking back to me, and then once again for talking back to our Firing coaches. He locked it up after that. You can't straight out punch someone outside of the house, so you have to jar their brain-housing group somehow. He locked it up after that.

Anyway. I had the choice of shooting first or second relay because of the number of recruits, so I picked first relay so I could get it done and over with. I didn't want to take the chance of worrying or psyching myself out so I put myself on deck. You're not supposed to keep score but just like all the pages of this book, I found a way. I wanted to know exactly where I was at all times. There was no way I wanted to have to wonder what my score was. Finally the range came to life. Deep breath, steady hands, let's go!

200 SITTING Slow Fire- My Heavy Hat says that's where you make your money and he was right. I made my money. Every shot was a 4 and 5, which gave me a solid start. Plus, my Kill Hat showed me how to keep from jerking the trigger. It turned a lot of the 4's I got last time into 5's today.

200 KNEELING Slow Fire - Still making money. One 3. The rest 4's and

5's.

200 STANDING Slow Fire - A 5 and a 4. The rest were 3's. That was pretty normal. The first day I shot that, I thought I was screwed. It's tough making 4's and 5's standing. I'm still good.

200 SITTING Rapid Fire- Back to making money. 10 shots in under 60 seconds. I made up for my 3's, which got me back on track.

300 SITTING and 300 PRONE- This kicked my butt a little bit. I didn't score any 2's but I had way too many 3's. Gotta stay cool. I'm still on track.

500 PRONE- This is where I came back. I took my sweet time. Or at least, I took all the time they gave me.

As soon as I got done, I tallied my scores. You gotta be smart about keeping score for yourself otherwise you'll get smoked by a Drill Instructor. My Rifle Log had lots of pages, so I just put my final scores for each range on different pages throughout the book. That way, it just looked like scores from Pre-Qual and you couldn't tell. When I was all done, I added the scores from the different pages and I was good to go. I Qualified!

I tried to keep my head on straight and stay cool, but to be honest; I had the 4th of July going on inside my head. I was done with Table 1 on the Range. Table 2 is coming, but I heard it's a lot easier than Table 1 so I was happy feeling relieved. All I could think was I made it. While everyone else was trading scores and hearing the "who got what's", I just sat back and smiled knowing I had qualified.

12 Recruits UNQ'd. That means they would have 1 more chance and then get dropped to another Platoon if they UNQ'd again. That would put their Graduation date on the 15th of February instead of the 1st. Staying here two more weeks... yeah. No thanks.

When we were stripping down on the Range, Boyd did the dumbest thing I have **EVER** heard of any recruit doing: and I've heard some stupid junk. When we took off our Blouses, Boyd was reluctant. He didn't want to do it. When he was forced, the Drill Instructors found that he was wearing a CIVILIAN SHIRT THAT HE GOT IN THE MAIL FOR CHRISTMAS!!!! As it turns out, he had gotten it as a present and it was supposed to stay locked up in the Big Gear Locker until Graduation. However, he somehow snuck in, snatched it, and wanted to wear it because it was crazy cold outside.

A civilian shirt! Holy Crap! The commotion got the attention of our Senior and when he saw that, it was over. How can you put into words the image of a Drill Instructor becoming so enraged that you would think they might literally explode? His face turned red. His lips turned white. He was literally shaking. He got right in Boyd 's face and just pointed at his face and mumbled jibberish through clenched teeth. The Drill Instructors gathered around and were anxiously waiting to see what direction he would go. Either our Senior would kill him, or he would let them. At this moment, he stormed off and said the Drill Instructors could have him. They started quarterdecking the piss right out of him.

We were eating lunch so no one dared look up to see what was going on. We just listened to the result of a mistake you should never make. 7 pit bulls on 1 recruit. It was ugly. All the sudden, our Senior flew in out of nowhere and sank his teeth in. He made Boyd pick up the full Igloo and march it around the thunder dome with his arms locked out. Boyd was screaming for his life and begging for mercy. Tears were drenching his clothes. The more his arms would shake, the more our Senior would yell and scream at him. Boyd would fall over and our Senior would force him back up over, and over, and over. We thought it might not end until finally it did. Boyd collapsed on the deck and the other Drill Instructors were cheering for our Senior. Our Senior made sure he was alive, and then walked off. Our Drill Instructors made him stand up, see the Corpsman, and then brought him over to sit with the Platoon. He would eventually be fine. He learned his lesson. We smiled.

Our Drill Instructors are crazy, but they aren't stupid. They make you do some over the top stuff but nothing that will truly injure you or hurt you. They know full well how to ride that line. They have found ways to put so much pain in your body without killing you out right. It's awesome.

When we got back to the house, I got quarterdecked for not shaving good enough. Grr! Then the UNQ's got quarterdecked for screwing up. Then the Platoon got it for having 12 UNQ's in the Platoon. Oh well. It's Boot Camp.

Evening chow was great, great, and more great. Our Heavy Hat gave us time to eat and that's always appreciated. And by time to eat, I mean he gave us a good 10 to 12 minutes. In boot camp, that's a long time. Today is a done deal. And it was a huge day. Rifle Qual is a bomb of a challenge. It is a huge deal. Huge!

Your Drill Instructors can teach you how to march and you can be the best technical marcher in the world. They can teach you all the knowledge in the world and you can know every single thing there is to know about the Marine Corps. They can even make you the best hand-to-hand combat guy out there.
But if you can't shoot, you'll never be a Marine!

20071230 Sunday
Igloo I Wuv You!

Staff Sergeant Assassin got us up. He was in good spirits. He remembered the T-shirt incident with Boyd so he decided to have some more fun with him. Boyd's new job was to carry that Igloo everywhere we went. Luckily, he didn't have to hold it out in front of himself with straight arms. As long as he marched it to the chow hall, filled it up with ice, and brought it back, he was good. However, as we were marching along to chow, Staff Sergeant Assassin would every so often holler out *IGLOO!*
Whenever he hollered that, Boyd had to say- **"IGLOO, I WUV YOU!"** And he had to say it like a little kid.

It killed us. We tried to keep a straight face but it was hysterical. When we would march by another Platoon, Staff Sergeant Assassin would make him do it, the other Platoon would start to laugh, and then their Drill Instructors would start screaming at them for losing their bearing. That junk made us laugh. Staff Sergeant Assassin would just grin at the chaos he could stir up.

Went to church. It was a typical Sunday. Sunday's are based on recruit performance. If you're stupid, you'll play stupid games ALL day. If you are taking care of business, the Drill Instructors will leave you alone.

We figured that whole deal out, and so Sundays everyone knew to be on extra good behavior.

Today, the scribe learned a valuable lesson! Our scribe's name is Abbett. He's a good guy and doesn't drive anyone crazy like some of the scribes in the other platoons. We had his back. We went to the chow hall and found ourselves in a volume battle with another platoon. They were actually really good. Normally it's a smoke fest but this time we were going back and forth with WINS. We ended up tied and needed to break it. So they made myself and the other Guide go at it. I got a big mouth and I'm used to raising my voice at the Karate school, so I brought back another point for our platoon. Then the Squad Leaders went at it. It was give and take. Then the Scribes went. Abbett got slaughtered. Poor guy man. So we ended up losing and the other Platoon went into the chow hall first. It was our first defeat! But it's ok. We had the scribe's back and didn't give him any static. Can't say the same for the Drill Instructors. Our Knowledge hat was livid!

As soon as the scribe got done eating, our Knowledge hat snatched him up and took him back to the house. Uh oh. We were scared for him to be honest. We didn't know what would happen to him. When we got back, we rushed up the stairs to see if he was getting quarterdecked, or passed out, or screaming, or Indy 500-ing, or if he was even still there.

As we were climbing the stairs we could hear something like screaming but it was weird. We couldn't make it out. As soon as we made it on deck I saw what was happening. Our Knowledge Hat was standing there with his arms crossed. In front of him was the scribe. However, our Knowledge hat put a trashcan on his head and was making him scream so that he could be heard with a trashcan on his head. All you saw was two little legs sticking out of the bottom. He wasn't a tall recruit and that trashcan was huge. We felt relieved, had a good laugh inside our heads, and that was that.

20071231 Monday
...Great.

Early rise at 0100. Apparently, some recruits from another

Platoon had snuck onto another deck, beat up the firewatch, and stole the Platoon's Guidon. A Drill Instructor from one of the other decks came onto our deck and just announced that if it was anyone from this Platoon, they should out themselves, take their licks, and let the rest of us go back to sleep. Nothing was going to happen to them as long as it stayed with the Drill Instructors. The moment it goes to the First Sergeant is when the trouble would really begin.

That's how everything has been in the Platoon. Keep it in the Platoon and no one gets in trouble. Let word break out outside the Platoon and everyone gets into trouble. He went on to say that they already had one name so just come out with the others. It sucked though because he made us feel guilty that we had done it. The fact was no one from our Platoon did. I slept right by the hatch. I sleep really light. I would have known if someone from our house did it. We were innocent.

He left and 10 minutes later, the Series Guns came on deck and he told us the same thing. Admit who did it and no one gets in trouble. Let it go to the First Sergeant and we're dead. He then took me to the side in private and grilled me about the Platoon. I said-

Sir, this recruit knows every single recruit very well. This recruit knows for a fact it was not any recruit from this Platoon Sir.

He looked at me real hard and then after a moment, he said- *Very well.* That was that. They all left. 20 minutes later, the beat up recruits and the First Sergeant came on deck and fingered Bell and Betze. We were shocked. They were double shocked. They were escorted off the deck by the First Sergeant. We went back to sleep. Or at least we were supposed to but no one could. 45 minutes later, Bell and Betze came back. Apparently, the recruits falsely accused them, the truth was found out, and our guys were released. 4 hours later, we found out it was 3013 who did it. They got KILLED! They were in the PIT or getting smoked on and off every 2 hours for the entire day.

When we formed for chow that morning, all the Platoons formed up at the same time. Our Senior was going to take us to chow, but before we left, he recognized the recruits that falsely accused Bell and Betze. He blew up on them. He got ALL in their face and didn't stop till after about 4-5 minutes of verbally annihilating them. It was great! Justice served.

We have a lot to do today. We had to IP our Uniforms for inspection, iron, starch, the whole 9. 12 went to the dentist. 16 did work at the RTR. The rest of us stayed in the Squad Bay and worked on the Platoon's Uniforms. Oh well. It could be worse. Ate lunch chow relaxed. For some reason, there wasn't a Drill Instructor on deck and so we were on autopilot. Then, our Senior came back on deck and told us we were lucky it wasn't one of us who caused the trouble. The only way it would have been OK is if we told our Senior we were going to do it. Then, he could have warned the other Seniors and when stuff hit the fan, we could keep it under the radar. Recruits getting beaten up is not that big of a deal and stealing another Platoon's Guidon is a righteous mission. However, you have to let the Senior know. Since the recruits didn't tell their Senior, everyone was getting worked over.

As for us, our Senior then started taking recruits in 1 by 1 and smoking them in Tekken 5. I was the last 1 to go. I went in, picked Yoshimitsu, and put him down. He said I was lucky. Some might call it luck, I'd call it... well luck but who cares. It was cool. Our Senior would do regular stuff with us every once in a great while to see how we were doing. Honesty is HUGE in the Platoon. As long as you're honest about everything, the Senior can help you out with just about anything.

He then asked me if I could do any of the kicks that were in the game. I said I could and so then he wanted to see something. I showed him a 540 and a Sideswipe. Most of them had never seen anything like that so it was cool. Our Heavy Hat walked on deck when I did the Sideswipe. He said-

Hey Guide, if you kicked me like that, I'd grab your foot in mid air, slam you on the ground and stomp your fuckin face in.

I said- *Aye Sir.* He's a funny guy. I then made sure to explain that those kinds of kicks were for show. It's like street ballers. You have your flashy street ball tricks, and you have your professional NBA moves. You use the moves that correspond to the right game. My Senior then asked about some ground fighting moves and we talked about sinking in the Kimora. I used Jewski and he was down with it. It was fun. Speaking of

309

fun, Harmon and Conrad sitting in a tree F-I-GHT-I-N-G!
Harmon just had PMS. Here's the deal-
49 recruits.
8 sinks in the head.
=6 recruits to a sink.
Harmon grabbed a sink.
Conrad moves in.
Harmon elbows him.
Junk escalates.
Fight ensues.
After a bit, we break it up. (Babies)

Came home from evening chow and got a letter from my Dad. I can't wait to see them again. After I read the letter, I walked over and told Conrad that they are going to work it out tonight. I then went over and told Harmon that Conrad was coming over to work it out. Harmon asked for 2 minutes then he'll work it out. Good to go. I bring Conrad over, he's cool, and then I call for Harmon. Now he doesn't want to come. He doesn't want to come without his little entourage. I told him to forget about it and get over here. He ignores me. I had enough. I told him he was the biggest pussy in the entire Platoon and stepped back to my footlocker. What a baby! No discipline. Oh well.

That's when the fun ended. Our Kill Hat wanted to screw with us so we stripped down, jumped in the shower, sat down on the deck, most of us weren't even under water, we got back up, and got out. He told us that's what we get for Harmon acting stupid.

Had a hygiene inspection. 46 failed because they didn't shave good enough. Only 3 passed. The 3 went to free time. The rest went and shaved again and stood online until our Kill Hat was good and ready to check again. 10 minutes were left in free time when all was said and done. It was time to hit the rack.

That was what we were supposed to do, but our Kill Hat wanted to play god. First, we played the On/ Off game. We took our Blouses off at least 35 times. Someone was always moving slow. The next game was to run from the line, to the bulkhead, and back to the line. Yeah, that went on for a while. The last game was our Kill Hat's favorite. He was totally into making us scream. We would run from one hatch to the other and scream "Spirit" and "Discipline". The 3rd Battalion motto. We screamed it over and over and over. All the games finally ended and that was that.

However, our Kill Hat had one more thing for us. He taught us a new diddy. He asked-

What do we do if someone from another Platoon comes on deck during lights out?

Inform the duty Sir!
Verify rank and inform the duty Sir!
Tell them to stop and identify themselves Sir!

Nope nope nope. All y'all bitches are wrong. From now on, when I ask you what do you do if someone comes on deck during lights out, you're going to say WOOP DAT ASS SIR!

AYE SIR!

What do we do if someone comes on deck during lights out?

WOOP DAT ASS SIR!

That night, our Kill Hat split us into 3rds. Each third put a different color lens in their moonbeams. We had clear, blue, and red. We were instructed to go to sleep but keep the moonbeam on our footlocker. At 11:57, he woke us all up and made sure we had our moonbeam in hand. He then told us that when he said GO, we were to point our moonbeam at the ceiling and flip it on and off non-stop until he said STOP. At the strike of 12:00, he said GO and we blinked our moonbeams at the ceiling. It looked really cool. It was recruit fireworks. That went on for about 10 seconds and then he said- STOP. *Get yo ass back in the fuckin rack!*
We said, **Aye Sir!** Just before he walked back in the office, he growled and over his shoulder he said-
Happy New Year bitches!

Happy New Year... I didn't even realize it.

Here are a couple famous phrases from our Kill Hat-
Nope, nope, nope.
He said this whenever we didn't make it by the end of a count down.
Even if we made the time, he would say this and then inform us we
didn't make the time. It drove us crazy.

This is a game we play but it's a game I win.
He just wanted us to know that we were playing the game but no
matter what, we would never win. He would always win.

20080101 Tuesday
Friggin Stahling

Early chow. Waffles, mmm mmm good. Today we got to go down
and talk to the Series Guns. He told us stories about pulling firewatch,
moral discipline, doing the right thing even when you don't want to, not
worrying about girlfriends at home, and he told us about his nightmare
road trip to pick up some drunk friends in Tiawana. He said some really
good stuff but he mixed it with funny junk so you couldn't really tell you
were learning a lesson until it was too late. Good stuff. The Series Guns
is awesome!

When we got back to the house, Staff Sergeant Assassin dropped
a bomb on us. He said he found a notebook and wanted to know who's
it was. Stahling recognized it and told him it was his. As it turns out,
Stahling was gay and he had written some love stories in the notebook.
Everyone knew Stahling was odd but now it all made sense. Staff
Sergeant Assassin then made him come up and read that junk out loud.
Stahling wouldn't do it though. So Staff Sergeant Assassin started
reading. Wow! It was jacked up. He then started asking Stahling some
questions-

(To Stahling)
Who's Cody?
Just a name Sir.

(He then asked the Platoon)
Is there a Cody here?
Kimble raises his hand and says- Here Sir!

(Talking to Stahling)
It says he's got brown eyes.
Stahling said- I made it up Sir.

(To Kimble)
What color eyes you got?
Kimble said- Brown Sir.

(To Stahling)
Amazing!

From that point on, it was bad for Stahling. He tried to deny it but Staff Sergeant Assassin was smart. It would have been better if he just admitted that junk. The recruits would have left him alone for being a man about it. But instead, he tried to hide it and got served. Like I said, it got bad for Stahling. I tried to keep him away from some of the recruits when I could but you can only do so much.

Moral of the story- If you're gay, there's no need to bring it up at Parris Island. The Marine Corps tells you from day 1 of being recruited about the "don't ask, don't tell policy", and if you follow it, the Corps won't say one bad thing about it at all. And if you do really want to be a Marine, that's totally cool as long as don't let it effect unit cohesion and the ability to accomplish missions. But if you show up to Parris Island and start acting stupid and fighting for your freedom to openly express yourself, Parris Island is not the place.

It **WILL** be **BAD** for you.

After dinner chow, Staff Sergeant Assassin made us play the On/Off game. We stripped down to our skivvies and put everything all back on. Over and over and over. Some recruits were moving slow so then he tried to get us to stand jailbird again. No one moved. He looked at me and said-

Anytime to-fuckin-day Guide.
Sir, the Senior Drill Instructor instructed this recruit to stay in his towel Sir.
Is that so?
Yes Sir!
Very well.
And that was that. We had passed the test of standing up to not doing stupid junk and from that point on; he didn't try the jailbird game again.

20080102 Wednesday
A Pretty Good Day

Early Chow. FRIGGIN COLD! No Beanies, No Gloves. Awesome. When we got back to the house, we headed off to the Dentist. I had to get 3 fillings. No big deal really. The Doc was great. I asked about there being a Starbucks on Parris Island. She said No, no Starbucks on Parris Island.

That was the reason why everyone was so mean on Parris Island. If there was a Starbucks, everyone would be more pleasant. She was great.

Wow, my mouth was numb. I took 400mg of Ibuprofen AKA Marine Corps M&M's. When we got back. Our Senior was on duty and he stepped us to chow. Before we left, he unrolled our Guidon signifying that we weren't on his Kill list anymore. Awesome. It had been rolled up for so long that it kept its shape when I took the boot bands off. That night, I washed and ironed the Guidon and got it back into shape.

Later that day, some recruits were asking our Senior if our Kill Hat was ever going to let up. He's been smashing us every day since we picked up. Our Senior told us that is his job as a Green Belt Drill Instructor with the Billet of "Kill Hat". With every cycle, he'll be able to move up until he becomes the Senior. Until then, his job is to instill Pain and Discipline. There are no breaks. As long as those lessons need to be taught, there is no Off Switch. Our Senior told us we really couldn't be upset if he came at us. The only reason he would is if we were being stupid. Then the question was asked, what about when a recruit is doing what he's supposed to do and the recruit next to him gets in trouble and is sucked into the vortex. Our Senior said we have to police our own. Meaning, if we are accountable for each other then chances are we can keep each other out of trouble. It's better to tell your brothers to lock it up than it get to the Kill Hat and he has to tell you to lock it up. BIG DIFFERENCE. The rules are simple. If you're undisciplined, you pay. It's easy. Don't be stupid, and you won't get jacked up. He's mean, but it makes you hard. It's his job and he does it well.

The scribe then asked what about when we are put on the quarterdeck for no reason at all. Our Senior said, "Well consider it a privilege to have a little one on one training time. Marines are machines. One day you're going to loo back and be proud of the time you spent on the quarterdeck because it made you that much stronger, meaner, and that much tougher. You didn't join the Marines to be a little bitch."

As a highlight, some of the recruits and myself have been working Jons, and he actually did 5 good pull-ups today. We got an extra Protein bar for helping him out.
Good stuff!

20080103 Thursday
FIGHT WITH PALLOC

I told Palloc to lock it up because he was talking too loud during "Free time". He gave me some static about it but he said he would quiet down. When I walked away, he started making fun of me when I turned my back. Palloc was a good recruit but we hadn't found that common ground of respect between us so he wasn't to inclined to do anything I said. I get it. But nevertheless, I wasn't about to pay for him so I had to get him to quiet down. He kept it up so I started yelling at him.

This got Staff Sergeant Assassin's attention. He called me to the house and asked what the problem was. I told him that Palloc and Bassikoff were talking too loud and I told them to lock it up. He then told me not to worry any more with it and that he was going to put them on firewatch. Good to go. Nothing speaks more than taking away sleep or chow.

The problem was that Graham was walking by the house and

heard what was being said to me and ran and told Palloc what was happening. This set Palloc off. As soon as I walked out of the house and made my way past the quarterdeck, I saw Palloc coming for me. Here we go.

He got right in my face not saying a word. I stared right back at him waiting to see if he was going to do something. Without saying a word, he pushed me but didn't swing. Interesting. Palloc is bigger than me, pissed off, but not committing. I got right back in his face and told him to push me again and see what would happen. With that, all the recruits started circling up. He then went to push me and as he did, I punched him in the face. Game on.

The first couple seconds were a blur. Then the tunnel vision set in and everything went back to normal speed. Someone said- **"Let 'em go! Let 'em go!"** and it brought things back to normal. Palloc was taller than me and had a great reach so I needed to stay in tight. Just as I moved in, he caught me in the mouth with a right. I knew there was a good chance of eating something getting close. Nevertheless, after that shot it got me in close enough and I hooked the back of his had with my left hand. Automatically, he tried to resist by standing up. When he did, I slammed my shin up into his nuts. That brought him back down. I immediately followed up with a knee to his stomach. The knee found its way home and it backed him up from me so he could attempt to recover. As he started to back up, I threw an overhand right into his head. Blood went everywhere. The recruits went, **"OOH!"** and that was it.

They separated us and Palloc and his buddy ran to the head. Just then, Staff Sergeant Assassin yelled- *GET ON LINE!* I started back to my spot when someone yelled- **That's what's up GUIDE!** I turned my head back and smiled bloody teeth. I think my teeth tried to take a field trip through my lip. That right Palloc gave me was no joke. I was shaking with adrenaline. Good times I must say. Once we were all on line, Staff Sergeant Assassin went back into the head. He walked in and said-

What the fuck are we doing in my head?
Bleeding SIR! (Everyone on line was trying not to laugh. That junk was funny.)

Were we being stupid?

316

Yes SIR!

Talking back to the Guide. Hmm. Very well. You need to secure that shit.
Aye SIR!

He came back out and walked right up to me from the side. He didn't
say a word. He just stared at me for a minute. He would do that to see if
you would lose your bearing. I just stared straight ahead. After that, real
quiet he said- *Let's just see what Senior has to say bout this.*

And that was it, he told us to hit the rack. I got into the rack and
all I could do was smile. About 15 minutes later, the Senior rolled into
the squad bay. He was talking to Staff Sergeant Assassin for a moment
and then he stepped out the door and yelled for Palloc and me. We
jumped out of the rack and hustled to the hatch. We went in the office
and Staff Sergeant Assassin closed the door and left.

Our Senior was wearing street clothes and told us that he was at a
club having a great time and now had to come up here. So this was
going to be short. He asked me what happened and I told him the story.
He then asked Palloc if there was anything wrong with what I said.
Palloc said no Sir. He then asked us if this was going to be it or if we
wanted to go some more. We both said we were good.

He then asked Palloc what he wanted to say about the cut on his
head. If he went to medical because of a fight, it would be bad news for
the Platoon. Palloc said the cut wasn't from the fight. He said he
accidentally slipped and cut it on the front site post of his M-16. And
that was that. We went out and he got everyone out of the rack and
into a circle. He explained to the recruits that it was a done deal. He
then told everyone the story with Palloc and asked if anyone had a
problem with that.

One thing for sure is that our Senior will always tell the truth
when it comes down to it, and if a recruit didn't want to go along with
the story, then that would be OK, and he would just have to deal with it
in another way. But for now, it would just keep heat off the Platoon
because the First Sergeant didn't like us as it was and he was looking for
something to pin on us. We were good to go.

Just so you know, from that moment on, me and Palloc worked
great together. We pounded it out and found ourselves on common

ground. We both gave up some blood and that did the trick.
As I closed my eyes, I noticed my hand was throbbing.
Great.

20080104 Friday
1st Phasers

Woke up. Great chow, but it wasn't enough. We found we as a Platoon are able to pound a lot more in less time. That's a good problem. We stepped from there and went to get plane tickets. That was awesome. Our Plane tickets would take us from our home to MCT. That means we're almost done.

After our tickets, we stepped to get haircuts. While we were waiting, we found ourselves facing 1st Phasers. GARBAGE! But hey, we used to look just like that. It's all good. They wanted to Battle us.
Drill Instructor- How bout it?
Our Heavy Hat- Get the fuck out of here. We ain't battling no 1st Phase fuckin recruits.
Drill Instructor- Are you scared?
Our Heavy Hat- Are your recruits any good?
Drill Instructor- Good enough to beat anything you got.

At this point, all the recruits started chesting up a little bit because of their Drill Instructor. Our Heavy Hat looked at us, looked at his watch, looked at us again, looked at the ground for a moment, and said-
All right all right. This shouldn't take too long.

The Drill Instructor looked 3 shades of cocky and ready to unleash his Platoon. He got them all jacked up with that whole *"Are you Ready?...* **YES SIR!** *Are you ready?...* **YES SIR!** Crap and then kicked the first general order.

SIR, THIS RECRUIT'S FIRST GENERAL ORDER IS, TO TAKE CHARGE OF THIS POST, AND ALL GOVERNMENT PROPERTY IN VIEW!

They were pretty good, but right at this moment we knew we had them. They just didn't know it yet. The Drill Instructor looked at us with a smirk. Our Heavy Hat looked at us and kicked the same thing.

SIR, THIS RECRUIT'S FIRST GENERAL ORDER IS, TO TAKE CHARGE OF THIS POST, AND ALL GOVERNMENT PROPERTY IN VIEW!!!

The only difference is we had VOLUME! It was crystal clear and we blew them out of the water! Our Heavy Hat looked at the Drill Instructor as if to say- *Whatcha got now sparky?*
The Drill Instructor looked at his Platoon as if to say- ...aw shit.

They kicked the diddy for the M-16a2 service rifle-
SIR THE CHARATERISTICS OF THE M-16 ARE UPPER RECIEVER, LOWER RECIEVER, BOLT CARRIER GROUP SIR!

We blasted them with the M-203.
SIR M-203 IS LIGHT WEIGHT SINGLE SHOT BREACH LOADED (CHIK CHIK) PUMP ACTION SHOULDER FIRE WEAPON ATTACHED TO THE M-16!!!
With that the Drill Instructor wigged out and said only 1st Phase Knowledge! Our Heavy Hat just smiled and spit on the ground shaking his head. *Very well* he said.

They kicked the diddy for Chesty Puller.
SIR 5 NAVY CROSSES IS COLONAL CHESTY PULLER SIR!
We blasted them with the Chesty Puller add-on.
SIR 5 NAVY CROSSES IS COLONAL CHESTY PULLER SIR!!!
(We all snapped our heads down and in a deep voice said)
MAY GOD REST HIS SOUL

That was that. They had nothing and they knew it. Our Heavy Hat just crossed his arms and grinned at the Drill Instructor. However, the recruits were impressed and it left an impression on them. When we left, they all gave us the nod and we nodded back.
When we got back to the house, it was time to do a trial fit to

make sure we knew how to wear our uniform correctly. It was no joke. There was a lot of stuff to do and no time to waste. But in the end, we looked sharp.

Before we hit the rack, our Heavy Hat taught us a new diddy as a reward for schooling those 1st Phasers. It was the Senior Drill Instructor's Motto for the "adjust" command. We learned it and later that night, we surprised our Senior with it. He yelled- *A-DJUST!* And we screamed-

WHEREVER HE GOES WE WILL FOLLOW
THE TASTE OF DEFEAT YOU WILL SWALLOW
THE PAIN IN OUR BODIES WE'VE LEARNED
RESPECT IS NOT GIVEN IT'S EARNED
WE ARE AN ENDANGERED SPECIES SIR!

20080105 Saturday
Cookie Monster Cometh

We started the day with a 7.5-mile hike. It was awesome. We were in stealth mode, which means for the first time, we didn't have to scream knowledge the whole way. All we did was hike in Platoon formation, it was great! I loved just being able to hike in complete silence. Nothing to do but listen to the sound of boots hitting the deck and everyone keeping in step. It was awesome! I sang church songs in my head the whole time. We sang them on Sunday and they have a Marine Corps twist so it makes them fun.

When we got back, we had the Company Commander's Inspection. It starts with Drill Instructors coming on deck and blasting you. Then after that, the Company Commander comes in and does the Inspection. They do that so you make your mistakes under pressure with the Drill Instructors and then you're squared away for the Commander. It works too because I failed the first time around. I accidentally spoke during a move. The Drill Instructor caught me fair and square. There wasn't a punishment. It was just a learning lesson. When the Commander came through, I was flawless.

That's one thing about being the Guide. Drill Instructors, Officers, everyone that comes on deck will start with you because you're the first recruit in line and you're the Guide. A lot of recruits got skipped because the Commander didn't stop at everyone. If you're the Guide, you'll always be first.

After he left, I got quarterdecked twice for screwing up. Once because I screwed up. And again because I was the Guide and screwed up. Grr! Did you really think there was such a thing as a learning lesson without a punishment?

It was Larson's Birthday and he turned 19. Our Senior snapped him in his nipples 19 times with a rubber band. Larson didn't know whether to laugh or cry. It hurt after a couple but it was funnier than anything else so in this game, laughter won. It was hysterical. I was standing right next to him and so the Senior snapped me 4 times because I was laughing at him. It wasn't that bad after the first couple times.

We got this recruit named Madigan. He got dropped back into our Platoon and only lasted 2 days. On the second day, he refused to get quarterdecked by our Senior. Our Senior yelled for the Guide and Squad leaders and we all got in his face and started screaming at him. We had turned into a Drill Instructor's Mini Me. We were just like the Drill Instructors except for the rank, authority, and smokey cover. But we sure knew how to rush someone and get in their face. We were taught well. He took about 10 seconds of it and then wigged out. He swung at our Senior, missed, and ran for the hatch. Our Senior unleashed us and told us to catch him. It's ON! He didn't even make it to the second deck. We tackled him in the stairwell and secured him. Our Senior caught up with Staff Sergeant Assassin as back up and told us to walk away. I don't know what happened after that.

A cool thing about being the Guide is that everyone knows you and everyone always greets you when you walk by whether they are in your Platoon or not. The recruits recognize you're the Guide by the Brassard on your arm. So when you walk by, they say- Mornin' Guide. In turn, as a Guide, you always say Good Morning back or whatever the proper greeting is at the time. It's a courtesy that in the civilian world is taken for granted.

I started to remember all the times I would cross paths with someone walking down the street and the persons eyes would stay locked to the deck or they would look busy so they wouldn't have to acknowledge your presence. It's garbage. Even though in the civilian world there is not the same hierarchy, the lesson learned for me is that saying Good Morning and acknowledging someone's presence has the power to pick them up. It's a simple moment in time where you made the choice to let them know they are not insignificant. That's going to be my thing from now on when I get back. Any time I have a chance to say Good Morning I will.

Today, we got a new hat on deck. He just graduated Drill Instructor school and joined us so that he would know what to expect for his first full cycle. We called him Cookie Monster because you could never understand what he said when he screamed at you. However, he was a Kill Hat and he was great at it!

HOLY CRAP! He was nuts! We were used to our Drill Instructors quarterdecking us but when Cookie Monster got a hold of you, you wanted to die. He was different. He was ruthless. He started out in our Platoon very quiet and only spoke when directly spoken to by the Senior. Today, he became unleashed. I guess he proved himself to our other hats and they took the chains off him. He was officially part of the family.

We had one recruit named Roscigno who was strong on the quarterdeck. He could last through anything. But even Roscigno broke today. We didn't see that coming. Cookie Monster killed him on the deck. As Roscigno was staggering back to the line, Cookie Monster caught Bryan talking. This time, Bryan got put in a world of hurt. He was strong on the quarterdeck too and started talking more on line because he didn't care about getting quarterdecked. This time, it was like he went back in time to Phase 1 and felt the fire of the deck. He got murdered. It hardened him this time. He didn't say jack on line after Cookie Monster got a hold of him. There was no sympathy in 3014 for the undisciplined. And cookie monster was the new enforcer!

20080106 Sunday
The Wisdom of Sergeant Brown

Last day at the Rifle House. Done for now. My hand is killing me. It can't be broken because I can still move it. But it's definitely jacked up because I can't push with it or squeeze anything. Oh well. No matter what, I can't let it slow me down. My faith says it'll be ok. So it'll be OK. Stepped to chow, came back and cleaned the house, and then we got ready to step to church. Church was great. It reminded me of what my dad would preach. The preacher asked us the 2 Big questions-

1-   On a scale of 0 -100, how sure are you that you are a Christian?
2-   If you were to stand before God right now, and he asked you "Why should I let you into my kingdom?" what would you say?

To most "religious" people, these questions really dig down in you and make you think about where you stand. If the first question's answer is anything but 100, you simply need to accept Jesus into your heart or rededicate your position as a Christian and need to get back on track. The second question draws out whether you believe it's through your good works you think you are saved, or if you believe that Jesus died on the cross for your sins no matter what good stuff you've done and it's through that promise of eternal life you are saved. It's good stuff.

When we got back from church, we found out we lost Gary. He dropped back because he UNQ'd on the Rifle Range. So long Gary. To pick up our spirits, we went down and had a class with Drill Instructor Sergeant Brown. Drill instructor Sergeant Brown was hysterical. He says 3 things ALL the time. Those 3 things were-

1- Fuckin
2- goddam
3- Say aye sir

He had a way of making sure that all three of those words and phrases were in almost every sentence he spoke. For example-

Hey, you're bout to have a special period of instruction with fuckin goddam Sergeant Brown say aye sir.
I'm gon tell you all you need to know about dem fuckin goddam condoms say aye sir.

I say it feels better without the bitch say aye sir.
I say dem condoms feel better without the goddam bitch say aye sir.
And fuckin goddam you gotta watch a mo' fucker say aye sir.
Dem bitches come with a mouf and teeth say aye sir.

(A recruit started laughing out loud)

Hey bitch. Don't you worry bout what I'm sayin. You country as fuck say aye sir.

When we were packed up we jumped on the busses and headed out to BWT. BWT stands for Basic Warrior Training. We'd be staying there for a few days and then who knows where we go after that. We packed up the entire house into a semi trailer and the rest was carried on our backs. No big deal.

The BWT site is only a 15-20 minute drive away but it seems like it's in a world of its own. Everything so far has been around buildings and civilization. Now, we are out in the middle of the woods with no paved roads in sight. It was great. The feeling was different as well. The Drill Instructors weren't screaming at anyone. They still kept the reigns tight but no one was getting quarterdecked. Welcome to Camp Combat.

As soon as we stepped off the bus, we got a bearing on our surroundings. There were trees everywhere and we were right in the middle of a small clearing that contained several rows of huts. On top of the door to our huts read: BWT. On the other side of the street was a row of huts that said: Crucible. This sight served as a duel area for BWT Training and the CRUCIBLE. Awesome.

At one point in the middle of the night, we saw a whole Battalion of recruits coming back from a day at the Crucible. It must have been around 2300 when they rolled in. We couldn't see them but we heard them coming in. They stayed for a couple hours and then they left just like that. For the recruits that had last firewatch, they would have never known they came and went. We never got to see any of the obstacles or courses from the Crucible during BWT, but the second night I actually got to see some of the recruits when they came in and they were wrecked. The got back at about 0100 that night and were gone well before we got up again. Holy Crap!

For now, each Platoon stayed in a "hut". All it is is a concrete slab with 4 walls, a hatch at each end, and a roof. No racks or running water. It was great. Very very basic. After we dumped our gear, we rallied up with the other Platoons and the Drill Instructors told us the basics of what we were going to be doing during our stay, the rules of the grounds, and how guard duty was to be performed and executed. AWESOME!

The Drill Instructors would then rotate giving us hip pocket classes anywhere from taking care of your brothers in the field, to the purpose of the 3-point combat sling. Even friggin Cookie Monster gave us a period of instruction. But his was more combat oriented. He introduced us to how to clear a house. And then we got to practice it a few times. Awesome!

They talked to us completely different out here. They made sure what they said was sinking in without just screaming at you. It was great. That night, we learned how to sleep with our rifle. It went everywhere with us in BWT. And I mean everywhere.

PHASE III

*Out of every **100** men in battle,*
Ten shouldn't even be there,
*Eighty are just **targets**,*
*Nine are the **real fighters**,*
and we are lucky to have them,
for they make the battle.
Ah, but the One,
*One is a **WARRIOR**,*
*he will insure the battle is **WON**,*
and bring the others back.
                      -Heraclitus 500 BC

20080107 Monday
BWT Day 1

Had box chow for breakfast and then cleaned up the grounds. Today was all about land navigation. We learned how to plot points, read maps, and how to read a compass. After that, we headed out deep in the woods. We had a 4-point navigation mission. We split up into teams of four. We call them fire teams. Each person in the fire team has a job. 1 recruit controls the map. 1 recruit controls the compass. 1 recruit treads the path. 1 recruit keeps track of the paces. My job was point man. I had the compass and pointed the way to go. It was no joke. You start at a box with a number on it, then you plow through this thick brush, around trees, over streams, and find your way to this little box with a letter on it. You jot down the letter and then move on to the next point. You repeat this process starting and ending at different points until you get to the last box. My fire team did great. We finished up and when we checked in with the Combat Instructor, we didn't screw up. Awesome!

That took just about the whole day. Your day is governed by the sun, so when it goes down, you headed back home. When we got home, Staff Sergeant Assassin was having fun with Bassikoff -

What kind of name is Bassikoff?
It's Russian Sir.

Are you Russian?
Yes Sir!

Speak Russian.
This recruit can't.

Bitch you ain't fuckin Russian.
Aye Sir!

That night, we headed to the RTF. Recruit Training Facility. It was the knowledge house out at BWT. We kicked a knowledge/volume battle with the other two Platoons. I'm proud to say we killed them. 3012 and 3013 were good but all those times we were pissed off at Staff Sergeant Assassin for making us scream all the time had paid off. Our Senior was proud of us. He saw we were coming with it so we boxed them in and blew them out. It was 51 Recruits surrounding 2 Platoons.

Right after that, a Combat Instructor came out and briefed us on our next mission. We were going to keep the same teams and do the same thing as this afternoon, but this time we had different starting points, no moon beams, and it was pitch black except for the stars. This should be fun. It was our first night creep and we did great. We all worked together and got to the finish in less than 2 hours. We turned in our coordinates and got everything right. The hard part was not knowing how far you had to go. It seemed like you just kept walking and walking and climbing around this and that and you always seemed to wonder if you were still on the right track. Not to mention the fact that since you couldn't see anything, you were always running into tree branches and getting poked in the face and racking your shins on stuff you couldn't see. But in the end, we followed the directions, worked together, and we found our confidence in the dark.

Before we left for that training event, we were warned by our Drill Instructors not to spread too far out because there was a Guillie Monster in the woods. The Guillie Monster is just one or two of the Drill Instructors suited up in Guillie Suits. They would hide among the brush and darkness and wait. When an unsuspecting fire team would walk by, the Guillie Monster would snatch the last recruit. It made things interesting. We stayed tight so we never got hit. When we got to the finish, we found that a few recruits got snatched. Good times!

We celebrated the night with MRE's. (Meals Ready to Eat) Yeehaw! Let me tell you something about MRE's. Not only do they actually taste pretty good depending on what you get, but they'll back you up for at least a week. You can forget about having to use the head for a while after eating those things. And in the woods, that's good to go.

20080108 Tuesday
BWT Day 2

We learned yesterday morning that we had a lot of stuff to pack up for the morning routine, so we decided as a Platoon to wake up extra early and knock that out so we don't have to rush so much. It worked out perfect. The firewatch got everyone up and we got right to work. When the Drill Instructors came in, they were glad to see it wasn't going to be a headache and that we were squared away on our own. After chow, we stepped to the airfield. We got briefed on our objectives by our Combat Instructor.

Today, we were going to low crawl, high crawl, back crawl, and day walk. This doesn't sound like that big of a deal but we were put into two man fire teams and thrown on a course. Me and Roberts were a team and we fired into the course. It was no joke. You pretty much crawl in some fashion the length of 2 football fields. But me and Roberts worked it hard and we made it through the crawls, through the Constantine wire, and finished the buddy rush first. Trust me, it pays to put out and try to be the first done in everything.

The Drill Instructors see that you're putting out and they won't play stupid games with you. Jons and Stahling got KILLED. They would jack it up and have to start all over, move too slow and start all over. Yeah, they got played with. When me and Roberts got to the start again, we were sent through again. That was actually cool because we learned what we needed to do so that this time, we would be a lot smoother and have to expend less energy, which in turn would make us faster. It was great. Roberts was a GREAT teammate. He was serious about the training and helped push the pace. We killed it.

After that, we had formation training. That's when everyone goes into stealth mode and learns how to do all the hand and arm signals. That was really cool. Except for when members of your fire team fight over who's in charge. In this case, Boyd and the Scribe were measuring johnsons and fighting over what was the correct call, and neither one of them was the fire team leader. As a result, they got their fire team killed and now they were on the Drill Instructor hit list. Not only does this drill teach you formations, but it also teaches you how to trust in the leader. You have to trust the leader!

MRE #2 was awesome! I got M&M's. I haven't had candy since I got to the Island. It was a small pleasure. After that, I got to take the

Platoon for a head call. That was a first. But here in BWT, it's not about the Drill Instructors wiping your nose; you have to learn to work together. When we got back, we formed up with the other Platoons and had a model making class. It was one of those clear an area, find some stuff in the area, and make a model of the grounds. It was cool. You'd find rocks to indicate roads and string to indicate power lines. It was cool to try and make a replica of the grounds with whatever you could find.

When it got dark, our Heavy Hat told us about the next 3 weeks. It would be less than a month and we would be Graduating. Now was the most important time to really buckle down and pay attention to the training we were getting. There's no time for coasting in. He was different this night. Normally he was yelling at us and throwing tantrums. This time it was all about preparing us for the final chapter. He still kept his elbow in our throat, but now, it was all about making sure we did what we needed to do so we could Graduate. He said the Crucible is where it's at. He told us it was no joke. He assured us we were going to feel broke off 100% of the time. But, if we wanted it, we would make it.

That night, we had our second night creep. This time, it was going through the same crawl/ movement course we did today but with a twist. We didn't really know what to expect until it happened. In the middle of the course, pyrotechnics went off in intervals. It's not that big of a deal except you have to know what to do. It's pitch black outside. No moonbeams at all. The moon lights up the course. It takes 10 minutes for your eyes to adjust to the dark so you can see. If a pyro goes off and you have your eyes open, you'll lose your ability to see in the dark for another 10 minutes. And you don't want to be the one to try and negotiate Constantine wire blind. It's all about making sure you close your eyes for the brightest part, and then when it fades, you open your eyes and continue on. Some recruits had a hard time with it. You just had to pay attention and gage the light with your eyes shut. At one point I was on my back going under Constantine wire and a pyro went off. I held my eyes shut for the first 15 seconds. I then started to peak with only one eye so if I was wrong I would still be good with the other eye. I just about opened my eyes when all the sudden I found that Cookie Monster was standing right over me and he said-

Hey boy, you might wanna keep dem eyes closed a bit longer.

He was right. Just as he said that, the pyro's came in a pair instead of one and I would have been stuck. I would have been blind for a few minutes under wire and that's a no go. So I waited a bit longer with my eyes tight, and then when it was clear, I took off. When I got to the finish, we formed up as a Platoon and headed back to the house first before the other Platoons. That means we had extra time to hygiene and square our stuff away. It pays to be first in this game!

20080109 Wednesday
BWT Done. Hello A- Line

We got up early again and that really helps when you don't have to rush everything. Less mistakes are made and recruits don't drag. Well today is it. BWT is in the bag and now it's on to A- Line. We grabbed our Flack, Kevlar, and war gear and headed to the range. We learned how to fire a controlled pair, hydraulic failure, and the failure to stop drill. It just means lots and lots of combat shooting. Instead of range shooting where you get in position and take your sweet time, this shooting is all about close range rapid firing. It's awesome!
During the class, we learned about tachypsychia (Tak-ip-sy-kia). It's when you're in a state of stress and your brain is processing faster than normal. It makes everything appear in slow motion.
During classes, you usually sit in some building and watch lots and lots and lots of slides while a Combat Instructor tells you what the slides say. We call it "Death by Power Point". You'll want to go to sleep. No matter what is being discussed, sleep will sneak up on you if you don't pay attention. Make sure you got a lot of water. Any time you feel sleepy, you can put some water in your mouth and just hold it there. Your brain will keep you awake because you don't want to choke on water. Another thing that helped me was hand sanitizer. It's got an alcohol smell to it and you are required to carry it everywhere you go. So when you get sleepy, put a dab of it right under your nose and the fumes will kick your brain in the nuts. No matter what, don't fall asleep.

They have sand pits on the range and the Drill Instructors have no problem taking you there between every single class.

After our class, we headed out to the firing line and did a BZO test fire on human silhouette targets. We practiced snapping in and it was tougher than I expected. After some practice, we moved into our new home, which is this supersized 1st Battalion deck. This thing is huge. It's easily twice the size of any squad bay we had been in. It's right there on Weapon's Battalion strip, which was familiar territory for us.

We also got smoked as a Platoon. It's like "Welcome to your new home... now get on your face!" It was a bad one too because our Heavy Hat was pissed off at some of the lazy recruits. Our Senior was gone and when that happens, anything goes. This time, we were holding our packs straight out on line while the 4 recruits were drag racing down the highway. He picked these recruits because they were the weakest in the Platoon and he was pissed that they hadn't started taking getting in shape seriously.

When they started giving up, our Heavy Hat made us bring our pictures of our families on line. He knew we had some and made sure they all came out. He grabbed some pictures from the recruits and told us that every time a drag racer dropped a knee, he would rip up a picture. Soon enough, a drag racer dropped a knee and true to his word, our Heavy Hat ripped a picture up.

A recruit scrambled for the pieces of his picture but our Heavy Hat was having none of it. The pieces just stayed there in the highway. This went on for a while. About 15 family pictures got torn up and littered the highway. Then our Heavy Hat took out the next picture and it was one of a little girl. Our Heavy Hat asked who's it was. It was Roscigno's daughter. Roscigno said it was his. Our Heavy Hat said- *Very Well.*

Our Heavy Hat walked over and stood right in front of Roscigno. He said that if the drag racers made it down and back, he would give the picture back. If they didn't, it was gone. With his eyes locked on Roscigno, he told our Kill Hat to let him know if they made it. The Kill Hat sent them. They got all the way down and on the way back, one recruit gave up and dropped a knee. Our Kill Hat said- *Nope, Nope, Nope.*

At that, our Heavy Hat ripped up the picture right in front of

Roscigno and then walked away. Luckily, he gave the pieces back to Roscigno. Roscigno later taped it back together. Needless to say, we had a heart to heart with the lazy recruits.

20080110 Thursday
Table 2 Pre Qual

Early chow. Awesome. No box chow. No MRE's. Yeehaw! After chow we stepped to the thunder dome. Right away it was me against my Kill Hat. I had to make a head call. There was no way I was going to leave the Guidon unattended with the Platoon. That's a huge no no. So I took the Guidon with me. It wouldn't fit in the head so I put it right outside out of sight. When I came out, I found that my Kill Hat had taken the Guidon and gave it to Jons. I rolled up to Jons and my Kill Hat stepped in between me and Jons. We got into it. He started telling me that I wasn't the Guide anymore and to walk away. I told him I wasn't authorized to follow that command and went after Jons. He started screaming at me and it was turning into a big deal.

At this moment, I had to walk away. When things get to a certain point where it draws attention to another Drill Instructors, you gotta be smart. So I walked away. But as soon as he turned his back and was halfway back to the other Drill Instructors, I ran over and snatched it from Jons. My Kill Hat couldn't catch me in time when I ran for Jons. Jons gave it up without saying a word.

We started firing for the first relay and it was awesome! However, one recruit from another Platoon was in the middle of his firing round and got served. His coach told him to stop firing because the round was over. The recruit looked back and when he did, his rifle went off and shot the ground about a foot and a half away from his front foot. Luckily it was down range. IMMEDIATELY, the tower simply said-

Drill Instructors Drill Instructors: negligent discharge on lane 13. Will you take care of that?

HOLY CRAP! What seemed like out of nowhere, 4 Drill Instructors jumped all over that kid. 3 got right in his face and the other ripped his weapon away and made it safe. As soon as they made it safe, they escorted the recruit to the yellow footprints. That's bad news right there. He stood there and the Drill Instructors lined up on him. They took turns one at a time tearing into him. As soon as they were done, a Drill Instructor escorted him out to the middle of the field. He made him sit there on the ground just watching the sun go down. Yeah, he was done. We never saw him again on the range.

After the practice relay, it was time for Pre-Qual. All the sudden the nerves came back. This was big. But just like before, you rely strictly on what you're taught, focus on the objective, and make it happen. I got through it and I was good to go. Now, I just have to repeat the same thing tomorrow for Qual and I'll be set.

Now, the next story I'm going to tell you is one that would change my life forever as a recruit. In one way it displays how serious Recruit training can appear, and on the other hand, it shows how meaningless everything truly is. It was the ultimate paradigm shift and final lesson to be learned during my stay on Parris Island.

When the firing was done, it was time to strip down and show we weren't walking off the range with anything. I stripped down and shook out my junk. Right in the middle of inspection, a Drill Instructor came over and told 6 of us recruits to go and help pick up brass off the lines because they were running out of time and it had to get done. All 6 of us started to get dressed. We were then told to keep our gear grounded in nice and neat piles, finish with the detail, and then come back for it. Nothing unusual about that. So we all took off. We finished the job in less than 10 minutes. When I got back, my Brassard was gone. I knew right away because I had secured it to my magazines just like always when we stripped down. Now it was gone.

I ran up to my Heavy Hat and informed him immediately. No response. Awesome. I ran back to the Platoon and told the recruits what happened. They said our Heavy Hat snatched it off my gear. My Heavy Hat took the brassard off my gear! We got back to the house and as soon as I stepped on deck, my Senior called for me. I ran up right away. He asked me where the brassard was. I told him that my Heavy Hat had picked it up. He didn't even bother to question my Heavy hat. He just asked why it was gone. I told him the story of getting yanked for duty. The other 5 recruits confirmed that we had been yanked right in the middle of strip down. He knew I wasn't lying. My Heavy Hat chimed in and said he took it straight off the deck. I told my Senior that was incorrect. But something had changed. My Senior didn't have my side. He started giving me this 50/50 that either I left it on purpose, or I forgot about it. Neither was true. I was ordered to ground my gear, perform detail in boots and ute's, and came right back. But this was going nowhere.

My Senior fired me right on the spot. He also fired the Squad Leader that confirmed my story. He immediately turned to Larson and Roberts and told Larson he was Guide and Roberts he was Squad Leader. There was no hesitation. Two were dumped, two were hired in an instant. 2 weeks before Graduation, I was fired as the Guide! I had been the Guide for 11 straight weeks. And now, it was all gone.

I was devastated. Right then and there, I was ordered to move all of my gear from the Guide rack all the way down to the end of GP (General Population). I took all my stuff and made sure I was on the very, very end. I didn't want to be in the mix with the recruits. I just wanted to be on the end. I wanted to be alone.
The Platoon was shocked. I was shocked. It was cool though because when I told them I was moving to the end, they were cool with that. The recruit on the end moved to Gary's rack because he was gone. The Platoon will never know how much I appreciated that. I didn't move to the end to throw a pity party for myself. I moved down there because I wanted to finally be able to relax just a bit. On the end, you weren't directly under the eyes of the Drill Instructors. You could fly a bit under the radar. Being the Guide was a crazy job. You were constantly on edge and always having to stay on point. I figured if I was fired, I was going to put myself in the best possible position. It was selfish in a way, but in a way I felt it was fair. I had led the Platoon for 11 weeks. The way I saw it, I was almost there. It won't matter in a few days.

For the rest of the day, all the recruits came by at different times and asked me how I was doing. I didn't know what to say. They knew it was horse crap. I just wanted to be left alone for a while to sort things out. No drama, no big deal. The recruits were cool with that. They let me be for the rest of the night. Palloc came up and showed me his smurf nuts. They were straight up blue. It's not that I wanted to see anything of his, but he just came up and said check this out. I looked up and I couldn't help but laugh at him. He said they've been like that since our fight but doesn't want to see the doc about it. I told him my hand still hurt but it wasn't going to slow me down. We laughed a bit more and then he took off. I hope my hand gets better before the Crucible. I don't know how that's going to work. But there's no way I'm quitting. I'm almost there.

After today, it all makes since why Marines are the best. The amount of time and value put on firing and the training that goes behind it is completely in check. Guys that I never thought would amount to anything are making multiple head shots from the 500 on Table 1 and smoking junk on Table 2. That's some good training.

Today was a bummer, but I kept my bearing. No drama from me. On the good side of being fired, I set myself right behind the Squad Leaders in formation so that I could always eat first. The Platoon didn't mind at all. That said a lot for them. If I had been garbage, they would have told me to stay in the back of the formation. But 3014 wasn't like that. We always helped each other out. And they knew it was bull crap. Plus, Larson needed help knowing what to do as Guide and I helped him out when I could. When I went to sleep that night, half of me wanted to fight tooth and nail to be Guide again, the other half said screw it, relax and enjoy the ride to Graduation. No more baby-sitting, no more games. All I have to do is finish the Crucible and Graduate. Tomorrow will be a new day.

20080111 Friday
Table 2 Qualification

Early chow. But this time I got to enjoy every bit of it. We came back and packed up the house. It was our last day. For the first time, I was relaxed. I was nervous about Qualifying, but that was it. My mind wasn't racing to remember everything that had to be done as the Guide. I let it all go. I missed it, but it felt great to have that pressure relieved.

When we got to the range, I was first relay and shot great! Table 2 was in the bag. I Qualified and that was that. It actually worked out better than I thought. I was totally relaxed for the shoot and it paid off. Now, the only thing that could keep me from Graduation was to get hurt in the Crucible. And that wasn't going to happen. My hand was being nursed as best as it could and I made due so far. My Kill Hat saw me wrapping it with duct tape and asked what was wrong. I said it got kicked when I was going through the buddy rush course. He studied me for a moment, and then later that day a tube of icy hot showed up for anyone that may need it. I jumped all over it when no one was watching. It helped with the swelling and Boyd hooked me up with some Ibuprofens he got from dental. it worked out.

The firing range was a done deal. I'm glad it's over. No more shakedowns. No more pressure. No more threats. We jumped on the bus and headed back to the BWT grounds. It's funny because everyone calls me Guide, realizes I'm not the Guide anymore, and then they call me "fired Guide."

That was my name until Graduation. Fired Guide. My Kill Hat almost broke my neck because I was walking off the range and he was calling for me from a distance. He came running up to me and yelled at me for not responding. I told him that I heard him yelling for the Guide, but that's not me. He understood. He didn't even know my name. He looked down at my name on my uniform and said-

Very well Killian, dat Guide shit don't matter anyway. Just hurry the fuck back to the Platoon and tell the new Guide his ass is gonna see me on the quarterdeck!
Aye Sir!

20080112 Saturday
BWT Endurance Course

Early rise. Had to finish packing our gear. Ate a box chow and got ready for some fun and adventure. Today was the Combat Endurance Course. We were told we were getting nasty. Sounds fun. It was the last objective in the BWT schedule. Staff Sergeant Assassin got us in formation and told us-

You gonna die up in this bitch!

It's rated as the most physically demanding event in BWT. Needless to say we were hungry for it. I was in the rabbit group- 3rd Team. They put us in teams with a Drill Instructor and we had to finish the course together. Wouldn't you know it? I was in my Senior's group. Great! Oh well. It'll be fun. We started with a half-mile sprint. We saw the 2nd group take off and my Senior told us we HAD to catch that group. We couldn't start until they got to the end of the half-mile sprint, and once they did, we tore off after them. We turned the corner at the end of the sprint and bounced across the rope bridge. No big deal. We sprinted to the next obstacle, which was the low crawl through the "poop shoot." And as a surprise, we caught the 2nd team. It's called the poop shoot because it's nothing but "knee deep fowl-ness that I don't want to know about". It smelled really bad and if you got some in your mouth, it was a no go. It was putrid. I saw 2 recruits from the 2nd team blow chow. I would throw up too but we had to fly. We had no time for that.

The barbed wire kept you in the mix so there was no high crawling through that junk. We were back crawling as fast as we could through that junk.

After that, we hit the cargo net and then found our way to the rope swing. That was tough because our hands were all wet and cold and it made it nearly impossible to hold onto the rope. But we made it. After that, we hit the inclined wall and we flew over that. More low crawling followed and we were almost there. The 1/8th mile sprint between all the obstacles was awesome because it gave us a chance to catch the other teams. Now was the time we were glad our Kill Hat made us play all those running games. It helped us out big time here. We finished in 1st Place!

It was just lots of fun in the rain and mud. We were Nasty! Our Senior and Heavy Hat did the whole course with us. Our Heavy Hat was awesome. He showed us how to blast through tough parts of the course and motivated everyone to push it. As for our Senior, everyone started to shoulder him. He was losing respect points fast with our team. While our Heavy Hat focused on us, he was focused on himself, which got old really fast. Our Senior said he did everything with us. That's garbage. He didn't carry a rifle or war gear through the course. He didn't even do all the obstacles. The fun ones he did, but when it came to the hard ones, he just stood off to the side and said we were going too slow.

As for our Heavy Hat, he did the entire course with gear and went through some of the obstacles twice to push the slower teammates or show them how to get through it faster. That's the difference. When we got back, the other team that was with Staff Sergeant Assassin said he straight up grabbed his Rifle and dove head first into the Poop Shoot. The Drill Instructors know how to have some fun and they aren't afraid to show you how to do it. That's awesome.

After the course, we stripped down on the airfield and cleaned up as best as we could. Then we collected our stuff, jumped on a bus, and headed back to good ol' 3rd Battalion Home sweet Home. We set up our stuff and it was awesome to be back to our original house. This is where it all started and now we were about to finish our training.

After we got set up, we went out to hit the Drill deck. We didn't even get started. Our Senior got pissed at us and took us to the Pit. Grrr! What are we supposed to do? We have a new Guide and Squad Leaders and they don't have a clue as to what to do. The Guide doesn't know the commands or how to march in the Guide spot. I'd been the Guide for all this time and so no one had ever taken the time to see what I had to do whenever we would march. It's a lot of stuff you have to remember. Since he doesn't know the commands, and the new Squad Leaders don't know the steps in the new positions, it was a mess. We got smoked for it. Awesome! Our Senior was banking that they would pick it up just like that and that didn't even come close to happening.

After that, our Heavy hat took over because our Senior stormed off frustrated and pissed. Our Heavy Hat saw what was up and told everyone what they needed to do. And sure enough, it began to make sense. There was no way they would have it perfect, but at least they could fake it through and not look stupid.

Our Heavy Hat always brought the best out of us on the Drill deck. He was proud of us. He made us what we were and we worked for him. He then took us to chow and we ate good, good, good. Put a fork in me, I'm done for today.

It's cool being back at the house where we started. So many memories cam back and it was really clear how far we had come.

20080113 Sunday
You Live and Learn

Early chow and it was off to church. A few more services and I'm out of here! The service was great. We talked to the newbies. It was their first Sunday and they were all shocked and paranoid. I gave them as much encouragement as I could. It was like giving them ammo. The confidence started to grow as they learned what to expect. They'll still have to feel the fire and fight through it, but at least they'll know what kind of beast they'll face.

We got back and hit the Drill Deck. Right now, that is the only thing that matters. No more shooting. More will come. But for now, it's all about drilling and popping sticks. Final Drill is right around the corner and we have SO much to do in order to get ready.

That night, the Platoon found out about the deal the Senior had made that ended in me and the squad leaders getting fired. Our Senior made a bet with another Senior Drill Instructor that he could fire his Guide and Squad Leaders and still win Final Drill. That sucks. Everyone was pissed about it. We were doing really good and marching was locked down and tight. Now that we had a new Guide and Squad Leaders, it was like starting all over again. It answered a lot of the unanswered questions. It didn't make any sense why we got fired the way we did. Now we all see. Oh well. There is nothing anyone can do about it now. We just gotta keep rolling and not sweat the stuff we can't change.

It was funny because during free time, we got into a group and they would tell me stories of what I had done from time to time. Conrad called me the Angel of Death. He said I was all nice to everyone until someone got stupid. Then I would go from 0-100. BAM! But not anymore. Now I'm just relaxed and focused on training hard. No more drama to worry about. Being the Guide was a big deal to me so I do apologize if you are tired of reading about it. But it's all about the lessons we learn. I learned more from being fired than I did from everything going the way I thought it would.

A wise man once told me the story of a Captain and his ship. The Captain would sail along enjoying the sun and the breeze, and in an instant, a storm would roll in and shake up the world that he had grown to love. In one moment he would be basking in the sun. In the next, his ship would be shattered on the rocks. He cried out to God-
Everything was going so well. Why has this happened to me?
And then God answered him and said-
It's not a matter of **why** a storm hits you, it's a matter of what you do **when** the storm hits you. Only one of the two you can control. And it's up to you to decide if you will let it leave you broken, or if you will learn from it and press on with one more lesson learned.

I felt broken, but I'm not beaten. It's just another lesson learned and Graduation is around the corner.
Game on!

20080114 Monday
Almost There

For the first night in a long time I slept really well. I woke up to the lights, lights, lights, with a smile on my face. After chow we stepped to the RTF for some classes. The class was on Land Navigation 2. As soon as the class was over, we were loaded directly onto buses, driven out to the middle of nowhere, dumped, split into fire teams, and told to get back home. It was me, Palloc, and Betze. We were one of the first 2 teams back. AWWYEAH! It's cool how me and Palloc work together now. They say you can't make an omelet without breaking a few eggs. Ever since the fight, nothing was ever an issue again.

I can't wait to finally Graduate. For now, I just have to keep pushing hard. I found out today that I still may receive a Meritorious Promotion. That would be awesome. In the Platoon, the Guide, Scribe, and Squad Leaders are typically given a Promotion. Even though I wasn't the Guide now, I had served long enough to qualify so I should be good to go. I Hope so.

My hand is finally getting back to normal. It's about time. We filled out the Crucible Pre-Scan sheet to prove we are physically ready to go for it. I'm praying every day that my hand will heal up. Ever since I hurt it, I have been downing Marine Corps M&M's 3- 4 times a day, putting Icy Hot on it, wrapping it up with tape, and doing everything I can not to aggravate it without my Drill instructors catching wind of it.

My Heavy Hat questioned me on it before we finished A-Line and I told him I busted it during the Buddy rush Course, but it was OK. He looked a bit harder at me and then said- *Very well.* And that was the end of it. I made sure to tell him the same thing I told my Kill Hat so if it came up they would have matching stories.

That night before we hit the rack, we were PT'd hard. The final PFT is coming and we have to be ready. As a reward, we got to sing the Marine's Hymn. We were told to memorize it. It may not seem like a big deal but it was to us. We were forbidden to associate ourselves with anything that was Marine related. It was pounded into us that we were not Marines yet. We were nothing but nasty recruits. So to be able to sing the Marine's Hymn was awesome. Especially when we got to the end. Staff Sergeant Assassin got us screaming **"OO-RAH!"** at the end.

20080115 Tuesday
8 More Days...

Early chow as always. But this time, the Drill Instructors reversed the formation so all of us in the front went to the back. It was cool. It gave the little end a chance to eat first. They were excited. 8 days till the Crucible!

After chow, we stepped for our Uniform final prep. It could be a long morning. I was right. It took all but most of the morning and afternoon to get us our final size and fit for our Uniforms. Box chow wasn't even that bad. We'll eat anything. There is no such thing as a picky recruit when it comes to chow.

I got put into the group of Artist Recruits. My job is to paint these Hat Racks for our Drill Instructors. I started with the Rack for my Heavy Hat. It's going to be awesome. I've got a great idea for my Heavy Hat, Kill Hat, and Staff Sergeant Assassin. I'm not doing one for the Senior because the other Artist Recruits were instructed to make him a footlocker. Not just a hat rack. A whole friggin footlocker. Have fun with that.

We marched in front of some newbies and they stopped to watch us. The Drill Instructors of their Platoon were busy pointing out stuff we did that they needed to do and told them that's how it should be. We weren't the best, but we had our stuff in check. They looked at us just like I looked at the 3rd Phase recruits when I was in 1st Phase. You're just floored. How are we going to become that tight in such a short amount of time? It's called an awesome Heavy Hat. We were a machine. We had made our big mistakes, paid for them. And now we were refining our game.

It's a hard step-by-step process but the end result is amazing. I would have never thought we would make it. But even the most garbage recruit finds his way and is able to get it all together. Granted, they may pay a lot more than the person that gets it within the first few times. But the big deal is that they get it.

I started thinking more about it and found that I could actually be just as much a motivator in GP (General Population) as I was as the Guide. In some cases, a bit more. As the Guide, you have a commanding presence and you can easily force recruits to do what you want them to do. It is often faced with a bit of a fight at times, but it gets the job done. It works in reverse when you're GP. In this case, you have to reason with the recruit so they clearly see that it's in their best interest to do the right thing. You can't make them. You can only guide them. Not to mention that the vast majority of the time is spent having to lead first by example. But, the big difference is that they are willing to do a better job when it's on their own. So it's a bit longer task but the result is superior to just out right making someone do something. There is a time for both. You have to know when to do which one.

20080116 Wednesday
Live and Learn Part 2

After chow, we stepped to the PT field. We were scheduled for a 3.1-mile motivational run. That's where you run in formation and sing cadence just like in the movies. It was AWESOME! Our Heavy Hat was the best. He sang some great cadence. It was obvious that he had done this a lot because there was absolutely no hesitation from verse to verse or between songs. Staff Sergeant Assassin came in on the 2nd Mile. And our Kill Hat got us on the 3rd Mile. Each one had a unique set of songs they would sing. Our Heavy Hat was all about boot camp songs. Staff Sergeant Assassin was all about having sex with hot Navy girls. Our Kill Hat sang about killing everyone! It was a lot of fun. We felt like we could keep going strong for another 6 miles but we had to wrap it up.

Big Problem. Tuller, Zanis, and Beale fell out on the run. When we got home, Cookie Monster got a hold of them. Tuller was crying like a little girl and there was no end in sight. To our Senior, this was shameful. How could you have a 3rd Phase recruit falling out on a motivational run? For that reason, he let them get smoked for a long...long time.

But soon enough it did finally end and afterwards we had a PT shower and got ready to step to the RTF. Wow, today is wicked cold. It's been cold before, but today, we had this wind chill that cut right through you. I was thinking forget about it. You're going to be cold today. Don't even bother trying to stay warm. Just grit your teeth and push on. I pulled road guard duty just so I could run from post to post and stay somewhat warm. That was the best I could do.

When we got back to the house, I missed the-

Put your fuckin beanie in your little fuckin daypack! - Issued by Staff Sergeant Assassin.

I froze my butt off for the rest of the day. We stood outside a lot. That's what happens. However, I was so mad at the situation of leaving my beanie that it actually kept me warm while everyone froze with it on. Then it hit me, if the Drill Instructors weren't wearing a beanie (which they weren't) and they weren't worried about it, then I shouldn't either.

At the RTF, we had classes on drug and alcohol abuse. It was pretty cool. After dinner chow, our Kill Hat ran us under water for fun while running back from the chow hall so now we were soaked and frozen. Good stuff. It just hardens you up every time you do something where you're miserable like that and after a while, you just don't care anymore. Bring it.

20080117 Thursday
Prep for Prac App

Yesterday, it was cold. Today, it's raining and cold. However, this time we were ready for it. We got to wear our Gortex and everyone made sure to pay attention to when we needed our beanie. We were waterproof and warm. At this moment, it occurred to me that if you have the right gear, you'll never be cold. You just have to know what to wear. Granted, Drill Instructors love to play with you and make you freeze, but to be honest, if you pay attention, they'll take care of you.

We went to the RTF and I got a big surprise. I ran into a familiar face. A recruit looked really familiar but I couldn't be sure. He saw me and when he had the chance, he came up and introduced himself. His name was Brian. When I lived in Florida, I opened up a Karate School in Gainesville for the ATA in 2001. He was one of my students. He started as a white belt and trained with me until he got his Black Belt. He was a

345

good kid. He had a tough road coming up with his family, but he fought his way to the top. After he got his Black Belt, I moved to Annapolis to my Martial Arts School. Before, it was a clear cut Instructor/ Student relationship. I taught him everything he needed to know to become a Black Belt.

Now, we were both recruits. We are on the same playing field and held the same rank regardless of our background. It's a small world.

I finished my Heavy Hat's hat rack. It looks great! That night, we had a big study session for our Prac App test. The test is tomorrow and I feel confident about it. It's pretty much going to include a Knowledge section, a First Aid performance section, a Land Navigation section, and an Oral section where you have to identify stuff. Should be good.

We broke up into teams and practiced the individual sections that would be found on the exam. Land Navigation was in the bag. So was the medical response stuff. The only thing we really had to work was the oral part. We were required to know how to check in/ check out and embark/ debark a ship. You just have to say the right thing and then make sure you know how to excuse yourself without looking stupid. A lot of recruits screwed up the dismiss. They kept stepping with the correct foot and then swinging the incorrect arm back. Our Drill Instructors didn't say a word.

At this point in training, it was up to the Guide and Squad Leaders to jump down a recruit's throat. If it didn't happen, of course they would step in, but we were usually good with helping each other out so it didn't come to that.

Oh yeah. Let me just tell you one HUGE thing about Boot Camp. In your Platoon, EVERYONE loves to be the one to correct you. Holy crap! You can take the most garbage recruit. The one that just sucks at everything. He always gets quarterdecked, he always says the wrong thing, and he always screws up everything. Go ahead and do the littlest thing wrong right next to him and let him catch you. He'll blast you as if he's the son of the Senior. It's the craziest power trip. Stupid recruits get in so much trouble for being stupid so they naturally just wait on the tips of their toes for someone to do something wrong so they can unleash the pint up aggression they have stored up. It's gay.

I'm not saying you shouldn't correct a brother in your Platoon. Just get used to EVERYONE, even the most garbage recruits, to jump all over you when you make a mistake. Get used to it.

20081018 Friday
Practical Application Exam

The Prac App exam is today and the final PFT is tomorrow. When we went to chow, they didn't have any milk. GRRR! I had just gotten some Fruit Loops and now we don't have milk. Great! So I took my Red PowerAde and used it as milk with my Fruit Loops. Improvise, Adapt, and Overcome! It wasn't the best, but those Fruit Loops went down the pipe. I could care less.

Right after chow, we headed to the RTF for the exam. This exam is Pass/ Drop. But given how much we had been practicing, we should all be fine. The first section was Land Navigation. They give you a map and some coordinates, and you have to plot the route. All you have to do is remember the formula and use the tools they give you. No big deal here.

After that, we headed for the First Aid. We had done this so many times that it was a blur. We didn't even have to think about what to do. They gave you a dummy, a situation, and you did all the appropriate steps. Cakewalk.

The last section was Oral. You looked at about 15 or 16 cards, identified what was on the cards, and you were good with that part. It was basically identifying rank insignias for all the branches, general orders, and a couple bonus questions. Not a huge deal.

The final stage was to report in. when you arrive to your first duty station, they want to know that you can present yourself as a motivated Marine. There is a desk with a Marine behind it, you walk up, say your lines, and then dismiss yourself correctly. This is the part that got a lot of recruits. It's easy to crack under the pressure and do something stupid. Fortunately, like I said we really hammered this stuff with Staff Sergeant Assassin so we were in and out. I scored a 100%. It's no big deal if you keep a level head and stay up on your studying.

When I got back to the house, I put the finishing touches on Staff Sergeant Assassin's Hat rack. If you're an Artist recruit, the only time you get to work on this stuff is during chow. You only have a maximum of 45 minutes to work on it per session and by this time, you don't have too many days left. Keep in mind that if you work on it during chow, the Scribe brings back who knows what for you to eat, and if you pissed off the Kill Hat, he'll get your chow. If he does that, stand by! It's always jacked up. The last time, we got noodles and green jello all mixed together.

So now, Staff Sergeant Assassin's rack was done. He saw it when it was black and white without color and it was the first time I ever saw him smile. He still hasn't seen it with color and I know he wants to because he's always trying to sneak up on us and get a peak at it.

We got a pick up today. The last one didn't last more than two days and so we'll see how this one does. Cookie Monster killed him. They saw that he was talkative with the recruits so the Drill Instructors silenced him. They just made him stand in the middle of the highway and scream non-stop until he lost his voice. It was annoying but it only lasted for maybe an hour until his voice was totally gone. He couldn't say a word after that. Then, Cookie Monster and our Kill Hat quarterdecked him because he was a PFT drop. Whenever we had a break, he was getting quarterdecked. All day long. They wanted to get rid of him and send him to medical but he was determined to just make it. You could tell in his eyes that he wasn't going to quit again. Everyone in the Platoon gave him props for that. He was welcomed to 3014.

20080119 Saturday
FINAL PFT

When we went to chow, our Kill Hat told us to eat light. We needed to eat, but this morning was about pounding chow that is hard to throw back up. So it was pretty much Eggo's and eggs. No milk or dairy products. After chow, we stepped back to the house to prepare for the PFT. This is the final PFT. By now, no one was really concerned about failing it and getting dropped back. In fact, we were charged and ready to go.

On the way back to the house, we got hit with some torrential rain. No big deal. That just means we'll have to do our Pull-Ups and Sit-Ups in the house, and then we'll hit the run whether it's raining or not.

Who cares about the rain?

For the Pull-Ups, our own Drill Instructors were not allowed to grade us on our performance. Other Drill instructors came in to check us out and ours went to other decks to look at their recruits. However, our Heavy Hat stayed back in our house to make sure the other Drill Instructors didn't play with us. We lined up for Pull-Ups and everyone did really well. Only 4 recruits did less than 10 and most importantly, everyone passed. Even Rich threw down and got a couple past the minimum. He failed the pre test PFT and we had really worked with him. He stepped up and made it happen for himself. Good man.

After that, we lined up with a partner and got ready for the Sit-Ups. We destroyed this. All you have to do is get 100 in two minutes and you're done. You're not really supposed to stop when you get to 100 so you throw in a couple more if you have a couple seconds left. When you're done, they just tell the ones that did less than 100 to stand up and report their number. The rest just get marked as max for Sit-Ups.

We got our Gortex and day pack and headed out to the track. It was still pouring with no end in sight. So we grounded our gear and spread our ponchos over the gear so it would stay dry. So we're standing our there with the rest of the 3rd Battalion Follow Series, we're wearing nothing but our PT gear which consists of a skivee shirt, skivee shorts, and our go fasters. It's freezing cold and pouring rain... and we're excited. Only on Parris Island will you find totally motivated recruits freezing, wet, and amped about running 3 miles as fast as possible. Yeehaw! But it's true. This was the last Physical Test outside of the Crucible. This was our last chance to just go for it!

We formed up in our running groups. The rabbits in the front and everyone else formed up behind. This was the last time that me and the other 3rd Battalion rabbits would be together to run. We were all shaking hands and bumping knuckles getting ready for the go. All the big wigs showed up to see how we did. It was a simple out and back and you could cut the adrenaline with a knife. Even the Drill Instructors were in a good mood. This was the last time they had to run with us. Everyone was set, the course was on point, and we were ready. We got the GO and fired out of the gate. We followed the 6-minute mile Drill Instructor and stuck with him as long as we could. Running in the rain was a lot different. Me and my running buddy stuck with him as long as we could. I'll tell you right now that that Drill Instructor was a friggin machine. Consistent and persistent to the 9's. He started to pull away from us. As long as we stayed in between him and the 7-minute mile Drill Instructor, we were good.

We kept to our pace and me and 3 other recruits I always ran with finished with a time of 20:19. Running a sub 7-minute mile for 3 miles in pouring rain with a nuclear head wind is good in my book. It wasn't my best time but given the circumstances, I was happy about it. I gave a high five to my running buddies and headed back to my Platoon. When we got back to the house, we got our scores. I had a 1st Class PFT in the books. Awesome!

After we got back to the house and showered up, we got a big surprise. Today was **Black Saturday**. It's the last day of recruit training that the Drill Instructors can quarterdeck you. After today, the quarterdeck will be closed. We had no idea. They split us into 4 groups.

Our Heavy Hat had the front Quarterdeck. Staff Sergeant Assassin had the other Front Quarterdeck. Cookie Monster and our Kill Hat had the back Quarterdeck. Our Senior took the PIT outside. This was the last time we would get smoked by our Drill Instructors. Needless to say, we were totally excited! For the majority of recruit training, we were terrified of the quarterdeck. By now, we didn't mind it at all. We knew we could survive it. We welcomed it. It was good training. My group started with our Heavy hat. We stayed there for about 10 minutes as they gave us the most miserable up, down, in, out, on your face, on your back, on your feet, faster/ faster/ faster work they could give us. Then we would rotate to the next quarterdeck. Each Drill Instructor had their own unique drills they would make you do so it was never identical to another Drill Instructor. Good times.

In Boot Camp, you are not allowed to say "thank you" to anyone. You say, "received sir" or "received recruit" if someone gives you anything. So, since we couldn't say thank you to our drill instructors for a great kill session, we all screamed **"RECEIVED SIR!"** when we rotated away from their station.

When we got done rotating through, we were smoked indefinitely. But we had smiles on our faces. We had learned the art of determination and we had only our Drill Instructors to thank for that lesson. In Phase 1, we would have NEVER been able to withstand 10 minutes of hard-core drills. (let alone 4 solid rotations.) We had come a long way!

However, after the Drill Instructors finished with us, they announced that we were losing a recruit. Beale was gone. He gave up on himself during the PFT and failed it. He complained of a leg issue and even though he was cleared by the Doc, he just gave up during the 3 mile run. I couldn't believe it. Now he's getting dropped back. That sucks. He was a good guy. Well, it won't slow us down. We can only move forward from here. Tomorrow is Sunday! Hallelujah!!

20080120 Sunday
Demo Team

This morning, we got an extra hour of sleep. Awesome! Not sure why but we didn't complain. By now, we had an automatic internal alarm clock and we got up before the whole Lights, Lights, Lights deal. When we woke up, we looked at the clock and saw it was passed 4AM. We started to stir and Staff Sergeant Assassin came out of the office and told us to stay in our racks. We didn't complain or question why.

For chow, I shoveled in the biggest breakfast to date. I had Cinnamon Toast Crunch, Pancakes, Hash browns, Cinnamon Roll, PB and J sandwich, Banana, Grits, Scrambled Eggs, Milk, and Red PowerAde. Yeah! I was hungry after yesterday!

After chow we stepped to church. We got to talk to the New Marines that just finished the Crucible. They still haven't graduated, but once you finish the Crucible and get your Eagle, Globe, and Anchor, you are considered a Marine. They were Marines now. They told us what to expect and based on their appearance, they weren't joking about it. They looked beaten and banged up. It was great to see them. You could see them radiating pride. It was inspiring.

After the Bible Study, we stepped to the actual church service in the chapel. We were sitting down and minding our own business when all of the sudden this 2nd Battalion recruit came up and starting ragging on us because we were wearing our leather gloves. He said-

It's not even cold. I've been here for 6 months. I had to shoot on the Rifle Range in just a skivee shirt.

I had enough! I saw his boots weren't bloused so I jumped on him. I asked-
Why aren't your boots bloused?
He just shrugged.

So you're going to dog on us for wearing gloves and you can't even blouse your own boots. You've been here for 6 months because the bottom line is you can't do anything right. You're garbage as hell. Walk away!

I didn't raise my voice because I was in church but I was serious and staring straight at him until he walked away. The recruits around me were shocked. I never said anything like that before but I was right so it was all good. However, I apologized for saying "Hell" in church. That was wrong. My bad.

When we got back to the house, luck had shined upon us once again. Our Kill Hat was looking for 10 motivated recruits. The only requirement was you had to have a 1st Class PFT. Obviously we jumped at whatever he wanted. He got us all together and explained that we were going over to Lima Company and we were going to be on our Kill Hat's Demo team. Demo team for what? He told us we were going to demonstrate how to get quarterdecked to the brand new recruits. AWESOME!!!

It took everything in us to not start giving high fives and lose bearing. We stayed cool. This was going to be awesome! Our Kill Hat told us what the order was going to be, that we were going to perform on 3 decks, and that we had to give it everything we had and scream like never before. Good to go!

We stepped over to the Lima Company Barracks and waited outside the hatch. Our Kill Hat went over the game plan one more time and we were set.

All of the sudden, our Kill Hat gave us the GO and we ran on to the quarterdeck and formed up. All the recruits were sitting on the other quarterdeck. We stripped off our blouses, emptied our pockets, and locked our bodies by the time their Drill Instructor introduced our Kill Hat. He then whipped around and gave us a 60 second heater. We did up downs, push-ups, sit ups, and arm circles at lightening speed and screamed to the top of our lungs. When we were done with our set, he locked us out and then screamed at us to get off the deck, and just like that (SNAP) we were gone.

On my way off the deck, I snuck a glance back and saw the faces of the recruits. They were shocked and paralyzed! They had the same look I had when those 3rd Phase recruits came on our deck and did the same thing when I was a 1st Phase recruit. It was an awesome experience. The funniest thing was the way the houses looked when we ran in. On 2 of the 3 decks, it looked as if the Drill Instructors had just gotten done playing with them. There was gear and shaving cream everywhere. They have no idea what's coming! We finished the 3 decks and went back to the house. That was so much fun.

8 weeks ago, I can't say I would have volunteered for that. I didn't get it yet. I didn't understand the purpose of the quarterdeck and how important it would be. It seemed as just a horrible punishment at first. Now, I understand. The quarterdeck is the secret weapon that drives 3rd battalion. The quarterdeck thoroughly instills SPIRIT and DISCIPLINE.

We finished the day by studying for our Final Knowledge Test. After that, we'll be academically done. This is the last chance to get dropped on a test. With that in mind, we studied our butts off.

20080121 Monday
Final Knowledge Test

Back to early chow. This time, our Senior made us stay back to work on stuff during chow. It was a bummer because morning chow is usually the one we cared the most about getting. Oh well. We got to work and everything is looking great.

After chow, we headed to the RTF for the final Knowledge test. This was it. This was our last academic test to take and then we were done with that. We got to the RTF, sat down, and got busy. To be honest, it was a lot easier than I thought it was going to be. Myself and a few other recruits got a 100%. Awesome! I wish I could say it was a lot harder but it wasn't. It was much easier than the Phase 1 and Phase 2 Knowledge test.

On the way back, Staff Sergeant Assassin had some fun with us. 3012 was in front of us and we were all kicking diddy's back and forth to see who was the loudest. 3012 kicked one of our diddy's. They stole that junk outright. But we had something for them.

The other night, Staff Sergeant Assassin taught us a new diddy. We didn't know why, but now we found out. It seemed totally odd and no one understood it until we kicked it. Staff Sergeant Assassin found out they stole our diddy and knew they would come at us with it. So after they kicked our diddy, Staff Sergeant Assassin yelled-

ESPIONAGE!

We used to say-
SIR, ESPIONAGE IS WHAT SPIES USE TO GATHER TOP SECRET INFORMATION SIR!

This time we said-
SIR, ESPIONAGE IS 3012 SIR!!!

3012's Drill Instructor was floored. Staff Sergeant Assassin was a Knowledge Hat for a reason. He was always one or two steps ahead of everyone else. They shut up after that. Good times.

When we got back to the house, we were about to pop sticks with the Senior and he dropped a bomb on us. He told everyone in the Platoon that he wasn't going to Meritoriously Promote any of us. He told the Guide, Scribe, Squad Leaders, and myself that none of us were getting promoted. The Guides, Scribes, and Squad Leaders in **ALL** the other Platoons were getting promoted except for 3014. WTF Over!

If you look in our Graduation program to this day, you'll see all the other Platoons promoting and recognizing recruits. Not us. Not 3014. Under Meritorious Promotion there is nothing but blank space. That was horse crap. Oh well.

At dinner chow, everyone turned on Larson for abusing his power as the Guide. Boyd had a question about the Hot Trays he had to take

354

back to the house, and instead of Larson listening to him and getting the job done, he sent him to the back of the line for trying to speak to him out of line. Boyd was pissed. I would have been too. It screwed the Artist Recruits because he wouldn't help Boyd.

Recruit Bryan also turned to the dark side of garbage. He yells at everyone to do the right thing, but then he is the first to do something mean to a recruit for fun. At this point, the tried and true hard recruits were getting stronger and rising to the top. Unfortunately, the garbage recruits were also making themselves known. This was the start of the making of the final product we'd see on Graduation day. We were all determined to make it. The difference was what the end result would be.

20080122 Tuesday
More Games... Yeehaw!

Tomorrow is Final Drill so it's easy to guess what the focus was today. You got it. Drill, Drill, and more Drill. That's all we did. We spent the entire day on the grinder outside of chow times. After dinner chow we were stepping back with Staff Sergeant Assassin and he was having some fun with us. McCool was laughing about something in formation and so Staff Sergeant Assassin made him run around the Platoon as we were marching back. He just kept running around and around. Then Staff Sergeant Assassin said-

Hey McCool, how you doin?
Great Sir!

Great, go check on the Guide and see how he's doing.
Aye Sir! (He ran up to the Guide and kept running beside him)
How you doing Guide?
Good. (He runs back to Staff Sergeant Assassin.)
Good evening Sir, the Guide says he's doing good sir!

Good. Go check on the Squad Leaders and see how they are doing.
Aye Sir! (He runs back to Squad Leaders.)

How you doing Squad Leaders?
#1- Good.
#2- Good.
#3- Good but my leg is bothering me. I'm ok.
#4- Good. (He runs back to Staff Sergeant Assassin.)
Good evening sir, all the Squad Leaders say they're good except for #3.
He says his leg is bothering him but he's OK.
Good. Go tell #3 to stop marching and run around the Platoon with you.
Aye Sir! He did what he was told. They ran around the Platoon the whole way back. When we got to the street, they stopped running, got back in formation, and that was that. It was hysterical!

20080123 Wednesday
Final Drill

Today is Final Drill. This is the last time we will go to the Grinder and march. It's the last chance for a Drill Instructor to earn bragging rights among the other Platoons. Yeah, no pressure. Today, it's all about walking a tight rope, align to the right, cover down, popping sticks, and no matter what, stay focused and DO NOT make any mistakes.

We were up early and got our Rifles out to pop sticks. The sun wasn't even up, we hadn't had chow, but we were ready to go. Our Heavy Hat was just as anxious as we were. We went through a few moves and then he stopped us. He walked into the house and came back with a CD player. He hit play and we got a full dose of Rage Against the Machine. Awwyeah! It pumped us all up.

After we practiced a bit, our Heavy Hat told us to get back in the rack until it was time to get up at our usual time. It was a great 45 minutes of down time before we started our daily routine. After that, we got up and got dressed in our Drill Cammies. Those were the cammies that we saved for just this occasion. They were immaculate. We got dressed up and our Heavy hat came out to take a look at us. He then announced he was going to give us a little bit of his magic mojo. He presented a small bottle of Aqua Velva. It's the color blue and he loves the stuff. He said it was the mojo we needed to rock on Final Drill. He then put it into a spray bottle and gave us a dose.

We then jumped on the bus and it took us to the Indoor Training Center. We would be performing our Final Drill indoors because it was pouring outside. That's cool. We popped sticks outside while we were waiting our turn and then it was on. We walked in, took position, and waited to take the deck. Our Senior was going to call Drill for us. We would have preferred our Heavy Hat but it's all good. We started up and we did OK. It wasn't our best performance but it wasn't our strongest either. It was a blur to me. I don't even know how or where we screwed up. All I know is that less than 3 recruits missed getting their bolts back so that was great. I'm sure 2 missed it. Our Heavy Hat went through the roof. He just stood up and stormed out of the Indoor Training Center and didn't bother watching the rest.

Weak recruits kill Platoons.

You may be perfect, but all it takes is a couple idiots and you're done. Oh well. Like I said, it was less than 3. After 3, they start docking points. Little mistakes don't really carry any weight EXCEPT for making sure you get the bolt back! Oh well. It was over and we made it through.

There were no serious train wrecks. When we got back to the house, our Senior gave us the rundown of how we did. We ended up getting 4th out of 5 places. That's cool. We didn't care about getting 1st. If our Heavy Hat was in charge and marched us, it might have been a different story. Our Senior screwed the Platoon more than a few times and so everyone relaxed on Final Drill. He then blamed the Squad Leaders for screwing up. I think that's crap. We all messed up a little here and there and even the Senior screwed up on calling cadence and he knew it. He forgot to go to Left Shoulder at the end of the deck and it threw everyone off because we had practiced everything in a precise order.

I found that weak people blame others when they fall short. A Marine takes responsibility for their own actions and learns from them with a sense of humility and integrity. After the Final Drill recap, we packed for the Crucible. That's all we cared about now anyway. The Crucible is tomorrow.

If we survive, we're home free.

20080124 Thursday
CRUCIBLE- DAY 1

*Due to the nature of the CRUCIBLE, some details have been omitted from this text.

LIGHTS, LIGHTS, LIGHTS came at 1:30AM. Needless to say, most of us were up already. Sleeping was a no go. We drifted in and out without being able to fall into full on sleep mode. The Drill Instructors rolled in and made sure we were ready to go. We were buzzing with anticipation and adrenaline.

As soon as we got the morning count, we got everything together and staged our gear on the grinder with all the other Platoons. It was on. 3rd Battalion Lead and Follow Series was getting ready to move. We had been issued 4 MRE's which were to last for the next 54 hours. If you break it down, that means we could eat 1 meal every 13.5 hours.

At this point, we weren't going to blow an MRE this early in the game. We had a 4-mile hike ahead of us so our Drill Instructors brought us a box of apples. We tore into them. When we were done, we asked our Drill Instructors where we needed to throw the cores away and they told us to eat them. Good to go. We could care less. We threw the stem on the deck but hoovered the rest.

The house was cleared, the gear was staged, and 3rd Battalion was ready to go. When we got the word, we picked up our gear and we were off. It was pitch black outside except for the Drill Instructors glow sticks they had strapped to their packs. The air was cool and no one was saying a word. All you heard was the sound of a full Battalion of motivated recruits on the move. Boots hitting cement. It didn't matter what they made us do, we were determined to fight to the death. For the first time in our recruit training, we were ready for this moment. We had become hard. We were disciplined. More importantly, we had finally become a team. When we first started, we would have thrown the person to our right and left in front of a bus and cared less. Not now. We had each other's back without needing to say a word.

For the first two miles I just sang songs in my head. There's nothing else to do and you have to keep your mind occupied. It's pitch black, your stomach's pretty much empty except for an apple, and you're warm from hiking with a full pack. Result- You're friggin sleepy. If you don't watch it, you'll start drifting into the recruit next to you and look stupid.

I was pretty good though because my stupid pack was making noise. There's a plastic buckle that was rubbing against something else and it kept going ree-ur ree-ur ree-ur with every step I made. However, I found that if I moved just right it would stop but if I forgot then it would keep up. So it just became a game. How many steps could I make without my pack going ree-ur ree-ur ree-ur? But before long, we were there.

We found ourselves in BWT town again. This time, we were in the other huts that were marked Crucible instead of BWT. So now it was simply Crucible town. We dropped our packs, set up our gear, and we were right back out with what we needed for the first day. It was still pitch black out. The temperature had dropped way down which meant the sun would be coming up pretty soon. That's how it was out here: it was really nice out and then always got super cold right before the sun came up. We formed up outside the huts and split up into fire teams and a Drill Instructor. I was psyched. My 15-recruit team was rock solid and my Drill Instructor was Cookie Monster. Awesome!

As it appears, we were going to be staying in this 15-recruit team for the duration of the crucible. That's cool. We had a pretty good mix of recruits and a variety of strengths to draw from. We had muscle, maturity, and intelligence. We were ready!

After we got formed up, we were given our start point, and we headed out to the Crucible. The Crucible is HUGE! There are over 25 events that you have to complete so all the teams can start on a completely different event and go from start to finish without seeing anyone else. It's wild. From beginning to end, you always hear this ambient noise over these hidden speakers. It's just sounds of people screaming that they're wounded and hollering. It's actually pretty disturbing at first but you get used to it after a while. Not to mention the machine guns and rocket explosions. It sounds live but I don't know where it's coming from... yet.

The rules are simple. Your team can fail no more than 3 missions. If you fail more than three missions, you fail the Crucible and have to pick up with the next Platoon the following week. That would suck. We understood this. We just have to stay focused and work together given it was unknown what we would face.

Our first event was a combat patrol mission. All we had to do was show that we knew how to make formations in stealth mode. We set up our team and went to work. We covered the course and Cookie Monster watched and graded us from a distance. He didn't interfere at all and let us work through a problem as a team if we hit one. It was a cool warm up event. I know it's going to get a lot harder.

Across the way, we saw another team with our Senior. He was playing games with them. We were glad to be with Cookie Monster. He didn't play with us. It was all business. Get the directions for the event, work it out as a team, and attack it. Afterwards, Cookie Monster would recap what we did, offer other possible solutions, and sometimes he would tell us a story of how he encountered the same thing or something similar in Iraq. First event- Passed.

Our second event was the Bayonet field. The objective was simple. Make 3 teams. Buddy rush correctly through all the obstacles, perform the correct attack on all the targets, and complete the course under the time allotted. Not too bad. I was the fire team leader and we were off. We buddy rushed all the way through and killed our targets. The bayonets were no joke. We stabbed and sliced through our targets easier than I imagined. We got to the end, received our time, and we were good to go. Second event- passed.

So far, we had a coordination event and a combat movement event. The next was based on strategy. Event 3 was nothing more than a suspended red/ black tire. The objective was to get all the gear and the entire team through the tire without touching anything but the inside of the tire. The inside of the tire was black and the rest of it was red. We found out then that any of these strategy challenges followed the same rule. You can touch the black. But if you touch the red, you either have to start over or you fail the event. We had to get everyone through under the given time frame. It was hard at first, but once we got the right strategy, we finished with a few minutes to spare. Third event- passed.

Eating falls under two categories- Big Chow and Little Chow. The way big chow works is you can take a meal break in which you have a certain amount of time for everyone in your team to eat. You have to set up a secured perimeter, post security, and then make sure you rotate everyone so that everyone can eat and everyone can pull guard. For small chow, you just keep a snack in your cargo pocket and you can eat it whenever you are not in a challenge or receiving directions. You just have to make sure you limit how much you eat at all times. If you're not eating, you are making sure your Rifle is in working order, your gear is accounted for, and your face is painted up correctly. IN THAT ORDER. Your Rifle always comes first. Chow is dead last. You can always eat later.

Our fourth event was a 3-story victim rescue. The primary objective was you had to buddy climb to the top, lower the victim from the top with a rope, and get down using the cargo net. You had to buddy climb without touching the red areas, you had to limit the number of recruits on each floor at all times, you couldn't talk, hand signals only, and you had to post a safety officer. And all this had to be done under a given time frame. It took us 2 restarts and then on the 3rd we got it with a minute to spare. We were lucky but we did it! Fourth event- passed.

At this point, Staff Sergeant Assassin joined our team and relieved Cookie Monster. It was cool because the Drill Instructors did everything with us except for the events. They carried their own gear. They stayed painted up. And the coolest thing was, they treated us differently. They didn't have their Smokey Hats. They were wearing beanies just like us. (except we had Kevlar Helmets) They talked to us to make sure we learned from these events. And if we made a mistake, they explained what we should have done and dropped it after that.

Our fifth event was a victim rush. We broke into 3 man teams. We had to buddy rush from cover, get back to cover when we were fired on, and move ourselves in position to grab a victim and get back to safe cover without getting in the line of sight by the gunman. The gunman was firing compressed air blasts through a 50-caliber machine gun.

WOW that thing was loud! If we got too high and he could see any part of us, we were dead and would fail the mission. My job was to grab the victim and carry him back to cover. Not too bad. My teammates kept me informed 100% of the time when I made my moves, and they kept me safe from getting shot. If it wasn't for our team really working hard together and staying focused, we would have failed hands down. Some teams did and that put them 2 strikes a way from getting dropped. It was EASY to fail. We paid attention, it paid off, and we made it through the first time. Fifth event- passed.

In between events, we would be taken to combat endurance courses and ran through non-stop. There is no down time what so ever. You have to keep your head in the game.

The next event was another strategy event. It was a wire challenge in which you had to get the entire team across the 3 wire bridges along with 3 weighted ammo cans. You got a length of rope to use with the ammo cans and that's it. You post security, get a team across, post security on the other side, get your team and ammo cans across in the correct order, and that's it. Sounds easy. Took us 2 attempts. But since we made it under the time limit, we were good. BAM! Done deal. Sixth event- passed.

Our next event was the WEAVER. It looks easy but when it comes down to it, you and your team better be ready to move fast. The Weaver is set up just like the weaver in the confidence course, except this one is super sized. It's huge! The Weaver is an A-Frame structure. It's about 25 feet high at the point. You have red and brown logs alternating up each side. You post your team on all the brown logs. The rest of your team has to pass over the brown logs and under the red logs. The gear has to go as well and it can't touch any red logs. Needless to say, if a single piece of gear falls, you automatically fail the event. If a piece of gear touches a red log, you fail. You have to do all this under a given time limit. Everyone can see how this works. The magic comes with the strategy you use to get the job done. It's not easy. But we got it done. 7th event- passed.

Our next was a joint Battalion event. We were taken to the rodeo ring and we were going to square off and do some fighting. AWESOME! We were hungry for this. Let me take a moment and try to describe the rodeo ring. I'll go from the inside out. If you're standing in the center, you are in a ring that is approximately 25 feet in diameter. Actually, it's not really a ring; it's in the shape of an octagon. The deck is sand. The walls of the octagon are 8-10 feet high. Around the top of the octagon is a walkway where the Drill Instructors can watch the matches from an elevated position. Now here comes the tricky part. There are 4 entrances to the octagon. Each entrance is covered by a tarp so you can't see anything until you walk through the entrance. If you were going out of the octagon, you would walk through the tarp and then you would find yourself in a corridor walkway.

Out of the 4 entrances, there are two long corridors and two short corridors. The long corridors and short corridors are positioned directly across from each other.

For the first round, we were split into Red and Black teams, and then put in order of weight from lightest to heaviest. We geared up with gloves, head gear, and flak jacket. The first round was a one on one body shot brawl. You could take the person down but the Combat Instructor in the ring would just stand you back up. So, in this case, you wanted to stay on your feet and just pound it out and see who had the weakest gut. It was crazy because while we were waiting, we couldn't see the action in the octagon. All we could hear was the body shots being delivered, the Drill Instructors yelling and cheering, and the sounds recruits make when they get hit really hard. We had no idea who we were going to fight until we ran through the tarp and saw them face-to-face.

When my turn came, I got my high fives from my team, and ran into the octagon. I faced my opponent and the Combat Instructor gave us brief reminder of the instructions. We nodded in understanding and he shouted FIGHT!

I knew my right hand was useless for punching so I came with my lead left hand hook as my primary weapon. I knew he was going to be coming with it so my goal was to hit him as hard as I possibly could in his sternum. With my left hook being thrown, that could work. I started to move while he came with an onslaught of punches, defended what I could, ate a few, waited for the right moment, and BAM! I slammed my hook into the soft part of his chest. It staggered him. Now, every time I came with my hook, he would be worried about it and cover up. He came with another blitz, I covered with my right and sank another hook, but this time when he covered, I followed with an onslaught of hooks that bounced between his upper and lower body. I didn't want to hit the same place twice. One of the hooks found its mark and he dropped a knee. The Combat Instructor jumped in and stood him back up. He was taller than me and would have gotten me if I stayed outside his range, but based on my strategy, it worked great. He couldn't keep me away in range and I was finding my marks by staying close. After the second round started, I took his wind with a hard shot to his soft ribs and he was done. The Combat Instructor called it and we touched gloves and ran out of the Octagon. I never saw him after that until we crossed paths at the chow hall just before Graduation. He was a great guy. We laughed about it and talked about the shots we landed. Good times.

The second round was Pugil Sticks. Now this was just friggin NUTS! It wasn't one on one. It was two on two. Two Reds against two Blacks. Each team member got in the short and long shoots. At the sound of the whistle, you would sprint down the shoot, through the tarp, and try to level the other person coming at you. It was nothing short of trains colliding full speed. The short shoots would hit each other first, and then the long shoots would fly in. To this very day, I have no idea how more recruits didn't get sent to medical. HOLY CRAP! The good Lord above was just watching out for us. That's the only thing that would make sense. I remember one recruit was just about to come through the tarp, when all the sudden his opponent actually came through his tarp and hit him cold turkey. He said it startled him because he didn't think he would get hit until he came through the tarp. Nope. He was leveled in his own shoot and didn't even make it into the octagon. It was awesome!

After that event, the sun was going down and we headed back to the house. We made sure our gear was in check and fueled up for the next event. The Crucible is very interesting in the way it challenges you. So far, today has been all physical training. The next event was the Night Creep. We had no idea what to expect.   For starters, we did this night creep in Battalion formation. So everyone was in the mix. We struck out when it became pitch black. We started in 4-squad formation and stepped to the tree line. When we got to the tree line, we switched to 2 wide so you were shoulder to shoulder down the trail. You couldn't see a thing once you stepped in the tree line. The only thing you could see was the glow sticks tied to trees that marked the way for the Drill Instructors to follow. Other than that, we just knew it was going to be a 5.1-mile hike. The trail would go up, down, around, and every which way. Every so often we would come out of the trees, walk across the airfield and go right back into the trees. It went on, and on, and on, and... it just went on. You couldn't say a word. All you could do was keep moving. At about mile 3, we made a head call. To be honest, I think the feeling of needing to use the head was what was keeping us awake. Because after that, recruits started walking into trees, falling over, walking into their buddies next to them, walking into the recruit in front of them. It became a mess. There was a combination of sleep deprivation and pitch black that made it tough. At times, it felt like you were walking in outer space. At times, you couldn't see the recruit in front of you. That was bad because that meant you were slowing down and didn't even realize it. It played with your head.

I think some recruits tried to close their eyes and hold on to the recruit in front of them, then they would just fall over. FINALLY, after what seemed like forever, we got back to the airfield and we were told to form back up. Hallelujah. From that moment, all the recruits referred to that event as the Sleepwalker.

5.1 miles of walking into pitch black nothing-ness.

We got back to the huts around 2430 (12:30am) and got ready to pass out. I would say hit the rack, but that's not it. We were totally exhausted from the day. Today was exactly what I expected. It was hardcore. It challenged us physically and mentally like never before. And this was just the first day. We posted firewatch. I got it first so I got to stay up for another hour. It was fine for me. I was relieved at 2AM. The Platoon got up the previous morning at 1:30AM and we all hit the rack at 1AM. That's a full day right there. Today was no joke. We were banged up, bruised, lying about not needing to go to medical to our Drill Instructors, and absolutely loving it.

20080125 Friday
CRUCIBLE- Day 2

Lights hit at 4AM. I got 2 hours of sleep. Awesome. It was cold. The thermometer read 20 degrees. To make things more interesting, I woke up sick. Great! I don't know if I was just exhausted from the day before or perhaps I had a bad MRE and needed to get it out of my system. But I knew I had to fight through it. Who cares? I just had to flush it out of my system as fast as possible.

We formed up and stepped out to the airfield. The Drill Instructors whipped up a batch of hot broth and so I downed 2 cups of it. I figured with the sodium content and it being warm would help out. After about 3 hours, I felt a million times better. In the meantime, our first event was another Battalion event.

It's called the Kesan Challenge. You get in Battalion formation and march 3 miles out to the Rifle Range. We were happy to march because we knew it would warm us up. I was near the back and when we started to inch worm, I didn't mind it at all. Running was good to go. Everyone was sore from the previous day and so this would loosen us back up. It made things interesting.

Sure enough, after 2 miles of marching we worked that soreness out. Once we got to the range, we set up a perimeter and posted security in our area. That just means you get down on the ground in the prone position, keep your rifle in your shoulder, and do whatever it takes to keep yourself awake. The ground was friggin COLD. There was frost everywhere so it made you stay awake. No big deal. Teams were leaving one at a time and we had no idea what to expect. When it was my team's turn, we stood up, and the Combat Instructor briefed us. Cookie Monster was our Drill Instructor again. That was great!

It started with us getting in fire team formation. We walked a marked trail in stealth mode. When we got to the end of the trail, we found ourselves at a new firing range. This one was cool. We were given our rounds, and made our way to the targets. We were given targets to fire at and instructions on how to come out of cover, hit them, and then immediately return to cover. We did exactly that and fired off the rest of our rounds if we had extra. No big deal. By now, we felt 100% confident in our ability to shoot. Firing just to fire without the pressure of failing a qualification shoot is a great feeling. After we dumped our rounds, we formed back up in fire team position and continued on to a new trail. Cookie Monster said we might get ambushed if we screwed up so we needed to stay focused. As it turns out, we didn't get hit and found our way through these buildings keeping position tight, buddy rushing around buildings, and we got our team to the end. The trail brought us right back to the rest of the Battalion. We made it. We had our last shakedown and that was it. However, this time the shakedown was-

Do you have anything?
No Sir!
Good. Get back on your gear.

No more games. Speaking of no more, this was the last time we would ever fire our weapon at Parris Island. While we were putting our gear together, it hit us. We wouldn't fire any more. This was it. We're almost there. After we all got back, we marched the 3 miles back to Crucible town. Just like before, we ran all the way back but it didn't matter to us. However, It did to the Drill Instructors. It flat pissed our Senior right off. Oh well. By the time we got back, my stomach was back to normal and my temperature was gone. I thanked the good Lord above for that.

Back to the Crucible Events. Our next event was the plank walk. It's all about communication and teamwork. You have a path to negotiate, and you have (2) 8-foot long ski looking boards with ropes tied to the boards. You are supposed to use the ropes to pick up the boards under your feet and walk forward to the end of the path. It's hard! If 1 person drops their rope, you can keep going, but they have to make sure they keep their foot on top of the board. If one foot hits the ground, you fail. It took everything we had to get our team across under the time limit. However, we made it and even though it wasn't pretty, we worked it out.

Event- passed!

The next event was the bar jump of trust. The set up is simple. There is a 3-foot high platform to stand on. About 6 feet away is a bar about 7 feet off the ground. Everyone stands in rows of two facing each other by the bar. The objective is to jump from the platform to the bar. Both hands have to lock on to the bar. The other teammates lock arms and catch you. The only way to get your hands to the bar is to jump with everything you have and lay yourself flat in the air. It's like a military stage dive. Once your hands lock on the bar, you have to trust your buddies will catch you. It's definitely one of those challenges where you look at it and it looks easy, but when you actually step up and have to go, it's a different story. Some recruits couldn't make the jump at first.

They wigged out and shorted it. 3 strikes and you fail the event. Luckily, everyone on my team went for it and we passed!

After that, we did the suspended plank wall. This was pretty tough until you figured it out. Imagine two red uprights about 15 feet tall and about 8 feet apart. There is a cross bar going across the top. There are two red ropes hanging down from the red cross bar. Attached to the red ropes is two horizontal 2x4's. One is 4 feet high, and the other is 4 feet above that. You cannot hold onto the ropes. Your objective is to climb up onto the first 2x4, and then climb up on top of the 2nd 2x4 without touching the ropes. Once you get up there, you have to get all the gear and the rest of the team up and over the top. This one wasn't as bad but it was a great challenge. It was the ultimate test in balance!

The next event was a HUE City tactical run. All you had to do was buddy rush as a team all the way to the end without getting shot. Not a big deal. You just better pay attention.

The next challenge was by far one of the hardest strategy events our team had faced. It's called ring around the pole. There is a 15' red pole. Your job is to get a tire up and onto the pole and all the way down to the bottom of the pole without the tire touching it at any time. You have 15 members on the team and only 12 can help because one is the team leader and the other two are safety officers.

We started out trying to figure out how to get that tire up high enough to get on the pole. The tire itself weighed a solid 80 lbs. So it would take 2 pairs of hands to get it up. That means 2 recruits have to be at the top of the pole. That would mean 3 recruits have to hold them on their shoulders. Which would mean 4 recruits have to be on the ground holding all of them on their shoulders. Got it?

The first step was to take the biggest 4 guys on our team and make them the base. The next 3 recruits climbed up on their shoulders. The extra recruits were used to help the other two recruits climb on top of the base recruits' shoulders and continue up to the next pair of shoulders. Once the top two were in place, free hands grabbed the tire and passed it up. We got it to the top and slowly lowered everyone down at the same time. BAM! Done deal. Step 1 complete. Now we have to get it back off. We got everyone in place and went to work. We got it all the way up and were just about to get it off when the time ran out. CRAP!!!

This was the first event we had failed.

We were so close. But there's nothing we can do. We gave it our best shot and almost got the job done. Later that day we would find out that we were 1 of 3 teams out of the whole Battalion that got the tire on. Only one team got it back off. In a way, that made us feel better. But still. We have to watch ourselves. We can't fail any more. With that in mind, it gave everyone a surge and it was a better motivator than if we had passed it. We could have gotten it on there no problem had we been fresh and feeling good. But it's not what you can do when you're perfect: it's what you can still do when you're totally smoked. Lesson learned.

The next mission was "Noonans Evac." Our task was to evacuate the helicopter, get in fire team formation, find the wounded pilot, and get him back to the helicopter under a given time frame. We started in the mock helicopter and set the game plan. Staff Sergeant Assassin gave us the go ahead and it was on. We flew out of the helicopter and started patrolling the path. We stayed in formation cruising along when all of the sudden our Saw Gunner got hit by a sniper. We located, identified, and killed the sniper and then carried on. We were down two. Our wounded teammate was helped back to the helicopter by another teammate. We still have 12 so we're good. Or so we thought. Right about then, 3 of our teammates got hit by an IED. They were dead. At this point, we couldn't risk losing six, so one stayed back to guard the dead, and we'd have to pick them back up on the way back.

It wasn't looking good. However, this time we located, identified, and killed the 2nd sniper before we were spotted. That made us feel a lot better. We just had to keep our eyes razor sharp. When we got to the end of the path, we found that another team on the same mission had evac'd the pilot and so all we had to do now was to high tail it back to the helicopter. We just had to make sure we weren't ambushed on the way back. As soon as we got back to the dead recruits, we picked them up and hustled them back to the helicopter. We had 45 seconds left, we were carrying three, and had 100 yards to the helicopter. With seconds to spare, we made it. Hallelujah we made it! Even if we carried the pilot back, we would have made it. The team was on fire. We all worked together, dug deep, and made it happen.

The last event of the Crucible is known as "Event -4". It's the works. It's got everything in it. If you die, you have to start all over. If you lose your 45 lbs. ammo can, you automatically fail. There's tons of low crawling, high crawling, buddy rushing, wall clearing and jumping, bridges to cross, culverts to negotiate, barbed wire, Constantine wire, fireworks, explosions, machine gun fire, and 50 cal. type fire going on 100% of the time. Not to mention the fact that this event is not a one team on the course at a time event. Everyone is charging through at the same time. It's nuts.

I started in and flew through the low crawl and the high crawl. I got to the barbed wire and back crawled beneath that. When I got to the Constantine wire, that was a different story. You can do it alone but it's not the smartest way. We learned that fact during the day we learned how to negotiate Constantine wire. If I'm first to the wire, then I'll hold up until the next recruit behind me makes it, then I'll go under while he secures it, when I'm through, I'll secure it and he'll come through. It's much faster and safer that way. If you do it alone, it'll take a lot longer and you take the chance of getting snagged. If you get snagged, you only have a 25% chance of getting through by yourself.

I'll never forget this one recruit that was 2 lanes over and he tried to get through on his own. He got under no problem but didn't secure the "X" with his rifle. It sprung back down on him and all the spurs dug into him. One of them had him by the eyelid. He was screaming for his life. He was completely helpless. Luckily for him, a Drill Instructor gave him a hand and then sent him back to the start. You have to work as a team. Even if you find yourself on your own, you have to think to yourself the difference of whether you could, or whether you should. I could attempt to go under the wire by myself. But that would be a mistake. I should wait 30 more seconds for another recruit to come up and we both get through it safely. I decided option B.

I got over the wall and continued on to the next series of crawls. By now, my arms were screaming from dragging this 45 lbs. ammo can along. But I had to stay focused. Some recruits were getting stupid. Their canteens would come out, and instead of putting them back in their cargo pocket, they started throwing them ahead. I know because I was crawling along and then got beaned in the head by a full canteen. It pissed me off. But a Drill Instructor saw it and set him straight. I was almost there. A few more sets of Constantine wire, a bridge, a day walk section, a culvert, and then I was home free. When I got to the culvert, I bolted from there to the tree line and ran right into Sergeant Brown. He said-

Fuckin goddam Guide. Why don't you just run right into a bitch? Goddam! Hey, you made it. Follow this path and form it up. You're done say aye sir.
Aye Sir!

I was done. It took everything I had just to keep my bearing. I followed the path and made it out of the woods. I turned in my ammo can, got in formation, and stepped back to Crucible Town. The day was done!
Today I got broke off. It was wicked nasty grueling hard. But I'm glad. If it would have been any easier I would have been disappointed. The Crucible puts to the test everything you've been taught during recruit training. The Crucible has a reputation and I'm glad that reputation held true. By this time, I felt confident in everything I had been taught. Finally. You never know what you can do until you are tested. It felt great!
But it's not over. That night, we packed up our gear because tomorrow morning we were hiking back. We weren't aloud to hit the rack until 2400 (12:00am). The Drill Instructors made us just sit there on our sleeping bags until it was time. That was tough. We were exhausted and all we wanted to do was go to sleep. But we couldn't. We had to stay awake. Finally, we got the lights order and we passed out. I don't think anyone was awake more than 2 minutes after lights went out. 2 hours later, we were up again.

20080126 Saturday
9 Miles to Freedom

It was 2 in the morning and we got the huts swept and cleared, our gear staged, and we were ready to go. We were bruised, dirty, blood was dried to our skin, but we weren't broken. We were alive.

Inside, we were all smiling. We had the last of our chow. For most of all of us, that was a snack we had saved just for the hike home. The rest of the MRE's were gone. But it was enough. We were going to make it. We got our packs on and formed up. When we started the Crucible, there was adrenaline in the air, the packs felt light, and everyone was excited. Now, we moved a bit slower, the packs felt heavy, our bodies hurt all over, but you could feel the determination. We had 9 Miles to go. All we had to do was hike 9 miles home.

We got the go ahead and started for home. Within the first mile, recruits from other Platoons started falling out. I have to admit that it was hard starting the engine, but once you got going, you were fine. I was thinking how someone could fall out when they're so close. The choice is easy, make the 9 miles, or do it all over again. 3014 was going to make it as a team. We silently encouraged each other and made sure everyone was moving. At 4.5 miles, we stopped for an apple and PowerAde. It was a nice break but we knew not to get too comfortable because we were only half way there. We started back up again and to be honest, I don't remember the next 2 miles. I was just singing songs in my head and daydreaming. It was still dark out and you couldn't see a thing.

All the sudden, you could see a horizon. Then a tree line. Then you could see trees. Then BAM! The sun came out of the tree line and the world came alive. That's when I got my head together and woke up. We were an hour away. We started to stand up a bit straighter as we marched. We knew we were getting close. When we finally got to a paved road, it finally hit us. We were 30 minutes away from being done. To our left and right, we saw recruits starting their day, some were on the PT fields getting a good workout, some Platoons were getting killed in the PITS by their Drill Instructors. One Platoon actually marched right passed us and they were staring at us. We must have looked entirely wrecked. But, we didn't care. We were back.

Just then, our Heavy Hat broke out with some Marching Cadence. *Mama mama can't you see...* kinda stuff. It was awesome! We were screaming it to the top of our lungs. Finally, we rolled up right in front of the Indoor Training Facility. It was the place we did final drill. We grounded our gear, and marched in. This was it!

We were given the order to fall in and we did in a flash. All the

Platoons were formed up in a horseshoe formation. The building was empty. The last time we were here, there were people watching the final drill in the stadium seating and all the lights were on. Now, it was just our Platoons, our Drill instructors, the First Sergeant, the Series Commander, and the Captain. The lights were dim and all was quiet.

The Eagle, Globe, and Anchor Ceremony is not meant for anyone but the recruit that earned the right to be there, and the men that brought them through the fire of recruit training.

The Ceremony started off with the colors. Then the chaplain said a prayer. And then the Star Spangled Banner played. After that, the First Sergeant said a few words to us. After that, our Drill Instructors started the distribution of EGA's. Over the speakers, you heard a very soft instrumental version of the Marine's Hymn being played over and over. The Marine's Hymn gave ambient noise to cover what the Drill Instructors were saying to the recruits and the tears of joy being shed by the recruits. Recruits are required to maintain bearing at all times. Exceptions are made during this moment. You deserve your moment. I was the first in line to receive the EGA from my Senior. He said-

You did it Killian. Even though I fired your ass, you made it. Good job.

I shook his hand and for the first time,
I said- Aye Staff Sergeant.
I made it!

I, Matthew Killian, am now, and forever will be, a United States Marine.

From that moment on, everything changed. The moment you receive your EGA, you are a Marine. No more Aye Sir! You call your Drill Instructors by their rank. You're not entirely out of the woods. You can still get dropped for being stupid. But outside of that, I am no longer a garbage recruit. I am a Marine.

At the end of the Ceremony, you are given the order of your dreams. The First Sergeant addresses the Drill Instructors and says-
Drill Instructors, take charge of your new Marines, and feed them a

warrior's breakfast!
AYE FIRST SERGEANT!!!

The Superman theme song came over the speakers and we walked out of the ITF as if the past 54 hours didn't even happen. Now was not the time for limping and gimping. Everyone was on top of the world. And now, we were hungry!

We were marched over to the chow hall and the directions were simple. Go through the line, get whatever you like, sit down, eat it completely relaxed, and repeat. We could go through the line as many times as we wanted!

HOLY CRAP! I have never eaten so much in my life. I wrote it down just to be sure-

2 boxes of Cinnamon Toast Crunch
1 box of Honeynut Cheerios
2 Waffles
1 plate of Sausage and Gravy
4 Cartons of milk
5 strips of bacon
2 French Toasts
1 box of Apple Jacks
4 Omelets
2 Steaks with A1
and 3 plates of Scrambled Eggs

But that wasn't even the coolest part. The Drill Instructors came and sat down and ate with us!!! What? Yeah. They would walk right up and sit down with us and talk to us like they were our big brothers. I was sitting with my buddy and he dropped his fork. He went to pick it up and when he looked back up from the floor, he was in our Kill Hat's way. He immediately scrambled to get out of the way and our Kill Hat said-

Take your time, your good.

It was like another world. You still had to watch what you said and did but not like before. Our Kill Hat and Cookie Monster sat down with us and we started to tell them stories of what we thought of them, what they did to us, all kinds of stuff.

It was hysterical because they denied all of it. We told our Kill Hat how he filled our Hygiene bags up with shaving cream and he said, *Naw, that wasn't me.* And he just smiled.

We told Cookie Monster that his nickname was Cookie Monster and he laughed so hard. He thought it was great! We told Cookie Monster one of our funniest stories about him-

When Cookie Monster picked up with us, he was NOTORIOUS for running recruits everywhere. When we were on the range, the head was located in between the 300 and 500-yard lines. We would be standing there getting our ammo. We would see some recruits walking to the head. They would get about a third of the way there. Then, across the entire range, we would see Cookie Monster spot them walking to the head. He would run all the way across the entire range at mach 5. When the recruits saw him coming, they tore off to the head. Cookie Monster was so fast, he would catch them as they were going into the head. You know he was in there screaming at them the whole time because they flew right back out a moment later and he chased them all the way back to the firing line. Recruits would always ask us who that crazy Drill Instructor is that chases everyone on the range. We would say yeah... that's Cookie Monster.

At that moment, they were still our Drill instructors, but now, it was different. From this moment on, we didn't have to ask permission to speak. We didn't have to talk in the 3rd person. We could now say "I" and "you". All the rules changed.

We still had to stay on the ball but just in a different way.

We were human again.

When we formed up after the Warrior's Breakfast, we were getting eyeballed by other recruits. They saw us call our Drill Instructors by their rank and it freaked them out. When we got back to the house, our first objective was to start the process of returning gear. All I could think of was how it felt like a flip of a switch. No more Drill instructor's yelling and screaming. No more quarterdeck. Everything seemed normal. It didn't feel like you had to watch your back like before. The Drill Instructors treated us like we were Marines.

It was awesome!

20080127 Sunday
Libo Sunday

Even though we claimed the title "Marine", we were still on the Island and had to follow the plan of the day. And the plan of the day said get out of the rack lickity split just like any other day. Everyone went to chow except for the Artists. We stayed back and put the finishing touches on our masterpieces. They're looking great!

After everyone got back from chow, we stepped to church. And this time we got to march there and march back by ourselves. We didn't need a Drill instructor keeping us in step babysitting us. We were squared away and had enough discipline to come and go as we were instructed.

This service was the one we were all waiting for. It had finally come. This was our last Sunday on the Island. Our little group had been faithful for every single Sunday. We never missed a service. And now, this would be our last. We went to the Bible study at the RTF. This time, we were the ones getting blasted with questions by all the recruits that were leaving the next week for the Crucible. We passed the word and wished them well. I have to admit; it felt good to be called "Sir" by the recruits. Or when I told them something, they would respond, "Aye Marine." I couldn't get enough of it. After the Bible study, we stepped to the Chapel. Upon arrival, we walked into the Sanctuary and headed straight to the coveted middle section where only Graduating Marines get to sit. We claimed our spot.

By the way, I feel I need to tell you about something I observed. Parris Island is a breeding ground for leadership training, testosterone guided pit bulls, and idiots on power trips. However, not everyone knows which one they have become or have the authority to portray.

Right before the service started, I had to make a head call. I walked back and saw one of the Marines I went through the Crucible with standing by the head and playing games with new recruits. He was telling them they had a time limit, only a certain number in at one time, and he said he had been posted there by a Sergeant to keep recruits in

376

line. The recruits were obviously doing exactly what he said without question. However, he didn't have the authority or reason to do stuff like that. He was wielding the power of his EGA like his daddy's gun. I didn't want to make a scene so I took him to the side and questioned him why he was doing that. He gave me the same stupid story about being posted and I told him he was full of crap. I told him that we hated that junk when we were recruits and simply told him to go back to his seat. He looked at me for a second and then it just hit him. He knew I was right. We hadn't gone through the past 12 weeks of being a recruit just to turn into a dickhead. The difference between an idiot and a man is knowing you have the power and having the sense of knowing what to do with that power. Being a Marine does put you at the top of the heap. But you have to consider what the recruits see when they look up at you. Don't be an idiot.

During the church service, I heard an incredible story that I would like to share with you. It exemplifies the difference between BELIEF and FAITH.

There was a man by the name of Charles Blonden who was a famous tightrope walker. Incidentally, his fame came from crossing Niagara Falls a number of times. Huge crowds would come to watch him perform this stunt. Charles would walk across it, ride an especially made bike across it, he even took a chair out and ate an omelet. One day, he decided to cross the Falls pushing a wheelbarrow. This seemed like an easy task compared to all the things he had done before. However, it would require both hands at all times and that alone raised the bar of difficulty. He addressed the crowd and asked if they believed he could do it. The crowd cheered of course you can. He asked again and again and the crowd became louder and louder. Through the crowd, Charles spotted a man that was by far the most confident in his claim that he could make it. So Charles singled the man out. He said Sir! Do you truly believe that I can cross the Falls by pushing this wheelbarrow. Of course you can the man proclaimed. I said, are you SURE? Do you believe I CAN? The man said, Sir! I have never seen another soul possess the same level of skill and I firmly believe you can push that wheelbarrow all the way across! Charles said very well. You Sir! Get in the wheelbarrow and I'll push you across.

The man believed he could do it, but it would take more than belief to make the man get in the wheelbarrow. It would take absolute faith.

At the end of the service, we got to sing the two songs that meant more than anything else to us. The first was "I'll Fly Away". For a recruit, that's all you want to do at Parris Island. Especially the verse where you sing, *"...just a few more weary days and then, I'll Fly away!"* We loved that verse.

To my right, were all the brand new recruits that had just gotten there. They looked shocked and horrified. They looked as if they couldn't sing. They wanted to, but they would just start to tear up. I had been there.

To my left, were all the Phase 2 recruits looking at us and wondering if they would ever make it to where we were. Mixed in with the Phase 2 recruits were all the Phase 3 recruits that knew they were heading to the Crucible this next week and then they would be here soon enough. They looked calm. Not exactly excited but they were just enjoying this time to relax. I'd been there too.

Now as we sat here in the middle, knowing this was our last Sunday on Parris Island, you couldn't help but finally understand how far you had come. It was an INCREDIBLE transformation. It was staggering. It's absolutely astounding what can be done in 13 weeks. Unbelievable.

After the service, Drill Instructors flew into the sanctuary and ran their recruits out. We got our stuff together and made our way out. It was hard to leave. That sanctuary saved our lives in more ways than one. It kept us strong mentally and spiritually. It kept us united and willing to encourage each other even when we wanted to butt smash a recruit in the face. It was like stepping into a portal that took us back home and helped us to feel human just for a moment. We walked out the doors, gave a nod to the struggling recruits doing everything they could to keep up with their Drill Instructors, looked back at the chapel one last time, then took a breath and headed back to the house.

When we got back to the house, it occurred to us that today was Libo Sunday! Liberty Sunday is the day that you get to walk around the Island for about 5 hours and do whatever you like. (Within reason) Our Heavy Hat gave us the rules and we were good to go. The rules were simple-

1. Don't do anything stupid
2. Be back at the appointed time
3. Purchase a timepiece (aka a watch)
4. Get the Senior something to go in his footlocker
5. Don't do anything stupid.

Simple enough. We got dismissed and FLEW out of the house. When we got outside, we met up with our buddies from the other Platoons and headed straight for the Commissary. We walked in and we had arrived in heaven. The Commissary is just a huge grocery store. Without saying a word, we split up and attacked. I got an Almond Joy, Peanut M&M's, Oreos, and an AMP Overdrive. I was getting smoke checked on sugar. For the past 12 weeks I had lived off of red PowerAde and water. Hello caffeine. You never looked so good.

Since you are prohibited from walking while eating and drinking on the Island, we sat outside on some benches and downed everything we had bought. It was fantastic! Mission 1 was complete. Our next mission was to locate the quick stop that sold timepieces. It was right around the corner and we found the timepieces right away. I got the cheapest thing I could possibly find.

The next order of business was to find the phones. I hadn't talked to family since Christmas and I was dying to hear a familiar voice. We searched for a bit and saw nothing but lines at every single payphone. This was a no go. We had to make a head call so we stopped in at the Marine Corps Museum. While I was waiting for everyone else, I was looking around and saw a light on and decided to investigate. I peeked in and it was nothing more than a small little room with about 6 phones sitting on a table. CHA CHING! I ran up to the information desk and asked the Marine if we could use those phones. He said yes and it was on like Donkey Kong! I ran back and got my friends. We quietly strolled back and started dialing. I called my parents and talked with them for a bit. They had a million questions and I answered them without going too much into detail. I told them I would fill them in when I saw them. My dad told me that all the arrangements were made and he was bringing my sister up to the Graduation. I was so happy.

After that, we headed over to the Exchange and I got a few souvenirs. I got a shot glass, a 3rd Battalion shirt, and a 3rd Battalion coin. I was set. While in the exchange, I ran into Drill Instructor Sergeant W. He was the Sergeant that told me that God doesn't exist on Parris Island during my first church service. Well, he might have been wrong bout that, but I won't hold it against him. This time, I said Good Afternoon Sergeant. He stopped talking to the other Drill Instructor and replied- *"Good Afternoon Marine."* And then went right on talking. Amazing. I looked at my timepiece and we were running out of time. We left the exchange, took a few pictures of some memorable sights, and then we headed back to the house. When we got there, we were required to bag all of our junk food and put our name on it. We knew we would never see it again and that was fine with us. We had a blast!

Later that night, the Senior saw the backs of the Hat Racks and said he didn't like them. He loved the fronts but didn't like the backs. What the fudge Over? Even the Platoon was floored. The Racks were awesome! I made sure the Drill Instructors got a peek at them to make sure they liked them and they were floored. Oh well.

He liked the fronts and wanted to keep that so I told the Artist Marines to come up with whatever they wanted for the backs. They didn't know what to do so they just gave it there best shot. I was done. Later that night we started packing gear. We would be leaving Friday and had A LOT to do between now and then. There was no time to chill out.

20080128 Monday
4 Days to go...

Lights as always and then we stepped to chow... like always. Nothing changed here. Then we got to the chow hall. It's so cool how all the Drill Instructors talk to us now. No yelling at us what so ever- unless your stupid. But even then it's minimal. In fact, a Drill Instructor was screaming at a new recruit outside the chow hall. Out of courtesy I said- *Good morning Sergeant.*

He stopped, looked at me, calmly smiled, and replied- *Good morning Marine.* And then he went right back to screaming at the recruit without missing a beat. Awesome!

When we got back to the house, it was time to unveil the Footlocker that was made for the Senior. We brought it out. It was all painted up and we were given instructions to fill it with all kinds of protein bars and energy drinks for the Senior. When he opened it, he took one look, slammed the lid, kicked the footlocker, and stormed into his office. Our Heavy Hat walked up and opened the lid. Apparently, only 4 recruits got the Senior an energy drink for the footlocker. There were 4 cans of NOS and 3 protein bars. He looked up and asked us if he told us to get him stuff to put in the footlocker. We all said, **Yes Sergeant.** He asked us what this stuff was. We told him stuff for the Senior. He got the idea and dropped it. He knew we were all pissed at him for one reason or another and so no one wanted to buy him anything. He let it go.

Later that day we got our PROS and CONS. The Senior is responsible for grading each and every one of us based on our effort in the training. Obviously he took the easy way out. Instead of grading us individually, he scored us by the following-

General Population got 4.1
Squad leaders and the Scribe got a score of 4.2
The Guide got a score of 4.4

Awesome!

Everyone was pissed but nothing can be done. He just doesn't care. Luckily we still have the other Drill Instructors taking charge.

Later that day, we got our Brown Bag of Civilian clothes back. We weren't allowed to open the bag, but it was sure cool to see it again. I remembered going through the warehouse trying to get my bearings on the new surroundings. I was cautious, paranoid, and scared. What a difference now.

Some of my buddies started telling their stories of where they were standing the first time they were there and what they were thinking not knowing what was ahead. It was crazy how we were all thinking the same thing.

When we turned in our LV pack, we were all talking about where we were in formation, who was getting yelled at, and what was going through our minds. The last time we were here, we had just gotten to the Island and it was going on 5 in the morning. We didn't know each other at all.

That night, the sleep schedule was turned off. There is a general time to hit the rack, but you don't get blasted if you are out of the rack. We set the firewatch list and the Drill Instructors will come and go depending on the night they have duty. Instead of a Drill Instructor being on deck the whole night, there will be two watching over all the decks. The amount of responsibility we are given now is incredible.

20080129 Tuesday
3 Days to go...

Lights as usual. But this time we got box chow. No chow hall? That's cool. We could care less about what kind of food we got. We started the day by helping 3010 clean their entire house. Their Final Inspection is today and then they'll be helping us tomorrow. It was strange walking into someone else's house. This was their home and even though the floor plan was the same, it was unique in it's own way. While we were cleaning, their Senior was going over the most frequently asked questions heard during the Final Inspection. It was good junk. We hadn't talked about it at our house so we ate it up while we were cleaning. Wow, did we field day that deck. My gosh. They'll be good to go.

After that, we formed up and went to pay our final bills. This included our class Platoon photo, our Rings, and a few other things we were able to get. While we were waiting to pay the bills, we found a vending machine. Obviously, the question on the table was, are we big enough Marines to rate using the machine, or are we still under lock and key and not allowed such pleasures? Hmm. Good question indeed. I had enough and busted out my change and hooked up some pop tarts. Someone had to go for it. Might as well be me. I got mine too. I didn't want to make too much of a scene so I strolled up like I owned the place, put my money in, took my pop tarts out, stuck them in my cargo pocket, and every so often I would pull out a piece of sugary heaven.

Yeah. That ended quick, fast, and in a hurry. Other Marines saw me do that and followed suite without the same level of covert ability. That led to a swarming of the vending machine and Drill Instructor Staff Sergeant P put a fork in that. He didn't blast us for it, he just said that the machine was for the people that worked there and we would respect that.

He then told us a story about doing what's right. He said when he was stationed, he kept a 9mm for a friend over a weekend. Now, firearms are strictly prohibited in the quarters of any Marine. When his room got inspected, he was questioned on the firearm and he said he was keeping it for a friend. He didn't get charged for the incident but he did get served. He had to fill 1005 sandbags full of sand and after he was done, he had to dump them all back out. That's A LOT of sandbags. He said that in the Marine Corps, it's either paper or pain. Either you get served paper with a UCMJ, or you'll pay in some way.

We came back to the house and cleaned for the rest of the day. And I mean thoroughly cleaned. Crazy, Q-Tip to every crevice clean. Our Final Inspection is tomorrow. If we fail, we'll miss Family Day. We'll still Graduate but everyone wants to see their family. That would suck if you failed the Final Inspection.

That night, we had our first Graduation practice. Yeah. That's a lot of standing, waiting, saluting, marching, saluting, waiting more, marching more, and then screwing it up and having to do it all over again. Get used to it.

One recruit from 3013 actually pissed himself right there on the parade deck. I guess he was daydreaming and then all the sudden realized it was too late. Our Senior called him on it and he tried to say something else but our Senior was hip to it. He knew what happened.

That night, I stayed up studying the Command structure. It's all the names of the people from our Senior, all the way to the President of the United States. It's about 15 names you have to memorize as well as their position. I got done with that and at 1:30AM I ironed my uniform one last time before tomorrow. The Final Inspection would be my last test on the Island. I wanted to Kill it.

20080130 Wednesday
2 Days to go...

Lights hit and we had box chow again. Yeehaw! Right away we got ready for the Final Inspection. The house was clean from bottom to top and all we had to do was get dressed. Our Senior and Heavy Hat took us through a few run and that helped a lot. We were nervous. There is no hiding that. This was a big test. Before the big dogs showed up, Sergeants from the other decks came on and grilled us. We did really well. We were completely different then when they came on during 1st Phase. We kept our bearing rock solid, we answered the questions with authority, and performed our Rifle Manual without hesitation. We were set.

After that, the Lieutenant Colonel came on deck and the show started. I was at the very end of the line and heard them go through a few Marines. He didn't stop at everyone. He just stopped at whomever he liked. He was escorted by our Senior. Then they got closer. Since I was last in line, I had a feeling he would definitely stop at me. I was right.

He walked right up to me, stopped, and faced me. Without missing a beat I snapped to attention, jerked my Rifle to port, Inspected it, and passed it off. So far, so good. He asked me a few questions about how old I was, why I was here, and what the hardest part was. He asked all the questions we learned the day before. Man was I glad I worked that cleaning detail!

Satisfied with my answers, he passed my Rifle back and it was over faster than it began. He finished his rounds and walked off deck. That was it! Game over! I'm Graduating!!!!

After that, we stripped back into cammies and took off for the armory. We marched up and said so long to our M-16. It had been with us from the very beginning and now it was over. Even though I didn't name my Rifle, it was very special to me. While we were waiting, myself and a few other Marines got to talking with our Kill Hat. I told him that I heard he was going to take us all to Backyard Burgers for chow. He looked at me and said

Bull shit. You better learn to say Backyard box chow.

After that we got our last haircut. And this time, we got to get a high and tight. Up until now, it was baldy cuts. Now we look somewhat normal.

Next up was another exhilarating Graduation practice. The Marine that runs the ceremony is a female Marine and our Senior Hates her!

HOLY CRAP. Whenever she would make us get back and start over, he would gesture or mock her and it started to become contagious. Luckily, we got it on the next run and we were done with that. Next on the agenda was a class with the First Sergeant. We headed to the RTF and he told us about what to expect when we got out of Parris Island. It was always good times with the First Sergeant. He was funny but he sure did know his stuff. One of his favorite sayings was an adjustment to a diddy we learned.
Ours was—

Fire Team Mission!
Sir the Fire Team Mission is to Locate, Close with, and Destroy the enemy by fire and Maneuver Sir!

When it came to females,
His was-- *To locate, close with, and tap dat ass!*

After the class, we formed back up outside and we struck up a talk with our Heavy Hat and our Kill Hat. We asked our Kill Hat what his MOS was before he became a Drill Instructor. He said he was a boot maker. And he was getting closer to his promotion of chief boot maker. Take it as you will.

We then asked him how old his kid was-
How do you know I have a kid?
We said we saw the car seat in his car. He said-
It wasn't a car seat. It was a quarterdeck device. If I'm quarterdecking you and someone walks by, I can fold it up real fast and no one will know I was quarterdecking you because it looks like a car seat you bunch of terrorists.

(Drill Instructors call you this when you start finding out stuff without being told directly by them)

My next question was-
Is it hard to go from wanting to kill us every day to having to treat us like fellow Marines?
My Kill Hat got real serious and said-
It's real hard you understand dat? A lot of you, I want to punch you in the face. Even now. A few times this cycle I was hoping one of you would take a swing. But the Marine Corps doesn't work like that you understand dat?

One thing you always say is that we play games, but it's games you win. Do you ever let your son win?
Never. I win at everything. It doesn't matter. Singing the alphabet, ABC's, I always win.
What if he ran faster than you?
He wouldn't. I'd send his ass to medical on race day.

We then switched gears over to our Heavy Hat. It went like this-
What's your MOS Staff Sergeant?
I'm not sayin.
We heard it was Cryogenics.
Fuckin terrorists. Who told you that?
The Senior Drill instructor.
Very well. Yeah. It's Cryogenics. It's turning oxygen into a liquid state.
Where would you use that in the Marines?
In cases like planes or where you might need life support.
We would like to get you something before we go. What would you like?
You ain't getting me shit. I don't need nothing from no fuckin private or PFC.

Back to our Kill Hat.
What do you do when you go home at night?
I sit back and think about quarterdecking you.
Do you have any words of advise you could give us?
Hmm. When you get into the fleet, don't be stupid. Life is full of "Oh

shits."
You get a girl pregnant- Oh shit.
You ain't got no money- Oh shit.
You going to Iraq- Oh shit.
Don't buy everything you see you understand dat. It makes no sense to have a 20,000 ride with 22's on it that you drive 2 miles to and from work and that's it. Don't be stupid. Save your money.

20080131 Thursday
Family Day

At 1:00AM, I pulled my last fire watch at Parris Island. I've had it every other day consistently since day 1. Man I'm glad that's over. However, the experience did give me some peace and quiet, time to memorize knowledge, and just think about stuff. But now that's done. I remember one time I was on fire watch with Bell during Phase 1 and he asked me if we made a mistake coming here. I thought long and hard and said-

No man. This isn't a mistake. It sucks now, but in the end, it'll be worth. We'll make it.

I didn't even believe half the stuff I was saying at the time but it made things feel better at the moment knowing you felt the same thing as the ones around you. That night, we talked about that conversation we had and now we were both graduating. It did suck. We did make it. It did get better. It was worth it. It wasn't a mistake. We said we would stick together and we did.

Lights came on at 5 and even though it was Family Day, we had stuff to do. We hit up the chow hall and got back to the house in a hurry. Today was the day. We would start off with the motivational run and then we would finally be able to see our families.

We headed to the Parade deck in PT gear and we were buzzing with anticipation. Families had shown up super early and they were lining the street we were coming down and they were all clapping and cheering for us. We couldn't wave at them or lose bearing in any way.

So to show our appreciation, we sang cadence as we marched. It jacked the crowd up because we were screaming that junk! It was awesome!!!

Families started showing up and filling the stands on the parade deck and I kept looking and looking for my family. I'll catch them sooner or later. No worries. Once the sun was up, we formed up in full 3rd Battalion strength and got ready to go. And just like that, BAM! We were off.

We started down the sidewalk toward the street and then we would take a 3-mile run around the Island. We were screaming cadence the whole way too. It was great! As soon as we got to the street, we turned the corner and started down the street. Not more than 100 yards down the street, I saw a Black pickup and a driver. I looked closer and it was my dad! In the passenger seat was my sister! I could have reached out and given them a high five when we ran by. I was supercharged. I finally got to see them!

We turned some corners, ran by the house, and then a few broke off from the pack and got to ring the 3rd Battalion Bell signaling our immanent Graduation. It was exciting. When we got back to the parade deck, we formed back up with our own Platoons and got ready to step back to the house. We grabbed our gear and started moving quick. My family parked the truck and found their way to the sidewalk that we would be walking down. They were smiling and waiving at me but I didn't dare smile or waive back. Instead I gave them a little wink and kept on.

When we got back to the house, we changed into our Charlies and got ready to go. We formed back up and took a bus to the ITF. It was there that we formed up in front of all of our families, received our instructions for family day liberty, and finally, we were released for a few short hours.

I had no idea where my family was so I just stood still and they found me. From there, we rolled out in a hurry. I got to show them around the Island a bit. We took some pictures by some famous statues and then I took them on a tour of everywhere I went my first days I was here. I showed them the RTF, the Chapel, the Grinder, and then we went up to the house and they saw my squad bay. I showed them the quarterdeck and introduced them to my Heavy Hat. After that, we left to grab a bite to eat. Along the way I told them stories of this and that but to be honest, I was just glad to see them. It was funny because at one point, my sister asked how the level of discipline was on the Island and right then we walked by two recruits guarding weapons and they snapped to attention and screamed-

GOOD AFTERNOON SIR GOOD AFTERNOON MA'AM!

at the top of their lunges. I said- *Does that answer your question?* She was shocked.

We went to Backyard Burger and ate and just enjoyed finally seeing each other again. And just like that, it was time to leave. We started walking back and my sister asked why they had beach volleyball courts set up with no nets. I said those weren't beach volleyball courts. Those are PITS. That's where you go if you do something stupid. And just like that, a Drill Instructor and a recruit came flying out of a hatch and he was stripping gear and diving into the PIT. The Drill Instructor was screaming at him, looked up and saw us, and then lowered his voice so only the recruit could hear it. Yup. He's in trouble.

We carried on and eventually had to part ways until tomorrow. I told my dad about where my gear would be and the best way to get off the Island. After that, I told them I'd see them tomorrow.

Later that night, we had the Dong Show. That's when all of us got to impersonate the Drill Instructors. We were rolling. It was so much fun being able to act out how the Drill Instructors were with us. They laughed too. We all had a good time. I also presented Staff Sergeant Assassin, our Heavy Hat, and our Kill Hat with their Hat Racks. They were floored. Before we hit the rack, our Drill Instructors laid out some journals and we were allowed to write what ever we wanted to say to them. All through the night, we would get up and write in one of them. It was really cool. As much as you HATE your Drill Instructors, they made you what you are and when all is said and done, you want to do nothing but thank them. To some of the fellas in our Platoon, our Drill Instructors were the only fathers they had. Having an unbreakable male role model to follow and guide you as a young man is universally paramount. Not only did our Drill Instructors make us Marines, in some cases, they also made a few men. You could hear a few of the fellas sniffle and work to keep their composure as they tried to express their thanks into written word. However, I think some of the tears that fell on the page said more.

That night I laid in bed and thanked God for getting me through everything. Without Him, I couldn't have done it.

I fell asleep with a smile on my face for the last time on Parris Island.

20080201 Friday
Graduation Day

We were all up and ready to go before the Drill Instructors came in. Right away, you could feel the difference in the air. Platoon 3014 started to realize all the "last times" that were popping up in our heads. This is the last time I will ever wake up to Lights Lights Lights. This is the last time I will ever wake up in this squad bay and have to clean it and maintain it. This is the last time I will ever see these Marines in this setting.

This is the last day I will be on this Island.

As much as you hated this place and so desperately wanted to get away from it, deep down you loved it. It became a part of you. All the hard times disappeared while all the good times filled your memory. Just for myself, I took out a white shirt and asked everyone in my Platoon to sign it and say something if they wanted to. They were happy to do it and left some great stuff. I even got my Drill Instructors to sign it and say a little something. They did. They were great. I'll keep that shirt as long as I'm alive.

Everything lifted. Marines who truly hated other Marines the entire time were giving each other a hug and saying thanks for the good times. No more animosity. No more games. It was all over. This was the end for 3014 here at Parris Island.

We spot checked the house for the last time, moved the gear to it's staging area, and we were off. This was it. We formed up outside of the ITF and got ready to make our entrance. All the families were there and music was playing. It was exciting. We were all laughing and joking with each other about what we were going to do after Graduation. Everyone wanted to meet up and go out one more time at Backyard Burgers. I told them-

Hey Marines, I appreciate the invite but this is my plan. As soon as our

Senior says dismissed, you're going to turn around to say goodbye and all you'll see is a puff of smoke from where I used to be. We're lucky we're inside because otherwise, my family would have the car running right behind me in formation.

Finally, we got the word and marched in. The crowd went wild. Then everyone settled down and the Graduation ceremony officially began. They went through a lot of formalities, we formed up perfect, we saluted the colors with pride, the Guides turned in the Platoon Guidons, Honor Grad awards were given out (Even though not ONE single Recruit got one in 3014!) And finally, after all was said and done, we were given our LAST COMMAND.

Our Senior turned around to face us and said the last words I ever heard him speak-
PLATOON 3014................ DIS-MISSED!!!!!!!!!

The next few moments were a blur. My Family met me outside, we hustled to the truck, I got in, we went to the 3rd Battalion "house" and picked up my stuff, I got back in the truck, we headed to the gate, went through the gate, we went over the bridge, we got to the final gate, passed through the gate, and just like that, it was all over.

Parris Island vanished in my rearview mirror.

Got that right!

The Present

I left Parris Island on February 1, 2008 as a United States Marine and as a better man. Mission accomplished! I was able to spend some good quality time with my family and I was able to tell them some of the stories I had. My mom actually conceded and allowed me to wear my Dress Blues to Sunday morning church service. Her distaste for the Military still rings true but I have to hand it to her. Not throwing a fit and allowing me to wear my Dress Blues to church was huge. Thanks mom!

And then I spent the rest of my 10 days leave working out. I knew I only had a few days from the time I Graduated until I had to leave again, so I really had to make the most of it. No time to chill out. It's easy to want to do nothing and let yourself go, but that's not me. I wanted to keep myself on the cutting edge and in shape.

After my few days back, I then went through MCT (Marine Corps Training) and Graduated. Which, by the way, is just another book all together. If you like this book, then I'll bust that one out too.

And then from there I was sent to Goodfellow Air Force Base and completed my training by Graduating the Combat Fire Fighter Program and earned the title of Distinguished Graduate.

I returned to Annapolis Maryland on July 25, 2008 and returned to teaching Martial Arts.
I deployed to Iraq in 2009.

Came back February of 2010.

In 2014, I opened 5 Peaks Martial Arts Academy, finished my 8-year contract, and was Honorably Discharged in June 2015.

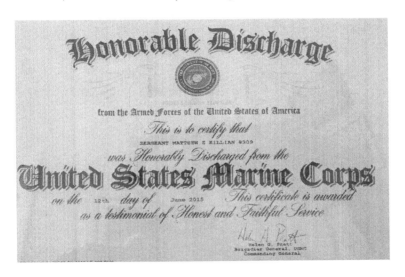

All throughout my Marine Corps Career, I had continually bounced back and forth between the most amazing of times and the absolute worst of times. There were moments when I was riding so high that I never ever wanted it to end. My goal was to make Sergeant (E-5) inside of 6 years and that's exactly what I did. Most of the fellas would finish up as Lance Corporal (E-3) or Corporal (E-4), but I wanted to make Sergeant. One of the happiest days of my life was to be promoted, have those pins smashed into my collar, and know from that day forward I was Sergeant Killian.

Then, there were days where I was counting days, hours, and minutes just to get through some hard times. I would often tell myself over and over that nothing lasts forever and that I was unbreakable. The Lord did not give me a spirit of fear but of Power. It would only be a moment in time.

Looking back now, I wouldn't trade any of the good or bad. I would take it all again. It got me thinking that we are given these days to live as a gift. If I would not have gone on the computer and searched up MARINES, I would have missed out on all these experiences. Sure, I would have had some great times doing what I was doing, but nothing like this.

Everything changed when I followed my heart, prayed for direction, and then attacked it.

Ever since I've been back, I've had lots and lots of people ask me questions about my life in the Marine Corps. So I figured I would put a few of the top questions and my answers here. If you have any more, by all means email me and I'll answer them to the best of my ability.

How did you record what happened every day during Boot Camp?
That was pretty difficult. I had a ton of close calls but I made it happen.

My first order of business was to find out **when** I would be able to write down what happened. I figured that if I had no time to write then it wouldn't matter. I found that I could write stuff during RTF classes, before church started, and at the end of the day if and when we had square away time. These 3 times were when I wrote down everything. Outside of that, there was no way I would have been able to get it all down in such detail.

My second order of business was to find out **where** I could write. Drill Instructors were notorious for dumping your footlocker and ruining everything you own. So I had to find things they wouldn't wreck. The green monster was awesome! It's the knowledge book we get and it's filled with hundreds of pages. I knew that couldn't be wrecked so I would write in the margins of that. I would write in bullets to remember key points of what I wanted to write. At the end of the day, I would fill out more detail from the bullets during square away time. If I didn't have much time during the week, then I would fill out the details before church started. I got a ton written before church started. So now I knew where and when I could write everything.

My last order of business was to find out how to get those pages I had written back home. This was tricky. I couldn't hoard the pages because if the Drill Instructors find out they would be thrown away. I also couldn't take the chance of them getting wrecked when the house got bombed. So I kept the finished pages in the back of my Bible where I knew they would be safe. Drill Instructors won't mess with your Bible. And I kept my Bible in a ziplock back so that if my footlocker got dumped, all the pages would remain in the Bible. Plus it wouldn't get wet from travel. I put my name on the front of my Bible and on the ziplock bag so there was no question as to whose it was.

When I had enough pages in the back of my Bible, I added them to my mail that I sent home. The Drill Instructors wouldn't touch my mail and it was not uncommon to send multiple pages in your envelope. I repeated this process all the way through Boot Camp so I had the whole story. When I got back, I started cranking out the entire story and it was a blast going back and remembering everything that happened. I didn't leave anything out that mattered and really tried to include not only my victories but my challenges and failures as well.

How was life in Boot Camp?

Life in Boot Camp is a matter of coping to a set environment. The beginning was very difficult. For the first 7 days, all I could think of was-
"What have I gotten myself into?"
"I've made a mistake."
"I don't want to be here."
But that's what you're supposed to think. That's what you're

supposed to feel. Boot Camp is supposed to seem like a nightmare. But then, if you can gut it out, it'll change and become somewhat tolerable. Like I said, it's a set environment. There are set rules and if you learn the rules and commit to living by those rules without reservation, you will find there is a light at the end of the tunnel. There are no comforts in Boot Camp. You're not supposed to eat well. You're not supposed to get sleep. You're not supposed to feel 100% when you have to perform. You're going to feel miserable. You're going to make mistakes and get blasted for it. That's just how it is. No matter where you come from, you will be broken, you will hit "the bottom", you will want to quit, you will become inspired, you will find you can make it, you will make it, and you will be born again a Marine.

Was it hard?

Boot Camp is as hard as you make it. At it's core, it's very hard. You go in knowing that. You prepare for that. But any extra difficulty that comes beyond that is entirely up to you. If you really push yourself and give it everything you got moment by moment, it'll be very hard. If you give anything less than that, you're going to get killed every time you turn around. The way I think about it is this: it's me against the Drill Instructors. I have to find a way to beat them using their rules. Not mine. I wanted to out run them. I wanted to scream louder than they did. I wanted to show them they could put me through anything and I'd claw my way to the top. I wanted to show them I was the most disciplined recruit in the Platoon. Most importantly, I had to do that every single day.

Are you allowed to fight in Boot Camp?

Absolutely. When you become a Marine, there are heavy consequences for bad conduct. However, in Boot Camp, all bets are off because you're nothing but a nasty recruit. The only "rules" is that you have to keep it in the squad bay and you can't send a recruit to medical otherwise you can get in trouble.

All that being said, even though you can go to swings with a recruit, it's rare. Most of the time, recruits are trying to just get by together and make it through another day of training. If you're a hooligan that fights all the time, you'll get separated and be on your way back home. The point here is that tempers do flair and everyone has a breaking point. When that happens, the Drill Instructors will let you get it out of your system and then break you off for being stupid. It's better to just stay cool and make it to Graduation.

What was the "Deal" your Senior made?

He made a bet against 2 other Drill Instructors that he could fire his Guide and #1 Squad Leader with only 2 weeks to Grad and still win 1st Place in Final Drill. It was just a game to him. As you know, that didn't happen. We got 4th out of 5th place. As a result, the Platoon resented him for playing a game using us as a bet and the Platoon fell apart. He always bragged that he was superman. This time, it backfired. It was personal to us because we took our positions seriously as the Guide and Squad Leader and Platoon 3014 was the most respected Platoon among the other recruits.

What is being quarterdecked?

It's actually called IT (Individual Training) it's when a Drill Instructor takes you aside and works you out individually, in a small group, or as a Platoon. But to the recruits, we call it being quarterdecked. You are sent up to a designated area in the squad bay, called the quarterdeck, with a Drill Instructor. You take off your blouse and empty your pockets. The Drill Instructor runs you through a high-speed mix of various exercises. The entire time, you are to scream to the top of your lungs all the commands given by the Drill Instructor. The time varies depending on why the Drill Instructor called you up.

Was it worth it?

Absolutely Yes. At times, you totally hate life in the Marine Corps. However, there is always a lesson to be learned or a silver lining to be discovered. You just have to take it for what it is. I learned so many priceless lessons that I would never trade a second back. Boot Camp didn't make me a man. But it did help me to become a better man. It taught me lessons that I would have never been able to learn as a civilian.

What's one of the hardest parts of life right after Boot Camp?

The top 2 are- Having to play stupid games for stupid Marines. The belief in the Marine Corps is that if one pays, all pay. This Sucks!!! One thing for sure is that you'll constantly pay for the bad Marines and rarely be rewarded for being a good Marine. It is what it is.

The second is garbage Marines that dishonor the Marine Corps. As soon as you get to MCT, you'll run into your first batch. There is a special Platoon called Legal Sep's. They are the ones that, for whatever reason, decided to get popped for drugs so they would get separated from the Marine Corps. These Marines are the worst of the worst. They went through all that training and all that hard work just so they could turn their backs on every single person that believed in them, and they gave the finger to the Corps.

The truth is, they couldn't handle it. They are garbage to the core and made a decision to give up on the opportunity to make a better life for themselves. These are known as the only Ex-Marines. You can't take away the fact that they made it through Boot Camp and got their EGA, but they are no longer of pure blood. They are outcasts. A Marine who has reached the end of his contract and discharged will still refer to himself as a Marine and NEVER an Ex-Marine.

Was there anything in particular that helped you through Boot Camp?

Yes. Two things. The first is church. Going to church is incredible. It heals a struggling spirit and God gives you exactly what you need to get through. The second is mail. Knowing you have someone counting on you and praying for you is paramount. You'll feel alone, but you're not. They're saying their prayers and counting on you to make it. You'll want to make them proud.

The Marine Corps is everything I hoped it would be. I had a lot of expectations going in, and it met each one of them. I also got a lot of extra surprises along the way. Ever since the beginning, I have said that I'm always trying to find challenges and ways to push myself to that next level. In most cases, all I've had to do is make a plan, attack it, and I was good to go. In this case, there is no way I could have done it alone. This experience has truly changed my life for the better. No longer will I ever have to worry about "what if's" in terms of the Marine Corps. I'm living it.

Before I wrap this up, I just want to thank you for sharing in this journey. A wise man once said that the journey is more important than the finish and the start. I truly hope you enjoyed the ride. I know I did. Only God above knows what's in store for the future. But for now, I can truly say-

I am living the dream!

Made in the USA
Middletown, DE
10 January 2016